The Romantic Generation of Modern Chinese Writers

HARVARD EAST ASIAN SERIES 71
The East Asian Research Center at Harvard University administers
research projects designed to further scholarly understanding
of China, Japan, Korea, Vietnam and adjacent areas.

Leo Ou-fan Lee

The Romantic Generation
of Modern Chinese Writers

HARVARD UNIVERSITY PRESS, CAMBRIDGE, MASSACHUSETTS, 1973

© Copyright 1973 by the President and Fellows of Harvard College
All rights reserved
Preparation of this volume has been aided by a grant from the Ford Foundation.
Library of Congress Catalog Card Number 73-75058 ✓
SBN 674-77930-4
Printed in the United States of America

To my parents and their generation

Preface

More than fifty years have elapsed since the Chinese students in Peking unleashed what has come to be called the May Fourth movement. Another shore and a time span of fifty years lend a different perspective to May Fourth. The distance reveals much about at least two generations of modern Chinese intellectuals, the May Fourth generation, now fathers, and a younger generation brought up by them in changed circumstances. For a member of this post-May Fourth generation, a study of the May Fourth movement is necessarily burdened not only with the issue of historical objectivity but also with that perennial phenomenon, the generation gap.

The original stimulus for this study in fact first came from my parents. As "emancipated" intellectuals fresh from college in the early thirties, my parents adopted a "modern" method in raising their first son, steeping him in Greek mythology and the music of Chopin. Western literature—Dumas, Lamartine, Byron, and Romain Rolland in Chinese translation—became the regular educational fare in my adolescent years in Taiwan. I can still recall with vivid immediacy how my father gave me special permission one night to read through *La Dame aux Camélias* until early dawn. And it did not take me much time to find out that the initial letter in my father's European name stood for Armand. There must have been countless Armands and Werthers in the more "modern" sectors of China in the twenties and thirties. And my parents, who went to college in Nanking in the thirties, must have been typical of young intellectuals in the coastal cities.

All these personal conjectures blended into my academic disciplines as I began the study of Chinese history in the United States some ten years ago. Memories of my upbringing predisposed me to modern Chinese literature and the May Fourth movement. For I am convinced that the student protest itself, on that memorable Sunday afternoon, May 4, 1919, would not have been so historic had it not been associated both by its *metteurs en scène* and by later scholars with what is broadly defined as the New Culture movement, in which New Literature played a central role. The importance of New Literature as a clue to modern Chinese social and intellectual history has been generally acknowledged but seldom seriously explored. An endeavor along this line thus becomes both an academic and a personal challenge, because my father, a musician by profession, was also a poet in his college years in Nanking.

What are the legacies of this May Fourth generation? We have been informed that tradition was swept away, new currents of thought from the West were introduced, young girls in high schools and colleges were emancipated, and New Literature, written in the vernacular *(pai-hua)*, became immensely popular. Aside from all these generalizations, which are by now no more than academic clichés, we have not learned anything from scholarly works as to how the paraphernalia of New Culture made inroads into the personal lives of young Chinese intellectuals in the May Fourth period. How did the exhilaration of iconoclasm and Westernism affect their life-styles, fashion their personalities, and condition their general outlooks? Insofar as "Confucian personalities" have become standard fare in Chinese studies in the West, can one perhaps suggest a new type of May Fourth personality? If so, what are its basic components? How is one to assess it in the context of its own time? And finally, to repeat, what are the legacies of the May Fourth movement in Chinese literature and life? I shall attempt to explore some of the preceding questions by examining the lives and works of a few of the writers representative of the time. The source materials are literary, but the questions and answers are historical. My present approach has to be a combination of both.

The conceptual category of the "generation" is not entirely out of place in a work like mine, but it must be flexible. The eminent French historian Marc Bloch has given the classic definition of a generation. "Men who are born into the same social environment about the same time necessarily come under analogous influences, particularly in their formative years. Experience proves that, by comparison with either considerably older or considerably younger groups, their behavior reveals certain distinctive characteristics which are ordinarily very clear. This is true even of their bitterest disagreements. To be excited by the same dispute, even on opposing sides, is still to be alike. This common stamp, deriving from common age, is what makes a generation." [1]

The purpose of this study is to explore some of the "analogous influences" and "distinctive characteristics" of the May Fourth generation of literary intellectuals. I take the May Fourth generation to mean those who were born at the turn of the century, grew up with the demise of the Manchu empire and the founding of the Republic, and reached manhood in the 1920s or early 1930s. Thus they became active on the literary scene following the Literary Revolution of 1917 and the May Fourth demonstrations of 1919. The choice of representative figures, which is entirely my own, reflects in large measure the development of a central theme, on which I will elaborate in the concluding part. For thematic purposes I have chosen to begin with two precursors—Lin Shu and Su Man-shu—who embarked upon their literary careers before the emergence of the May Fourth literary scene but who nevertheless had an enduring impact on the young men and women of the May Fourth generation. Yü Ta-fu and Hsü Chih-mo are the principal protagonists of my study, as is Kuo Mo-jo. I have not discussed Kuo in detail because of David Roy's recently published book on Kuo's early years. [2] My treatment of this important figure is therefore more thematic than biographical. I discuss Kuo together with Chiang Kuang-tz'u and Hsiao Chün as three prominent writers whose individual lives epitomize the fate of the romantic turned leftist. The leftward drift of New Literature concludes my story and ushers in a new phase in the history of modern Chinese literature, which has been admirably studied in the West by, among others, the late T. A. Hsia and Merle Goldman.[3] I include Hsiao Chün, who takes the story forward in time and somewhat beyond the scope of my study, in order to demonstrate certain continuities between my work and theirs.

I would have liked to include a chapter on women writers in the May Fourth period. But some preliminary research has convinced me that the subject is much too vast and important to be treated summarily. In view of the recent upsurge of movements for women's liberation in the Western world, a separate book devoted exclusively to women writers in modern China may well be a worthy subject for academic pursuit. Although the present study is not graced with women writers as central figures, the validity of my over-all theme is not, I hope, drastically hampered. For these men and women, living in the same historical milieu and practicing the same profession, were inevitably bound together by their shared experience.

1. Marc Bloch, *The Historian's Craft* (New York, Knopf, 1953), p. 185.

2. David Tod Roy, *Kuo Mo-jo: The Early Years* (Cambridge, Mass., Harvard University Press, 1971).

3. T. A. Hsia, *The Gate of Darkness: Studies on the Leftist Literary Movement in China* (Seattle, University of Washington Press, 1968). Merle Goldman, *Literary Dissent in Communist China* (Cambridge, Mass., Harvard University Press, 1967).

Acknowledgments

My interest in modern Chinese literature and history began at the University of Chicago under the guidance of Professor T. H. Tsien. The present book is a revised version of my Ph.D. dissertation at Harvard University under the supervision of Professors Benjamin I. Schwartz and John K. Fairbank. My intellectual debts are mainly to these three outstanding teachers.

Like many students of intellectual history, I am profoundly indebted to Professor Schwartz, whose erudition and insight have exerted a strong influence on my work, and I hereby gratefully acknowledge its many "Schwartzian" elements in both conception and approach. Professor Fairbank has always been patient with the erratic progress of my research. Without his constant encouragement and perceptive criticism of the various preliminary drafts this book would never have been completed.

I have also benefited from the wisdom of Erik H. Erikson, whose seminar on psycho-history I attended as a layman and whose theories have added a new angle to my analytical thinking. The scholarship and instruction of Professor Jaroslav Průšek have also left their imprint on this work; it was his pioneering research on the subjective tendencies in modern Chinese literature that led me to my thesis.

Many scholars and friends have helped me in the research stages of this book. Professor Liu Wu-chi kindly allowed me to draw upon his authoritative work on Su Man-shu. David Roy's book on Kuo Mo-jo made my task much easier. Robert Compton warned me of many errors in the translated titles of Lin Shu. Gary Melyan brought me up to date, especially with Japanese scholarship, on Yü Ta-fu. Martin Bernal helped me to find Hsü Chih-mo's academic record at King's College, Cambridge. Mr. Leonard K. Elmhirst placed at my disposal his private collection of some twenty letters from Hsü Chih-mo, which have never been published. The late T. A. Hsia, who taught me English literature at National Taiwan University, continued to advise me on Chinese literature. My chapters on Chiang Kuang-tz'u and Hsiao Chün are but an extension of his work. And finally, my former colleagues and "protégés" at Dartmouth College—particularly Marysa Navarro, Manon Spitzer, and George Wen—assisted me gallantly in editing and research of the final part of the manuscript.

Among scholars who have taken pains to read through the entire manuscript, I am especially grateful to Professors David Arkush, Cyril Birch, Jerome Grieder, Frederick Mote, and Jon Saari. They corrected my numerous mistakes and gave me invaluable comments and suggestions. I was also honored to spend an afternoon of pleasant reminiscence about Hsü Chih-mo with Professor I. A. Richards. I am indebted to Sir Isaiah Berlin for a brief, but rewarding, lesson in European romanticism.

The staff of the Harvard-Yenching Library and the Hoover Library at Stanford permitted me to use their impressive resources. The Harvard-Yenching Institute and the Council on International and Regional Studies of Princeton University provided financial support when I needed it to survive and to work. I am grateful to these institutions.

In a book on romantic writers who defied conventions, it is perhaps appropriate to depart from the conventional practice of scholars to thank their tireless and long-suffering wives. Rather, I would like to share the joys of this first book with Ellen F. Soullière, who has given inspiration to my work and to my life.

Contents

CONTENTS

Part One The Setting

Chapter 1
The Emergence of the Literary Scene

On February 1, 1917, Ch'en Tu-hsiu first raised the banner of the Literary Revolution in the pages of his *Hsin ch'ing-nien* (New youth) magazine. What followed is now familiar history. Polemics were successfully directed against a none too formidable enemy by the "Army of the Literary Revolution," which consisted initially of Ch'en Tu-hsiu, Hu Shih, and Ch'ien Hsüan-t'ung. The vernacular language *(pai-hua)* gradually came to enjoy nationwide usage, literary journals mushroomed, and the so-called New Literature was brought into being.[1]

Before *New Youth* was founded first in Shanghai in 1915, the publishing industry of this city had at least two decades of growing prosperity. To find the appropriate setting for this exciting drama of the Literary Revolution—perhaps the most splendid facet of the May Fourth Movement and one of its most momentous legacies—one must first probe into the publishing market and its vanguard, journalism.

Treaty-Port Literary Journalism

Since the T'ang dynasty there had existed, in one form or another, a kind of official newspaper which served to communicate imperial decrees and court events for the capital area.[2] In the late Ch'ing period, especially in the last decade of the nineteenth century, some unofficial and semi-official newspapers had also been published, at the suggestion of missionaries like Timothy Richard, John Fryer, and Gilbert Reid.[3] These publications in Peking often provided the reform-minded officials and literati with a ready channel for voicing political opinions and comments and therefore were banned sporadically by the court.[4]

Western missionaries also pioneered in developing nonofficial newspapers in China. Robert Morrison set the first example by founding in 1815 the *Chinese Monthly Magazine* in Malacca. Foreign language newspapers and journals mushroomed in the second half of the nineteenth century in the treaty ports, culminating in the widely popular *North China Herald* of Shanghai, founded in 1850. Shanghai thus became one of the first cities to witness the beginning of Chinese newspapers under the tutelage of Western missionaries and journalists. Wang T'ao had pioneered successfully in Hong Kong in the 1870s. In Shanghai, the two most famous Chinese newspapers at the turn of the century were *Shen pao* (Shanghai news; founded in 1872) and *Hsin-wen pao* (News tribune; founded in 1893), both of which were supported in the beginning by foreign capital.[5]

In 1896, Liang Ch'i-ch'ao founded *Shih-wu pao* (Current affairs) in Shanghai, thus setting the precedent for using journalism as the most powerful medium to instill new ideas and instigate social and political change.[6] Moreover, he was not alone in the field. In 1904, a returned student from Japan, Ti Ch'u-ch'ing, founded *Shih pao* (Times), which in 1905 played an important role in promoting the boycott against American goods in protest against the unfavorable treatment of Chinese workers by an act of Congress.[7] As the impending revolution was gathering momentum, Liang and Ti were joined by revolutionaries of various shades. Chang Ping-lin edited the famous *Su pao* (Kiangsu tribune) in Shanghai; when he and other editors were arrested and imprisoned in 1903 other members founded the *Kuo-min jih-jih-pao* (National people's daily), to which Su Man-shu contributed his articles. Yü Yu-jen, another revolutionary, published a succession of four newspapers, including the short-lived

Shen-chou jih-pao (China daily).[8] With the founding of the Republic, more newspapers joined the ranks, the best known of which was *T'ai-p'ing-yang pao* (Pacific news).

These treaty-port newspapers served not merely as political weapons; they also provided the breeding ground for a new genre of mass literature which was gradually emerging after the turn of the century. Since the very beginning of nonofficial journalism, it had been common practice to spice up news items with a few poems or some leisurely comments on local customs and the theater. In 1897 one of the Shanghai newspapers established a special supplement titled "News of Leisure," thus ushering in the phenomenon of the literary supplement *(fu-k'an)*, which soon became a regular feature of all the major newspapers. As more demand was felt in the market for literary supplements, some more enterprising journalists began publishing independent magazines which were, in fact, expanded literary supplements now separate from the newspapers. Li Pao-chia (Po-yüan) founded *Yu-hsi pao* (Playful news) in 1897 and more magazines followed.[9]

It was in these literary supplements and "little magazines" that the new "mass literature" burgeoned and prospered. Edited by a hybrid group who might be called journalist-littérateurs—men who had an inkling of Western literature and foreign languages but a more solid background in traditional Chinese literature—these publications featured a plethora of pseudo-translations, poetry, and essays which, although claiming to awaken the social and political consciousness of the people, served also the purpose of entertainment.

The idea of mass literature magazines as well as their ideological window-dressing was obviously taken from Liang Ch'i-ch'ao, who in 1903 had founded the influential *Hsin hsiao-shuo* (New fiction). By way of an inaugural manifesto, Liang published his celebrated essay, "On the Relationship between Fiction and People's Sovereignty." Drawing upon examples from the West, he asserted forcefully that the novel performed a crucial function in renovating the social, political, religious, and moral conditions of a nation.[10] The contents of *Hsin hsiao-shuo* presented an interesting mixture of fiction carrying political and social messages, plays, poetry, songs, and translations of

Western science fiction and detective stories of doubtful quality. The portraits of Tolstoy, Hugo, Byron, Shelley, Goethe, Schiller, Maeterlinck, and the Polish romantic writer, Henryk Sienkiewicz (1846–1916) appeared on the front pages of its issues, although no translations from their works were attempted.[11]

It was in this important magazine that Lin Shu later published his translations of H. Rider Haggard and some of the most talented treaty-port journalist-littérateurs made their debuts. Wu Wo-yao (Yen-jen), perhaps the best known of them, wrote a masterpiece of social and political satire, *Erh-shih nien mu-tu chih kuai hsien-chuang* (Strange things witnessed in twenty years). Li Pao-chia, editor of the fortnightly *Hsiu-hsiang hsiao-shuo* (Illustrated fiction), had not only perfected the traditional satirical story in such serialized favorites as *Kuan-ch'ang hsien-hsing chi* (Exposés of officialdom), *Wen-ming hsiao-shih* (Short history of modern times), and *Huo ti-yü* (Living hell) but also dabbled in translations and popularized Western history, such as *T'ai-hsi li-shih yen-i* (Popular explanation of Western history; *yen-i* was a common term in traditional titles of chivalric or historical fiction). A third man, Chou Kuei-sheng, who collaborated with Wu Wo-yao in editing *Yüeh-yüeh hsiao-shuo* (Monthly fiction), was also a pioneer translator whose works included, among many others, Sir Arthur Conan Doyle's Sherlock Holmes stories, *The Arabian Nights*, and *Aesop's Fables*.[12]

These writers wrote feverishly in order to meet deadlines and profusely to make money. It was by no means uncommon to find that the editor of a magazine was the author of every piece in an entire issue. The works of such writers reached a wide audience: the literate or semi-literate segments of the urban population.

The popularity of these journalist-littérateurs and their new brand of treaty-port literary journalism represented a phenomenon of great historical significance. Long before the modern vernacular literature appeared with the Literary Revolution, a half-modernized form of mass literature had already sneaked onto the treaty-port scene through the back door of journalism. With the proliferation of literary supplements attached or unattached to newspapers and their growing reading public, a market had already been established for the May

Fourth practitioners of New Literature. Moreover, the treaty-port journalist-littérateurs, in their arduous efforts to make money, had also managed to establish a new profession. Their commercial success proved that literature as a vocation was not only possible but also lucrative. It remained for their May Fourth successors to establish further the convention that to be a literary man was not only economically feasible but also socially prestigious.

Journalism and Literature in the May Fourth Era

When Ch'en Tu-hsiu talked a Shanghai publisher into funding his new journal, most of the literary supplements were still under the control of journalist-littérateurs. By the first decade of the Republic, the most popular genre of mass literature as practiced by them had degenerated from social and political reformism to what came to be known as the Saturday School of "Butterfly" fiction.[13] The literary supplements of the three major newspapers in Shanghai—*Shen pao*, *Hsin-wen pao*, and *Shih pao*—were under the editorship of such Saturday littérateurs as Chou Shou-chüan, Chang Hen-shui, Yen Tu-ho, Hsü Chen-ya, and Pao T'ien-hsiao. Their stories of "talent meets beauty" vied for attention and popularity with detective stories, pseudo-translations, and more sentimental fiction written by other journalist-littérateurs and printed in a host of popular semi-literary magazines—*Yüeh-yüeh hsiao-shuo*, *Hsiao shuo lin* (Forest of fiction), *Hsiao-shuo shih-chieh* (World of fiction), *Hsiu-hsiung hsiao-shuo*, *Hsiao-shuo shih-pao* (Fiction news), *Hsiao-shuo yüeh-pao* (Fiction monthly). All enjoyed large circulations.[14] To compete with such established publications was no easy matter.

As *New Youth* raised the clarion-call for New Literature, the authors needed more channels to publicize their cause and to try their pens. Fortunately, they found ripe soil in three influential newspapers. In Shanghai, the Kuomintang's *Min-kuo jih-pao* (Republic daily) lent its support via its literary supplement *Chüeh-wu* (Awakening), in which one of the newly established modern Chinese poets, Liu Ta-pai, first experimented with his semi-vernacular love poetry.[15] Notable contributors to the supplement included Ts'ai Yüan-p'ei, Hu Shih,

Chou Tso-jen, Lu Hsün, Kuo Mo-jo, John Dewey, and Bertrand Russell.[16] New Literature found another outlet in *Hsüeh-teng* (Academic lamp), established in March 1918 as a literary supplement to the *Shih-shih hsin-pao* (The China times), an organ of the Yen-chiu hsi (Political studies clique), which was composed of Liang Ch'i-ch'ao's followers. Its first editor, Tsung Pai-hua, became Kuo Mo-jo's good friend through correspondence and propelled Kuo to nationwide fame by publishing every poem which Kuo sent him. Yü Ta-fu's early work, "Silver-grey Death" was also first serialized in *Hsüeh-teng*. In 1921 another literary journal, *Wen-hsüeh hsün-k'an* (Ten-day literary publication), edited by Cheng Chen-to with contributions from members of the newly founded Association for Literary Studies, began publication as another supplement to this newspaper. Thus it can be said that the early talents of the two most important literary organizations in the 1920s—Literary Studies Association and the Creation Society—were nourished "parasitically" by this powerful journalistic organ of Liang Ch'i-ch'ao.

The third champion for New Literature was the *Ch'en-pao* (Morning news) of Peking. The tremendous prestige and influence of its literary supplement was due to the efforts of one dedicated littérateur, Sun Fu-yüan, who derisively called himself "a writer without works."[17] With proselytizing zeal he championed the works of new writers in the Peking area, especially those of the Chou brothers—Lu Hsün (Chou Shu-jen) and Chou Tso-jen. Lu Hsün's "True Story of Ah Q" was first serialized in this supplement. In 1923 Sun resigned abruptly in a fit of temper over Lu Hsün's satirical poem, "My Unrequited Love," which was taken out by another general editor without Sun's prior consent as it was ready for print.[18] But the reputation of this prestigious journal remained and in 1925 reached new heights of glory under the editorship of Hsü Chih-mo. After Sun Fu-yüan left *Ch'en-pao*, he took over the literary supplement of the *Ching-pao* (Capital news) in Peking and turned it into another bastion of New Literature.

With the pioneering efforts of these three newspapers, others soon followed suit. Hundreds of "literary supplements" and magazines were founded specifically for the propagation of New Literature;[19]

other already existing ones were wrested from the hands of the Saturday School littérateurs and transformed for New Literature. *Hsiao-shuo yüeh-pao*, published by the Commercial Press and an established arena for Butterfly fiction, was taken over in 1921 by the Association for Literary Studies and made into one of the most popular journals of New Literature. The literary supplement of the *Shen pao*, *Tzu-yu t'an* (Random talk), underwent a similar transformation. Thus the old stage which had been constructed by the journalist-littérateurs was decorated anew and new acts were performed.

The Peking "Aggregate"

Along with the mushrooming of literary journals came the proliferation of literary societies. Mao Tun estimated that in the period from 1922 to 1925 there existed in the major cities more than one hundred literary societies with such youthful and dynamic names as Star, Infant, Roses, Light Grass, Green Waves, Smile, Sprouts, Spring Wind, Dawn, Flames, Rainbow, Morning Glow, Clouds, Storm.[20] The majority of them were organized by students in colleges and secondary schools. The lead was taken, of course, by professors and students in the Peking area. The editorial committee of *Hsin ch'ing-nien* after January 1918 consisted initially of Ch'en Tu-hsiu, Hu Shih, Ch'ien Hsüan-t'ung, Li Ta-chao, Liu Fu, and Shen Yin-mo, all professors at National Peking University. In December 1918 Ch'en and Li established in Peking the *Mei-chou p'ing-lun* (Weekly critic). In November some students of Peita, notably Fu Ssu-nien and Lo Chia-lun, established the Hsin-ch'ao (New Tide) Society with the assistance of Ch'en, Li, and Hu Shih and began publishing a monthly under the same name.[21] Other members of the New Tide Society included Chu Tzu-ch'ing, poet and prose writer, Yeh Shao-chün, novelist, Li Hsiao-feng, publisher and owner of the Pei-hsin bookstore, and Sun Fu-yüan. Before Sun took charge of the literary supplement of *Ch'en-pao*, its first editor was Li Ta-chao. The supplement was instrumental in promoting the works of such subsequently well-known writers as the Chou brothers, K'ang Pai-ch'ing, Yeh Shao-chün, Hsü Chih-mo, and Shen Ts'ung-wen.

The journal editors and contributors in Peking constituted a very loose grouping of New Culture advocates which may be called the Peking aggregate. One literary historian has branded them academicians, for most of them were directly associated with Peking universities.[22] In the first half of the 1920s, this grouping, though amorphous in organization, evinced a certain esprit de corps as leaders of New Culture and New Literature. But gradually, factions began to emerge within its ranks. With Hsü Chih-mo assuming the editorship of *Ch'en-pao's* literary supplement in the winter of 1925, a new line-up was formed which consisted chiefly of men with English and American educational backgrounds: Hsü, Ch'en Yüan, Chao Yuenren, Wen I-to, and their close disciples or associates, like Ling Shu-hua (Mrs. Ch'en Yüan) and Shen Ts'ung-wen. Hu Shih, after having broken with Ch'en Tu-hsiu and his *Hsin ch'ing-nien* colleagues in 1921, joined this new group, which subsequently formed the core of the Crescent Moon Society. The remaining ones, clustered around Lu Hsün, Chou Tso-jen, and Sun Fu-yüan's journals, became the backbone of the original Peking aggregate.

With few exceptions a kind of scholarly urbanity characterized both groups. The Anglo-American group was Western oriented in its political and literary outlook, but the core group was more interested in classical Chinese learning and gradually adopted the characteristics of traditional scholars—knowledgeability, sophistication in tastes, temperance in politics, and a preference for research and expository writing than for poetical or fictional creation. Some of them, like Yü P'ing-po and Ku Chieh-kang, withdrew from the literary front altogether and devoted themselves to re-examining the "national heritage," thus providing the only remaining link between this group and Hu Shih, who also confessed to his "historical habits."

The core of the Peking aggregate—the Chou brothers, the Sun brothers (Fu-yüan and Fu-hsi), Li Hsiao-feng, Liu Fu, Ch'ien Hsüan-t'ung, among others—were the founders of the subsequent Yü-ssu (Thread of talk) Society and the *Yü-ssu Weekly* (1924–1930). While professing "freedom of thought and critical judgment,"[23] they were content with picking a few bones and throwing a few darts at contemporary manners, morals, and personalities while shunning radical slogans or constructive proposals. This celebrated *Yü-ssu* style is very much reminiscent of the "pure talk" (ch'ing-t'an) tradition of Chinese literati of the past. The exception was, of course, Lu Hsün, whose association with this group, despite his attempts to dilute the ideological connotations,[24] remains one of the many paradoxes of his personality. And because of Lu Hsün's participation, the Yü-ssu group has received undeservedly temperate treatment from leftist and Communist historians.[25]

The Peking aggregate did not monopolize the Peking literary scene, nor was their dominance unchallenged. According to Lu Hsün, a small literary society, Mang-yüan (Wild fields), was formed in 1925 by a few novice writers and students out of dissatisfaction with Sun Fu-yüan's Ching-pao supplement.[26] Lu Hsün was invited to be the editor of their weekly, which was also attached to the Ching-pao. But internal strife soon followed. Kao Ch'ang-hung, one of their flamboyant leaders, formed another short-lived society in Shanghai under the grand romantic title of K'uang-p'iao (Sturm und Drang). Lu Hsün was also associated with another small group called the Wei-ming (Unnamed) Society, which, led by Wei Su-yüan, Li Chi-yeh, and others, seemed to be an extension of Mang-yüan but asserted its independence because of personal conflicts with Kao Ch'ang-hung.[27] Similar short-lived literary societies abounded in Peking and Shanghai. With the growing power of the Association for Literary Studies and the Creation Society, however, the initial scene of confusion and amorphousness gradually gave way to the seeming confrontation between two powerful literary organizations.

The Association for Literary Studies

In November 1920 several people interested in New Literature met at Peita to discuss the possibility of organizing a literary society. The possibility became a reality when Mao Tun (Shen Yen-ping) was appointed editor of Hsiao-shuo yüeh-pao and offered his friends in Peking a chance to renovate thoroughly this established journal of Butterfly fiction. On January 4, 1921, the Association for Literary Studies was officially inaugurated in Peking. A total of twenty-one persons—twelve founding members and nine new members—attended the inaugural session at the Chung-shan Park.[28] A week later the first issue of the revamped *Hsiao-shuo yüeh-pao* appeared in Shanghai. This new issue (Vol. 12, No. 1) published a constitution and a manifesto which enumerated three fundamental principles governing the formation of the association:

"To unite in fellowship." The founders of the association saw dissension between practitioners of old and new literature and even among the ranks of new literary men. "Therefore, in organizing this association, we hope that all (members), meeting frequently and exchanging opinions, may achieve mutual understanding and create a unified organization of writers."

"To advance knowledge." Knowledge to be gained should come from foreign countries. "Those who re-examine the old literature must use new methods, while those who study new literature are even more dependent upon foreign materials." Therefore, the association aimed to "establish gradually a library, research center, and publishing department to aid in the advancement of individual and national literature."

"To establish a foundation for a professional union of writers." "The time has passed when literature was taken as amusement in periods of elation or diversion in periods of depression. We believe that literature is also a kind of labor and, furthermore, an urgent kind of labor for man. Persons engaged in literature should consider it a life-time occupation."[29]

This manifesto should be regarded as something of a milestone. It proclaims, in its first principle, the formal emergence of modern Chinese men of letters who were to be united in a fellowship for new literary endeavors. Second, it echoes the proposition in *New Youth* that the old Chinese literary tradition is inadequate and that modern literary men should borrow from the West. Third, it asserts a new stance, truly unprecedented, that literature ought to be regarded as a serious, independent, and honorable vocation. Their predecessors in the treaty-port newspapers had laid the groundwork, and the association, as envisioned by its founders, was to consolidate it and promote the interests of writers by posing as a union in embryo.

The twelve founders of the association were writers: Chou Tso-jen,

Mao Tun, Hsü Ti-shan, Wang T'ung-chao, Yeh Shao-chün; editors and translators: Sun Fu-yüan, Keng Chi-chih; scholars: Cheng Chen-to, Chu Hsi-tsu, Ch'ü Shih-ying, Kuo Shao-yü; and even one military man, Chiang Pai-li. All of them were then located in Peking. Thus in the beginning the composition of the association reflected some over-lapping with the Peking aggregate. But as membership expanded and branch offices were established in Canton and other cities, the outlook was so broadened as to seem sufficiently vague.[30] Moreover, although the association's formal address was in Peking, its periodicals—*Hsiao-shuo yüeh-pao, Wen-hsüeh hsün-k'an, Wen-hsüeh chou-pao* (Literature weekly), *Shih* (Poetry)—were either published in Shanghai or affiliated with the *Shih-shih hsin-pao* of Shanghai. As a result, the Peking influence was further diluted. The first significant contribution of the association, therefore, was to widen the scope of the literary arena.

The association's second contribution lay in consolidating and popularizing the new role of the practitioners of New Literature. Its publications, particularly the *Hsiao-shuo yüeh-pao,* enjoyed increasing prestige and wider circulation among the youth, so much so that to have one's articles published in one of the association's periodicals was tantamount to admission to the elite circles of literary men. Compared to the Creation journals, the association's publications were quite open to new outside talent.

A third contribution—somewhat doubtful—was the association's introduction and translation of foreign literature. One of its most ambitious undertakings was the projected Association for Literary Studies Series. A total of 101 titles was announced, out of which 71 were to be translated works.[31] Complete data are unavailable on the final results.[32] In general, Russian and East European works predominated, but French authors were not neglected. Special issues of *Hsiao-shuo yüeh-pao* were devoted to Tolstoy, Tagore, Byron, Hans Christian Andersen, Romain Rolland, the literature of "oppressed nations," "antiwar literature," French literature, and Russian literature. Turgenev, Chekhov, Dostoevsky, Gogol, Maupassant, Zola, France, Blake, Yeats, Loti, Merimée, Johan Bojer, D. H. Lawrence, and even Dante and Virgil were also introduced. The long list of authors indicates clearly that the association did not champion exclusively the literature of any particular author, type, or nation. Its extensive coverage also reveals the society's own lack of intensiveness and depth. The association reached its peak of activity by 1925 and thereafter declined steadily until its noiseless demise in 1930.

The Creation Society

The Creation Society (Ch'uang-tsao She) grew out of a group of close friends consisting initially of Kuo Mo-jo, Yü Ta-fu, Ch'eng Fang-wu, and Chang Tzu-p'ing. As students at Tokyo Imperial University, they decided after a series of informal discussions to publish a magazine to disseminate their own brand of New Literature. When they returned to China, the manager of a small Shanghai publishing firm, T'ai-tung, was the first to capitalize on their talents. In the summer of 1921, the T'ai-tung Book Company published the first Creation Society Series of four works. The formal founding date of the Creation Society was traced by Kuo Mo-jo to July 1921, when a meeting was held at Yü Ta-fu's residence in Shanghai where the abovementioned four founders together with Ho Wei and Hsü Tsu-cheng decided to publish a quarterly, entitled *Creation* at the suggestion of Kuo Mo-jo.[33] The society lasted a decade until February 7, 1929, when it was closed down by the government.

The initial emphasis of the Creationists was, indeed, on creation. In the six issues of *Ch'uang-tsao chi-k'an* (Creation quarterly; 1922–1924), original poetry and fiction overshadow criticism and comments. Few translations were published; there was one issue (Vol. 1, No. 4) devoted to Shelley. With the appearance of two new periodicals, *Ch'uang-tsao chou-pao* (Creation weekly, May 1923–May 1924) and *Ch'uang-tsao jih* (Creation Day, one hundred issues, July 21–October 31, 1923, attached to the *Chung-hua jih-pao*), translations and introductions of Western literature assumed equal importance. Major figures from Western literature and philosophy introduced in the two journals were: Nietzsche, Romain Rolland, Max Stirner, Alexander Herzen, Tagore, Walter Pater, Rossetti, the "Yellow Book" group, Maeterlinck, Heine, Goethe, Shelley, Wordsworth, Lamartine, Hugo,

Maupassant, and Theodor Storm. The list reflects a decidedly Romantic outlook and partially overlaps with a similar list which can be compiled from the leading Western writers introduced by the Crescent Moon Society. Accordingly, the first period of the Creation Society, from 1922 to 1925, has been generally called its "romantic period."[34] One member of the society later reminisced that Kuo, upon being queried about the society's orientation, answered unequivocally, "neo-romanticism."[35]

With Kuo's conversion to Marxism in 1924, the society is said to have made its celebrated shift to the left—"from literary revolution to revolutionary literature"—in its second (May 1925–June 1928) and third (June 1928–February 1929) periods.[36] The issues involved were not merely ideological but also organizational.

A group of younger members of the society, consisting of Chou Ch'üan-p'ing, Ching Yin-yü, and Ni I-te, managed to found a new fortnightly, *Hung-shui* (Deluge) in 1924, partly to publish the extra articles which were left over from *Creation Weekly*. It ceased publication after a few issues. One year later, in September 1925, the magazine was revived by the same young group to serve as a "public platform for youth" and to attack "whatever hinders the development of youth's mind—in thinking, in life, politics, and economics."[37] The magazine, therefore, laid the basis for a subsequent "usurpation" of power by the younger Creationists from the older founders. Half a year after the revival of *Deluge,* its increasing sales encouraged Chou Ch'üan-p'ing to have the magazine published independently. Chou was also in charge of the publications department of the Creation Society, which was open for business on April 1, 1926.[38] Earlier in March, Kuo Mo-jo, Yü Ta-fu, and Wang Tu-ch'ing, who had just returned from France, went to Canton. Ch'eng Fang-wu was there waiting for them. Cheng Po-ch'i and Mu Mu-t'ien also joined them a few months later. Thus almost all the founding members of the Creation Society had clustered in Canton, leaving their old headquarters in Shanghai to the care of their "junior partners." A widening chasm began to extend between the old and the new Creationists. The three earlier Creation journals having been terminated, the old members founded a new one in February 1926, *Ch'uang-tsao yüeh-k'an*

15

(Creation monthly), which lasted until January 1929. But the junior partners were in firm control of the publications department. Chou Ch'üan-p'ing brought in his friend P'an Han-nien, who reprinted "meaningless books" on his own initiative without having the prior consent of the founding members.[39] The masters were enraged by their irresponsible apprentices and sent Yü Ta-fu to Shanghai to "clear things up." Because of his drinking bouts, Yü merely managed to get himself evicted from the society.[40]

The ranks of the younger Creationists were further strengthened in 1928 by the return from Japan of a group of young radicals including Li Ch'u-li, Chu Ching-wo, Feng Nai-ch'ao, and Li T'ieh-sheng, who had persuaded Ch'eng Fang-wu to use the society publications as an "ideological stronghold . . . to expound dialectic materialism and historical materialism."[41] Moreover, mutual misunderstanding and dissension among the older members had wrecked the foundation of the society, making it easier for the younger members to consolidate their power. After 1928, a series of short-lived journals were issued by them: *Wen-hua p'i-p'an* (Cultural criticism), *Huan-chou* (Mirage), *Jih-ch'u* (Sunrise), and *A 11*. Their ideological framework was definitely Marxist.

The "leftism" of the Creation Society in the second half of the 1920s was instrumental in bringing about a changed atmosphere: the slogans concerning "proletarian literature" came initially from the younger Creationists and their associates. But it was also in the second half of the decade, as the power and influence of the association gradually waned, that the proud, headstrong Creationists met formidable challengers. The tone of Lu Hsün's critical *tsa-wen* against the younger Creationists in the years 1928–29 bordered on sheer nastiness.[42] The Yü-ssu group added disdain to Lu Hsün's distaste. But the positive challenger, the group which offered an alternative posture to the younger Creationists' radical leftism, was the so-called Crescent Moon Society, founded in 1928.

The Crescent Moon Society

In 1924 a private club was formed in Peking. Its name, Hsin-yüeh (Crescent moon), was borrowed from the title of a collection of Tagore's poetry. Composed mainly of returned students from England and America, the Crescent Moon was first created as a dining and entertainment club.[43] Its guiding spirit was Hsü Chih-mo, who had recently returned from England. In 1925, Hsü became the editor of Ch'en-pao's literary supplement and presumably some members were drawn into literary creation. Hsü also befriended Ch'en Yüan (Hsi-ying), a professor at Peita and editor of Hsien-tai p'ing-lun (Contemporary review). Although the weekly was not literary, it devoted enough space to literature and promoted the works of Ling Shu-hua, a student of Yenching University, who later became Ch'en's wife.[44] When Ch'en was embroiled in a personal feud with Lu Hsün over a student protest incident at the Women's Normal University, Hsü Chih-mo somewhat reluctantly published his friend's letters criticizing Lu Hsün.[45] It was these two personal groups which formed the backbone of the Crescent Moon Society.

In 1927, the forces of the Northern Expedition reached the Yangtze. The alarmed warlord government, in confusion, was unable to supply salaries for the professors of the national universities in Peking. The chaotic situation forced the exodus of members of the club along with some other professors. They all sought protection in Shanghai, where they were joined by two young professors from Nanking, Liang Shih-ch'iu, a literary critic, and Yü Shang-yüan, a dramatist. A discussion group was formed at the house of P'an Kuang-tan, a sociologist, for the publication of a literary journal. The group included Hsü Chih-mo, Liang Shih-ch'iu, Yü Shang-yüan, Hu Shih, Wen I-to, a poet, Ting Hsi-lin, a dramatist, Jao Meng-k'an, a translator, and Yeh Kung-ch'ao. Hsü Chih-mo was again the mastermind and fund raiser. He managed to squeeze enough money from his friends to set up the Hsin-yüeh bookstore early in 1928.[46] On March 10, 1928, the first issue of Hsin-yüeh was published. The magazine lasted until 1933 and published an impressive total of four volumes and forty-three issues.

Most of the Crescentists had studied at Columbia University. Their journal reflected a decidedly Anglo-American orientation, the English elements being the personal imprint of Hsü Chih-mo. The format of the magazine was supposed to be a replica of the famous English journal, the *Yellow Book*, published from 1894 to 1897 with contributions from Henry James, Edmund Gosse, Max Beerbohm, W. H. Davis, Ernest Dowson, and others.[47] And throughout its six years of publication, *Hsin-yüeh* introduced Shakespeare, Byron, Shelley, Keats, Rossetti and the Pre-Raphaelites, Burns, Blake, Elizabeth Browning, Mansfield, Swinburne, Hardy, W. H. Davis, Lytton Strachey, Galsworthy, Shaw, Masefield, A. E. Housman, O'Neill, Poe, O. Henry, Tagore, Ibsen, Baudelaire, and Maurois. The list is predominantly Anglo-American. In the heated atmosphere of the late 1920s, when the leftist outcries for proletarian literature and Marxist slogans filled the air, the *Hsin-yüeh* could not but convey a highly "ivory-towerish" quality. The Anglo-American authors seem to have imparted a strong dose of poetry over prose, and fantasy over realism. In poetry, Hsü and Wen were more concerned with rhymes and meters than with thematic content. Disciples like Ch'en Meng-chia and Fang Wei-te followed their lead. In fiction, the two most frequent contributors were Ling Shu-hua and Shen Ts'ung-wen. Miss Ling, whose romance with Ch'en Hsi-ying curiously reminds one of that between Katherine Mansfield and John Middleton Murry, consciously modeled her style after the English authoress, and she was as fond as Katherine Mansfield of subtle explorations of the female psyche. Shen Ts'ung-wen, a poor student who had gained sponsorship from both Hsü Chih-mo and Ch'en Hsi-ying in Peking, wrote about fifteen short stories and a long novel for the magazine. Most of his stories described the romances and life styles of his favorite southern Chinese countryside.

When by the force of circumstance the *Hsin-yüeh* finally turned to politics in late 1929, its political outlook remained Anglo-American. Hu Shih's plea for the immediate promulgation of a constitution by the Kuomintang government and Lo Lung-chi's exposition of the "politics of specialists" on the model of the American civil service clearly revealed the American type of pragmatic liberalism. But their mild criticisms and suggestions proved futile vis-à-vis the government and downright reactionary in the eyes of the leftist writers.[48]

In November 1931, Hsü Chih-mo died suddenly in a plane crash. After its "soul" disappeared, the Crescent Moon Society deteriorated rapidly, but not without having relegated to posterity a poetry journal (*Shih-k'an*, to be distinguished from a poetry supplement to *Ch'en-pao* bearing the same name) of five issues and about a hundred volumes of poetry, fiction, literary criticism, essays on various subjects, and translations of Western—mainly eighteenth and nineteenth century English—fiction and drama.

Polemics and Personalities

With the formation of these four large literary groupings and the interplay among them, the new literary scene in the 1920s was punctuated by a series of major and minor skirmishes, both ideological and personal. The rearguard actions by the defenders of the classical tradition and the literary style *(wen yen)*—like Chang Shih-chao and his *Chia-yin* (Tiger monthly) and the group around the *Hsüeh-heng* magazine—had been easily crushed by the combined New Literature forces. The more exciting drama, however, came from within the new literary circles, among which the two predominant and antagonistic camps were naturally the Association for Literary Studies and the Creation Society.

Much has been written about the dichotomy in literary theory between the two groups in terms of two clichés: "art for life" versus "art for art." But in the primary documents of this period, this theoretical antagonism seems more apparent than real.

An examination of documents from the Association for Literary Studies is illustrative. In a candid memoir written in 1924, for instance, Mao Tun, one of the prime architects of the association, said the following about its "ideology":

For a while, the members of the Association for Literary Studies were regarded as proponents of "art for life's sake." Especially after the founding of the Creation Society, many people considered the Creation Society as an "art clique" in opposition to the Association's "life clique" . . . When I went to Canton in the spring of 1926 the young people there were still asking about this and they said: "Why doesn't the Association for Literary Studies expound art for life's sake now? What does the Association advocate now?" I remember replying something like this: "The Association for Literary Studies has never advocated anything, but the principles of the individual members of the Association have been many. If you want to ask me my personal opinion I'll be glad to explain it." [49]

Chou Tso-jen, another leader and theoretician in the association, is representative of the "art for life" theory. As early as 1918 he had published in *New Youth* an essay titled "Humane Literature." After a confused and pretentious analysis he concluded that "this humane literature, which we have called literature for life . . . is for an individual as a member of humanity to express his individual feelings with artistic means." [50] In another article, "The Demands of New Literature," he elaborated on the same point: "The proper interpretation (of the life school) still regards art and literature as its ultimate aim but they should have contact with life through the writer's feelings and thoughts. In other words, the writer should use artistic methods to express his feelings and thoughts toward life so that the readers will obtain esthetic enjoyment and an explanation of life." [51]

This "proper interpretation" by Chou Tso-jen serves an important function in clarifying the amorphous truism of "art for life." In the temper of the early twenties when the association was active, Chou's view was an adequate reflection of a general attitude. Where should a writer reflect his own feelings and thoughts, that is, his personality, if not in his life? How could a new author write with real substance and no pretense if he did not write about life, especially his own life? Therefore, the cliché of realism, which Ch'en Tu-hsiu put on his banners of Literary Revolution and which many contemporaries and later scholars have attributed to the association, seems to be mere common sense. [52] The possible variation of this common theme may have come from Mao Tun's "naturalism": he was intent on writing about other people's lives whereas most of his colleagues wrote about their own. [53] The "realistic" works of Yeh Shao-chün, Ping Hsin, Wang T'ung-chao, Huang Lu-yin, and Hsü Ti-shan—all members of the association—are related to their own or familiar experiences. What is at stake in the creative output of his period is not so much "life" in general as the writer's "feelings and thoughts toward life." In a brief preface to Volume 15, Number 2 of *Hsiao-shuo yüeh-pao*, Cheng Chen-to, another prominent man in the association, remarked: "When we differentiate between good literary works and works not qualified to be literature we cannot use rational and moral standards. We only look to whether the sentiments expressed by him [the writer] are sincere and earnest, whether his techniques of expression are meticulous and beautiful." [54]

Opposed to the slogan of "art for life" was the prevalent notion associated with the early Creationists, "art for art." Like the leaders of the association, the Creation founders never fully acknowledged the term as the official motto of the society, despite their fondness for Oscar Wilde and the French symbolists. Kuo Mo-jo stated and Ch'eng Fang-wu reiterated that "this little society does not have any set organization. Nor do we have any regulations, nor bureaucracy, nor unified doctrine. We are but a random gathering of some friends. Our doctrines and ideas are not in full accord; nor do we demand accord. What we have in common is simply to engage in literary activities in accordance with our inner demands." [55]

In another essay on the "Mission of New Literature," which is comparable in standing to Chou Tso-jen's article, Ch'eng made further clarifications:

The so-called art for art school is this: they think that literature has its own inner meaning and cannot be counted into utilitarianism . . .

At least I think that the pursuit of "perfection" and "beauty" divested of any utilitarian calculations deserves the possibility of our life-long endeavor. Moreover, a literature of beauty, even if it has nothing to teach us, gives us a sense of bliss and comfort from beauty whose regenerating effect on our daily life we cannot but acknowledge.

Furthermore, literature is not without some positive benefit to us. Our epoch has taxed our reason and feeling too heavily. Our lives have reached the end of dry boredom. We are thirsty for having a literature of beauty to nourish our beautiful feelings and to cleanse our lives. Literature is the food for our spiritual life. How much joy of life, how much vibration of life can we feel! [56]

It is not necessary to quote other similar pronouncements from Kuo Mo-jo and Yü Ta-fu to discover the crux of this "art for art" argument. Far from the French symbolist notion that art not only re-structures life but also constructs a new edifice into which the artist can escape from life, Ch'eng's arguments point in fact to the other pole: his esthetics are founded on the solid groundwork of life. The pursuit of "perfection" and "beauty," which Ch'eng defines as art, is ultimately to nourish life, to provide, as Chou Tso-jen has mentioned, "esthetic enjoyment." Moreover, life in Ch'eng's schema is not de-fined in the abstract but refers to "our daily life" as perceived through our "feelings and thoughts," that is, through experience. The differ-ence between Ch'eng and Chou is the difference of perspective and preoccupation. "Individual feelings" for Chou Tso-jen may have been conceived on a more rational and realistic basis, whereas the Cre-ationists, in their pre-Marxian phase, had more ecstatic views of their "daily life." They may have idolized the creative process, but their esthetics is also based on their own life experience. In short, Ch'eng Fang-wu's argument may be interpreted in this way: art, although having its own inner meaning and value, is originally created on the basis of life and ultimately serves life by giving it pleasure. In both instances of "life," Ch'eng was thinking of his own.

Kuo Mo-jo summarized sardonically the whole range of theoretical justifications from members of the two groups by saying that "there were no fundamental differences between the Association for Literary Studies and the Creation Society. The so-called life school and art school were but window-dressing." [57]

The real problem with the rivalry between the two groups lies in the clash of personalities. The labyrinthine mesh of personal relation-ships among modern Chinese celebrities—particularly the politicians and the writers—is perhaps the most formidable task for a historian of another age to tackle adequately. But even a sketchy outline reveals its immense complications. Kuo Mo-jo recounted in his memoir about the Creation Society that initially the founders of the association, especially Cheng Chen-to, did invite the Creationists to join them. A letter of invitation had been sent to T'ien Han in Tokyo, which, for some unknown reason, was neither answered nor referred to the other Creationists. In Shanghai, Cheng Chen-to and Mao Tun treated Kuo to dinner and again urged him to join. Kuo, upon being told of such a letter, surmised that T'ien Han turned down the invitation and accordingly Kuo declined the request in order not to harm the feelings of his good friend.[58] The seeds of disharmony were thus sown.

However, the initial relationships between the two groups remained cordial. In 1922, to celebrate the anniversary of the publication of Kuo's Goddesses (Nü-shen), Yü Ta-fu held a grand dinner party to which some of the association members—including Mao Tun, Cheng Chen-to, and Huang Lu-yin—were also invited. Mao Tun made an encouraging speech and photos were taken. The real cleavage occurred when Yü Ta-fu put in an ad for the forthcoming Creation Quarterly, in which he referred to one group as "monopolizing the literary scene." Some members of the association were naturally incensed. References to Yü as a "decadent depictor of carnal desires" and Kuo and T'ien Han as "blind translators" began to appear in the association's publications.[59] The Creationists counterattacked. Yü Ta-fu wrote a satirical piece parodying Mao Tun, Cheng Chen-to, and their brand of "blood and tears literature." Kuo Mo-jo and Ch'eng Fang-wu resorted to further carpings on translations. Storm's peaceful Immensée provided the unexpected battleground for members of both camps to flaunt their knowledge of German. A careless misreading of "atheism" into "Athenianism" by one association translator was sadistically magnified by Ch'eng into a doctrine—Athenianism—of translation.[60] From criticism of translations the Creationists moved to downgrading of their opponents' creative work. Himself never a first-rate poet, Ch'eng Fang-wu wrote a scathing survey called "The Defensive Battle of Poetry," vilifying such notables as Chou Tso-jen, Yü P'ing-po, K'ang Pai-ch'ing, Hsü Yü-no, and even Hu Shih.[61] In terms of aggressive daring, the Creationists seemed to have won the first round. But their youthful impetuosity also gained for them more foes than friends.

The Creationists' clash with the "gentlemen" of the Crescent Moon followed a similar pattern. The Crescentist leaders—Hu Shih, Hsü Chih-mo, and Liang Shih-ch'iu—were initially on friendly terms with the Creationists. Hsü and Liang's letters were published in the Creation Weekly; Liang Shih-ch'iu even contributed a story from America.[62] The scuffles began when Hu Shih found fault with Yü

Ta-fu's German, which distressed and infuriated Yü so much that he contemplated suicide. Although he failed to muster enough courage to jump into the Huang-p'u River, he did write a rebuttal. Hu Shih wrote back, and Kuo and Ch'eng joined the skirmish. Hu's friends Chang Tung-sun, Ch'en Yüan, and Hsü Chih-mo lent their pens. Ch'en Yüan attacked Kuo concerning the translation of *Immensée*. Hsü referred casually to Kuo's "torrents of tears" [63] and brought upon him the wrath of Kuo's friend Ch'eng Fang-wu, who published an open letter to Hsü in *Creation Weekly* and lamented with disillusionment: "Chih-mo! I can never imagine that the hypocrisy of man has fallen to such depths! . . . You have criticized us as 'false men' . . . but only you qualify as a 'false man.' And I hate most of all false men . . . " [64] To be called "false" must have been more than a sting for a man who took pride in his sincerity and openness.

Except for Yü Ta-fu, the Creationists—both old and young members—had never been in favor with Lu Hsün. Although both lived in Shanghai, Kuo Mo-jo and Lu Hsün seemed to have purposefully avoided each other.[65] In Lu Hsün's long essay, "A Glance at Literature in Shanghai," the Creationists earned the incomparable title of "dilettantes and rogues," and Ch'eng Fang-wu was accused of "displaying a kind of extremely left-leaning and fierce face." [66] The younger radicals were not spared the old man's vindictive sprees in another essay full of Lu Hsün's typical earthiness: "On the battleground of 'revolutionary literature' I am one 'behind the ranks.' Therefore, I can't see what happens at the center and on the front. But looking in the direction of their asses, one sees Commander Ch'eng Fang-wu's *Creation Monthly*, *Cultural Criticism*, *Flowing Sand*; the *Sun* with Chiang Kuang-X (sorry I have yet to know what word he has changed to now) in command, Wang Tu-ch'ing . . . young revolutionary artist Yeh Ling-feng . . . young revolutionary artist P'an Han-nien . . . " [67]

The venom hidden in the old master's fangs remained unmatched by anyone in the field. The many battles Lu Hsün fought were a clear indication of the muddled relationships among the complicated configurations of literary groups and individuals, who were, in one way or another, all embroiled in endless feuds.

24

The background factors behind this complicated pattern are as complex as the pattern itself. One way to look at it is through the two axes of education and geography. The Crescent Moon Society was an Anglo-American group. In arguments its members still affected the manner of "gentlemen" debaters. In contrast, the Creationists were, with few execptions, all Japanese-educated students who regarded the Anglo-American group with a mixture of envy and disdain. Others who had never gone abroad, like some members of the association, harbored similar feelings against both. Within the same Japanese "tradition," the situation was complicated by age and rank: earlier "drop-outs" like Lu Hsün and Chou Tso-jen could hardly stomach the arrogance of a group of Tokyo University upstarts. Within the European "tradition," the problem seemed to be one of culture. French-educated Wang Tu-ch'ing would not venerate English-educated Hsü Chih-mo, although the continental tradition seemed acceptable to the Creationists, perhaps because of Japan's own tradition of continental borrowings, particularly German, since the Meiji Restoration.

Geographically, the configurations conveyed a totally "Chinese" flavor. In Peking opera there has long existed a kind of dichotomy between the so-called Peking (*Ching-p'ai*) and Shanghai (*Hai-p'ai*) schools. These two broad terms may also be applicable to the literary men. The Peking school has been termed by one connoisseur as generally "classicist" whereas the Shanghai school may be thought of as "romantic";[68] the Peking school "traditional" and the Shanghai school "modern." Being more learned and hence proud of their cultured tastes, the Peking school often looked down upon the shallow, philistine "poets on the Shanghai beach."[69] Lu Hsün, Chou Tso-jen, and other elderly members of the Peking aggregate can be taken as the best representatives of the Peking school, whereas in their eyes the Creationists, with their "machinations, vacillations," their wine and women, and especially their hankering for fame and profit, are typically in the compradorial "Shanghai style."[70] Thus the association was generally able to maintain peace with the prominent members of the Peking aggregate like the Yü-ssu group while the Creationists often found themselves fighting against both. The Crescent Moon group presents a similar pattern with the association and might have found some degree of accord with the aggregate academicians had they not distinguished themselves by their Anglo-American education.

Ultimately, the polemics and groupings result from personal temperaments. The more urbane and tolerant ones like Hsü Chih-mo and Hu Shih are bound together by more than their similar educational backgrounds. The Creation founders, each different in his own fashion, are linked together by a common ebullience and concept of self-heroism; even Yü Ta-fu's "decadence" was a self-perpetuated heroic vision. The connoisseur's appreciation of rare books and rare scenic spots characterize the essays and life styles of Chou Tso-jen and the Sun brothers, who are among the best essayists and travel writers of modern China. Finally, Lu Hsün, the most tormented and the least trusting soul among them, was also the loneliest—a solitary giant who defied all alliances and attributes. Although he was widely respected, few could gauge the depths of his psychological tribulations. He remains an enigma, unique and unclassifiable.

Born in 1881 to a gentry family in rapid decline, Lu Hsün was brought up in the twilight splendor of the Chinese tradition. As he gradually assimilated Western learning in Japan by studying Western medicine, he reacted against what he came to regard as the superstitions and stupidities of his childhood milieu. He abruptly dropped out of the Sendai medical school in 1906 after having watched news slides depicting Japanese soldiers decapitating Chinese in Manchuria. He chose literature as a medium to cure the "souls" of his compatriots. Back in China in 1909, he became a depressed observer of the 1911 Revolution. When the *New Youth* raised the banner of Literary Revolution in 1917, Lu Hsün was drawn out from the long spell of his despondency. Somewhat reluctantly, he joined the ranks of the new literary men by publishing a short story, "Diary of a Mad Man." Other stories and miscellaneous essays followed and Lu Hsün was thrust into the forefront of the New Culture movement.

But while fighting consciously against the forces of tradition and traditionalism, Lu Hsün was seized by periodic attacks of spiritual nihilism. He seemed unable to shake off the inner ghosts of tradition that continued to haunt him. After teaching and writing for fourteen years in Peking, he journeyed south in 1926 to Amoy. In 1927 he moved from Amoy to Canton and finally settled down in Shanghai, where he became something of a doyen on the literary scene. Although hailed by the young as their master, he suffered from ambivalent relationships with the young writers who sought his guidance. Willing to help them, he was unwilling or unable to point out the way for the future; generous and considerate in his efforts to promote new authors, he was often bitter and irascible when his disciples propounded theories with which he could not agree. Thus in the late twenties Lu Hsün found himself fighting on all fronts. His 1928 debates with the younger Creationists on proletarian literature drove him to translate some works of literary criticism by Plekhanov and Lunacharsky, thus further entrenching him ideologically on the left. The League of Leftwing Writers, founded in 1930, proclaimed him a leader, but his relations with this Communist dominated group were not harmonious. He died in 1936, a desperate and tormented man, alienated from those who later deified him.

Chapter 2

The Phenomenon of
Wen-t'an and *Wen-jen*

I have attempted to delineate a pattern of evolution of literary activity, from the treaty-port newspapers and popular magazines at the turn of the century to the major societies and publications dedicated to New Literature in the 1920s. The geographical setting was mainly in two cities—Shanghai and Peking, with Shanghai obviously the largest center of journalism and publishing and Peking the revered seat of learning. Canton, despite its importance as a "revolutionary base," paled in a cultural comparison. It was no wonder that when some of the leading literary people from Peking and Shanghai—Lu Hsün, Yü Ta-fu, Kuo Mo-jo, Ch'eng Fang-wu, Mao Tun—came to Canton in the mid-1920s the place proved a great disappointment. The city of political cliques and military coup d'états could offer only military men and politicians whose uncouth and unkempt ways the cultured, pampered, and sophisticated literary men from the north regarded with repugnance.

Although the May Fourth movement was first launched in Peking, one can detect a gradual shift of literary activity from Peking to Shanghai. The cultural assets of Peking—palaces, museums, universities, the splendor of its past history—were offset by the chaos, corruption, and instability of a succession of warlord regimes. Because of this political confusion a degree of intellectual freedom did exist by default in the beginning, thanks mainly to the ineptitude of the warlords. In the spring of 1926, however, shortly before Chang Tso-lin's army stormed into Peking, the alarmed Tuan Ch'i-jui regime threatened arrest of more than fifty "over-radical" professors and other intellectuals, thus forcing their mass exodus.[1]

Lu Hsün was among this group and left Peking in 1926. After brief stays in Amoy and Canton, where he became disillusioned with "revolutionary youth," he moved back north and settled in Shanghai. His movements typified the patterns of hundreds of other New Culture "radicals" who forsook the cultural pride of Peking and plunged themselves in this "ten-mile foreign settlement" (shih-li yang ch'ang) of Shanghai. In 1927, because of the salary shortage at national universities, another wave of intellectuals emigrated from Peking and made their home in Shanghai.

Shanghai, this largest treaty-port with its paraphernalia of native and alien cultures—French cafes, British and American banks, White Russian prostitutes and massage parlors, mass dance halls, a city orchestra composed mainly of foreigners, numerous Peking opera and K'un-ch'ü theaters, gambling houses, opium dens—became the center of literary activity after the mid-twenties. The city offered two kinds of ready facilities which proved congenial to these new-style intellectuals. First, the foreign concessions, ironically, provided them with a haven from the warlord scuffles and, after 1927, Chiang Kai-shek's "white terror." Second, Shanghai's publishing establishment was unrivaled anywhere in the country. The largest firm, the Commercial Press (Shang-wu yin-shu kuan), owned the Hsiao-shuo yüeh-pao and published the works of the Literary Studies Association and other writers. T'ai-tung, a small and obscure company, made a fortune by teaming up with the Creation Society. The Creationists and the Crescentists later also set up their own publishing companies. In addition, some enterprising book companies, such as K'ai-ming, Sheng-huo, Ya-tung, Kuang-hua, and Pei-hsin, did great business by catering to New Culture under enlightened leadership.[2] Most of them were willing to take risks with unknown writers, although they would pester established writers for their new works. The first printing of a work did not usually exceed more than one to two thousand copies, but a popular work could conceivably run to tens of printings.

The Phenomenon of Wen-t'an

The literary societies, journals, newspapers, and publishing companies formed the necessary background of a phenomenon generally known as *wen-t'an* (literary scene). Nobody ever attempted a definition although everybody presumed its existence. The term came into widespread use when the Creation Society in 1921 charged that some persons had "monopolized the literary scene," an unjust implied reference to the Association for Literary Studies. But the charge did seem to corroborate one of the visions of the association: they were indeed endeavoring to establish a congenial literary scene where all practitioners of New Literature could write and publish with a sense of esprit de corps. The challenge from a "militant band" of "pedantic, dogmatic, and bellicose" writers shattered this rosy "commonwealth" vision.[3] The literary scene since the early twenties, to participants and observers alike, seemed to consist of nothing but petty clique squabbles, personal feuds, ideological polemics, production of "fashionable" literature, and foppish aping of foreign literary fads.

A summary of the *wen-t'an* in the 1920s would focus on its setting in Shanghai. The scene would in general reflect the interplay among at least four groupings—the Association for Literary Studies, the Creation Society, the Yü-ssu group, and the Crescent Moon Society. If the term were extended beyond the confines of New Literature, *wen-t'an* might include the Saturday School of Butterfly fiction with their half dozen publications and such extremists as "Dr. Sex" Chang Ching-sheng and his Beautiful Bookstore (Mei-ti shu-tien). Both enjoyed immense popularity in sales. There was no undisputed leader on the literary scene, although Lu Hsün in the latter half of the decade, fighting single-handedly on all fronts but winning the grudging esteem of friend and foe alike, appeared as something of a dean of letters. His prestige gained him access to quite a few publishing firms and under his sponsorship many new works by young authors were brought into the market, especially in the early thirties.

It was on this literary scene that new trends and fashions were set and popularized. The predominant role, in this respect, belonged to the Creation Society. Their rise to fame from poverty, self-induced "suffering," and maltreatment by publishers established the typical pattern, a kind of Horatio Alger myth for the 1920s. A few friends, united by a common urge to write, would form a literary society and get a small printing firm to publish at least one issue of their journal. It would contain works of their fellow members (*t'ung-jen*) and be sprinkled with self-inflating manifestoes and personal notes and comments. When the journal sold well, the members would hold big celebration banquets where contacts could be made with other established writers. But in most cases, such publications would seldom last for more than a few issues.

The Creation Society and its affiliates were also mainly responsible for coining literary and political slogans. In the early twenties, Kuo Mo-jo and "Big Gun" Ch'eng Fang-wu vented their creative energy by flaunting terms like inspiration (*yen-shih p'i-li ch'un*) and muses (*miao-ssu*). As the Society moved from "literary revolution" to "revolutionary literature" in the late 1920s, it introduced such borrowed or coined fancy terms as *ao-fu he-pien (aufheben) yin-t'ieh-li-keng-chui-ya* (intelligentsia), and *p'u-lo* (abbreviation for proletariat). Thus the name proletarian literature came into fashion around the years 1927–28 before any substantive examples were created. The style of leftism was again largely the work of Creationists and their associates.

The literary scene was also the seat of what may be called *étrangerie*—foppish imitations of foreign manners and morals, both literary and social. With the massive introduction of foreign literature by the Association for Literary Studies, foreign writers and foreign literary trends were popular: Tolstoy, Tagore, Dostoevsky, Turgenev, Byron, Shelley, Keats, Maupassant, Zola, Hugo, Romain Rolland; classicism, romanticism, neo-romanticism, realism, naturalism, humanism, Tolstoyism, Marxism. A superficial knowledge of these big names and big "isms" bestowed status. This fashion was first popularized by the early Creationists and was carried further by returned students from Europe and America. Wang Tu-ch'ing, after a tour of Europe, wrote a book about it and bragged about his meeting with Anatole France.[4] Ching Yin-yü came to know Romain Rolland by correspondence and displayed the French master's short letter everywhere in print. Hsü Chih-mo wrote glowing memoirs of his visits to Thomas Hardy and Katherine Mansfield. Liang Shih-ch'iu and Mei Kuang-ti taunted the radicals with their own master, Irving Babbitt, under whom they had once done seminar work at Harvard. Gradually, precious real-life experiences, recounted ad infinitum, paved the way for false legends. The lecture tour of Tagore glamorized Hsü Chih-mo and Lin Hui-yin. George Bernard Shaw's brief visit to Shanghai brought him together with Lu Hsün, who had to deny with discomfort subsequent inflated accounts. Shen Ts'ung-wen, his native sensibilities incensed by this excessive *étrangerie*, wrote a long scathing novel called *Alice's Travels in China (A -li-ssu Chung-kuo yu-chi)* in which Alice and her rabbit friend were given the following suggestion by a Chinese literary man: "In order to make the acquaintance of the Chinese intellectuals, you can merely ask somebody in Europe who knows any big name in literature. Get a photograph of that literary celebrity and sign his name as if he had given it to you. Once you are in China, no matter whomever among the professors you meet, just show the photo to him and he will get you publicized tomorrow and everybody will ask you to give lectures."[5]

The foreign Alice also found the Shanghai scene disappointingly "un-Chinese": "The things displayed in shop windows are foreign merchandise; the houses are in European style; the people walking in the streets or riding in cars are for the most part Europeans."[6] This exaggerated parody referred of course to the so-called modern (*mo-teng,* in its chic Chinese transliteration) people, of whom the literary men and women were both the fashionables and the fashion setters. K'ang Pai-ch'ing, one of the early new-style poets, opened a cafe in Shanghai,[7] and Hsü Chih-mo's first wife was in charge of one of the largest women's dress shops.[8] In men's clothing, while the traditional Chinese scholar's long gowns were not out of fashion, it was stylish to wear under it a pair of Western-style trousers. French-educated men would not forget to wear their French berets in autumn and winter. Western suits, in general, were considered à la mode, so were French garters. The following passage is a summary portrait by an observer in 1926: "One of them wears a stiffly ironed Western suit; the folds of his trousers are like iron wires. His shining and pointed leather shoes are of low cut, revealing gleaming silk socks. Under his hard collar hangs a silk cravat, which is placed in front of his pongee shirt. His hand holds a 'civilized stick' and, as he steps inside the front court over the stone lintel, he takes off from his head a brand new straw hat . . . I think he must be a returned student." [9]

The fashionable women in the early years of the Republic "had been disfigured by a succession of lumpish modes until about 1926 a dressmaker of genius, needless to say in Shanghai, hit upon the idea of transforming the Manchu bannerman's robe into the 'split skirt.'" [10] There were constant shifts in the height of the split as well as the length of the sleeves. High, stiff collars were fashionable for a while for both men and women. A student returning from America found to his pleasant surprise that "here, there, and everywhere on the streets high-heeled shoes adorned the dainty feet of young women. When one heard quick heels tapping the sidewalks one felt at once that the rising generation were radically different from their mother." [11] Another more experienced old hand in Shanghai writing in the early thirties drew the following profile of a *mo-teng* woman: "She must wear a short *ch'i-p'ao* (split skirt) . . . high-heeled shoes and flesh-colored silk stockings, with her hair given a permanent wave. Her eyebrows are drawn thin and long, her face is covered with thick powder, her lips painted with blood-colored lipstick. She wears short underpants and carries a leather pocketbook . . . Unfortunately her breasts are not big, her hair is not blonde, her nose not high, and her eyes not deeply encaved." [12]

Less exaggerated than this caricature of the modern literary woman is the following sketch of a "girl student": "Her hair has been cut by half. To her loose short hair is fastened an ivory butterfly [ribbon]. Her breasts inside her snow-white gauze shirt are very flat; obviously she is wearing a tight brassiere . . . Under her short and open black silk skirt are a pair of short legs in white silk stockings. Further down are her dark high-heeled leather shoes, which make her limbs wave and writhe when she walks." [13]

The short hair and flat breasts were the typical features of independent, emancipated girl rebels who were taken by the general public for "female revolutionaries" (nü-ke-ming) because the short hair was supposedly introduced from Soviet Russia.[14] The outward appearance was very much a part of the new Nora prototype: young girl students who escaped from their traditional family background and migrated into the cities under the influence of New Culture, especialy the Hsin ch'ing-nien brand of Ibsenism introduced first by Hu Shih. As teachers in secondary schools or college students with a yen to write, they would daringly visit and befriend young literary men on their own initiative. The literature of the 1920s was filled with stories of how an independent Nora met and flirted with a pale and pensive young man at a café or how a group of nature-loving girl students bumped into a handsome art student doing a landscape painting at the West Lake near Hangchow. Names would be exchanged in a welter of English appellations—Mister (mi-ssu-t'o), Miss (mi-ssu), darling (ta-ling)—and romances soon followed, punctuated as they often were by incessant love letters, furtive rendezvous at restaurants and hotels, breaking-up of earlier arranged marriages, vows of devotion and infidelities, and comic or tragic endings either in new-style marriages, or in weeks of "interminable" suffering and self-pity. Western literature—a few names they read about or a few poems they managed to memorize—became stage props in these numerous romantic dramas. The life styles of these young fashionables in the coastal cities, in the popular phrase applied usually to studying abroad, were "gilded with gold," with the wonder and glamor of the West.

The life stories of these young men and women who joined the literary scene in the twenties and early thirties disclosed a typical pattern. He or she was born at the turn of the century in one of the more prosperous provinces in southeastern China. After a few years of old-style education, in which the youngster devoured the Four Books and Five Classics with half comprehension, new-style schools were opened in the provincial capitals and some other big cities. So our young novice first migrated to these new urban centers, having left a traditional environment in rapid decay. The curriculum of the new-style schools included such untraditional subjects as geography, mathematics, and sometimes foreign languages. During free hours, he or she would be immersed in the world of Yen Fu's translations of Spencer or Huxley and Lin Shu's world of Western romantic heroes and heroines. Liang Ch'i-ch'ao's essays, written always with "a touch of emotion at the tip of the pen," also became favorite reading among the young and bred their initial consciousness of nationalism. The 1911 Revolution, although changing very little of the rural landscape, often led to a kind of revolution in life styles. Our young man or woman became emboldened. The students staged strikes which sometimes forced out unpopular old-style administrators but often brought punishments upon the rebel leaders. He began to write love letters surreptitiously to a girl schoolmate he hardly knew; she fell secretly in love with the new teacher of Chinese literature. If their parents objected too much, they had a further excuse to break away from home for good and stay permanently in cities.

The publication of *Hsin ch'ing-nien* crystallized and popularized their radicalism. Everybody was reading the magazine and numerous other New Culture and New Literature magazines began to appear. Bursting to find an outlet for the accumulated creative urges, he or she gingerly tried creative writing. A pseudonym was generally used. Once the young writer's works appeared in some of the more prestigious places, he or she was already a self-styled *wen-jen*. Our young authors might also be bold enough to form their own literary societies and publish their own journals.

Sometimes when he or she became known provincially or even nationally, a further migration was made to Shanghai or Peking, presumably to study or teach but actually to loaf around, to meet people and be introduced to the literary celebrities. It was in the treaty port of Shanghai, often in the International Settlement or the French concession, that they met one another and fell madly in love. The experience provided new material and new incentive for further creative writings. Thus more works were written and published. He or she became a celebrity.

The Phenomenon of Wen-jen

The foregoing description brings us to another significant phenomenon closely related with the *wen-t'an*—the emergence and proliferation of *wen-jen* (men of letters, literary men) or, derogatively, *wen-kai* (literary beggars or rogues).[15]

The term *wen-jen* can be traced back as early as the Han period. But in the socio-political context of traditional China the usage was quite undifferentiated. It might refer to the broad category of "civilian" people as contrasted to the "military" men *(wu-jen)*.[16] But within the civilian category, a *wen-jen* had the further, and more concrete, connotation of practitioner of one or several genres of belles-lettres. In this narrower definition, the point to be noted is that belles-lettres could seldom be a socially accepted vocation. The early professional court painters and the writers of popular fiction and drama since the time of the Sung dynasty may have taken literature as a vocation, but it was never socially popular and, especially in the latter case, was entered only with considerable reluctance and regarded with substantial embarrassment, for most were frustrated scholar-officials. In the "great tradition," however, to be a famous *wen-jen* might bring a certain degree of social prestige but never political power nor financial well-being. A poet or an essayist never made money out of his works, nor was he willing to write for commercial purposes. Thus *wen-jen* in its most elevated form was but the more elegant and literary side of a scholar-official, and literature was more often than not a pastime or avocation.

The treaty-port journalist-littérateurs made literature a commercially viable vocation. They were the immediate ancestors of the modern men of letters. The New Literature movement marked the end of the era of the proto-literary men and catalyzed the modern *wen-jen* into existence. The charter of the Association for Literary Studies not only formalized their new status but also led the way toward literature as a serious and esteemed vocation. The Creationists made the modern *wen-jen* fashionable. And numerous young men and women, attracted by their life style and the popularity of their works, made literature their life ambition. The editors of literary journals were besieged with letters from youthful aspirants such as the following:

I am a 20-year-old youth and have received secondary-school education . . . I dare not say that I am versed in literature (or have literary talent). But I love literature and plan to dedicate myself to literature. Accordingly, I am asking for your instructions. How to study literature? What books of literary theory can I read? How to write? . . .

I am a young man of ambition, but circumstances have forced me to run around to make a living. I cannot but forsake my books. But my desire for knowledge does not submit itself to environmental pressures. Moreover, I want to do something beneficial to human society. So I have chosen literature. I intend to use literature to plead against the darkness of society and the sufferings of mankind, to convey my own thoughts and feelings, to portray the brightness of future. But I am a layman as regards literature and would like to ask you for instructions as to how to realize my goal . . .[17]

The notion that literature is a medium "beneficial to human society" and a tool with which to fight social ills and human suffering is both ancient and modern. But our young man's conceptions in this letter were most likely influenced by two more contemporary sources. The first was Liang Ch'i-ch'ao's famous view concerning the relationship between literature and people's sovereignty. Another possibility was Lu Hsün's account of his own decision, made while he was a medical student in Japan, to engage in literature as a result of watching documentary slides of Chinese peasants being beheaded by Japanese soldiers.[18] For the May Fourth men of letters, literary endeavor did not end with craftsmanship. Their sense of mission impelled them to see themselves as social reformers and spokesmen for the national conscience. This is entirely consistent with the prevalent ethos of nationalism in the May Fourth era.

Chinese tradition also holds that wen-jen are "mutually depreciative" (wen-jen hsiang-ch'ing). But the original inventor of this phrase, the poet Ts'ao P'i of the Six Dynasties period, certainly had in mind a different interpretation from its modern implications. "Depreciation," in Ts'ao Pi's time, concerned matters of literary styles and genres. As each was various and numerous, few wen-jen could master them all. Thus each "criticized" the shortcomings of the other on the basis of his own specialties (ke i so ch'ang, hsiang-ch'ing so tuan).[19]

This criticism of styles of literature gradually degenerated into "depreciation" of personal styles. Attacks in the 1920s became clique fighting. Insofar as the phrase still reflected its traditional connotations, its modern usage meant simply that the best works were works of one's own. The more arrogant would regard his own works not only as the best but also as the most "modern," that is, current with the most fashionable trends from the West.

A modern *wen-jen*, like his traditional counterpart, was more than a practitioner of literature. In both ancient and modern times, a *wen-jen* was often identified with *ming-shih*, a man of style whose life was bound up with wine and women.[20] Li Po, Su Tung-p'o, Yüan Mei, and the modern *wen-jen's* favorite, Huang Chung-tse, come easily to mind as past representatives. Through Su Man-shu, Yü Ta-fu, and many others, the modern men of letters perpetuated this tradition. A similar but slightly pejorative connotation was attached to a *wen-jen* —either traditional or modern—when he was compared to a *ts'ai-tzu*, a scholar with a "talent" for literature and, more important, a knack for love. The major difference between a modern *wen-jen* and a *ts'ai-tzu* in classical novels or Butterfly fiction was that the former was "modernized" with foreign fads and new-style thinking, whereas the old-style *ts'ai-tzu* might still weep over Black Jade's poetic burial of her withered flowers in the *Dream of the Red Chamber* or find his passion inflamed by the furtive rendezvous between the two lovers in the *Romance of the West Chamber (Hsi-hsiang chi)*. The new-style *wen-jen* preferred to invoke the love affairs of Byron, the sad ending of Keats or Shelley, or even the daring amours of George Sand. The so-called new-style thinking, popularized and vulgarized in the twenties, could be achieved, it was commonly believed, by meeting the following qualifications: subscription to *Hsin ch'ing-nien* and a few more New Literature journals such as *Creation Quarterly*; knowledge of Western intellectual and literary trends as gleaned from Liang Ch'i-ch'ao, Yen Fu, Ch'en Tu-hsiu, Hu Shih, and the major literary journals; an anti-warlord and pro-Canton stance before 1927, but a stance against Chiang Kai-shek's "white terror" afterwards; fascination with Russian nihilism and the Soviet example but not necessarily with theoretical Marxism; and, for new-style short-haired woman, a thorough espousal of Ibsenism, that is, a rejection of family and society, an emotional identification with emancipated heroines like Kollontay, Sophia Perovskaya, Emma Goldman, or Ellen Key.

A seasoned old hand in the 1920s wrote a book on how to succeed on the literary scene in which he proposed the following qualifications:

1. *Initial qualifications.* The minimum requirement is simply the ability to "read a few words." Equipped with this basic tool, a *wen-jen* should possess, in addition, the conviction of his own genius, idiosyncrasy, physical beauty, experience in love, brazenness and flexibility against attack, a little learning in traditional literature, especially the popular novels, and a ready memory of twenty names of Western authors.

2. *Temperament.* A modern *wen-jen* should be bohemian, amorous, boastful, lazy but tricky, complaining all the time, and emotional rather than rational.

3. *Life.* He should like modern, fashionable clothes, have gourmet tastes, indispensable habits of drinking and smoking, peripatetic residences, gamble and patronize brothels, have debts, an illness (especially tuberculosis and syphilis), and the ability to chat and meditate.

4. *Social intercourse.* He should have up-to-date knowledge of major trends and configurations on the literary scene, visit literary celebrities, form societies, engage in factional fighting, be able to retain friendly links and make new friends—both national and international.

5. *Writing.* A *wen-jen* had better keep a study in his house; maintain a willingness to know a little rather than nothing, write originally, especially about his own romances and, if creative writing is impossible for him, translate; pick fashionable "isms" or doctrines, choose subjects and themes from his own personal experiences—especially love—and write with an individual style in the following genres: poetry, drama, fiction, autobiography, diary, love letters, random sketches, short essays, travel accounts, and literary criticism.

6. *Publishing.* To make himself famous, he should contribute articles to other journals or newspapers, publish his own magazines and books, get to know and manipulate some publishers.

7. *Advertising.* He should print calling cards with full titles, use

stationery with personal letterheads, take photos, make announcements in newspapers, attend meetings and give long speeches, supply information of his own whereabouts to the information columns of literary journals or fabricate it.

8. *Preservation of achievements.* He should sponsor new writers, hire hack writers, examine the "national heritage," translate foreign classics, build a new house or redecorate an old one, compile collections.

9. *Readiness for change.*[21]

This comprehensive but devastating survey has conjured up a composite image of the modern Chinese man of letters in which one can detect traces of some of the eminent figures mentioned here. Yet this composite portrait in sarcasm hardly penetrates the surface. The external modes of behavior would have been less significant had they not been expressions of certain predominant inner feelings and thoughts. It is the interplay of the inner and outer sides of a *wen-jen* that intrigues historians of another age, for it reveals an important theme in modern Chinese literature and history—the evolution of a romantic temper. The following chapters are intended to develop this theme through biographical studies of seven men.

In treating sentiments, I aim only at acquiring
the right sentiment.
—Lin Shu

Chapter 3

Lin Shu

Lin Shu (1852–1924) was born in the village of Nan-t'ai, near Foochow, of a family who had been farmers and "good people in the
locality" for generations.[1] When Lin was four, his father went to
Taiwan to seek employment, and the whole family of nine members
often went without food for five or six days in a month. Four years
later, Lin's father was still in Taiwan and was absolutely penniless.
The family strove desperately to survive on some tiny allotments
from Lin's uncle and on the earnings from needlework done by his
mother and elder sister.

Lin's education began in 1862 at the age of ten. Financed by his
uncle, Lin became a favorite pupil of a poor local scholar, with whom
he avidly read the essays of Ou-yang Hsiu and the poems of Tu Fu.
Later on in the same year, his father finally obtained a job in a yamen
in Taiwan and was able to send money home. Relieved of the threat
of starvation, young Lin managed to save a few pennies and bought
some old fragmentary copies of *Han shu* (History of the former Han
dynasty) by Pan Ku and the works of pre-Ch'in philosophers. In five
years he had filled three closets with used classical volumes. At the
village school he also gained access to the *Shih ching* (Book of poetry),

the *Tso chuan* (Tso commentary), the *Shang shu* (Book of history), and Ssu-ma Ch'ien's *Shih-chi* (Records of the grand historian), which became his special favorite. By the age of twenty, he had read over 2,000 volumes of classical Chinese literature.

Lin's industry in study finally found reward in two degrees: he became a *hsiu-ts'ai* at the age of twenty-seven and a *chü-jen* at thirty. But he subsequently failed seven times to obtain the higher degree of *chin-shih*. Progressively thwarted by his repeated failures in the regular route to officialdom, Lin gradually gave up the prospect of an official career and reconciled himself to teaching. He held posts at various schools and, in 1905, when the civil service examination system was abolished, he joined the Faculty of Peking Imperial University where he taught until 1913. Educated in the Confucian tradition, Lin gradually distinguished himself as a master of the *ku-wen* (ancient) style and attained renown for his scholarly erudition in the works of the so-called Eight Great Masters of the T'ang and Sung dynasties. According to his own account, he had spent forty years studying the works of Han Yü, Liu Tsung-yüan, and Ou-yang Hsiu.[2] Wu Ju-lun, perhaps the last master of the T'ung-ch'eng school, praised his classical style,[3] which some others regarded as superior even to that of Wu himself.[4]

Among Lin's many essays none seems to exude as much warmth as his many reminiscences (often in the form of condolences) about his family members. There are essays on his mother, his grandmother, big brother, sister, uncle, his eldest daughter, his wife, and his concubine. It is obvious that Lin was very close to his family, which had such an emotional hold on him as to exceed the ritualistic expectations in the Confucian framework of social relations. At the age of eighteen, Lin grieved over the successive deaths of his grandparents and his father. Shortly afterwards he contracted tuberculosis and vomited large quantities of blood.[5] In late 1895, his mother fell seriously ill. For nine successive days he rose early in order to pray for his mother, vowing to sacrifice his academic degrees in exchange for a peaceful death for his mother. He even prostrated himself in torrents of rain. His fervid prayers seemed to be answered: his mother died quietly with no traces of blood from her ailing throat. In the sixty-day period

Lin Shu

of mourning at home Lin wept every night. For the next six years he frequently fell ill and had fainting spells.[6] During these unfortunate years, Lin was transformed by his sorrow into something of a bohemian. Ignoring his relatives, he indulged himself in poetry and songs, with the result that his fellow townsmen regarded him as a "wild scholar" and shied away from him.[7] In 1897, his wife, who had tended the ailing Lin with devotion for eighteen years, died of tuberculosis. In the next two years, he also lost his second son and eldest daughter.

The manifestations of grief over the passing of his family members bespeak Lin's highly emotional personality. It seems that his Confucian moralism is much more emotional, springing from his experience with his family, than it is academic. He was at times irritable and morose. His title "wild scholar" was also partly derived from his compulsion to engage in debate. In order to behave in accordance with the established code of the classics, especially as he approached middle age, he had to restrain his impetuousness.[8]

It was unusual for a traditional Confucian scholar to abandon himself to personal emotions within the prescribed bounds of propriety. But Lin proved himself truly exceptional: through a fortuitous encounter with a Western novel, he became deeply ingrained with Western fiction and attempted to justify his own emotionalism by both Chinese and Western examples. He became China's first major translator of Western literature and left an unsurpassed record of some 180 translated works.

La Dame aux Camélias—The World of Sentiment

Lin Shu's first exposure to Western literature was quite accidental. In the years when Lin was shattered by the loss of his mother and his children, a friend by the name of Wang Tzu-jen, a cadet from the Naval Academy near Foochow, brought to Lin's attention a French novel, La Dame aux Camélias. Perhaps with a view to diverting Lin's grief and loneliness, Wang, who knew French, suggested a joint translation of Dumas's novel. Since Lin did not know any foreign language, Wang first translated the sentences orally, and Lin then rendered them into classical Chinese prose. The two men wept profusely over

Marguerite Gautier's miseries. When they came to the most maudlin passages, the sounds of their sorrow were reportedly heard even outside the house.[9]

The novel not only moved Lin to tears but also became one of the most popular translated works in China. One wonders why, for a moralistic prose essayist thoroughly rooted in a tradition in which romantic novels seldom attained recognition in circles of "high culture," a Western work depicting a courtesan could have exerted such a strong appeal. Obviously Marguerite bore no resemblance to Lin's recently deceased wife. And the frivolous dandy, Armand, hardly fits the image of a Confucian gentleman.

Many speculative explanations could be offered to account for the initial appeal of this French novel to Lin Shu personally. For a more plausible interpretation, one must first go back to Lin Shu's biography. Lin had written one strictly autobiographical essay—"The Biography of Leng hung-sheng"—in which, of all possible themes, Lin chose to dwell upon a depiction of his own emotional nature, a rather uncommon gesture for a Confucian literatus. He admitted in the beginning of the essay that he was "stubborn and irritable," with an "undistinguished appearance." He then proceeded to describe his experience with prostitutes. Shortly after his wife's death, Lin found himself the object of the amorous attention of a charming prostitute. An admirer of his talent, she tried to ingratiate herself with him but received no response. When his friends jokingly reproached him for his cruelty, he defended himself thus: "I am not repaying her good sentiments with hatred. But because of my narrow-mindedness and excessive sense of jealousy, once I became fond of someone I would devote myself to her until the day of my death. People may not appreciate this, and therefore I want to disentangle myself at the very outset."[10]

To frequent houses of prostitution was certainly not taboo for a traditional scholar; many literary men—including one of Lin's favorite masters, Ou-yang Hsiu—often spent part of their after-hours in the houses of sing-song girls, where some of the best lyrical poetry was first conceived. But to treat prostitutes with the kind of serious attention shown in Lin's essay was rare in traditional China. It is apparent that Marguerite, a charming courtesan with a heart of gold, could easily win Lin's sympathies. One may even venture the argument that Marguerite's life story comes very close to exemplifying the Chinese popular notion that beautiful women lead miserable lives (*hung-yen po-ming*). But these surface affinities could merely reinforce a more deep-rooted emotionalism in Lin's personality. In this regard, Lin Shu's personal attitude toward prostitutes does, it seems to me, offer something new in the context of tradition: whether consciously or unconsciously, Lin Shu was attempting to merge the two traditionally separate worlds in the life of a Confucian scholar-official —the world of social and political commitment based on correct moral behavior and expressed in state service, and the less serious world of esthetic cultivation, of temporary withdrawals into nature, of casual and often flippant flirtations with sing-song girls. In other words, Lin Shu, as a moralistic Confucianist, attempted to bridge the gap between morality and sentiment by imbuing sentiment with the same degree of seriousness that he had accorded moral behavior. To him, sentiment (*ch'ing*) is more than the "inner" reflection of propriety (*li*) as prescribed in the *Analects*; sentiment *is* morality.

Lin himself admitted his unabashed attention to sentiment. He was reported to have said smilingly upon reading his own translation of *La Dame aux Camélias:* "If I can describe things to such an extent, how can it be said that I, stubborn and morose as I am, harbor hatreds toward sentiments?" [11] And his sentiments were not merely bestowed upon fallen women. The members of his family are the focus of many of his profusely emotional essays. His concubine received the same kind of warm respect. In 1924, on the occasion of her fiftieth birthday, he wrote an essay praising her frugality and diligence, and boastfully proclaimed that he was the first Chinese literatus to write a formal essay in honor of a concubine. He had no objection even to his son's suggestion that she be elevated to the position of his lawful wife. It was the concubine herself who declined the offer.[12] His devotion to his family led him naturally to emphasize filial piety. It was also in filial piety that Lin saw the perfect epitome of the merger of emotion and morality.

Dickens—The World of Ethics

In 1903, Lin and his family settled down in Peking, where he made the acquaintance of Wei I, his colleague in the Translation Bureau (Ching-shih i-shu chü). In 1907 and 1908 translations of five novels by Dickens were issued as a result of their collaboration: *Nicholas Nickleby (Hua-chi wai-shih), The Old Curiosity Shop (Hsiao-nü Nai-erh chuan), Oliver Twist (Tsei shih), David Copperfield (K'uai-ju yü sheng lu)*, and *Dombey and Son (Ping-hsüeh yin-yüan)*.

The appeal of Dickens to Lin Shu was explicitly discussed by Lin himself in his prefaces. Lin admired first Dickens' literary skill, which he compared to that of his favorite master, Ssu-ma Ch'ien.[13] Furthermore, Lin saw Dickens as a serious, and often tragic, social critic: "Dickens was a sorrowful man of the past. He was, according to his biography, of lowly social origin and brought up in poverty. Therefore, he was able to depict the characters of the lower strata of society; his pen neglecting nothing and encompassing a whole range of sentiments and sins in stark reality. Once a book was completed, the sight and sound [of social reality] could hide nowhere." [14]

A third feature he finds in Dickens' novels, a feature that obviously appeals to him most, is their ethical significance. While there were crimes and cruelties in Victorian society, there were also people like Dickens who upheld ethics. The sentimental and humanistic side of Dickens finds a warm endorsement in the heart of his Chinese translator.

Dickens' sentimentality is notorious and often mocked by sophisticated critics. Aldous Huxley, in commenting on the *Old Curiosity Shop*, remarked cynically: "Whenever in his writing he becomes emotional, he ceases instantly to use his intelligence." [15] This cutting remark typifies a whole trend of shifting taste on the part of the Western reading public. But in Dickens' own time, thousands of Victorians had cried over the death of little Nell, and the *Old Curiosity Shop* was one of his most popular best-sellers. Lin translated the title into Chinese to read: "The Story of the Filial Girl, Nell," thus not only echoing the response of readers of Dickens' own time, but turning the pathetic Nell into a glorious personification of filial piety. A simple sentimental story is given the additional weight of ethical exhortation.

Lin Shu's moralistic-sentimental interpretations of Dickens point to a very important question about Dickens himself. To what extent was Dickens a painstaking critic of society who used his satirical humor mainly as a means to a serious end? And to what extent was he (as the warm portraits of E. M. Forster and G. K. Chesterton show him) a good-natured middle-class writer impugning his society out of a sense of humanistic passion? There are grains of truth in both interpretations. Like most sensitive Victorians, Dickens was perhaps torn by divided feelings. Proud of being a member of a society making gigantic strides in material progress, he was nevertheless deeply embittered at the spectacle of human miseries that this progress created. Witnessing the various forms of social abuse, Dickens sometimes raised his voice in strong protest. But what, then, was his prescription for this social malaise? He had none, except an abundance of benevolent feelings and compassion—of what the French scholar Louis Cazamian has aptly called "la philosophie de Noël." [16] It was a philosophy of social ethics based on sentiment, on the conviction of the innate goodness of man. Thus it can be said that the reason Dickens remained Lin's most admired writer lies in an interesting parallel between the two men. Dickens, too, is a sentimental moralist, attempting to buttress his claims for social justice on the basis of his profuse sentiments of human decency. The difference between the two lies in their different social contexts. Whereas Dickens' morality and sentimentality arose as a reaction against human misery and social injustice caused by industrialization, Lin Shu's response sprang mainly from the tradition of Confucian ethics. Therefore, although Lin accepted Dickens as a social critic, the more "materialistic" aspect in Dickens' social criticism largely escaped Lin's attention. The best example is *Dombey and Son*.

Generally regarded as the first masterpiece written by the mature Dickens, *Dombey and Son* highlights the transition from Dickens' early works, with their humor and relatively innocent satire, to a more serious concern with social problems. The novel was published at the time of the railway mania of the 1840s, and its chief character, Mr. Dombey, is an enterprising businessman. It seems quite reasonable to Edgar Johnson to assert that "Mr. Dombey is the living symbol of the nineteenth century theory of business enterprise and its social philosophy."[17] Most Western scholars agree that the theme of *Dombey and Son* is the callous inhumanity and social evil engendered by industrialism. But the novel discloses more than this; it illustrates Dickens' ambivalent attitude toward material progress. While castigating all the social evils resulting from industrialism, Dickens was not unaware of the positive values of machines and the implications of power and wealth attached to them.

Two quotations from *Dombey and Son* will help exemplify this ambivalence. In Chapter Six, for instance:[18] "In short, the yet unfinished and yet unopened Railroad was in progress; and, from the very core of all this dire disorder, [it] trailed smoothly away, upon its mighty course of civilisation and improvement" (p. 95).

But in Chapter Twenty, which describes Dombey's journey on the train, there are several passages like the following:

Louder and louder yet, it shrieks and cries as it comes tearing on resistless to the goal: and now its way, still like the way of Death, is strewn with ashes thickly. Everything around is blackened . . . There are jagged walls and falling houses close at hand, and through the battered roofs and broken windows, wretched rooms are seen, where want and fever hide themselves in many wretched shapes, while smoke and crowded gables and distorted chimneys, and deformity of brick and mortar penning up deformity of mind and body, choke the murky distance (p. 314).

Perhaps as a result of the carelessness of his oral collaborator or perhaps because of Lin's own inability to grasp their "symbolic patterns," in the Chinese version these two passages are entirely omitted. Lin's inserted comments hardly touch on the merits or evils of industrialism. For him, England's material wealth was already an established fact. What he saw in Mr. Dombey was not the symbol of utilitarian mercantilism or industrialism but simply a man, whose icy callousness (note the metaphor in the Chinese title, "the affinity of ice and snow"; also, Lin's own deceased daughter was named *Hsüeh* —snow) was finally melted by the purity and warmth of Florence's love and filial piety. When he read Cousin Feenix's speech describing Mr. Dombey as "a British merchant—and a—and a man" (p. 476), Lin could not help inserting a word of joy: "splendid!"[19]

But to Lin Shu, the engrossing figure in *Dombey and Son* is undoubtedly the daughter. It is in the image of Florence that sentiment and ethics are combined into one. Near the end of the book, when father and daughter were reunited and Florence cried (p. 860): "Never let us be parted any more, papa!" Lin again could not prevent the overflow of his emotion: "As I write this sentence, I am crying for the third time!"[20] Florence's prime virtue is certainly her filial piety. The epithet *hsiao-nü* (filial girl) appears constantly in Lin's translation. When Dickens praises Florence through the mouth of her maidservant: "Miss Floy is the most devoted and most patient and most dutiful and beautiful of daughters" (p. 638), Lin translates it simply as, "This girl is unusually filial."[21] When Dickens exclaims, with an over-exuberance of emotion:

> Awake, unkind father! Awake, now, sullen man!
> The time is flitting by, the hour is coming
> with an angry tread. Awake!
> Awake, doomed man, while she is near. The
> time is flitting by; the hour is coming with
> an angry tread; its foot is in the house. Awake! (p. 632).

Lin's translation, combining the two paragraphs into one, runs: "Heartless, stupid brute! Sleep if you will. When you are awake and want to see this exceedingly filial daughter of yours, it will no longer be possible. Even if you can find her, your death-hour is coming near!"[22]

Lin Shu's discovery of a glorification of filial piety in the novels of Dickens mirrors an interesting contrast between Chinese and Western ethical codes. In Western societies filiality of course also exists. Dickens himself has stressed "the cult of the elementary domestic affections,"[23] and filiality is often incorporated into his advocacy of "the fulfilment of all natural spontaneous emotions in the family."[24] But in the Judeo-Christian tradition of the West, filiality is only one of the Ten Commandments and perhaps not the most important one. Its very enshrinement in the Christian religion leads to its decline in importance along with the general decline of religious fervor in modern times. It is therefore no wonder that Edgar Johnson observes in regard to Florence: "Imperceptive readers who have resented Florence's sufferings have found her gentle humility unconvincing. But given the initial bent of her disposition and her childhood in that cold house . . . it is inevitable that she would blame herself for failing to win her father's affection and build up a feeling of forlorn guilt." [25]

This analysis in terms of a guilt complex would hardly seem convincing to Lin Shu. In China's Confucian tradition, with its strong family nexus, filial piety is often the most basic of all ethical principles, partly because the "this-worldly" orientation of Confucianism has transformed filiality into a social custom. Consequently, for Lin Shu, bred as he was in this tradition, Florence's sufferings are also quite understandable. Isn't her "gentle humility" a clear reflection of that cardinal virtue of woman which, as early as the Han dynasty, the historian Pan Chao had already advocated in her renowned *Lessons for Women*? For she wrote: "Let her fear disgrace, let her even endure when others speak or do evil to her." [26]

Haggard—The World of Heroism

Lin Shu's reading of filial piety in the works of Dickens has not merely sentimental value to himself but also has significance of a far wider scope. To Lin, filial piety is the all-abiding sentiment in his own life as well as a link between ethics and politics, between China and the West. The extension of Lin's ethics can be found in his translations of the 25 novels of H. Rider Haggard (1856–1925), the largest number of works translated by Lin from a single author.

In *Montezuma's Daughter*, whose title in Chinese Lin rendered as "The Story of an English Filial Son's Revenge on the Volcano" (*Ying hsiao-tzu huo-shan pao-ch'ou lu*), the hero's pursuit of his mother's murderer is taken as proof that "not all Westerners are unfilial," that "he who knows how to fulfill filial obligations by avenging the murder of his mother certainly knows how to be loyal and to avenge the shame of his country." [27] This interpretation suggests plainly that filial piety can indeed be extended beyond family bonds to serve the purpose of national wealth and power—a view held by his good friend Yen Fu, another important translator. [28] Since "not all Westerners are unfilial," Lin further admonished, "we cannot commend

51

China and depreciate foreign countries." The reason "Western learning has not spread all over China" lies precisely in the mistaken
notion held by a few conservatives that "Westerners know no
fathers." [29] To find such a progressive view in a Confucianist devoted
to filial piety is indeed surprising.

Lin Shu is essentially not a political thinker, nor are his views on
politics in his translations as important as Yen Fu's. But the fact that
Lin could grope toward the same kind of conclusions as Yen Fu reflects a changed historical context. The attempt to come to terms with
the West was no longer confined to a few *yang-wu* experts like Li
Hung-chang. Both Yen and Lin had definitely rejected the Sinocentric
isolationist stance; they had accepted the presence of the West in
China as a fact of life and tried to grapple with it. Nor is the long
prevalent theory of "essence-utility" *(t'i-yung)* sufficient for them and
their generation. It is no longer possible to confine oneself to borrowing such "utility" items as guns, ships, telegraphs, railways, or even
institutions while keeping away from the realm of Western ideas and
ideologies. Lin is in fact tackling Western "essences" in his translations. Although Lin approaches them from a generally Confucian
standpoint, the step itself is of immense significance as a harbinger
of the more daring trends to come in the May Fourth period.

If in the context of the May Fourth iconoclasm Lin appeared as an
arch-conservative, he was at least a progressive in the context of his
own time. Lin was born and brought up in a China torn by foreign
encroachments and domestic unrest: the Anglo-French invasions, the
Taiping Rebellion, the Nien and Moslem revolts, the trials of the
T'ung-chih Restoration, and the tribulations of "modernization." Foreigners were in charge of the Maritime Customs; foreign steamships
roamed the inner waters of China. Right near Lin's own home town,
Foochow, a shipyard was built with French aid. Immersed as he was
in his perusal of the classics, Lin was nevertheless keenly sensitive to
the shock and shame of his country. In 1884, while the Sino-French
War raged in nearby seas and French warships destroyed the Chinese
naval forces and shipyards at Foochow, the thirty-two-year-old Lin
Shu, furious at inept Chinese military officials, boldly submitted in
person a letter of protest to Tso Tsung-t'ang when the latter arrived

at Foochow.[30] When he was in Peking for his last *chin-shih* degree examination in 1895, Lin sent a memorial to the Ch'ing court protesting China's cession of Taiwan and the Liaotung peninsula to Japan. Although he did not join the group of reformers led by K'ang Yu-wei, he was certainly convinced of the urgent need for reform. In 1898, after the German seizure of Kiaochow, he asked in another memorial for the abdication of the Ch'ing emperor in the interest of political, military, and financial reforms.[31]

After returning home from Peking, Lin became associated with a group of people with similar views, discussing current affairs and continuing to advocate reform. In 1897 he published a collection of thirty-two satirical poems in which he castigated foot-binding, pedantic scholars, and social corruption, and argued for the education of women, reduction of taxes, adoption of a realistic diplomacy, military training, and the betterment of the condition of the lower classes.[32]

While these suggestions smacked of reformism and were not radically different from the views of the late Ch'ing reformers, Lin later in his translations went beyond this practical reformist stance. Again, the novels of H. Rider Haggard provide the best illustration.

It has often been argued that Haggard's adventure stories are no more than slavish imitations of the medieval romance. The mission of his heroes, as of old, is always noble: "Sometimes to rescue a damsel in distress, sometimes to help a friend, sometimes to right a wrong, sometimes to seek adventure and try one's strength."[33] But as his biographer has ably pointed out, Haggard also "helped to Victorianize the medieval romance."[34] The search for riches in an unknown land was indeed a reputable Victorian pursuit and one of the basic motives of British empire-building. For Haggard, who came from the so-called "squirearchy" class (the original backbone of the British Empire) and who had participated in the Boer War, the British Empire was a "given"; to defend it or serve it on behalf of its interests was an unquestioned duty. This attitude was shared by Kipling, Stevenson, and a host of other late-Victorian writers.[35]

Haggard's contemporary, Lin Shu, saw clearly this imperialistic assumption in Haggard's works and seized upon it to advocate a

forcefully positive view. On the one hand, Lin finds a common "predatory" (chieh) motive underlying all the Western fiction of adventure.
From individual acts of robbery, this motive can be magnified to pil-
laging on the largest scale: the conquest of countries and continents.
The early spying and exploratory process is merely a necessary prelude to the gory grand finale. Was it not Columbus who, following
in the wake of his pirate predecessors, led to the plunder of America?
Is not China, viewed in this light, merely a recent victim in this long-
predatory tradition? "We must know that, since the white man can
annex America, he can also swallow China and Asia." [36] On the other
hand, is it not exactly this barbaric tradition of aggressiveness that
accounts for the strength of the Western powers? What a threatening
contrast it presents to the traditional Chinese ethos of "yielding!" In
his preface to The Spirit of Bambatse (Ku-kuei i-chin chi), which he
dedicated to Liang Ch'i-ch'ao, Lin Shu summarized his views about
Haggard's stories:

> They encourage the white man's spirit of exploration. The blue-
> print has already been drawn by Columbus and Robinson Crusoe.
> In order to seek almost unobtainable material interests in the bar-
> barian regions, white men are willing to brave a hundred deaths. But
> our nation (tsu), on the contrary, disregards its own interests and
> yields them to foreigners. We have invited the guests to humiliate the
> hosts and to subject a multitude of 400 million to the mercy of a few
> whites. What an ugly shame! [37]

In another essay he elaborated on this theme in greater detail:

> The Westerners' consciousness of shame and advocacy of force do
> not stem entirely from their own nature but are also an accumulated
> custom. Once the custom is formed, those who act against it are con-
> demned by all . . . In China, this is not so. Suffering humiliation is
> regarded as yielding; saving one's own life is called wisdom. Thus
> after thousands of years of encroachments by foreign races, we still
> do not feel ashamed. Could it also be called our national character? [38]

The many variations on the theme of national shame in his Haggard prefaces indicate that Lin Shu, like his good friend Yen Fu, was
also "groping toward the notion of China as a society-nation rather
than a culture." [39] Chinese culture, insofar as Lin thinks it still pos-

sesses intrinsic ethical values, becomes a subsidiary to a final goal of all-abiding importance. This goal is manifestly the defense of China, not on grounds of cultural tradition, but by the application of force.

Lin Shu's nationalism, like Haggard's imperialism, is tinged with racism. The whole picture seems to be painted on a grand canvas of white-yellow polarity with the barbaric vitality of Western man overshadowing the civic languor of the yielding Chinese. The implied racial drama of competition for survival cannot but lead one to wonder at the possible impact on Lin Shu of Social Darwinism, as seen through the glass of Yen Fu's translations.[40] This, however, should not blind us to the prime attention given to the individual white man, whom Lin Shu admires despite his feelings of racial animosity.

The early model of the "white hero" is found in *Robinson Crusoe*, which Lin also translated. His main features are dynamism, independence, adventurous spirit, defiance of death, and practicality—the ingenuity and resourcefulness with which Robinson Crusoe overcame the most adverse circumstances. Lin regarded Crusoe as having demonstrated the real essence of the Confucian "golden mean" (*chung-yung*), which gave the lie to that trouble-dodging, fence-sitting, play-it-safe attitude in Chinese social practice, which Lin called "the golden mean of the mediocre."[41]

This Robinson Crusoe tradition was inherited by Haggard's heroes, of which the most representative is Alan Quartermain. The difference lies in the fact that, while Robinson Crusoe only conquered nature, Alan also conquered men. This interpretation of the Haggard heroes puts Lin's view in interesting contrast to Haggard's own notions. Whereas Haggard's original portrayal of Alan Quartermain projects the author's own romanticism in his subconscious craving for a release from Victorian conventions, the Alan of Lin Shu's translation is really the embodiment of individual vitality, which is the key to all the assertions of Western superiority. Unlike Ku Hung-ming, who rejects with disdain the brutality of the heathen Europeans, Lin Shu imbues it with a positive meaning. The defiance, the bravery, the brutal intrepidity characterizing this Western "bandit spirit," Lin pleads, "if applied to defend ourselves against foreign encroachments, cannot but perform a useful function for society."[42]

This emphasis on adventure and heroism in Western fiction is therefore not without justification. In fact, it reminds one of the heroic tradition in Chinese popular novels such as *Shui hu chuan* (The water margin)—to which Lin may likewise have been attracted, since, in his elucidation of the Western predatory motive, he also remarked: "All heroes, Chinese or foreign, in antiquity or in modern times, are of bandit origin."[43] The fact that this "little tradition" failed to dispel the inertia of the Chinese populace in a weak, stagnant society may have been the reason why, in confronting this Western vitalist ideal, Lin was struck with mixed feelings of envy and admiration. It is interesting to find that both Yen Fu and Lin Shu have come along different paths to a similar destination. The basic concepts of "energy, dynamism, struggle, self-assertion, and the fearless realization of all human potentialities"[44] that Yen found in Herbert Spencer's scheme of things all exist in Haggard's novels, when they are personified, dramatized, and surrounded by an aura of brigandish heroism.

Epilogue

Lin Shu's career would have been unthinkable for a Confucian scholar in early nineteenth century China. From his urge to write prefaces justifying his efforts, it can be inferred that Lin himself felt quite uneasy. His activities in the Republican period can be interpreted in the same light.

It is well known that Lin argued against the use of colloquial language and debated heatedly—even writing a nasty imaginary story as a personal attack—with the proponents of New Culture.[45] It is also widely known that Lin made eleven pilgrimages to the grave of the Ch'ing Emperor Kuang-hsü. Had Lin become ridiculously anachronistic as Ch'en Tu-hsiu and Ch'ien Hsüan-t'ung had depicted him? His essays describing his pilgrimages make it clear that his gesture was much more personal than ideological. In one moving essay he recounted how he arrived at the grave in the midst of heavy snow, how he could no longer restrain his tears even before prostrating himself, how he wept so hard after nine prostrations that he lost his voice, and how the two guards, deeply moved, wanted to usher him into the main court but were refused by the humble subject of the late dynasty.[46] The melodramatic act served as a release for his pent-up frustrations as a Confucianist. For, indeed, in the context of the venerable "three bonds" (san-kang), his life experience had only inflicted one frustration after another. Loyal to his emperor, he failed seven times to serve him in office; filial to his father, he suffered from his early death; devoted to his wife, he became a widower at the age of forty-five. Moreover, he had to make a living in a field of endeavor hardly legitimate and respected in the Confucian tradition and became quite rich. Lin is anachronistic only in the sense that he attempted to dramatize his Confucian leanings in an age of increasing anti-Confucianism. It was emotional nostalgia that lay at the root of his demonstrations of loyalty to tradition. Later historians can readily perceive how Lin was inevitably engulfed in the temper of his times. They also have the vantage of hindsight to assess Lin's influence both on his generation and on subsequent ones.

The Pandora's box of Lin Shu's translations has released a swarm of legacies of which he himself was unaware, and subsequent chapters will testify to them repeatedly.

Ask me not whether our parting is for life or
  death!
A lonely monk, I wander like clouds floating and
  water flowing.
For no reason at all, I madly laugh and then
  loudly wail.
Although a warm and glad heart I had, it is as
  cold as ice.
—Su Man-shu

Chapter 4

Su Man-shu

Su Man-shu was born on September 28, 1884, in Yokohama. His
father, Su Chieh-sheng, was a Chinese comprador who had come from
the Su family's home town, Hsiang-shan, Kwangtung province, to
become the manager of the British-owned Wan-lung Tea Company
in Japan.[1] It was not unusual during this time for enterprising Chinese, especially the Cantonese, to go to a country which, after the
Meiji Restoration, provided lucrative markets for merchants. As a
result, sizable Chinese communities were formed in commercial centers like Yokohama. Nor was it unusual for the more successful Chinese merchants to acquire Japanese concubines. Su Chieh-sheng had
one, in addition to his Chinese legal first wife and two Chinese concubines. Although Su Man-shu cherished a warm respect for his
father's Japanese concubine, Kawai-sen, familiarly known as O-sen,
recent scholars have established that Su Man-shu was not her own
son. Rather, Man-shu's real mother is reported to have been a Japanese maid by the name of Owaka, age nineteen, possibly Kawai's
niece.[2] Three months after the boy's birth, she returned home, never
to go back to the Su family.

Su Man-shu (whose original name was Chien) was brought up by

Kawai, whom he regarded as his mother, in his father's Yokohama establishment. His happy life with his Japanese mother was cut short in 1889 when the six-year-old boy was taken back to China to grow up among his kinfolk at Li-ch'i village in the fifth district of Hsiang-shan county. Three years later, upon the failure of his tea business, Su Chieh-sheng also returned home with his two Chinese concubines, never to go back to Yokohama again. Kawai was left behind. Man-shu did not see Kawai until he was twenty-four, when Kawai had married an elderly Japanese of a good and wealthy merchant family.

Man-shu began his education at home in 1890, where at the village school he learned the rudiments of Chinese classics typical of the time. Nothing else is known about his studies. In 1898, after two years' sojourn in Shanghai, Su Man-shu returned to Yokohama with his cousin and entered the Ta-t'ung (Universal Harmony) school, established by the Chinese community there, the name being given by K'ang Yu-wei. The young Man-shu spent four years at this school, where he studied Chinese mainly with the followers of K'ang Yu-wei and English with Chinese graduates from Queen's College, Hong Kong. It is reported that "Confucius was worshipped every Sunday when students were required to kneel in front of the sage's image, refusal to do so being punishable by expulsion."[3] Nationalistic slogans were also chanted regularly, such as the following:

> Our national humiliation has not been avenged,
> And the people's life is still full of hardships.
> Do not forget it every time you take your meals.
> Oh, young men, exert yourselves diligently![4]

The atmosphere at school reflected, of course, the temper of the reformers after they failed in their hundred days of office in Peking in 1898. The school was considered such a hotbed of K'ang's reform faction that in 1902 a band of hired rowdies invaded the school compound and classes were disrupted. Su therefore went to Tokyo, where he plunged headlong into the vortex of revolutionary fervor among Chinese intellectuals. While he took a Senior Preparatory Course at Waseda University and enrolled in 1903 at the Ch'eng-ch'eng (Seizo Gakko) Academy to study military science, he also joined three revolutionary organizations founded by Chinese students in Japan: the

Su Man-shu in Western dress

Young Men's Association, a small group whose formation was apparently inspired by Mazzini's La Giovine Italia (Young Italy) and whose members included Feng Tzu-yu, Chang Chi, and Ch'en Tu-hsiu; the Chinese Students' Anti-Russian Volunteer Corps (to protest Russia's armed occupation of Manchuria); and the Association for the People's Military Education. Swayed by the revolutionary spirit, Man-shu left Japan in 1903 to start actual revolutionary activities in his native country. But who would have expected that this fledgling revolutionary would drift farther and farther away from the revolution?

He landed in Shanghai in September 1903, in time to join his former fellow members of the Young Men's Association in working for their newspaper, Kuo-min jih-jih-pao (National people's daily). For this paper Su contributed two patriotic poems, two articles—one eulogizing the famous American anarchist, Emma Goldman, the other castigating his fellow Cantonese for their lack of national consciousness and their ingratiating servility toward the foreigners—and a partial translation of Victor Hugo's Les Misérables. But the newspaper was closed down in December. Su went south, to Hong Kong, where with a letter of introduction from Feng Tzu-yü, he found temporary lodging at the headquarters of Sun Yat-sen's newspaper, The China Daily. Then, unobtrusively, he disappeared. When he reappeared at the China Daily office, his colleagues found with great dismay that "he had already shaved his head to become a monk and changed his name to Man-shu" (after Manjusri, a Bodhisattva).[5]

He refused to go home for his father's funeral in 1904, but went to Shanghai and then took a trip to Siam and Ceylon for a few months and started to learn Sanskrit. Upon returning to China in the fall of 1904, Su embarked on a life of perpetual drifting: from one city to another—Soochow, Hangchow, Tsingtao, Hong Kong, and his primary city of sojourn, Shanghai—back and forth between China and Japan, and between the monastic and the mundane. From 1909 to 1912, he even made an extended trip to the South Sea Islands and taught English at a Chinese school in Java. He later talked about going to India and, as soon as the war was over, to Europe.[6] But these plans were never realized. When the 1911 Revolution broke out, he was far away in Java. He returned in early 1912 and joined the editorial staff of the *Pacific News*, where he published his most famous autobiographical novel, *Tuan-hung ling-yen chi* (The lone swan). The last six years of his life, between 1912 and 1918, he spent in China and Japan. He taught English at various schools, frequented restaurants and brothels, made surprise visits to his friends for money and food, wrote, and painted.

Legend

The above brief sketch of Su Man-shu's life does far less justice than either the first English treatment of Su by Henry McAleavy or the full biography by Liu Wu-chi. For the purposes of this chapter, however, it is the legend of Su Man-shu rather than the real Su that appeals to us, as it did to millions of Chinese readers. The life of this most interesting figure at the turn of the century has remained a fascinating enigma posed by a string of incidents and anecdotes as recounted by his friends and by a kaleidoscope of images and accounts masterminded by himself. No scholar can claim full knowledge of the inside story of Su Man-shu.

We learn that he is immensely versatile. "He is versed in the arts, especially painting."[7] He writes old-style poetry. He is a translator and knows at least five languages: Chinese, Japanese, English, French, and Sanskrit. We are then told by his friend Ch'en Tu-hsiu that Su never studied Chinese carefully in childhood and Ch'en taught him how to write classical poetry.[8] According to another friend, Chang Shih-chao, he became an established master in no more than two to three years. Ch'en Tu-hsiu therefore considered him "truly a genius."[9]

Then, there is his self-perpetuated reputation for gourmandism. From his many letters to friends we know that his favorites included steamed meat dumplings, sweet wheat cakes, "eight-precious rice," fish, seasoned ham, "moon cakes," beef, and particularly cigars and candies. He was addicted to Manila cigars, and often consumed three or four boxes of a special brand of candies called "Mo-erh-teng," which, according to our learned epicurian, was the personal favorite of La Dame aux Camélias.[10] He would end a letter with a phrase like "Written by the side of roasted beef, chicken slices, and fish."[11] He would pull out the gold fillings in his teeth to exchange them for candies.[12] When he was in Ceylon, for one whole month he had supposedly eaten nothing but fruits and consequently contracted dysentery. He would groan with stomach pain after an oversized meal. His death was caused, according to one account, by his having eaten sixty meat dumplings in order to win a bet. When he finished about fifty, his friends were alarmed, but he insisted and finished the last ten with a cup of coffee.[13]

He gave himself a great number of names (32 altogether; his English name, Pev Mandju) some identifiable, some not. He loved to send his friends photographs of himself, when he was not making surprise visits and begging them for loans. Once, a friend saw him in Canton with his beard "as long as a full inch"; some time later, Su sent him a photo from Shanghai in which he appeared as a clean-shaven, dashing dandy.[14] Another admirer one day saw a young man wearing a cassock, with his woolen underwear sticking out, and sitting at the edge of a cliff.[15] Then, the young hero would be transformed, according to another account, into a disheveled monk sitting with his face toward the wall and wearing a shabby, dust-laden cassock, in a shattered wooden house hidden under the trees behind a monastery, as if he had not set foot outside for a whole year. The poor monk turned out to be the same person who only three days ago had lived in comfort and luxury in Shanghai.[16] Sometimes he would simply disappear for months, leaving no traces for his anxious friends.

Was he indeed a man of such profound sorrow that from time to time he had to seek temporary solutions in solitary meditation? To an outside observer, his many poses impart an air of narcissistic affectation, as if the adulations of his friends—especially females—were not enough. The many anecdotes supplied by his friends and admirers only lead us to suspect that he was craving a lofty style of life. To be both a monk and a poet conjures many glamorous images in the Chinese tradition. But Su did not seem satisfied with emulating one model. He experimented and, with his ingenuity, invented. The result was, of course, the picture of a melancholy genius whose thoughts were too unique and whose sensitivities were too acute to be wholly

Su Man-shu in a monk's robe

understood by his age—a posture that many self-styled men of letters were later to adopt eagerly. Su Man-shu was among the first men to exemplify the idea that the style of a man is, both to himself and his public, as important as the man himself. The fact that Su Man-shu could gain popularity from his personality and life style as much as from his literary accomplishments reflects an even larger phenomenon —the gradual erosion of the established norms and customs of behavior, which made it necessary for men like Su to create new ones. The traditional image of an intellectual would still fit the portrait of Lin Shu; but Su was already far from the Confucian prototype.

The Lone Swan

Styles, appearances, and idiosyncrasies are the stuff of legends. Su Man-shu, however, has added another component: his fictional writings. Since most of them are imaginary reconstructions of many actual events in his life, they are of the utmost importance for a historian. The most popular and the most closely autobiographical of his fictional works is undoubtedly *The Lone Swan*. Thus it serves as a logical beginning for additional probings into the Su Man-shu legend.

The story begins with the hero, Saburo, a Sinified Japanese (described in the first person) already completing his training as a monk, in a secluded monastery on the coast of southern Kwangtung. A chance encounter with a boy leads him to find his former nurse, who recalls how she came to be employed by a cultured Japanese lady, Saburo's mother. She also tells him that his father was a well-respected Japanese from Tokyo who died a few months after Saburo was born. She then describes how his mother was ill treated by his stepfather's Chinese concubines. Filled with emotion, he decides to travel to Japan in search of his mother. Saburo also meets, quite accidentally, his childhood fiancée, Hsüeh-mei (Snow plum), whose father has retracted their marriage contract after the death of his stepfather. In order to have Hsüeh-mei enjoy the happiness of another marriage, Saburo has decided to become a monk. But he finds his former fiancée still very devoted to him.

65

Saburo's trip to Japan is financed by Hsüeh-mei and Reverend Lopez of Madrid. The reunion of mother and son is one of the most lachrymose parts of the novel. Saburo visits his aunt and meets Shizuko, his cousin. Shizuko falls madly in love with him, but being a monk he cannot repay the intensity of her feelings. Nor can he accept the offer of marriage to Shizuko from the two kind ladies. Accordingly, after much mental self-torture, he finally resolves to leave surreptitiously for Shanghai. In a farewell letter to Shizuko, he reveals the secret of his monkhood:

Alas! You and I shall never meet again! A Buddhist monk ordained in the grand precepts of the law, I can never have the life-long companionship of any woman. But, being neither wood nor stone, how could I not be grateful for your gracious and generous sentiments, your lofty virtue that reaches high to the skies? Born under the ill-omened Waterstar, I have encountered in this life unutterable sorrows . . . With a monk's staff in my hand, I shall now roam afar as a mendicant. In this dusty world, chances are slim of our seeing each other again. I beg you, elder sister, to let me drag out alone my lingering existence. What else could I do? [17]

Upon returning to China, Saburo immediately changes into his monk's attire and goes back to his monastic life. During a service at which he officiates, he meets a brother and sister named Mai who happen to be his former classmates. From them he learns that Hsüeh-mei has committed suicide. He goes to the village burial ground but fails to find her grave. The story ends with our hero wailing among a heap of desolate mounds. "Readers, please consider, how could my sorrows at this moment be matched anywhere in this human world? Now my tears have been exhausted. I feel my heart is like wood and stone. I have made up my mind to return to the monastery of my original teacher. I do not know how much more sorrow is in store for me." [18]

Three themes clearly present themselves: the hero's monastic bent, his search for his mother, and the triangular relationship of the hero with two women devoted to him—themes which give a clue to an understanding not only of Su's works but also of his life, or the legend of his life.

Although we are unable to ascertain the reasons for Su's monk-hood, we can still accept it as a fact of his life and attempt to gauge its role in the structure of the novel and the legend of his life. Many critics have noticed the similarity in the pattern of characterization between *The Lone Swan* and *Dream of the Red Chamber (Hung-lou meng)*. Both portray a fragile, sensitive hero wavering between two heroines. It is almost certain that Su, like most writers of the so-called "talent-beauty" stories *(ts'ai-tzu chia-jen)*, owed a great debt to this greatest novel in China. Not merely in the superficial pattern of char-acters but also in the basic ethos, the two novels are very much alike.

In one sense, *Dream of the Red Chamber* could be regarded as a microcosm of the conflict between Confucianism and Buddhism. Pre-ordained, in the popular Buddhist sense, in his previous karma, the hero Chia Pao-yü descends into this mundane realm to suffer the trials and temptations of the "red dust," the setting of which is a large family imbedded in long-established Confucian norms. Love—both aggressive and tender as represented by Hsüeh Pao-ch'ai and Lin Tai-yü—is treated in this dual context. Its flow has to be curbed by the rigors of Confucian ethics, but it is also, in the Buddhist frame-work, merely an ephemeral, kaleidoscopic bubble or gleaming grain of sand in the red dust that evaporates into nothingness.

Su Man-shu seems to belong thoroughly to the *Dream of the Red Chamber* tradition. But unlike the *Dream* and Lin Shu's works, the Confucian elements are much more diluted. The "curse" that the hero Saburo carries is almost the same as Pao-yü's, but he is not subject to the torture of that grand matrix of Confucian relations—the big gentry-official family. The problem of filial piety, so heavily empha-sized and glowingly depicted by Lin Shu, is symbolized in Su's novel by Saburo's somewhat nostalgic attachment to his Japanese mother, a well-respected woman, of course, but from a different cultural tra-dition. If one compares Su's fictional portrait of his mother with his real life experience with his mother, the implications that could be drawn would seem more vaguely Freudian than strictly Confucian.

Su Man-shu was very detached from his father. He even refused to go home for his father's funeral. Was it due to his distaste for the comprador class? No serious scholar is in a position to give a convincing interpretation of Su's relationship with his father because he himself has written almost nothing about his father. His mother, however, presents an entirely different case. If Liu Wu-chi's chronology of Man-shu is to be trusted, Su left Kawai, whom he always thought of as his mother, in 1889 at the age of six, and did not see her until 1907 when he was twenty-four. This indicates clearly that during his entire adolescent period he was without a mother. The lack of a normal family milieu, especially the loving care of a mother, perhaps underlies his self-image as a lone traveler stricken with "unutterable sorrows." The sorrows could be compounded if, indeed, Su had been torn by his quandaries about the identity of his real mother. It is in this context that Man-shu's nostalgic attachment to and loving idealization of his mother has to be viewed. Not only in *The Lone Swan* but elsewhere the image of a cultured Japanese lady has been perpetuated. She has allegedly written in Japanese a preface to a collection of her son's paintings,[19] but some of Su's biographers and friends strongly suspected that the real author was Su Man-shu himself.

Women and Love

The central role of his mother in Man-shu's life leads us naturally to the baffling question of women in his life, always a major component of his legend. Every reader of Man-shu's fiction would be immediately struck by a recurring phenomenon: the hero is always the object of single-hearted devotion of two women—one tender and docile, the other more passionate and aggressive, both loyal and self-sacrificing. Does Su Man-shu crave certain psychological compensations for the lack of female attention in his real life?

Even given the possible existence in real life of Man-shu's two or three early loves, the traces of their idealization in the stories are clearly discernible. This can be seen in Su's last story, *Sui-tsan chi* (Tale of a broken hairpin). Set in two coastal cities—Shanghai and Hangchow—where foreign merchandise and foreign fashions were becoming the vogue, the story presents, as usual, two lovely girls clinging to a fragile, vacillating, often bedridden young man. One of them, rich and more aggressive, wears chic Western dresses and carries opera binoculars to attend Western-style plays.[20] One wonders why she should be modern and fashionable in appearance but traditional in her devotional virtues. Such heroines might have indeed existed, but it is more likely that his heroines are composite figures combining what Su himself considered as reigning ideals. Thus the dual personality of his heroines represent Su's own feeling of ambivalence toward women in general. On the one hand, he cannot totally break away from the Chinese tradition. Born outside China and not adequately educated in Chinese culture, he may have harbored more intense yearnings for the best in Chinese culture. Hence, like Lin Shu, Su gives a highly emotional coloration to the traditional womanly virtue of devotion. Like the older Lin Shu, Su also looks with distaste at the erosion of traditional virtues and the invasion of Western manners. The cynicism exhibited in some of his critical essays about "modern women" is the cynicism of a man who finds his idealized images increasingly shattered by the reality around him. "Let this humble monk respectfully admonish our fellow female countrymen. Henceforward you should not follow the fashion of high breasts and slender waists. Rather, the motto at your dressing mirror should be: a gentle woman should marry for virtue and not appearance . . . The virtues of women are fidelity and chastity."[21] Yet, on the other hand, having been exposed to foreign influences through his reading and traveling, Su may not have been content with the uneducated and parochial types of traditional women. Hence the femmes fatales in his novels, who combine the still Chinese virtues of devotion with somewhat foreign attributes of passion, aggressiveness, and sensual abandon. (Shizuko, the more passionate heroine in *The Lone Swan*, is a Japanese.)

But Su seems not equipped to cope with such women. In *A Broken Hairpin*, he wrote, "All women under heaven are the sources of calamity." In another work one finds the following slanderous words: "There is nothing more fearful than women, tender and charming in appearance but viciously evil at heart. Women are the harbingers of hell; when they utter beautiful speech, they are in fact pouring poison."[22] Such utterances reflect more than the cynicism of a man "who reacted violently in moments of bitter resentment against the evil forces of society"; they verge on the pathological. Are we to suppose, with McAleavy, that Su was born with a sexual incapacity?[23] Further conjectures could be made with regard to Su's attitude and behavior toward prostitutes.

Sing-song girls—refined prostitutes—had been an established part of the glitter and sophistication of Shanghai society. Su Man-shu, a frequenter of this city, was known for his patronage of the sing-song girls. Many anecdotes have been told by his friends. It is said that he often lavished large sums of money on them and attended dinner parties in their company. After calling the girls to the party, he would attempt to practice meditation to the chagrin of his female companions.[24] In one revealing account, Su fell deeply in love with a prostitute and practically lived at her place, but he never attempted sexual intercourse. When the women asked him for an explanation, he reportedly said with solemnity:

Love is air for the soul. The soul can live forever when nourished by love, just as the body relies on air in order to live. In our daily humdrum lives, we have all the time been swimming in the sea of sentiment. It is said that the sea of sentiment is the sea of calamity; a few steps into it and you will be drowned. This statement mistakenly confuses the sea of desire with the sea of sentiment. But things, when pushed to the extreme, often have opposite effects . . . Sexual desire is the extremity of love. We love each other but do not reach for abandon, so as to preserve this sentiment forever . . . After reaching abandon, the fervor of passion will recede . . . I do not intend to seek pleasures of the flesh at the expense of love of the spirit.[25]

This reported statement might serve to confirm McAleavy's conjecture. For our purposes, however, it rather provides the best perspective to summarize Su's ambivalent attitudes toward women.

The treatment of women in Su's fiction is but one aspect of the basic outlook that Su shares in common with Lin Shu. The themes of Buddhism, mother, and women all revolve around one leitmotif, that of sentiment. Su Man-shu, like Lin Shu, is a man of strong emotions. Whether imaginary or real, the basic story line in Su's fiction and some of his poetry is the odyssey of a sensitive soul in the sea of sentiment. One of his own remarks profoundly summarizes the fundamental concerns of his life: "I am sad because I seek the way [implying perhaps the Buddhist path] through sentiments" (wei-ch'ing ch'iu-tao).[26]

In the imaginary world of his fiction—the world of his dreams—he aspires toward that quintessence of sentiments, love. But he is overpowered by the physical aspects of love—the sea of desire—as personified by women who commit their whole beings to the seduction of the gentle weak hero. Therefore the hero either escapes from the mundane web of entanglements into the serene sanctity of the monastery or opts for the gentler and more traditional woman, thereby causing the suicide of the seductress but too late to save the gentle heroine from sacrificing herself also. But to lead a life without love is tantamount to death of the soul, and to enter the gate of Buddhism means the rejection of mundane life, hence death of the body. Thus the tragedies in his fiction are invariably the tragedies of love and death, of love consummated in death. At its best, Su's treatment of this theme is reminiscent of Wilde, as some of his more learned friends hastened to point out. In his short story, "Chiang sha chi" (Tale of crimson silk), Hsüeh Meng-chu (quasi-homophonous with Su Man-shu) was once in love with Hsüeh Ch'iu-yün but later became a Buddhist monk. The narrator accompanied Ch'iu-yün to a Soochow monastery to seek him:

When we got there, the pine shadows covered the front gate, it being the night of the full moon. I noticed that the door was ajar; so I asked Ch'iu-yün to wait outside as I entered the temple. Inside, the courtyard was empty, the night still, and only the light of Buddha's lamp flickered on the four walls. I continued forward to a side room, which was also quiet and vacant. Thinking that Meng-chu had not yet returned, I retraced my steps until I caught a glimpse of a white-faced idol at a corner of the courtyard corridor. As I approached, I saw that it was Meng-chu himself, sitting there lifeless with his eyes closed and grass growing between his knees. I called him but got no reply. I pulled at his hand and it was as stiff as iron. Only then did I realize that Meng-chu had met a Buddhist death.

I hurried out to tell Ch'iu-yün. She entered and stood silently in front of him, without uttering one word. All of a sudden, she saw a corner of a crimson silk kerchief protruding from the lapel of his cassock. She pulled it out with her hand, looked around, and turned it over. Then she nestled herself in Meng-chu's lap as she embraced and kissed him with streaming tears. All this time I stood still. Suddenly, I heard the rustling of the wind as Meng-chu's corpse dissolved into ashes, only the piece of crimson silk remaining in Ch'iu-yün's hand.[27]

Here is the nirvana of Man-shu's ideal sentiment, the intensity of his passion—the kind of passion which arises not so much from the exertions of the flesh as from the depth of the spirit, of emotion condensed and sublimated in tranquillity. This ideal points toward many ramifications, embracing many elements from both Chinese and foreign traditions.

Byron

The literary fame of Su Man-shu rests, in addition to his poetry and fiction, also on his translations; he was the first to introduce Byron into China. According to Liu Wu-chi, Man-shu's interest in Byron started in early 1908. During the two months of February and March he did little else but read Byron's poems.[28] In late 1909, the *Selected Poems of Byron* was published, a volume which included "The Ocean," "The Isles of Greece," "My Native Land, Good Night," and a few shorter poems: "To A Lady Who Presented the Author with the Velvet Band Which Bound Her Tresses" (how many ladies had presented Man-shu with personal gifts!), "Live Not the Stars and the Mountains," and "The Maid of Athens." Some of the pieces, especially "The Ocean" (from *Childe Harold*) had been polished by Chang T'ai-yen. The collection also contained two prefaces, one written in English by the British diplomat John B. Fletcher, and the other in Chinese by Su himself.

His own account has a more exotic flavor. In 1909, while traveling in the South Seas, he was ill. "Hsüeh-hung [Snowy Swan, that is Señorita Lopez, daughter of Reverend Lopez], a poetess from Spain, came to visit me on my sickbed and personally presented me with a lovely portrait of hers, a volume of Byron's poetic works, and a bunch of camellia flowers and sensitive plants. Very solicitously she urged me to make plans for a trip homeward. Alas! Early in my youth I shaved my head to learn the Buddhist Law but failed to accomplish anything. Whenever I think of my life, I have no words to express my pain. So, ill as I am, I write down these twenty-eight words on the front leaf of Byron's book. This sentiment will be appreciated only by Snowy Swan." [29] These words constitute a preface to a poem titled, "Inscribed on Byron's Poetic Works":

An autumn wind blows over the sea in the darkening twilight;
Alone, I bewail Byron's fate as I pore over his poetic remains.
You, poet, and I are wanderers, fluttering like reeds in the storm.
May I beckon to your soul from across a strange land? [30]

It is apparent that from the very beginning Su was attracted to Byron on account of the affinities between them. Both are wandering free spirits; both spent a portion of their lives in a foreign land (Su chose to translate among Byron's longer poems, "The Ocean," "The Isles of Greece," and "My Native Land, Good Night"); and both are emotional poets with a host of female admirers. One admirer wrote: "He has introduced Byron to us because he loves Byron, loves the similarities between Byron and himself, loves the Byron in Greece like himself in Japan. In letting China know of Byron, Man-shu inwardly also wants to make us understand himself." [31]

What are we to understand of Man-shu through Byron? In his preface to the *Selected Poems of Byron*, he praised his hero in the following words: "As a poet who conveyed in his songs the sorrows of departure from his own country and who would not claim any credit for helping the people of another country, Byron vied for glory with the sun and the moon." [32] Man-shu could easily reciprocate the "sorrows of departure" from his own country. But unlike Byron, a dandy poet turned self-styled revolutionist, Su was a frustrated revolutionist who became a self-styled wandering poet. Thus Byron, like the heroes and heroines in Su's fiction, represents a composite image of what Su could identify with and for which he could only yearn. Byron's later experience may remind Su of his early years. But he could only admire Byron as a heroic fighter. This kind of heroic pose represented by Byron, introduced by Su Man-shu but perpetuated by Hsü Chih-mo and others, was but another of his favorite imaginary poses, like that cassock-clad youth sitting at the edge of a cliff. Moreover, the problem of the Su Man-shu legend is also in a sense reminiscent of that of Byron. Through the popular accounts of his time and his own works we have inherited a legacy of Byroniana, a hero with many masks. Was Su aware that the headstrong, impetuous, and pretentious dandy might have his weaker and more sober side, that the Byron in *Childe Harold* might be quite different from the Byron in *Don Juan?* Did he notice that Byron's physical defect might have reinforced his heroic pretensions? Most likely, Byron's Chinese translator was more fascinated by the legend of Byron than by the real Byron himself, and the legacy of Chinese Byroniana, begun by Su Man-shu, has perpetuated this English poet in the glittering image of the Byronic hero.

In the preface to *Ch'ao-yin chi* (Voices of the tide), written originally in English, Man-shu attempted to compare Byron with Shelley, another favorite Western poet:

Byron and Shelley are two of the greatest British poets. Both had the lofty sentiment of creation, love, as the theme of their poetic expressions. Yes, although both wrote principally on love, lovers, and their fortunes, their modes of expression differ as widely as the poles.

Byron was born and brought up in luxury, wealth, and liberty. He was an ardent and sincere devotee of liberty—yes, he dared to claim liberty in every thing—great and small, social or political. He knew not how or where he was extreme.

Byron's poems are like a stimulating liquor—the more one drinks, the more one feels the sweet fascination. They are full of charm, full of beauty, full of sincerity throughout.

In sentimentality, enthusiasm and straightforwardness of diction, they have no equal. He was a free and noble hearted man. His end came while he was engaged in a noble pursuit. He went to Greece, where he sided with the patriots who were fighting for their liberty. His whole life, career and production are intertwined in Love and Liberty.

Shelley, though a devotee of love, is judicious and pensive. His enthusiasm for love never appears in any strong outburst of expression. He is a "Philosopher-lover." He loves not only the beauty of love, or love for love, but "love in philosophy" or "philosophy in love." He had depth, but not continuance: energy without youthful devotion. His poems are as the moonshine, placidly beautiful, solemnly still, reflected on the waters of silence and contemplation.

Shelley sought Nirvana in love; but Byron sought Action for love, and in love. Shelley was self-contained and quite engrossed in his devotion to the Muses. His premature and violent death will be lamented so long as English literature exists.

Both Shelley and Byron's works are worth studying by every lover of learning, for enjoyment of poetic beauty, and to appreciate the lofty ideas of Love and Liberty.[33]

This preface summarizes perfectly Su Man-shu's reactions to Byron. His juxtaposition of Byron and Shelley presents, in fact, two sides of his image of love which in turn reflects, like the heroines in his fiction, two sides of his temper. He admires and may indeed have imaginatively longed for the tempestuous outbursts of Byron. But Byron's volcanic dynamism is much too overpowering, like "stimulating liquor," for his gentle soul. He has to seek the more contemplative Shelley in whose serenity and depth he finds the "nirvana of love." Like Lin Shu, he noticed and glorified the potentialities of dynamism, but he was not quite ready for it. The total release of these potentialities came later.

The preface also reveals that Su's response to the works of these two romantic poets is highly emotional rather than intellectual, as befits a man of sentiment. The similarity with Lin Shu is again striking. Both reacted to Western stimuli by seeking similarities in their own temperament and experience. While Lin still attempted to justify his emotional response with Confucian tenets, Su became more intuitive, employing such sensory and visual metaphors as "a stimulating liquor" and the "moonshine, placidly beautiful, solemnly still." Lin Shu still retained his intellectual acumen as he sought to compare the styles of Ssu-ma Ch'ien and Dickens. The analogies which Su found in Chinese literature were not based entirely on literary style. That he paired Byron with Li Po and Shelley with Li Ho or Li Shang-yin seems to disclose an impressionistic effort to grasp affinities in temper and atmosphere between these literary men in the East and the West.[34]

Su Man-shu did not achieve an output of translations equal to Lin's. Besides Byron, he translated only a few scattered poems by Shelley ("A Song"), Burns ("A Red, Red Rose"), and Goethe. His translation of Les Misérables was notoriously deficient, containing merely portions of the original and long chapters of his own.[35] But

Su was nevertheless quite critical of Lin Shu, of whose translations he had only read *Robinson Crusoe* and Haggard's *Cleopatra*.[36] He was reported to have told the editor of a newspaper that Lin Shu's translation of *La Dame aux Camélias* "had too many omissions and was far from complete," that some day he would, for the benefit of readers, undertake a retranslation. The editor predicted, "Now with a man born of sentiment to translate such a book, I am sure of its prestige and popularity."[37] Like many of Su's promises, the task was never carried out.

Su Man-shu died on May 2, 1918. His last words, as reported, were: "Love embraces all; as for impediments, there are none."[38] During his lifetime he may never have met Lin Shu, nor corresponded with him, although both were eminent members of the same generation. If Man-shu had met or written to Lin Shu, a phrase which Su used in his letter to another friend on their mutual interest in Byron might have applied: "You, too, sir, are a man of emotions."[39] In spite of differences of background, the two men shared a common emotional denominator, which, as the May Fourth movement raged on, would prove to be of great consequence.

Two Precursors

The central theme which underlies the life and works of these two literary figures is, of course, that of sentiment. From a historical perspective, their originality lies in their shared belief that sentiment is the product of genuine personal experience. The primacy of sentiment thus becomes inherent in their works and does not represent the result of mere literary embellishments. In other words, Lin and Su can be seen as the precursors of an intensely subjectivist trend in modern Chinese literature and life.

Both Lin and Su shared a common cause, but in different contexts. Brought up in the old tradition of Confucian learning, Lin Shu propounded his new message in the general framework of the Confucian tradition, seeking to instill new blood into a gradually decaying body of orthodox doctrines and to widen the mental horizons of his fellow Chinese literati by introducing elements from the West. But he was, from historical hindsight, breaking new ground. He was quite sensitive to the question: given the prescriptions of propriety and the "golden mean" in personal behavior, including emotional expressions, what if the accumulated intensity of "correct" emotions threatens to reach excess? To this he had to give a dangerously unorthodox answer: "A man is afraid only of having no heart. I certainly cannot give rein to excessive sentiments which nevertheless stem from correctness by resorting to the ways of a Confucianist." [40] It was left to a later generation to reject all restraints and carry sentiments to excess.

Su Man-shu tackled the problem of sentiment from outside the Confucian tradition. Longing for the ethical virtues that Lin advocated, Su, however, wavered on the borderline. There were already elements in him which could not be measured by Confucian yardsticks. Buddhism provided a convenient escape, but it did not solve the problem. Thus in his last novel he concluded: "The most difficult thing to solve in the world is none other than sentiment (ch'ing)." [41] While Lin could still be self-righteous in justifying his views, Su Man-shu was struck with "unutterable sorrows."

Unable to solve his problem, he dramatized it, in his works and in his personal behavior. While Lin wrestled with it in theory, Su enacted it in practice. Lin Shu was renowned in his own day for the style of his writings; Man-shu became popular by virtue of his style of life. Both men exerted great influences on a later generation. Lin Shu's translations became the essential nourishment that fed the literary imaginations of numerous writers in the twenties and thirties. Although Su Man-shu's literary achievements failed to impress Hu Shih, he enjoyed the adulation of a large circle of admirers. [42] When he died in 1918, countless young men and women made special trips to his grave in West Lake near Hangchow; girl students hung his photo in their summer mosquito nets. [43] His niece even committed suicide. [44] The contribution of Su Man-shu to posterity, from a historical point of view, is the evolvement of a personality and style of life which not only, because of his popularity, shaped the manners and morals of his age but also inspired members of a younger generation to follow suit. One of the prominent members of this younger generation, Yü Ta-fu, perceptively remarked: "In sum, his poetry translations are better than his own poetry; his poetry is better than his painting; his painting is better than his fiction. But above all, his romantic temper and his behavior and style derived from it are better than everything else." [45]

When one puts Lin and Su in sequence, one is surprised to see how fitting they are as representatives of a transitional age. Lin Shu, still steeped in the centuries-old tradition, lived to be frustrated because he failed to fulfill the goals set for scholars in traditional Chinese society and was finally drawn to the West after the collapse of the ritual paraphernalia of tradition—the monarchy, the examination system, the classical prose style. It is more than symbolic to regard Lin Shu as both among the last Confucianists and the first real Westernizers.

Some thirty-two years Lin's junior, Su Man-shu epitomized a later period of this transitional age. He was born too late to be prepared for the civil service examination system, and too far away to fit into the nexus of traditional society. His revolutionary views and activities in Japan mirrored the rising power of a new group of Chinese intellectuals who were to hold sway over Chinese life and politics in the first half of the twentieth century—the Japanese-educated Chinese students who emerged at the seat of power not through the traditional channels such as the examination system but through new avenues: military academies, Japanese schools and universities, and literary and journalistic endeavors. The list of Su's many friends and acquaintances reads like a who's who in literature, thought, and politics in early Republican China: Sun Yat-sen, Chiang Kai-shek, Chang Chi, Feng Tzu-yü, Ch'en Shao-pai, Liu Ya-tzu, Liu Pan-nung, Chang T'ai-yen, and Ch'en Tu-hsiu. Moreover, the setting of his later fiction and life—the treaty ports and coastal cities—became also the major arena for the contest and conflict of traditional and Western ideas, fashions, and morals. Su Man-shu, through his style and his art, not only "personifies a happy union of the age-old literary traditions of China with the fresh invigorating romanticism of the West" but embodies the listlessness, commotion, and bewilderment of the general mood of his transitional age. The stage is set by men like Lin Shu and Su Man-shu for our main protagonists who have emerged from the "Literary Revolution."

Part Two Two Protagonists

So flieht für neues Leben
Mir jeder Hoffnung Schein!
—Wagner's "Tannhäuser"

Pitiable is my solitary existence!
That pretty flower in the mirror
　　has turned into a bubble.
—Free translation by Yü Ta-fu

Chapter 5

Yü Ta-fu: Driftings of a Loner

Yü Ta-fu once wrote a moving story called "Alone in the Journey," which recorded a few days of his life. The title may be a fitting epithet for the forty-nine years of his whole life. A celebrated *wen-jen* and one of the founders of the Creation Society, Yü Ta-fu was a leading representative of May Fourth literature. His autobiographical stories were among the earliest crop of the new literary harvest and left their imprint on the minds of a whole generation. Since most of these stories described only himself, Yü was able to establish firmly the convention, first begun by Su Man-shu, that a writer's art should reflect his temper and reinforce his behavior and life-style. He was truly a protagonist.

Yet for all his fame and popularity Yü saw himself as a loner in life's journey, which would lead him inevitably, as it did in fact, to a tragic end. He considered himself to have suffered along every stage of his life and wrote profusely about his suffering. In the first half of his life, he was constantly on the move—drifting, as he would put it—from one school to another, one job to another, from books to wine, from friends to foes, from one city to another city, from one day to another day, one year to another year. When he finally decided to settle down around age forty, his suffering was gone, together with his creative impulse and the impact of his literary product. At journey's end in Sumatra under the Japanese occupation, he was forced to give up altogether his literary career and identity.

Yü's life is nevertheless significant because he traveled the historical length and geographical breadth of the May Fourth literary scene.

Biography via Autobiography: Yü's Childhood, 1896–1913

From December 1934 to April 1935, a noted journal edited by Lin Yutang, *Jen-chien-shih*, published fragments of Yü Ta-fu's autobiography. Though incomplete, these fragments contain much valuable information about Yü's childhood and adolescence.

According to this account, Yü was born "on the third day of the eleventh month of the twenty-second year of Kuang-hsü (1896), at midnight." [1] Like Lu Hsün's family, the Yü household in Fu-yang, Chekiang province, had declined to the point of dilapidation by the time he was born. The infant was perennially ill from malnutrition. "Everybody in the family was exhausted by this little life. Sometime between spring and summer in the third year after my birth, father was brought thereby to illness and death." [2] His widowed mother was out working every day, his two brothers were studying far away from home, and his grandmother was seen day and night "moving her toothless, flat mouth and chanting Buddhist sutras." [3] "In my solitary childhood years the only person who was with me every day, who sometimes told me stories, sometimes quarreled with me on account of my odd temper, but nevertheless loved me dearly, was that devoted maid Ts'ui-hua," [4] a maid ten years older than he with a charming name which literally means "flowers worked with kingfisher's feathers."

Poverty was the keynote in Yü's reminiscences of his childhood. Yü seemed to feel that his loneliness, his extreme sensitivity and sentimentality, had been a direct outgrowth from this poverty-stricken childhood environment. Poverty caused illness, which accounted in turn for his father's death. His widowed mother, who had to take over his father's work but was often exploited by relatives in land and harvest transactions, left the younger Yü Ta-fu to face the outside world alone. Inured to solitude, weighed down by poverty, the young child, as recollected by the middle-aged writer, had become shy, timid, and withdrawn.

Yü entered a private tutor's school at the age of six (seven *sui*). Six years later, he was transferred to a modern-style elementary school in Fu-yang. Of all the students in the school, Yü was "the smallest both in body and in age."[5] At the end of his first year, his academic average exceeded eighty points and he was therefore immediately promoted to the third grade, bypassing the second and creating a sensation both at school and at home.[6] In describing life at this new-style school, Yü wrote very little about what he was taught to read, except for a brief paragraph about the craze among his classmates for English grammar. He graduated in 1909 when he was thirteen and reaching the age of adolescence.

From Fu-yang Yü went by boat to Hangchow; it was the first time that Yü was away from home. Once in Hangchow, Yü easily passed the entrance examination at Hangchow Middle School. But he soon spent most of his money in sightseeing and frequenting restaurants. He had to go to a less expensive school in Chia-hsing. Yü spent half a year there, lonely and homesick. His only remedy was reading and writing poetry. Three books influenced him greatly: a collection of poetry by Wu Wei-yeh (Mei-ts'un, 1609–72), a book describing the Boxers by an anonymous writer, and a collection of essays, poetry and memorials written during the Sino-Japanese War in 1894, entitled *P'u-t'ien chung-fen chi* (The righteous indignation everywhere under heaven).[7] Yü's impressions after reading these books revealed his heroic pretensions. "I hated being born too late; I could neither befriend a poet as early as Wu Mei-ts'un nor experience the two great calamities of 1894 and 1900, so as to charge at the enemy and savor the taste of battle."[8]

According to another source, he had read the Four Histories and T'ang poetry in his primary school days and, in the summer after his graduation, *Hung-lou meng* and *Liu ts'ai-tzu* (Six talented ones). In middle school he first came into contact with two popular books of classical fiction: *Hsi-hu chia-hua* (Interesting tales of West Lake) and *Hua yüeh hen* (Scars of romance).[9] It can be readily seen that Yü's literary sensibilities were in large part bred in Chinese classical litera-

Yü Ta-fu in 1934

ture. These books, by no means first-rate as literary masterpieces except *Hung-lou meng,* account for Yü's apparent ease and success in depicting traditional characters against an essentially traditional, albeit decaying and decadent-looking background.

Yü went back to the First Middle School of Hangchow after half a year of sojourn at Chia-hsing. The time was from late 1909 to 1910. Confronted by foppish young men from rich urban families and repulsed by homosexuality among his classmates (Kuo Mo-jo indulged in it in his high school years), Yü again sought escape in books and poetry.[10] He had begun to read Yüan and Ch'ing drama and write poetry for newspapers.

As more and more of his poems appeared in the newspapers, Yü became confident that his mastery of Chinese had already surpassed the level of his peers and studying with them at a routine pace was no longer necessary. As science did not enjoy enough prestige at the time, Yü decided to concentrate on English. Accordingly he enrolled in a missionary school run by a branch of the American Presbyterians.[11] But he soon found himself bored with prayers and involved in student movements. The pattern was a familiar one: first, for some petty grudges, a general strike was declared by the students who refused to attend classes; then a few "traitors" defected to the administration's side. Classes were resumed and the "tough" ones were ousted from the school. In this case the catalyst for the student revolt was a cook who had beaten a non-believer student. Yü belonged in the "tough" group. Thus, two months after he enrolled he was expelled. The competition among missionary schools was such that Yü found himself received by a Baptist school like a hero.[12]

Yü was soon disillusioned with the educational merits of the missionary schools. In early 1911, he had decided to quit school altogether and to engage in study at home. At the age of fifteen, Yü disciplined himself by setting up a tight schedule of studies; he would read English for one hour before breakfast and study Chinese classics (mainly two collections of T'ang and Sung poetry and Ssu-ma Kuang's famous *Tzu-chih t'ung-chien*) until noon. In the afternoon he would read science books. The whole day of studies would be followed by a walk in the countryside.[13]

Yü's autobiography does not mention, however, that in these years (1911–1912) he had also composed poems in his diaries, one of which was a narrative poem in the style of *Hsi-hu chia-hua*.[14] He had even written stories in which he imagined himself to be an amorous hero who fell in love with the two daughters of a rich neighbor whom he portrayed as of noble descent. The landscape of his hometown was transformed by his zestful imagination into a pastoral idyll. Sometimes on impulse he would try to translate the stories into simple English.

He had also subscribed to a Shanghai newspaper in order to keep up with the hectic current events. As he read about the Canton uprising, the Szechwan railway scuffles, and finally the outburst of revolution in Wuchang, he could only express his feelings of anxiety and exaltation on paper. Impatiently he waited for the revolution to sweep through his hometown. "Finally on one cloudy and cold afternoon, a few boats with white flags arrived from Hangchow. Some tens of soldiers, in grey uniforms and armed, came on shore. The magistrate had left the day before . . . Some big shots from the merchants' union and a few reputable members of the gentry . . . jointly put out a notice and held a meeting to welcome those soldiers."[15] Thus the revolution had come to Fu-yang. But the young Yü Ta-fu could not participate: "In my study I had thought only of charging at the enemy, plunging into battles, sacrificing myself for the people and dedicating my efforts to the country. Such a revolutionary comrade like me, at this crucial opportunity, could finally do nothing but stand outside the whirlwind, hold fast my fists, and shed a few noble tears of the observer."[16]

The theme of these autobiographical sketches seems to be that of a "superfluous hero" (Yü had developed a certain affinity to Turgenev and was extremely fond of "The Diary of a Superfluous Man"), whose tragedy lies in his total insignificance and uselessness. Yü considered himself left aside by life: first by his father, who died, then by his mother, who was not always at home, later by his classmates, whose foppish ways he detested, and finally by history, which "confirmed" his position as a superfluous man. Left out by external events he turned inward into his own heart and dissected himself through his fictional writings.

Yü's autobiography is also a document in sentiment. His profusion of sentiment and sentimentality is partially an outgrowth of his sensitive nature. It is also nourished by the many classical sentimental novels and poetry he read as a student. The awakening to the power of sentiment seemed to be a common form of the puberty experience in Yü's generation. Yü was unique among his contemporaries in that he had not in his high school years read any translations of Western fiction by Lin Shu. Yü made this point very clear in the reminiscences of his writing career,[17] implying that Lin's translations belonged in the category of adulterated and low-class literature on a par with the works of the "Saturday School." While times were changing and China was in the jerky process of "modernization," Yü Ta-fu's mental world remained traditional. It was only during his years in Japan that he developed a certain "modern" outlook and imbibed strongly Western literary influences.

Student Life and Sex in Japan, 1914–1922

Two years after the revolution, in September 1913, Yü Ta-fu went to Japan with his eldest brother, who was sent by the new Chinese government to inspect the Japanese judicial administration.[18] Yü's brother stayed until the summer of 1914, when Yü was admitted to the preparatory class of the First Higher School of Tokyo. In autumn 1914, Yü at the age of eighteen again found himself alone in a foreign land.

Japan in the first decade of this century was, like America in the 1950s and 1960s, a haven for Chinese students. The Ch'ing government, in the last throes of its "reform," had begun to send hundreds of students to Japan annually and the practice was followed by the early Republican government. Added to these students on government scholarships were even larger numbers of Chinese students in Japan on private funds—mostly dandies from rich families who wanted to escape from the storm that was raging in their homeland. The Japanese government made all possible arrangements for these students: accelerated classes in Japanese language, preparatory classes for regular government students (such as the one Yü attended), and even special and easier sections in some schools for the rich. It was in Japan that most of these Chinese youths came into unrestrained contact with foreign ideas, foreign habits, and Japanese women. The guest houses that catered especially to the Chinese clientele were usually run by poor Japanese families and the old landlady invariably had a daughter. There were always geisha houses, restaurants, and tea houses offering an endless array of sensual enticements for those somewhat belated adolescents. A fantastic world had been created by two governments for the young Chinese intellectual elite, who, still dazzled by the strangeness of their new experience, were beginning to consider what they would do in life.

Five higher schools were covered by Chinese government scholarships, provided the Chinese students were first admitted by these schools. Among them was the First Higher School of Tokyo where Yü first entered and met Kuo Mo-jo.[19] The courses were divided into three sections: humanities and social sciences, natural sciences and engineering, and medicine. Yü Ta-fu enrolled in the first section but soon changed to the third, perhaps on the advice of his eldest brother.[20] Upon completing his first preparatory year, he transferred (in 1915) to the Sixth Higher School in Nagoya where he began a major in natural sciences but changed back to the humanities in 1916. After finishing up his three-year high school education, Yü was admitted to the faculty of economics of Tokyo Imperial University, where he finally graduated in 1922.

We know relatively little about Yü's life during this most crucial period. From his own accounts, we learn that on the intellectual level he was initially attracted, like Lu Hsün and others, to Western science: "I began to realize the greatness and profundity of modern science—whether physical or metaphysical."[21] But his interests soon shifted to Western literature. When he was attending high school in Nagoya, he consumed more than 1,000 volumes of Russian, French, English, German, and Japanese fiction,[22] probably all in Japanese translation. He wrote old-style poems and sent them to newspapers, a practice he began as early as 1909. He also experimented, when he was in Nagoya, with writing a story about a love affair between a Chinese student and a Japanese girl.[23] But it was during his university years that he turned more and more to creative writing. The result was a collection of three short stories, *Ch'en lun* (Sinking), which subsequently created a storm on the new literary scene in China.

Thus it was in the schools of Japan and in the books about the West that the young Yü Ta-fu passed his years of late adolescence— a period in which, according to Eriksonian psychology, the problem of identity and identity confusion become dominant in the development of a man's personality. In this period of "moratorium," the young man gropes toward relating his past experience to future expectations in order to define his role in life.[24] That Yü shifted his majors three times in three years shows the degree of his identity confusion. Although he finally completed his studies in economics and returned to China to teach the subject, it was in literature that he ultimately found his true vocation. This process of confused choices and rapid changes in deciding upon a career, which was by no means uncommon among Yü's compatriots, reflects further the precariousness of a transitional age. It also compounded the sense of quandary in Yü's sensitive mind.

His general mood in his Japanese years Yü characterized as "hypochondria." "What I felt, thought, and experienced can be summarized as nothing but hopelessness, nothing but sadness."[25] He further stated that the root of his hypochondria lay in his deeply disturbed psyche and was related to "the various kinds of complicated attractions between the sexes" and a sense of humiliation at "China's low international position."[26]

Sex is naturally part of the mental and physical growth of an adolescent maturing into a man. What made Yü's case interesting was that his sexual awakening should have taken place in a foreign land with foreign women. With photos of semi-nude actresses in magazines, daring reports of sexual scandals in the newspapers, candid portraitures by naturalist writers, and finally the numerous Japanese coeds that one met in buses and trolley cars[27]—the sexual dose must have been too strong for a sensitive young man.

Yü's first sexual experience, according to him, occurred in the winter of 1915–1916. One afternoon, at the end of his first semester at the Sixth Higher School, when exams were over and it was snowing, Yü jumped on a train to Tokyo, had a few small bottles of sake, and got off at a small station. "After being received by the madam, I picked a fat and white-skinned prostitute . . . Following wild singing and drinking I broke my virginity." When he woke up the next morning he was seized with remorse: "Worthless! too worthless! My ideals, my ambitions, my passionate devotion to my country—what is left now? What is left?" [28]

How are we to account for Yü's recurrent feeling of excessive guilt with regard to sex? C. T. Hsia remarked: "The guilt and remorse of Yü Ta-fu is to be understood in the framework of a Confucian ethic, which had conditioned his upbringing. Even when engaged in casual amorous pursuits, Yü Ta-fu or his fictional alter ego always suffers from the acute awareness of his truancy as son, husband, and father." [29]

This explanation may be applied to Yü's attitude toward sex after he returned to China. But it can still be argued that even in a Confucian framework, for a scholar to while away his leisure hours in a brothel has always been an accepted custom. Moreover, Yü was always acutely aware, whether or not he was engaged in amorous pursuits, of his truancy as son, husband, father. The genesis of his guilt feelings must be seen in the context of the Japanese setting.

It has been noted that Yü's Japanese period coincides with the period of identity confusion in an Eriksonian scheme. While Yü was shifting between sciences and humanities to arrive at a discipline which might become his definite profession, he had also to define himself as a Chinese in a different and discriminating society. "The majority of these people—the Japanese race—were not courteous. They seemed to shout bluntly, in their manners, speech, and actions: 'You inferior people, abject breed of a defeated nation, what are you doing here in our great Japan, which controls you?' " [30]

It is indeed traumatic that at an age when he felt the sexual urges in his body, Yü's attempts at finding his identity had to be made in the form of physical contacts with the opposite sex of an alien race. To feel himself drawn irresistibly to the fair maidens of a nation which considered him inferior—especially to succumb to their temptation in brothels—must have been a psychological problem that Yü felt acutely but found it hard to articulate. Hence sex, racism, and even nationalism are all intertwined in his psyche as in his stories.

The young Yü Ta-fu, as he woke up in the arms of a fat Japanese prostitute, and the young hero at the end of his short story "Sinking," when he talked to his own shadow in self-pity, must have been seized by the same feeling that the numbing effect of abusive drinking and depravity would only be replaced by another sobering attack, a piercing reminder of his identity as a forlorn Chinese in an alien land. The nationalism of Yü Ta-fu in Japan was therefore personal and psychological, not exclusively political or ideological, as has been alleged by some Communist scholars.[31] He felt guilty toward his own country because he had developed a high degree of ambivalence toward his guest country: he was "humiliated, despairing, saddened, enraged, and pained" by the Japanese race, especially when he heard the derogatory word "Shina" uttered "from the mouths of young maidens";[32] but, like a drunkard, he was also taken profoundly by his foreign liquor, so much so that he had developed, in the eyes of his Japanese acquaintances, a real "feel" for the Japanese way of life.[33] This feeling of ambivalence reached its peak at the point of his final departure from Japan in 1922, after he had successfully passed the graduation examinations. "I have lived in this island country for ten years, this alien land where my youth like the spring dew has withered away. Although I have suffered many disgraces from her, although I do not want her to kiss my feet again, this sense of abhorrence is so deep as to, at the time of my leaving, give rise to a feeling that I could not bear to leave her for good."[34]

Yü had voluntarily delayed his date of departure in order to revisit many places and "to wipe off again the blood stains of my defeated romance." As the ship which Yü boarded at Kobe on July 20, 1922, stopped at Moji, he went ashore to buy a souvenir—a new book titled *Kimono* by John Paris—and to stand at the door of a brothel, "devouring the over-ripe female flesh."[35] The last invocation of Japan in his farewell piece reads: "Japan, ah Japan! I am gone. And I won't return even if I die [a promise he subsequently did not keep]. But— when I have to commit suicide under the oppression of my own society, the last image that may arise in my mind will be you! Ave [sic] Japan! My future is darkening!"[36]

Wanderings in China, 1922–1925

When Yü set foot on his native soil in Shanghai, ready to plunge himself into the newly founded *Creation Quarterly*, the activities of the Association for Literary Studies were in high gear. Scathing criticism was directed against the Creationists and Yü Ta-fu in particular, who was labeled as "a writer of carnal desires."[37] Moreover, the manager of the T'ai-tung Publishing Company, which was then supporting the *Quarterly* and Kuo Mo-jo, treated them in the manner of a condescending philanthropist. The sales record of the magazine was depressing: the first issue sold only 1,500 copies in two to three months.[38] The two disgruntled men wandered in the streets of Shanghai at midnight. "Mo-jo," Yü said, "let's go and have a drink!"

Hand in hand, they went from one bar to another, drinking a grand total of more than thirty bottles. Finally, totaly drunk, the two lonely figures tottered home along a street in the foreign concessions. Cars, with foreigners in them, whipped past them. And they began to curse the foreigners and foreign capitalism. Suddenly, Ta-fu ran from the sidewalks to the center of the street and, raising his hand toward a car that raced toward them, he yelled: "I'll deal with you with pistols!"[39]

A month's wandering and drinking in Shanghai soon left Yü penniless. He was forced to take up a job that Kuo had procured for him: to teach English at a school of law and administration at An-ch'ing, in Anhwei province. Before leaving for An-ch'ing, Yü decided to visit his family in Fu-yang. He pawned his wedding ring for travel expenses.[40] He had married a girl in 1920 when he returned home from Japan for the summer vacation. After a few days' stay with his bride, he left for Japan again. Now, two years later, the fatigued prodigal son was returning home again.

Having suffered for eight years from humiliation and alienation in Japan, Yü, upon returning home, found himself alienated from his mother, whose traditional mode of thinking enraged him. Obviously, the mother expected her son to come back with wealth and glory, but her son returned carrying only two suitcases. The widowed woman, now reaching old age, had grown bitter. Yü's wife, on the other hand, was caught in the universal conflict of wife versus mother-in-law. Neglected by her husband, she was antagonized by her mother-in-law on account of him; taught to be docile and obedient, she could only bear intermittent vituperations from the old woman with silent tears.

Perhaps because of a sensitivity nurtured by his intensive reading of traditional Chinese fiction and poetry, Yü had a profound sympathy for the victims of traditional society. Through this sympathy he could often attain keener insights than most of his rebellious contemporaries who believed that the old family system was wholly evil and who, in defiant acts of escape, often severed their ties with tradition for good. By contrast Yü found himself irretrievably entangled with it through his wife. Her hopelessness and docility released a deluge of warm feelings from him, and he brought her to An ch'ing, where their first child was born: the "seed of weariness" sown in those few days of the family reunion.[41] During the months when she was pregnant, Yü, easily irritable, inflicted upon her the pent-up feelings of frustration and indigation that were incurred by his encounters with the school authorities. Copious tears were shed after many quarrels between husband and wife. She finally even attempted suicide. The winter of 1922 saw Yü's mood reaching a low ebb. He toyed with the idea of becoming a laborer in Russia; he walked along the Yangtze River contemplating suicide.[42]

In spite of Yü's depressions at home, his career was thriving. The Creation Society was reaching the zenith of its popularity with two new publications: *Creation Weekly* and *Creation Day*. In 1923, Yü also brought his family from An-ch'ing to Shanghai. In September, Yü accepted an offer from Peking University to replace a professor of statistics. On his way north in October, he wrote back four letters. In the last letter he pondered the alternatives for his future: "Should I go to Peking to become a vagabond or return to my home town to become a hermit?"[43] Should he float with the currents of an evil and corrupt society to seek fame and fortune or should he cut himself off from this society altogether in order to preserve his personal integrity? The question and Yü's answer in late 1923 were prophetic of the future course of his life: "Naturally to be a hermit sounds better in name, but in actuality drifting along is more interesting." [44] So he drifted to Peking.

Yet Yü's life in Peking did not please him. In a letter to Kuo Mo-jo, dated March 7, 1924, Yü indicated that he was far from happy and content in Peking. He said he and Kuo had been "divorced from art" and could come back to it only through "restoring the original feeling of loneliness." [45] He wanted to leave his teaching position and come back to Shanghai in order to get back to his home province and "realize my long cherished wish to retire in the countryside." [46] The vagabond was already wearied and yearned for the life of a hermit.

Although Yü wanted to return to Shanghai in June, obviously his plan was not realized. In early 1925, he was invited to teach in the humanities faculty of the Normal University at Wuchang. In Wuchang, Yü again found himself in campus politics—an experience not dissimilar to that at An-ch'ing. Half a year later he quit. He was again engulfed in deep depression. "Since I started my writing career there have never been experiences of such bad moods as in this year. In this year I felt many disillusionments, raised many doubts. I thought from now on my creative power would disappear for good." [47] "In this year I neither read nor wrote . . . I drank and wandered impulsively, with the result that I was taken seriously ill in winter." [48] He returned from Wuchang to Shanghai, and from Shanghai to Fu-yang, a weary and fatigued vagabond who longed for the peace of the countryside to convalesce from his illness. As he was enjoying a temporary rest as a hermit, a younger group of new Creationists gradually took control; they started publication of a new journal, *Hung-shui* (Deluge) and, on April 1, 1926, founded the new Creation Publications Department. In the society Yü was, three years prior to severing ties with it, already a veteran.

Biography through Diaries: Wine and the Creation Society, 1926–1927

On March 18, 1926, Kuo Mo-jo, Yü Ta-fu, and Wang Tu-ch'ing

together boarded a ship from Shanghai to Canton—then the "cradle" of revolution—to join Ch'eng Fang-wu and lecture at Canton University. The old order's exodus southward marked the end of the first phase of the Creation Society and beginning of the second. Although Yü was for a while officially the editor of *Deluge* and the newly founded *Creation Monthly*, his mind and heart were no longer pre-occupied with the society but rather with more personal things and events.

In Canton Yü began a series of intermittent diaries, published under the title of *Jih-chi chiu-chung* (Nine diaries) in 1933, consisting of nine segments and covering a period from November 1926 to July 1927. Later on, nine more segments were published, recording sporadically Yü's life from October to November 1932 and from 1934 to 1936.

As the diaries began on November 3, 1926, Yü's mood was far from elated. Earlier in June that year, his son had died.[49] On this first day of his diary, he wrote: "Ah! my son is dead. My woman is ill. My salary has been snatched away. And finally I cannot even keep a few boxes of my most treasured books. I really don't know whether there is any justice in this world; I really don't know where there is any human feeling left. I want to cry, I want to curse, I want to kill."[50] His salary was held "by these politicians." His few boxes of treasured books, put under the custody of the university, were found divested of their contents. "I really regret having come here, regret having come to this barbarian place."[51] The chaos and ferment in this revolutionary base which held the alliance of KMT and CCP in precarious balance had proved too tough for Yü's sensibilities. Whereas Kuo Mo-jo joined the Northern Expedition in July, merely four months after he arrived in Canton, Yü could only indulge himself in drinking. His two diaries in Canton registered a long sequence of his drinking bouts, his mental resolves, and his inevitable relapses into drinking again. His habit of drinking, like Samuel Johnson's celebrated sloth, continued to be a life-long trait until his last years in Sumatra. Here are a few examples:

November 8: Took a bath. From tomorrow on, I'd better pull myself together. In the past two or three years I have been too depraved. A pitiable pity (p. 6).

November 11: Had a glass of wine . . . Today I am tired, too tired. Starting tomorrow, I plan to work hard (p. 7).

November 15: Getting old, too old. My heart is drier and lonelier than that of a Chinese 60-year-old (p. 10).

November 20: Had a bath and changed clothes. From today I want to exert myself. In the past week I have been too depraved, too irregular (p. 13).

November 24: Dinner with the faculty in the big bell tower. Having drunk a few glasses too much, I had a headache (p. 17).

December 3: In the evening, many young students and my admirers held a farewell dinner in the city . . . I alone drank too much and got drunk (pp. 26–27).

December 7: After 3 P.M., went to the party. There were more than 20 men and women who had gathered to celebrate my thirtieth birthday. After all it was a pompous affair. I got drunk again. (p. 31).

December 14: In the evening I asked Tu-ch'ing and two other young men for supper. Got 80 percent drunk. This time, after I go to Shanghai, I shall cut out smoking and drinking and make efforts. The success or failure will depend on whether I am firm in my resolution from now on. I disdain competing with philistines; I disdain particularly competition with the so-called politicians today. A hundred years from now, there may be some who can understand me. From now on I shall exert myself in creative writing (p. 35).

The diaries convey a ring of authenticity precisely on account of these repeated notes of drunkenness in plain and undecorative language. While Yü might have had vague intensions to publish them, the straightforward style leaves little doubt that he had not edited his daily entries.[52]

Yü's diaries vividly reflect some of the main traits in his life style and personality: sporadic vicissitudes of mood, self-indulgent excesses of a few habits, and, above all, a high-strung sensitivity toward his life which he considered caught in a time out of joint with his ideals. Given his personality and outlook, Yü was least capable of handling administrative affairs of the Creation Society. Yet this was precisely what the other veteran Creationists wanted him to do. He was instructed to go to Shanghai and clear up the mess with the power-seeking "junior partners" in the publications department of the society.

Yü left Canton on December 15 and arrived in Shanghai on December 27, 1926. On January 1, 1927, he wrote in his diary: "Today is the first day of 1927. I want very much to start from today to create anew, to undertake again the task of Jehovah in the Genesis." [53] At first glance we tend to assume that he was referring to the reorganization of the society. Then he added: "In the past few days I have been dissipating myself too much, with the result that my head is torpid and confused." [54] As we read through the many incidents of inebriation in his diary, we find that he talked with the junior partners from time to time and checked accounts occasionally. This only made him "feel more depressed at heart and realize all the more the despicable nature of the Chinese." [55]

Yü asserted that he finally succeeded in "clearing up the society within a society and entrusting the total financial assets of the Creation Society to the care of a relative of Ch'eng Fang-wu." [56] But judging from the temperamental way with which Yü dealt with the affairs of the society as revealed in his diaries, we are not so sure of his ability to clear up the mess single-handedly. The truth of the matter was that among the old members of the society, a degree of disharmony had also arisen after Yü published two controversial articles in *Deluge*;[57] both were critical of Chiang Kai-shek and the right wing of the KMT. The first article enraged both Kuo, who was then serving as a political commissar among the Northern Expedition troops under the KMT, and Ch'eng Fang-wu, who wrote a review in *Deluge*. They wrote angry letters to Yü charging that it was highly impertinent to write such an article at a moment when the forces of the Northern Expedition were pushing toward the Sun Ch'uan-fang controlled Kiangsu area. Yü noted in his diary: "Got a letter from Kuo Mo-jo . . . reprimanding me for my bad inclinations. I am afraid that he will be reined in by the rightists. We shall probably go our separate ways." [58] "Got a letter from Fang-wu saying that Mo-jo had also written to him and scolded me for that Canton affair article in No. 25 of *Deluge*. Mo-jo, because of his position, had to echo Chiang Kai-shek . . . After reading this letter and Fang-wu's short article . . . I felt unhappy. I think it's time to speak out for the people rather than echo the warlords and bureaucrats or the new warlords and new bureaucrats who are struggling for power." [59]

Yü's "inopportune" articles and thoughts illustrated dramatically the ideological and political confusions of his time. Although later Communist scholars jump at this instance to vindicate Yü's leftist loyalties,[60] in 1927 Yü could only enrage Ch'eng Fang-wu and embarrass Kuo Mo-jo. The three had come to Canton just in time for Chiang's surprise coup against the Communists in Canton (March 20). And Yü wrote his second article, "En Route to Changed Directions," only four days before Chiang's famous massacre of Communists on April 12, 1927. His diary of April 12 noted: "Before dawn I could hear the din of rifles . . . Went to visit friends in the afternoon. When we talked about Chiang Kai-shek's high-handed suppressive measures this time, everybody dared only to show anger but dared not speak."[61] Ten days later he wrote: "I came back and bought a foreign newspaper to read. Chiang Kai-shek split with the leftist clique and set up his own personal government in Nanking . . . Hateful rightists, they have caused the national revolution to halt at half-way. Henceforward I want to struggle, struggle for the country. I will not be self-depraved any more."[62]

Although these intimate thoughts had not yet been published, Yü's sentiments in the two published articles were sufficient to alarm the KMT authorities in Shanghai. Rumors that the Shanghai authorities would close down the Creation Society had spread. Early in January, Yü had heard a rumor of possible suppression. He had been on friendly terms with Hsü Chih-mo. Therefore he wrote a letter to Ting Wen-chiang, the famous hero in the science versus metaphysics debate in 1923 who was close to the high command of Sun Ch'uan-fang's forces in Shanghai, and asked Hsü to forward it to him. On January 18, Yü was informed by Hsü that 150 men were on the list to be arrested.[63] The alarm turned out to be premature.

In late May, Yü's article for a Japanese magazine *Bungei sensen* (Literary battleline), which was even more outspoken, aroused more threats, and he retreated to Hangchow for a month. In July, an inspector from the military command came to the Society office presumably to make arrests. Yü was not there and the younger members all fled. Ch'eng Fang-wu, who soon arrived in Shanghai, further reprimanded Yü for having caused alarm and damage to the society.[64] On August 15, 1927, Yü put a notice in two major newspapers in

Shanghai—*Shen pao* and *Min-kuo jih-pao*—cutting off entirely his relationship with the Creation Society.

Yü Ta-fu and Wang Ying-hsia, 1927–1935

The diaries of Yü Ta-fu after 1927—and his life—were dominated by one figure, Wang Ying-hsia. So far no serious scholar of Yü has ever given adequate attention to this woman, to whom Yü dedicated the first volume of his *Collected Works* (published in 1927) and whose name he wanted to leave for posterity together with his work.[65]

Wang Ying-hsia was a native of Hangchow, a city renowned for the beauties of its scenery and its girls. She was, indeed, a beauty by all accounts, and a famous one. When she was attending a girls' middle school, she won the title of "Miss Hangchow." Later, she was praised in social circles as the reigning queen of the four celebrated beauties from Hangchow.[66] Her limpid eyes, slightly large and sensual lips, her white skin (hence her nickname "water chestnut white"), and above all her elegant manners and speech have been singled out by friends for special commendation.[67]

In the second half of 1926 the forces of the Northern Expedition had gradually reached Chekiang and clashed with Sun Ch'uan-fang's troops. To escape the dangers of war, in December she moved into Shanghai with a couple, Sun Pai-kang and his wife, and sought the protection of the foreign concessions. Sun Pai-kang, her family friend and host in Shanghai, was a minor literary man himself and often visited the Japanese "Nei-shan" bookstore. One day early in January 1927, Sun met his old friend Yü Ta-fu in the bookstore.[68] A few days later, on January 14, Yü wrote longingly: "Went to the French concession to see a fellow townsman, Mr. Sun. There I met Miss Wang Ying-hsia from Hangchow, and my heart was stirred by her. I shall do my best to proceed with this, hoping to be a permanent friend of hers."[69] A few days later: "At noon, I played host and treated them to drink to their hearts' content, and I was drunk, too. Ah, ah, lovely Ying-hsia! I am thinking about her here; I don't know if she is also thinking about me over there."[70]

Thus began the courtship by a celebrated man of letters for the hand of a celebrated beauty. This romantic idyll, however, was marred by a few unpleasant facts. Wang, albeit still a beauty, was reaching thirty; Yü was thirty-one and already a married man. Shanghai in 1927 could hardly be a perfect romantic setting. Moreover, it was not love at first sight on both sides: Wang's initial reaction, not documented in any secondary source, may not have been too favorable. She knew he was married. Even Sun himself was surprised by Yü's unusually agitated mood. After Yü had paid numerous visits, he finally confessed his passion for her to Sun in Japanese, in a state of intoxication. Wang's response to Yü's outburst of emotions, after Sun's wife related Yü's feelings to her, was a simple expression: "He looks pitiable." [71]

Yü's infatuation with Miss Wang must be seen in the context of his mood. From his diaries we know he had not shaken off the despondencies of his Canton days. He was still unable to disentangle himself from the pattern of excessive drinking, followed by remorse and unfulfilled resolutions. His associations with Miss Wang in the beginning only served to aggravate this pattern. A tiny act of concern by her would send his heart to ecstatic heights; her hesitations and refusals would plunge him into the abyss of mental torture which led inevitably to more excessive drinking. A few excerpts:

January 16: At the dinner table . . . Miss Wang treated me very kindly . . . If I could obtain Miss Wang's love, probably my creative power would be stronger. Ah, life is still worth while, and some meaning can be still gained from it (p. 58).

January 20: Ah, ah, I am really happy. I truly hope that this time my love can succeed (p. 63).

February 9: Wrote a letter to her telling her about my disappointment and sorrow; this may well be goodbye for good (p. 89).

February 11: Plan to go out and get drunk tonight. Henceforward, I'll cut out smoking, cut out drinking, and cut out serpent-like women (p. 91).

February 16: Tonight I drank too much, and my body wasn't well. My real termination of drinking will start from tomorrow (p. 97).

February 28: Ah, Ying-hsia! You are truly my Beatrice. My ugly and depraved thoughts are all purified by you (p. 111).

March 3: If Ying-hsia could accept my request and carry out my plan, I think my life from tomorrow would undergo a great transformation. My real La Vita Nuova will probably begin tomorrow. Starting tomorrow, I plan to translate Dante's *La Vita Nuova* in two months so as to make it a souvenir of my marriage with Ying-hsia (p. 117).

March 5: She vowed to love me and remain faithful till death. And I laid bare my whole sentiments of love to her (p. 119).

March 7: Today is the first day that she consented to my kisses (p. 120).

March 8: Starting today, I am going to give up drinking and smoking, and devote my efforts to my work (p. 121).

March 31: Woke up at eight. Unclean thoughts arose again. And the resolution to strive and work of the past month was totally overthrown. Today I want to . . . drink a little, and re-enact the weaknesses in my life once again. And from tomorrow I'll start a new life. *Ah, Tomorrow, the hopeless tomorrow!"* (p. 121). [The italicized words appeared in the original in English.]

As these lines were written, Yü was also involved in the inner struggles of the Creation Society. He was reading, writing, and seeing friends. He passed through barbed wire and heard gun shots. But his whole life was increasingly intertwined with Wang Ying-hsia. All his other activities remained outside, on the outskirts of his life. Wang Ying-hsia had penetrated into his inner life. His many resolutions and relapses, while following the same pattern as in Canton, sound more imbued with tensions of inner conflict. For the first time he was grasping at something substantial—her "rich and opulent physique and the crystal and beautiful pupils in her eyes." [72] The mirage of love that he had searched for since the time of *Sinking* was being turned into a reality. He had said five years before *(Sinking* was written in 1921): "I want neither knowledge nor fame. All I want is a 'heart' that can understand and comfort me, a warm and passionate heart and the sympathy it generates and the love born of that sympathy. What I want is love." [73]

The development and transmutations of Wang Ying-hsia's feelings toward Yü Ta-fu are harder to follow. Since she has written nothing about this period (except later in her long denunciatory letters to the editor of a Hong Kong magazine in which she summarily dismissed the episode of courtship as that of an old wolf trapping an innocent girl), we can merely construct a few hypotheses. She may indeed have taken some pity on him. But vanity seems also to be implicated: she was, out of pity, going out with a famous author. That she had long had the reputation of being a reigning beauty indicated that she w. s not inactive in the local social circles, her family being well-known in Hangchow. Moreover, her grandfather had enjoyed the reputation of being a poet in the classical style. Family upbringing may have predisposed her toward talented men of letters, and Yü was a fairly good classical poet in his own right.[74] (He wrote a whole group of classical poems for her after their marriage.) In short, her declared "love" for him may very well have had a tinge of vanity and the pride of conquest.

From Yü's diaries we know that she declared her love for him on March 5 and granted him his first kiss on March 7, about two months after they first met. More physical intimacies followed. On March 14, Yü went to Hangchow to visit the Wang family. The next day he met her grandfather, Wang Erh-nan, and the two men obviously enjoyed each other's company.[75] On June 5, Yü and Miss Wang held their engagement party to which more than forty guests were invited. Yü noted in his diary: "The matter with Ying-hsia has been decided tonight. The problem in the future will be how to manage Ch'üan-chün (his first wife)."[76] Sun Pai-kang asserted that Yü and Wang began living together sometime in the summer or autumn of 1927. In February, 1928, Sun received an invitation card from the two lovers for "dinner"—to be held on February 21 in a restaurant in Tokyo.[77] It seems highly unlikely that they could have gone to Tokyo for their wedding ceremony. A possible explanation may be that Yü could not and did not divorce his first wife legally and hence never held a wedding ceremony at all. The general public, however, accepted them as being married.

After their engagement, they moved back to Shanghai where Wang was soon pregnant and gave birth to a boy. For a short period Yü did have a very orderly life. Wang Ying-hsia's influence on Yü's life was such that he wrote, on August 1, 1927, in the foreword to the second volume of his *Collected Works*:

I moved back to Shanghai at the end of 1926. I lived idly for half a year and witnessed the increasingly malignant machinations of the warlords and tasted the bitterness of being betrayed by friends and close associates. I should have sunk to the bottom: either to become a monk or to drown myself in a big river. But around this time I acquired an external force of assistance, which brought my entire soul and body to salvation. For my gratitude to this helping power, I want very much not to record with my pen and ink but rather to commend by my actions in the latter part of my life . . . All in all, I have been groping in the darkness for half a lifetime. Now I seem to have found a path to light.[78]

Of course Wang Ying-hsia did not change Yü Ta-fu into a completely different family man. Her influence served to dilute the intensity of solitary melancholia and self-indulgent depravity, but reinforced the more traditional traits in Yü's personality and life style.

The years 1928–1930 can be regarded as the afterglow of Yü's leftist phase of 1926–1927, after which he gradually withdrew from leftist politics and relapsed into his more traditional habits. Having left the Creation Society, he became in 1928 a co-editor of Lu Hsün's *Pen-liu* (Running currents) magazine and initiated another journal of his own, *Ta-chung wen-i* (Literature for the masses). In 1929 he joined Lu Hsün, Ts'ai Yüan-p'ei, and Sung Ch'ing-ling in founding the "Great League of Freedom for the Protection of People's Rights." In 1930, he was invited to join the League of Left-Wing Writers.[79]

In May 1930, Yü's grandfather-in-law, Mr. Wang Erh-nan, died. Yü wrote a biographical essay in his memory in which he reminisced: "Since we had become acquainted . . . I often talked with him about poetry and learning over a bottle of wine. A meal usually lasted for three or four hours. Sometimes we would get up at midnight, light the lamp, drink wine, leaf through books, and talk about the past and the present; often we would sit together until dawn."[80] At the end of the essay, Yü stated: "The gradual dilution of the misanthropic tendencies of my early years is due to his cultivating influence."[81]

Wang Erh-nan and his granddaughter did not, to be sure, restore Yü to optimism. What they had succeeded in instilling in Yü's life and personality was the sense of complacency of a cultivated traditional gentleman. The gradual emergence of this life-style can be seen in his diaries and writings from 1932 to 1935. In October 1930, Yü again moved to Hangchow to be treated for tuberculosis. He stayed in a resort hotel near the West Lake from October 6 to 13 and then moved into "West Lake Hotel." In the midst of natural beauties, he read Nietzsche and Turgenev (*Diary of a Superfluous Man*) and translated Rousseau's *Promeneur*.[82] But more often he went sightseeing alone or with friends, and composed classical poetry and wrote letters describing his experiences to his second wife. He continued to drink.

In his published works, we see a growing number of essays on his travels written with great care and a remarkable grasp of scenic details. A famous account in this genre is his *Hsi-yu jih-lu* (Daily records of a western excursion) included in his diaries and describing a group outing financed by the Chekiang provincial government featuring such well-known connoisseurs of taste as Lin Yutang, Hu Ch'iu-yüan, and P'an Kuang-tan. Yü and Lin praised the glories of nature with exclamations taken from Goethe's "Dichtung and Wahrheit"! One of his later books, *Chi-hen ch'u-ch'u* (Footprints here and there), published in 1934, is a collection mainly of travel notes and diaries and, in the opinion of a literary historian, "shows strong affinity with the older travel literature."[83] Another book, *Hsien shu* (Idle notes), published in 1936 and containing his essays written between 1933 and 1934, reveals the peace of mind of a middle-aged man and the joy of a connoisseur in art and poetry. There are, for instance, an essay praising the charm of autumn in Peking, another eulogizing the winter scene in the southern provinces, essays on poetry, on the local customs of Fukien, and a special group of poems written "to please Hsia."

All these manifestations in Yü's life since he married Wang Ying-hsia point to the dominance of the "hermit" side of his life as opposed to his earlier "vagabond" wanderings. He even acquired a piece of land for his burial place.[84] After the spring of 1933, the Yü's decided to live in Hangchow permanently. Through the help of local friends and mainly masterminded by Wang Ying-hsia, a project was gradually underway to construct a residence in an area at the eastern corner of the city.[85] Yü originally intended it to be a shabby thatched hut as befitting a Taoist recluse. The house, when completed in 1935, turned out to be a modern compound of two big buildings with a raised tower on the front facing south. Yü called his modern edifice "thatched hut against wind and rain," *(feng-yü mao-lu)* and the tower "tower of the setting sun" *(hsi-yang lou)*—very stylized traditional names which hardly reflect the reality, yet in a symbolic way prove quite adequate for Yü's images of this part of his life. He was a hermit far from the crowd and from the storms of social and political unrest. And, whether he was aware of it or not, the sun of his writing career was also setting; he was moving toward the twilight of his life. After 1930 his works did not sell so well as before.[86] He had also withdrawn himself from the League of Left-Wing Writers. As he told a reporter from a local Hangchow newspaper: "The Communist Party was very dissatisfied with me, saying that my works were too individualistic. This I admit, because I am from a bourgeois background, this is inevitable . . . Later on, the Communist Party wanted to assign me to practical work. I told them that I couldn't do things like distributing propaganda leaflets. So they became more displeased with me. Hence I have voluntarily struck out the name of Yü Ta-fu from the list of the League of Left-Wing Writers."[87]

Not only had he left the main stage of leftist literary activities, he began to write mainly for Lin Yutang's magazines after 1934. From 1936 to 1937 he became the editor of *Lun-yü*, one of Lin's most successful journals, dedicated to discourse on everything under heaven except politics.

Journey's End, 1936–1945

The erection of the "thatched hut against wind and rain" held great significance in Yü's life. The building, symbolically speaking, can be regarded as a monument marking the mid-point of his life. He wrote in a piece called "Some words about my residence": "Previously I liked traveling, especially in deserted regions unreached by trains, airplanes, steamships and all those effective vehicles of modern transportation . . . Once in a wide and thinly populated area, you could sing and hum, lay bare your body, and wash off all the false etiquettes and rigid manners of society . . . But this kind of disposition for traveling and drifting has gradually been diminished in recent years."[88] In his study with six or seven thousand copies of books in Chinese,

English, Japanese, German and French, he resembled more and more the old Mr. Wang Erh-nan: he drank wine, wrote poetry, and even began to learn Chinese painting.[89]

The first phase of development, of constant mental and emotional suffering and striving, and therefore of surging creativity, had come to an end. In 1935 he started to write segments of his autobiography for Lin Yutang's magazines, as if he had reached a point in his life where he could afford to look back and regard his past as the sum total of his entire life. On November 28, 1935, his fortieth birthday, he jotted down in his diary a poem with a sentence of self-commentary: "When one reaches forty and is still unknown to the world, there is nothing to be feared any more; Confucius was really a very experienced sage."[90]

In 1936, Ch'en I, Governor of Fukien Province, invited Yü to "visit Fukien," that is, to serve in the provincial government. Yü arrived in Foochow on February 4. His diary of February 6 noted: "At 9 o'clock called on governor Ch'en and had a lengthy talk . . . He said he would appoint me as an adviser to the provincial government with a monthly salary of 300 dollars. Am I going to be a military counselor in a barbarian court?"[91] The last reference calls to mind Chu-ko Liang of the period of Three Kingdoms, or the *mu-yu* custom in traditional China. It was, indeed, a long way from being an alienated wanderer to becoming a member of the establishment. Yü's decision to take this office may have stemmed from economic considerations. He was several thousand dollars in debt because of the construction expenses of the new house. Like most traditional-minded people, he regarded officialdom as automatically a lucrative channel. But his flirtations with governmental service proved to be disastrous for his private life. The Fukien Provincial Government, due to many years of wars, was still financially squeezed. As a result, salary payments were delayed and Yü received only a hundred dollars after serving for two months.[92]

Wang Ying-hsia, whom Yü left behind in Hangchow, began an affair with the son of a local official. As the impending clouds of war against the Japanese hovered over China, Yü's domestic strife was also raging. Although Wang's activities and sentiments in this period are not carefully documented in any source except Wang's own highly impressionistic and pejorative open letters in 1939, accounts by their friends and acquaintances generally agree that Yü's carelessness and lack of consideration for his wife and Wang's social vanity were the main causes for their marital disharmony.[93]

Wang's complaint was justified when she referred to Yü's careless and capricious ways, such as visiting his first wife and patronizing prostitutes.[94] Obsession with an outer life-style had gradually replaced his earlier penchant for introspection. No longer did he feel the creative urge to weave his inner tortures into a story; rather, he wrote a series of stylish classical poems about his marital crisis with his own commentaries, which he sent to a Hong Kong magazine, *Ta-feng,* in 1939 and asked the editor, Lu Tan-lin, to forward copies to people like Chiang Kai-shek and Yü Yu-jen. With Wang's rebuttals also in print (in which she still addressed him as "My still esteemed romantic man of letters"),[95] a private marital problem was consciously turned into a national scandal: this issue of the magazine went through four editions.[96]

As the Sino-Japanese War broke out, Yü joined in propaganda work in Wuhan in 1937, and even went to the front lines to visit the troops. But with Wang Ying-hsia living with somebody else and the ravages of war reaching his home town (it was reported that his mother was left to starve to death as the Japanese occupied Fu-yang), one wonders whether Yü was as dedicated to his work as he appeared to be. From Wuhan, Yü moved south via Hunan province, Foochow, Hong Kong, and finally reached Singapore in December 1938. Wang Ying-hsia soon joined him, after the two had reached certain understandings. Yü's reason for moving to Singapore can only be surmised. The *Singapore Daily (Hsing-chou jih-pao)* had formally invited him to help in propaganda work there. His personal motive might be to move his wife far away from her lover. But their marriage was not saved: in March 1940 they agreed on separation. Before Wang left Singapore for Chungking, Yü held a dinner party for her and composed a special poem for this occasion. She later served in the Ministry of Foreign Affairs before marrying a businessman.

Yü had once met Wen Tzu-ch'uan, a Chinese poet from Malaya in 1929. After reading two poems by Wen describing the tropical landscape of the South Seas, Yü had reportedly said: "Ah, South Seas, this place is extremely interesting; I must visit it if I have a chance."[97] He had also mistakenly identified Nan-yang with Stevenson's Pacific and pointed out that Stevenson had spent his last years there and had written some significant works.[98] Yü's dream was finally realized ten years later, but the South Seas was no longer as idyllic and peaceful as Stevenson's Pacific islands. When the Pacific War broke out in December 1941, Yü served as chairman of the Anti-Japanese League of the Chinese Literary Circles in Singapore. On February 4, 1942, he was forced to evacuate Singapore. In April he reached a little town called Pajakunbuh in southern Sumatra where he changed his name to Chao Lien and assumed the camouflage of a wine merchant. The last years of Yü's life were not without a certain literary afterglow. He grew a beard. He wrote numerous poems in the traditional style, some of which are among the best of his poetic output. He served as a translator for the Japanese military police, while secretly helping many Chinese in the area. As a wine merchant who also owned a paper-making factory and a soap factory, Yü came to be known as one of the local Chinese notables. People called him "Chao Beard."[99] Rumor had it that before the Japanese occupied Sumatra Yü had had a girl friend, a radio announcer (one line in one of his poems is said to refer to her beautiful voice), and had also been on intimate terms with a society girl and two Dutch women.[100] In September 1943 he married for the third time a local Chinese girl (the match was arranged by his friends) in order to avoid suspicion by the Japanese. Yü changed her name to Ho Li-yu (of beauty possessed), which conveyed a more literary flavor. On their wedding night, Yü reportedly was pleasantly surprised to find she was still a virgin.[101] She bore him one boy and one girl. (Yü had one son and two daughters by his first wife and three sons by his second wife.)

He had resigned his job as an interpreter in early 1943 on the pretext of having contracted tuberculosis. In 1944, his real identity was gradually confirmed by the Japanese military police. On the morning of August 14, 1945, he learned from unknown sources that the Japanese were going to surrender. Overjoyed, he went around and told his friends, with whom he also discussed plans for the future.[102] On the night of August 29, he was invited out by a native, presumably on the orders of a Japanese military police officer and never returned.[103] Possibly the Japanese military police had discovered his true identity and killed him in order to wipe out an articulate witness in the trials of war criminals. The "tragedy" of Yü's life was thus supplied with a highly heroic yet ironic ending. That alien race which had both lured him and humiliated him now became his executioner and sealed his fate.

All literary works are autobiographies of their
authors.
In my opinion . . . because art is life, life is art,
why should we separate the two?
—Yü Ta-fu

Chapter 6

Yü Ta-fu: Visions of the Self

For Yü Ta-fu, all literature is autobiography; the reverse seems also
applicable, that all autobiography—at least his autobiography—is
literature. This autobiographical impulse is the motivating force for
most of his creative output. Yet precisely because Yü identified art
with life, and life with art, biographers of Yü Ta-fu must be constantly on guard: behind the simple unity of his life and works lies
a maze of ambiguities between reality and appearance, between the
self and visions of the self.

From the very beginning of his creative life, Yü had embraced, together with his ebullient autobiographical impulse, a strong element
of self-deception. Scholars of Yü Ta-fu have all emphasized "his constant need to describe himself,"[1] but few have noticed his equally
persistent need to describe himself beyond himself—to construct
visions of himself. Literary creativity thus performs an emancipatory
function for Yü: to free his soul from the confines of his real self and
take on attributes which he deems desirable.

"Sinking" and Ernest Dowson

This interplay between the self and visions of the self is evident in Yü's first collection of stories, *Sinking*, written in 1921 when Yü was a junior at the Tokyo Imperial University. The collection contains three short stories, the most popular of which is the story that bears the collection's title, "Sinking." In his preface to the collection, Yü himself gave the following explanation of its content: " 'Sinking' describes the psychology of a sick youth. It can be called an anatomy of hypochondria. It also describes as a broad theme the suffering of modern man—that is, sexual need and the clash between soul and flesh . . . In several places I have also mentioned the discrimination of Japanese nationalism against our Chinese students there. But for fear of its being regarded as propaganda, when writing I did not dare to exert my efforts and merely put in a few sketchy touches." [2]

The Japanese scholar, Itō Toramaru, in his paper on "Sinking," debates the importance of hypochondria in the story. He points out the influence of Sato Haruo, one of the leading Japanese "Neo-romantic" writers, to whom Yü was introduced by T'ien Han in 1920, one year before the story was written. Itō is certainly correct to note that the young novice reiterated Sato's prevalent theme of hypochondria and owed a great debt to the theories of Sato and the so-called "I-novel" (*shi-shōsetsu*). In fact, Itō argues, the real theme of the story is Yü's feeling of sexual guilt as connected with national and racial humiliation. [3]

Thematically the story was among the first works in Chinese literature in which the author had brought forth with all seriousness a problem which had been treated as a subject of either social taboo or secretive and often flippant fun. Even Lin Shu and Su Man-shu had either side-stepped the problem of sex or submerged it in a stream of sentiment. "Sinking," therefore, represents the first serious effort by a Chinese literary man to merge sex with sentiment, in unveiled and unadorned frankness.

And yet Yü preferred to describe his sexual frustration as "hypochondria," a term fraught with allusions to both Japanese and Western romanticism. It may be said that together with autobiographical honesty Yü also brings in a degree of artificiality—an artistic design influenced by the works of Sato Haruo. It may also be said that, in Yü's mind, hypochondria was an essential feature of the romantic hero. In other words, at the same time when Yü was writing about his inner self he was incorporating an "outer" self into his story. The hero in "Sinking" is a stylish young loner; as he roams the pastoral landscape of Japan he is able to recite many lines of poetry from Wordsworth, Heine, and Gissing. In the opinion of C. T. Hsia, "a Wertherian self-pity exaggerates alike the hero's love for nature and the ache in his heart."[4] The shadow of Rousseau can also be readily seen in this self-image.

Another story in the *Sinking* collection, entitled "Silver-grey Death" ("Yin-hui se ti ssu"), presents more concrete evidence. The hero is again a Chinese in Japan, "aged 24 or 25, 5 feet 5 inches in height, thin, haggard, with high cheek bones and with his hair, several inches long, hanging in disorder on his forehead."[5] He wanders in the streets of Tokyo, seized by bitter memories of his wife's death. He visits the house of a young Japanese waitress whom he has befriended. Upon hearing that the girl is going to get married, he pawns his few books to buy some ribbons and ornamental hair pins plus two bottles of violet perfume as her wedding gift. He drinks an excessive amount of wine at her place and disappears, only to be found dead the next morning with a book of Dowson's poems in his pocket. At the end of the story, Yü added a postscript in English: "The reader must bear in mind that this is an imaginary tale. After all the author cannot be responsible for its reality. One word, however, must be mentioned here that he owes much obligation to R. L. Stevenson's 'A Lodging for the Night' and the life of Ernest Dowson for the plan of this unambitious story."[6]

The design of the setting is taken from Stevenson; the theme of the hero in desperate love with a young waitress is taken from Ernest Dowson's courtship of Missie, a Polish waitress of barely fourteen years of age, in London, 1892.[7] But the physical features and details of the plot belong to Yü Ta-fu himself. We learn from his own account: "Every day, if I was not reading novels, I spent most of my time in coffee houses seeking girl companions to drink wine with me."[8] We also know that he had married, in 1920, a Chinese girl.

The story is, therefore, neither strictly imaginary nor strictly realistic, but a delicate blending of the two. With a heavily imitative technique and an emerging autobiographical impulse, the young writer attempted to accomplish two tasks: to paint the contours of an imaginary figure based on his own image and to inflate this fictional personality to the proportions of an ideal, larger-than-life vision.

Possibly, Yü came to Dowson through Sato Haruo. But what attracted Yü to Dowson seemed to be less his poetry than his life and personality. In a long article on *The Yellow Book* group written in 1923, Yü not surprisingly focused on Dowson's unrequited love of the Polish waitress, which, according to Yü, led to his indulgence in drinking and his death.[9] He must have responded, though he did not mention it, to Arthur Symons' portrait of Dowson as possessing "a sort of Keats-like face, the face of a demoralized Keats, and something curious in the contrast of a manner exquisitely refined, with an appearance generally somewhat dilapidated."[10] Yü must also have found a precedent to his own patronizing of prostitutes in Dowson's association with female companions of doubtful background: girls named Dulcie, Essie, Missie. He may even have justified his later drinking with the example of Dowson. But certainly he was not aware that Dowson's recklessness in drinking and in dallying with girls of doubtful repute might be "in large measure the result of his lack of confidence in his own ideal."[11]

While Dowson might have used decadence to camouflage his inner uncertainties about his life and art, the young Yü Ta-fu was looking for an ideal after which he could model his own. This impression is further substantiated by Yü's attitude toward his favorite Chinese poet, Huang Chung-tse.

Huang Chung-tse and Yü Ta-fu

Huang Chung-tse (original name, Huang Ching-jen, 1749–1783) was one of the "lyrical" poets of the Ch'ien-lung period. A descendant of the Sung poet, Huang T'ing-chien, he was born in Kao-ch'un, Kiangsu province. "When he was three years old his father died, and early education devolved on his mother and his grandfather. At seven he moved to Wu-chin and then first met Hung Liang-chi, a neighbor three years his senior, who later became a writer and life-long friend. In 1760 Huang's grandfather died, and the family became poor."[12] In 1765, Huang took his *hsiu-ts'ai* degree but failed repeatedly in the provincial examinations. Thus he could only move from one post to another, acting as secretary to those who appreciated his literary talents. In 1771, Huang was engaged as a secretary by Chu Yun, commissioner of education of Anhwei at An-ch'ing. In the third month of the next year, Chu Yun gathered many literary celebrities in the Hall of Li Po at Ts'ai-shih chi, where the eminent T'ang poet had presumably died by drowning, for a poetry competition. Huang, at the age of twenty-three, was the youngest of the guests. "Wearing a white jacket and standing under the shadows of the sun, he in a moment came out with some hundreds of words. As they were shown to all the guests, they all stopped writing."[13]

While Huang thus distinguished himself overnight, his lack of a higher degree and his volatile temperament precluded any possibility for a steady and lucrative job. In 1775, he went to Peking where he passed a special examination under the Emperor Ch'ien-lung. Thus he obtained a post as a copyist in the Imperial Printing Establishment. He remained in Peking until 1780 when he became secretary to Ch'eng Shih-ch'un, commissioner of education of Shantung. In 1781 he went to Sian, Shensi, where he sought financial help from the scholarly governor-general, Pi Yüan. Upon his return to Peking, his rank was raised to that of assistant district magistrate but he had to wait for a vacancy. In 1783, although ill, he was forced by his creditors again to seek help in Sian, but died on the way at the age of thirty-four.

His entire life, as summarized by Chang I-p'ing, was burdened by poverty and illness.[14] As the only son in the family (his brother died when Huang was fifteen), he could not even support his widowed mother and his wife. Of fragile build and often bedridden, with the beautiful face of a woman, he dissipated his life in traveling, which he liked very much, reading and writing poetry, sometimes throughout the night, and drinking.[15] According to his own short autobiography, at the age of twenty-five he often "gasped for breath as if unable to support his own body."[16]

Huang's poetry is characterized by a simplicity and lyrical sentimentality uncommon in the Ch'ing period when most poets engaged in slavish imitations of T'ang masters. While clearly a follower of the famous Ch'ing poet Yüan Mei, Huang, owing perhaps to his sensitive nature, could instill into his poetry an exquisiteness and intimate immediacy seldom encountered in the poetry of his period. He had reportedly fallen in love at the age of fifteen with a cousin who lived nearby.[17] But he eventually married a different girl, at the age of eighteen, to whom he seemed equally dedicated.[18] Many of his tender and daring love poems were supposedly written for these two girls in his life.

On November 20, 1922, Yü Ta-fu completed a short story which he titled "Ts'ai-shih chi" (The cliff of colored rock). The story begins with Huang Chung-tse at the age of twenty-two (23 sui), in An-ch'ing, where he was attached to the yamen of Chu Yun. His excellency the commissioner of education was very fond of him, but was too busy to comfort him when he was in his "silent and mopish" moods.[19] And the 40 to 50 clerks and secretaries in the *yamen* never wanted to approach him. Those who barely knew him said he was too proud of his gifts; those who didn't know him at all thought he had no talents but dared to exhibit his tantrums by relying on the prestigious patronage of his boss. "Thus his reputation and friends had dwindled year after year, and his hypochondria which he had developed since childhood was aggravated year by year."[20]

He was a sad and solitary genius, unappreciated by all except his good friend, Hung Liang-chi, who, deeply impressed by his literary gifts, knew how to cope with the undulations of his mood. Most times, however, Huang liked to wander alone, composing his poems and losing himself in memories. One night in autumn, as he was taking a solitary walk in the dewy, moonlit garden, he suddenly recalled a vivacious young girl whom he had loved and left in his home town. She had always "stared at his thin and fragile body with her limpid eyes."[21] At their parting she had wept for half an hour and had given him a yellow silk handkerchief as a souvenir. He felt cold with the autumn dew but could not afford to buy a fur coat. He also thought that he should send some money back to his old widowed mother. Grieving for himself, he chanted spontaneously a new poetic line that had just come to his mind: "With endless days to come and my sorrows as deep as the sea . . ." [22]

The next morning Huang woke up late. He finished a poem, and went out for a walk. A sudden impulse inspired him to go up in the hills and look for the grave of Li Po. He finally found the grave, which was desolate and buried in the midst of wild grass. "Ah, ah, Li T'ai-po, Li T'ai-po!" he shouted involuntarily, and his tears rolled down. He sat there for a long time, "pondering on the lonely existence of the poet, his own situation of being maltreated by others, his tears flowing down intermittently." [23]

By the time he came back, his poem commemorating Li Po was already completed. Hung Liang-chi came to greet him and told him that Tai Chen, the celebrated master of textual criticism, had just arrived. At the banquet in his honor, Tai Chen had criticized Huang's poetry as "flowery but lacking in substance." [24] The label proved to be too much for Huang's sensitive temper and his feeble physique. He relapsed into illness, which lasted until next spring.

As spring came, Huang also gradually convalesced. But his "proud and suspicious disposition" had not changed. He felt that his patron had no longer been cordial to him after Tai Chen's visit. On one sunny day, Chu Yun was holding a sumptuous feast in the Hall of Li Po at the Cliff of Colored Rock that overlooked the Yangtze River. In the crowd of invited men of letters stood a young poet. Huang, "slim, tall and thin . . . wearing a white spring jacket, stood in the midst of the crowd, as if afraid of being blown away by the wind. The two red-tinged spots on his white and hollowed cheeks imparted an air of slight inebriation." [25] As Huang and his friend approached the Hall of Li Po, his patron asked: "Have you finished your poems?" Never yielding in any competition, Huang answered: "I have finished." He was merely joking out of his competitive nature. But Chu, observing the proud expression of the young man, said: "If you have finished so fast, I shall grind the ink, and you will write it out." [26]

116

As Chu prepared the ink and rolled out the paper, Huang's instant inspiration had already crystallized in his mind a long poem, which his hand, holding the brush, put to paper.

The story is typical of many of Yü's short fictional works, with its multilayers of past and present woven into one impressionistic whole, its lingering invocations of mood arrested in time, its fragmentary threads of memories which undulate with the slow progression of the plot—or nonplot—and finally its very anecdotal and incomplete quality.[27] But it is also one of the very few stories that is not set in a contemporary background; he was writing a fictional biography for a historical figure, a poet he admired above everyone else in the recent past. Yü in this short story was again creating a vision of himself.

Obviously Huang Chung-tse and Yü Ta-fu were kindred spirits, separated in time. Yü first encountered Huang when he was a student at the First Higher School in Hangchow in 1909. On Sundays he often frequented bookstores. Once he bought a copy of Huang's poetry collection merely to show to the clerk that he could afford it and to impress upon his older classmates his ability to read such an obscure and difficult poet. In fact, at that time, he was totally incapable of appreciating its merits. He read it again more than ten years later, when he taught at the School of Law and Administration in An-ch'ing. "Free and having nothing to do, I wanted to read more classical thread-bound volumes. So I again bought a copy of *Liang-tang hsüan ch'üan-chi* and read it twice from the beginning to the end. What moved me most deeply, besides the many poetical lines which cried out with hunger and poverty, were his solitary and ungregarious attitude and his premature death following a life of abject poverty."[28]

Thus Yü's response to Huang was similar to his previous fascination with Ernest Dowson: an emotional gesture of identification. It was reinforced by even more coincidental similarities in their separate lives.

In his autobiographical fragments Yü mentioned that his father "died in the third year after my birth." Huang Chung-tse's father died, too, when he was three years old. And throughout the early part of his life, Yü was plagued, like Huang, by disease and poverty.

As Yü had contracted tuberculosis, he wanted to believe that both Huang and Huang's wife had died of the same disease.[29]

In his autobiographical fragments, Yü described in a beautiful scene the evening of his graduation from elementary school: the two young lovers gazed into each other's eyes as "a sense of contentment, profundity, and intoxication enveloped my entire body as did the moonlight around me"[30]—a scene that corresponds in both mood and detail to the scene in which the solitary Huang Chung-tse recalled his first love. When Yü was in Japan, he had once joined a Chinese poetry society organized by the Japanese. During one gathering around the time of the Chinese mid-autumn festival, Yü, too, astonished the Japanese members by instantly composing a poem on the prescribed rhyming patterns of Yüan Mei.[31] Back in China and teaching at the School of Law and Administration at An-ch'ing, a place where, 150 years before, Huang Chung-tse had worked as secretary to the commissioner of education, Yü must have visited "Ts'ai-shih chi" and Li Po's grave. The description of Huang's search for the grave must have been based on Yü's own experience.

Both Li Po and Huang Chung-tse, like Yü Ta-fu himself, suffered from the humiliations inflicted upon them by a philistine society which could never appreciate true genius. In the literary circles, moreover, members of the Literary Studies group had begun to throw darts at them. Hu Shih had also written an article in which he carped at Yü's knowledge of English on the trifling issue of translating a work by Eucken and summarily dismissed Yü's associates as "unconscious of their silly superficialities."[32] Yü was so affected by the jeering condescension of this scholar-tycoon that he wrote to Kuo Mo-jo wanting to drown himself in the Huang-p'u River.

It was during this period when Yü was moping his days away in frustrated wrath that he re-read the poetry of Huang Chung-tse and wrote the story, "Ts'ai-shih chi." That Yü had projected into it his own accumulated feelings seems clear. Behind the fictionalized characters one senses the correspondences with real personages: Chu Yun and the manager of the T'ai-tung Publishing Company, Hung Liang-chi and Kuo Mo-jo, the unappreciative colleagues in the yamen at An-ch'ing and in the members of the Literary Studies Society; the haughty, spiteful, yet talentless magnate on the current cultural scene, the great master of textual criticism, Tai Chen, was paralleled by the new master of the "Reorganization of the National Heritage," Hu Shih (who reportedly felt elated to find himself compared to the great Ch'ing master).[33] And who could be that solitary, suffering genius but Yü Ta-fu himself?

The many felicitous coincidences and correspondences were such as to infuse the real with the fictional and confuse the historical with the contemporary. Yü used Huang Chung-tse to tell his own story, but Huang Chung-tse provided an extension of a vision that Yü had been constructing. It is apparent that both Huang and Dowson share similar features. Both were of fragile build; both possessed the face of a beautiful woman; both drank recklessly; both contracted tuberculosis and died young; Dowson at the age of thirty-three and Huang at thirty-four. Most important, both suffered from lack of public acceptance. While Yü could easily find enough similarity in his own temper and experience to identify himself with them, the glamor of his vision could also penetrate his "real" life and personality. The result was a tendency for him to imitate this ideal vision of himself, thereby making the real Yü Ta-fu what he publicly "confessed" himself to be—an image already gilded with imaginary contours.

Yü Ta-fu: Two Visions

Ernest Dowson and Huang Chung-tse have combined to conjure up one central image, that of a frail and lonely genius, frequently ill and melancholic, dissipating his life and talent in a society which alienates him. Some of Yü's favorite authors—Turgenev ("with his mild appearance, his eyes tinged with sadness"),[34] Rimbaud, and Verlaine— also fit very well into this image.[35] Despite its Western borrowings, it is quite akin to the ts'ai-tzu prototype in traditional Chinese fiction. Obviously, Yü had embodied it in both his life and his art. The many stories he wrote in the 1920s, whether about himself or about his fictional self, contain the same image of this subjective hero. Even in his autobiographical fragments written in 1934–1935, the "hero" is a "superfluous man" à la Turgenev.

119

Viewed in more detached perspective, the facts of Yü's life need not make him continuously melancholic. His own life experiences were quite typical of the life pattern of his generation. Though tinged with sadness, it was not, as he conceived it to be, "a tragedy badly structured." He must have had many happy moments playing with his childhood companion, the maid Ts'ui-hua; he was very active in student movements in school; his bohemian life in Tokyo was quite leisurely and carefree: "nobody wanted to study hard."[36] Even his life with his first wife need not have been so pathetic. His traditional wife was both literate and understanding, and he was not really devoid of love toward her. It was Yü's own vision of himself as a perennially suffering hero manqué drifting gloomily in the darkening landscape of life that caused him to be discontented with many aspects of his real life.

Curiously enough, as Yü was discontent with himself, we sense in some of his writings that he was no more content with this Ernest Dowson–Huang Chung-tse vision of himself. There lurked in his mind an opposite image which he could only admire from a distance but could not embody himself. It is the more positive, dynamic, and Western image of a strong and vital hero who wants to master life. The representatives of this image, as can be found in Yü's works, are Max Stirner ("Ego is all; all is ego"),[37] Alexander Herzen ("If we want to act, we should first have the courage like Herzen's to die in a foreign land"),[38] Romain Rolland ("who advocated striving to the utmost until the end of one's life"),[39] Henri Barbusse ("who initiated the movement of light, intending to burn out all the evil societies in the world with a blaze of fire"),[40] and, ultimately, also Rousseau ("the poet of rebellion, the upholder of liberty and equality, the proud son of nature").[41]

The two visions of male prototypes also have their female equivalents. Itō Toramaru has divided Yü's heroines into two types: the "persecutors" and the "persecuted." The former—fat, sensual, voluptuous *femmes fatales*—dominated Yü's stories in his Japanese period. The latter—frail, docile, pitiable victims of society—more frequently haunted his stories after he returned to China.[42] The "persecutors" aroused him sexually and he often yielded to their temptations, only to be torn with guilt and remose afterwards. The "persecuted" elicited his sympathies and released his sentiments; he was drawn into their miseries, but could only share their hopelessness. As was the case with his hero opposites, emotionally he could not help being attracted to persecuted women but physically he craved the persecutors. A very revealing report has it that in his only long novel, *Mi-yang* (Stray lamb), he originally intended to portray sympathetically a "La Dame aux Camélias" figure but eventually carved out, unsuccessfully, an amoral *femme fatale* that "reduced the confidence on the part of readers." [43] Even more revealing is the fact that in real life Yü had thrown in his lot with his first wife, a victim of traditional society but preferred to live with a more modern woman who proved to be, in fact, a "persecutor" and practically ruined his creative life.

The presence of polar opposites in Yü's mind and life recalls also the preoccupations of his predecessors, Lin Shu and Su Man-shu. Lin Shu responded sentimentally to the feminine charm of the Lady of the Camellias but at the same time could not prevent himself from admiring the masculine releases of energy in the heroes of Haggard. Su Man-shu, likewise, worshiped his hero Byron but undertook to perpetuate for himself the image of a rambling monk-hermit. Vacillating between an opposite pair of heroines—one more aggressive, the other gentler and more docile—his fictional alter ego invariably was drawn, belatedly, to the sentimental devotions of the latter. Like his two predecessors, Yü Ta-fu opted also for the more sentimental and the less dynamic.

In this respect, Yü was more traditional than his contemporaries, Kuo Mo-jo and Hsü Chih-mo. In fact, with his pale face and long gown, his habits of drinking and smoking, his associations with prostitutes, and, above all, his excellently composed classical poetry, Yü would have met the approval of Lin Shu and Su Man-shu.[44] What would have disturbed Su and provoked Lin's anger had they met Yü might have been his self-conscious and self-perpetuated air of decadence. Friends and critics have all been intrigued by, in commonsense standards, an "odd" trait in Yü noted by his good friend Kuo Mo-jo: "Ta-fu is a strange fellow; he likes to expose his bad traits." [45] Why was he consumed with the urge to confess his weaknesses? Why was he persistently and purposefully decadent?

As mentioned before, self-image building accounts much for the air of melancholia and decadence in Yü's writing and life-style. The inner urge for such an image may have sprung from an inborn pessimism which, according to one eminent Chinese critic, was conditioned by the death of his father.[46] Yü might have been afflicted with the feeling that he had carried a "curse" to his family, that he should not have been born at all. He was, in his own mind, superfluous to and different from the normal crowd of mortals. But to be burdened with a curse or stigma is by no means uncommon among sensitive men of letters. Su Man-shu repeatedly referred to his "unutterable sorrows." Lu Hsün had suffered from an even more traumatic experience vis-à-vis his father when, at fifteen, he was called upon to witness his dying father's last throes between life and death.[47] Erik Erikson has also noticed this aspect of a "curse" in the lives of Martin Luther and Gandhi.[48] But in the minds of great men, a sense of being accursed often breeds a sense of mission; it may become the motivating force behind individual creativity and leadership. The acts of many great leaders in literature, religion, and politics are in many ways "reenactments" of their personal afflictions; their successes and failures often depend on their historical context, the degree of response from their audience. In modern Chinese literature, Lu Hsün must be regarded as the prime example of a great man reenacting his own "curse" in his life and work.

Yü Ta-fu followed a similar path in his Japanese years. His identity confusion closely resembled Lu Hsün's: both shifted from science to literature. His experience in Japan was shared by Lu Hsün and many other Chinese students. What makes Lu Hsün greater than Yü Ta-fu seems to be the different ways in which they confront their inner afflictions. Lu Hsün managed with an almost superhuman effort to keep his inner conflicts and tensions to himself, to subject them to intense and agonizing self-scrutiny, and to condense them into crystallizations of profound insight in his works. Yü Ta-fu chose to write in order to exorcise, to drive out his inner demons by exposing them to his imaginary audience. Confession was his catharsis; after laying bare all his weaknesses, he would feel better.

But Yü did not stop at mere confessions. Rather than confront his "curse" in a lonely battle with himself as Lu Hsün had done, Yü "relieved" himself by finding and imagining kindred spirits. The cases of Ernest Dowson and Huang Chung-tse demonstrated that by resorting to historical figures similar to himself, he had created his own legend—a personality and life-style intended for mass consumption and imitation by his reading public just as he had imitated Dowson and Huang. He had not reenacted his "curse," but had rather pursued its image. The popularity of his works had made him a public figure, thereby inducing him further into a vision of himself. He had to be decadent. Thus manners begot mannerisms; habits turned idiosyncracies. His personal weaknesses became public assets. The chasm between image and reality revealed itself when, at middle age, he was neither poor nor lonely. His exuberant power of literary creativity sagged and he relapsed into the complacency of an old-style scholar—connoisseur—certainly a regression and the source of his real tragedy.

All my life experiences have their clues in emotions.
—Hsü Chih-mo

Chapter 7

Hsü Chih-mo: A Life of Emotion

When Yü Ta-fu was attending the Hangchow Middle School in 1910, he met a "naughty boy with a big head and gold-rimmed glasses" who always read novels but invariably scored highest in Chinese composition tests.[1] This naughty boy later turned out to be Hsü Chih-mo, one of the foremost poets of modern China.

While remaining friends throughout their lives, Yü Ta-fu and Hsü Chih-mo went their separate ways after they graduated from the same middle school. Yü went to Japan and became a lost soul afflicted with "hypochondria," whereas Hsü took a long journey to America to study banking, moved to England, and returned a burgeoning poet exultant with acquired European tastes. With their different experiences abroad, Yü and Hsü may be viewed as representatives of the two major groupings of returned students: those educated in Japan and those educated in the West. The thought and behavior of Hsü Chih-mo, however, reflect further the Anglo-American strand of Western tradition, although he had sufficient contact with French culture to communicate with those who had lived and studied in France and Germany.

Possibly as a result of differences in their educational background and their personal temperaments, Yü Ta-fu and Hsü Chih-mo are representative in another way. Both are intensely emotional men, but their individual treatments of emotions are different. Both Yü and Hsü, as prominent literary men in the 1920s, may be said to have occupied two significant positions: while Yü Ta-fu expands the subjectivist trend with his confessionalism and his "visions of the self," Hsü Chih-mo, in his tempestuous pursuit of love, brings it to new heights.

Youthful Promises

Hsü was born in the same year (1896) as Yü Ta-fu and in the same province, Chekiang. But unlike Yü, Hsü was assured of an easy, affluent life in a China torn by war and poverty. His father, Hsü Shen-ju, was a banker and industrialist, head of the merchant guild of his native town, Hsia-shih, and a friend of the famous entrepreneur, Chang Chien.[2] The Hsü family had for generations engaged in commerce. Hsü himself once remarked: "I have checked my family record. Since the Yung-lo reign (of the Ming dynasty) no single poetical line worth reciting had been written in this household."[3] Hsü Shen-ju was perhaps the most successful in a long line of enterprising merchants. He ran a bank in Shanghai. As the 1911 Revolution swept through Chekiang, he secretly helped the revolutionaries by supplying arms for the takeover of Hangchow.[4] Through the foresight and acumen of his father, the young Hsü Chih-mo (named Hsü Yu-shen at that time) was able to enjoy a happy and peaceful childhood unaffected by the social and political turmoil around him. The only family tragedy was the death of Hsü's grandfather when the young boy was barely six. "That was the first frightful experience in my life. But as I recall my feelings at that time, they are no more profound than those of that highland lass in Wordsworth."[5] Thus, unlike Lu Hsün and Yü Ta-fu, Hsü was brought up in a family milieu which shaped his sanguine and outgoing personality unladen with guilt or suspicion.

Hsü began his traditional type of education as early as the age of four and studied with a local tutor. At eleven, he was enrolled in a modern school in Hsia-shih and distinguished himself as the best in his class. The title "boy wonder" was given to him. When he graduated in 1909, the 13-year-old boy could already reproduce an imitative but impeccable classical style. In 1910 he entered the Hangchow Middle School and became Yü Ta-fu's classmate. The shy and introverted Yü could only admire the achievements of this sprightly and prankish boy who soon became class president by virtue of his academic record.[6]

The intellectual atmosphere in the new-style schools around this time was definitely dominated by the ideas of one single personality, Liang Ch'i-ch'ao, who later became Hsü's mentor. Thus in Hsü's earliest writings, the traces of Liang's influence was indelible. He contributed articles to the school publication, among which was an essay on "Radium and the History of the Globe," another essay was titled, "On the Relationship between Fiction and Society"—clearly an echo of Liang Ch'i-ch'ao's celebrated article, "On the Relationship between Fiction and People's Sovereignty."[7]

Hsü's talent was recognized by Chang Chia-ao (Chang Kia-gnau), who as the secretary to the Chekiang military authority visited the school one day in 1915 and was immediately impressed by a piece of Hsü's composition. Convinced of the youngster's promise in the future, Chang promised the Hsü family a match with his younger sister. The Chang family was equally prominent in the neighboring Kiangsu province. Among Chang's brothers were Chang Chün-mai (Carsun Chang), later eminent as a philosopher and Chang Chia-chu, who later became Hsü's close associate in the *Crescent Moon* magazine. Chang Yu-i, their sister, was only fifteen when she was married to Hsü Chih-mo in 1915. Hsü's father had made lavish arrangements, but at the request of his beloved son, the wedding ceremony was a modern one.[8] Hsü seemed to like his new bride, who was after all well-educated, well-mannered, and progressive in outlook.

Hsü graduated from Hangchow Middle School (renamed the First Middle School of Hangchow after 1911) in 1915. From Hangchow he moved to Shanghai, where he attended Shanghai University for a while before he went farther north to Peiyang University in Tientsin. In 1916, the law faculty of Peiyang University was incorporated into Peking University and Hsü Chih-mo became a formal student of law and politics at this renowned institution.[9] It was in Peking that Hsü, through the introduction of his wife's family, became a personal disciple of Liang Ch'i-ch'ao. It was reported that during the interview Hsü's usual eloquence was overcome by his sense of dazed uneasiness in front of this giant intellectual figure.[10] After the interview, he wrote a humble letter to Liang expressing his reverence and devotion. Liang later acknowledge Hsü to be among his favorite disciples. At this time, Hsü had also begun to devour Liang's works. He was so overwhelmed that quoting a line from the *Dream of the Red Chamber*, he proclaimed: "My own works should be burned."[11]

In the spring of 1918, a son was born to the new couple. As the whole family rejoiced in the new addition to the family line, Hsü found himself, in the summer of 1918, traveling on the high seas across the Pacific en route to the United States. The heaving waves inspired his youthful ambitions, which he described in a long letter to his friends and relatives. The style of the letter was elegant classical Chinese; the content reflected the influence of his mentor, Liang Ch'i-ch'ao. The last part reads:

In this age of domestic disorder and external disasters men of ambition should all arise. This is when time will make heroes of us all . . . Chih-mo is imbued with sadness, and inadvertently his words are deepened and his air excited . . . And he canot but give utterance to his foolish thoughts and submit them for consideration in front of his elders. Chih-mo is young and illiterate; he is ignorant of the immensity of the world. But he feels the evil currents of society and is worried lest we should lose our virtues and embark on the path to drunken depravity. This is why he leaves no time for self-pity but disciplines himself to be diligent and sincere so as to carry out the promises that he has just stated today. What he with good fortune will achieve can only answer infinitesimally what you gentlemen are expecting of him. On this day, the thirty-first of August, Hsü Chih-mo registered these words aboard a ship in the Pacific Ocean."[12]

This stereotyped letter revealed nothing more than a vague and naive sense of political commitment, which was quite typical of young men of his age. Since his father sent him abroad with the expectation that he would continue the family business of banking,[13] he enrolled at Clark University in the fall of 1918 and majored in banking and sociology. The choice of sociology might reflect Hsü's resolve to reform "the evil currents of society." The choice of Clark University was perhaps based on other motives.

Founded as a graduate institution in 1887 by Jonas Gilman Clark, a merchant, and Granville Stanley Hall, an educator, Clark University soon distinguished itself as one of the two earliest graduate schools in the states, the other being Johns Hopkins.[14] Under its first president, Dr. Hall, Clark University attracted a number of brilliant scholars, including Sigmund Freud, who was invited by Dr. Hall to give five lectures on psychoanalysis in 1910. By the time Hsü enrolled, however, Clark had also developed a three-year intensive undergraduate program with funds provided in the will of Mr. Clark. Scholarships were made available to students with limited financial sources and entrance requirements were informal. It is possible that Hsü and other Chinese students were lured to Clark for these practical reasons. Since Hsü had only had three years of college education in China, he must have been admitted to Clark College on a transfer basis. As high standards of academic work were needed to remain in the college, Hsü was determined to put himself to the test by devising with his four Chinese roommates (one of them being Li Chi, the famous archaeologist) a rigorous daily routine: "Get up at six, morning meeting at seven (to stimulate our sense of national shame); in the evening, sing the national anthem and go to bed at ten-thirty. During the day, besides studying diligently, do exercises, run, and read newspapers."[15]

Although on foreign soil, Hsü still lived in the shadow of his Chinese mentor. Besides taking courses with Frank H. Mankins in sociology and Harry E. Barnes in history, he was also engrossed in a book by Liang Ch'i-ch'ao, *I-ta-li san-chieh chuan*, (A biography of the three heroes of Italy), which recounted to the Chinese readers the heroic feats of Cavour, Mazzini and Garibaldi.[16] In one of his letters to Liang, he registered his initial impressions of Worcester, Massachusetts: "There are no more than a hundred Chinese here, among whom only ten are students. People of this town are very concerned with the war. Their united spirit and patriotic zeal are worthy of respect. The supplies of this town, however, are getting scarcer day by day, and the prices are rising. Life is difficult."[17] The end of the European war engulfed him in the general enthusiams of his fellow townsmen, but he was soon stirred to patriotic indignation as Germany transferred its rights in Shantung to Japan at the Versailles Peace Conference. While his compatriots broke out in stormy protest on May Fourth, 1919, Hsü could only echo their fury in a corner of New England.

In June 1919, Hsü graduated with high honors from Clark and went to Columbia University to study political science, where he received his master's degree the next year. His political orientation continued unabated. He had reportedly organized a number of extracurricular activities for the Chinese students and was possibly an active member of the "Chinese Students Association in Support of the Washington Conference."[18] His bookshelves were lined with books on Soviet Russia, which earned him the title of bolshevik in the eyes of his fellow students. Intellectually he was also drawn to socialism. "The type of socialism I was first exposed to was the pre-Marxist school of Robert Owen. It was a combination of humanitarianism, philanthropism, and utopianism. It just fitted my temper because I was easily emotional."[19]

This radical streak in the young Hsü Chih-mo, then twenty-three years of age, was characteristic of Chinese students of his generation. Their political ethos was directed toward a "new" China which could be fashioned in accordance with blueprints taken from abroad. Political radicalism, as manifested in the young Hsü Chih-mo, was geared to state service, not against it. For Hsü as well as for his fellow Chinese students abroad, the academic experience in a foreign land was conceived as a stage of practical training before he returned to China to take on a position of responsibility. Hsü's sense of mission exhibited in his letter, his disciplined routine at Clark, and his assimilation of Western socialist literature all pointed to this "practical" orientation. With his family background and connections, Hsü could well have pursued a political or financial career without suffering from the sense of frustration felt by Yü Ta-fu. That he later shifted from politics to poetry was, by his own account, purely accidental:

"Before the age of twenty-four, my interest in poetry was far less than my interest in the theory of relativity and the *Social Contract* . . . My greatest ambition was to be the Alexander Hamilton of China . . . That a man like me could have really become a poet—what more can I say?" [20]

Cambridge, England

In the fall of 1920, Hsü gave up his Ph.D. studies at Columbia and crossed the Atlantic to England. The motive for this momentous decision, according to Hsü himself, was his desire "to be a follower of Russell." [21] In his own mind, the move signified not a rejection of his previous goals, but rather a further reinforcement; he would be better equipped by studying with a world-renowned philosopher. It is, however, doubtful whether he had any clear idea of Russell's philosophic theories. When he arrived, Bertrand Russell had just been ousted from Trinity College of Cambridge University. Disappointed, Hsü spent half a year at the London School of Economics where he may have attended the lectures of Harold Laski.[22] The departure of Russell thus brought on a major psychological crisis in Hsü's life—a crisis that both Lu Hsün and Yü Ta-fu had experienced in Japan. In a more subdued tone than Yü's, Hsü recalled this period of identity confusion as "whiling away half a year, feeling depressed and contemplating a change of path." [23] The fact that Hsü could avoid Yü's "hypochondria" was due to fortuitous circumstances. Of course, his family wealth preempted the immediate worries of poverty which had pestered Yü. But it was through the "intrusion" of three personalities into his life in this period that he was able gradually to steer his new "path" to literature.

First, Hsü was indeed fortunate to have met, at this critical juncture, Goldsworthy Lowes Dickinson. From E. M. Forster's loving biography of this colorful figure, we know that by the time he met Hsü in 1921 Dickinson had just completed his spiritual pilgrimage to China. In fact, the process of Dickinson's intellectual development was curiously Hsü's counterpart, only the roles of China and the West were reversed. "At the beginning of the century," Forster informs us, "he was in a restless state of mind . . . He wanted to make some fundamental criticism of western civilization, which should be read by the general public, and should have some kind of artistic form . . . China was in the foreground politically, owing to the Boxer riots and the European expeditions to suppress them, and he had read Giles' 'Gems of Chinese Literature' and 'La Cité chinoise' by Eugene Simon." [24] The result of Dickinson's attempt was *Letters from John Chinaman*, which became immensely popular. Although he had written the book for the Western public, in the tradition of Swift and Montesquieu, he was himself drawn to China, believing that "in a previous existence, I actually was a Chinaman!" [25] In late 1912, he embarked upon a lengthy visit to China, which brought him in 1913 to the major cities as well as Mount T'ai and the grave of Confucius. After he returned, he became the great champion of China in England. "He began to attract Orientals who were visiting England, particularly students. An Anglo-Chinese Society was formed at Cambridge . . . The Chinese amused and charmed him in a way in which the Indians did not." [26]

Obviously, an interesting personality like Hsü who had embarked on a spiritual journey from the other pole would never fail to impress him. It was Dickinson who, as a fellow of King's College, brought Hsü to his alma mater in 1921 as a special student. The friendship of the two men became legendary in Cambridge. It was said of Dickinson that in his later years, "when he was feeling the draught, which was often, he wore a little Chinese cap. The first of these series of caps was given him by his friend Hsü. Foreign trimmings do not as as rule suit the Britisher, but the little cap seemed natural and harmonious in his case even when it broke the line of tufted heads which compose the High Table at King's . . . But if the legend-mongers ever do work him up it is on his mandarin's cap that they will concentrate, and perhaps they will relate how Confucius placed it on his brows in return for a copy of 'John Chinaman.'" [27] Another legend, more colorful than accurate, concerns the first encounter between the two men. One sunny afternoon, as our Chinese poet, wearing his long blue gown, lay under the shadows of a willow tree on the "backs" of King's College, a little old Englishman wearing a Chinese cap approached him, and the two became good friends.[28]

Legends aside, this "special student" did in no time become quite a popular figure in the Cambridge community. E. M. Forster "has since described his meeting with the young poet as one of the most exciting things that happened to him."[29] Among other noted scholars he had made friends with was I. A. Richards, who was then a member of the Heretics' Club, a literary circle dedicated to prosody and translation. Hsü was invited to join in their activities, especially in translating poetry. When Richards, James Wood, and C. K. Ogden published their joint book, *Foundations of Aesthetics*, in 1921, Hsü was given the honor to adorn a front page with two Chinese characters— "chung-yung," the "golden mean"—in his own handwriting.[30] In one of his letters written to his parents, Hsü had remarked: "Your son likes to associate himself with British gentlemen of repute, from whom he has benefited immeasurably. It can really be said that there is inexhaustible wisdom to be gained."[31] Cambridge thus represents also an intellectual break in Hsü's life. As he later recalled:

My eyes were opened by Cambridge. My desire for knowledge was stirred by Cambridge. My self-consciousness tooks its embryonic form in Cambridge. I spent two years in America, and two years in England. In America I was busy attending classes, listening to lectures, writing examination papers, chewing gum, going to the movies, and cursing. In Cambridge I was busy with walks, punting, riding on bicycles, smoking, chatting, drinking five o'clock teas and eating buttered cakes, and reading at random. If I was a pure dunce when I came to America, I remained unchanged when I left the Goddess of Liberty. But if I was unenlightened in America, my days at Cambridge at least made me realize that previously I was full of ignorance. This difference is by no means little.[32]

Intellectual stimulation might facilitate the burgeoning of a creative mind. But how does one account for the fact that Hsü's creativity was channeled into literature? For a possible clue, we must plunge into his private life. When Hsü first came to Cambridge in 1921, he led a leisurely existence with his wife, who had traveled all the way from China to join him. They rented a house in Sawston, a small town some six miles southwest of Cambridge. "Every morning I would take the bus (somtimes ride on my bicycle) to the college and come back in the evening. Thus with this kind of life I passed a whole spring . . . What I knew consisted of a library, a few classrooms, and two or three cheap restaurants."[33] But this idyllic atmosphere of blissful peace soon gave way to the storms of a marital crisis, which involved a young girl named Lin Hui-yin.

While in London, Hsü had met Lin Ch'ang-min, who was some nineteen years older than Hsü and father of Lin Hui-yin. Lin Ch'ang-min had been a close associate of Liang Ch'i-ch'ao and together with Liang had served briefly in the warlord cabinet under Tuan Ch'i-jui in 1917. Lin had come to London as a member of the Chinese Association for the League of Nations. After Hsü met Lin, they immediately became close friends. Kindred temper may indeed be the central link that forged the lasting friendship between the two men. For example, Lin had spent long hours with Hsü talking about his early love affair with a Japanese girl in his student days in Japan, which Hsü later turned into a short story.[34] They had also jokingly exchanged "love letters," with Hsü assuming the role of a married woman and Lin another married man.[35] It was Lin who introduced Hsü to Dickinson. It was through his associations with this man of sentiment that Hsü became aware of his own emotional nature.

When Lin Hui-yin arrived in London with her father in 1921, she was barely seventeen, a budding beauty endowed with intelligence and literary talents. It could be conjectured that if the father had unveiled Hsü's emotional temper, the daughter was responsible for unleashing the torrent of Hsü's emotions. A recent biography of Hsü Chih-mo based in part on information supplied by Hsü's first wife has confirmed that Lin Hui-yin was in fact the primary cause of Hsü's divorce.[36] In 1921, while Hsü lived with his wife in Sawston and Miss Lin was with her father in London, they exchanged letters every day. As a precaution, Hsü designated a local grocery store as his mailing address. Thus, every day at the expected mail time, he would go on his bicycle to the grocery store under the pretext of having a haircut.[37]

Hsü did not mention Miss Lin in his divorce proceedings. In a letter to his wife written in March 1922, demanding a divorce, Hsü had chosen to champion his cause in more grandiloquent terms. He declared that a marriage not based on love was intolerable, and that "freedom should be repaid by freedom."[38] He then presented his wife with a few exhortations: "Real life must be obtained through struggle; real happiness must be obtained through struggle; real love must be obtained through struggle! Both of us have boundless futures . . . both of us have minds set on reforming society; both of us have minds set on achieving well-being for mankind. This all hinges on our setting ourselves as examples. With courage and resolution, with respect to our personalities, we must get a free divorce, thereby terminating pain and initiating happiness."[39]

The letter not only betrays Hsü's simple idealism but also serves as his first romantic manifesto. It initiated the interesting process whereby his own life and personality were made to exemplify his ideal. With Lin Hui-yin and his divorce, Hsü began his emotional journey in search of love.

Hsü's understanding wife left Cambridge in the fall of 1921. After a brief sojourn in Paris, she stayed in Berlin where their second child, Peter, was born in February 1922. Yet in spite of the birth of a new son and objections from Hsü's parents, Hsü finalized his divorce in March 1922.[40] But Lin Hui-yin had already returned to China with her father. Thus alone in Cambridge since the fall of 1921, he finally "had a chance to be close to real Cambridge life for a whole academic year" and he "gradually 'discovered' Cambridge."[41]

Hsü's favorite spots in Cambridge were the "backs" of the colleges —Pembroke, St. Catharine's, King's, Clare, Trinity, and St. John's— which he likened to the paintings of Corot and the music of Chopin.[42] On the soft, green grass of the "backs," he passed countless mornings and evenings, "sometimes reading, sometimes gazing at the water, sometimes lying on my back and looking at the clouds in the sky, sometimes lying in a reverse position and embracing the softness of the earth."[43] He considered the famous River Cam which circled around the "backs" as "the most beautiful river in the world."[44] He often tried punting on the river, and failed awkwardly to get the boat to float straight. But perhaps more often he was on its banks: "To spend an evening on the banks of the Cambridge River is a panacea of the soul. Ah! that sweet solitude, that sweet leisureliness, as night after night I leaned on the railing of the bridge in a trance and stared at the western sky."[45] The serenity and splendor of Cambridge converted Hsü into a fervent nature worshiper and the adoration of nature became a recurring theme in his works. "Nature is the greatest book," he later proclaimed. "Only when you alone run to the embraces of nature, as a naked child jumps into the arms of his mother, do you realize the joys of the soul."[46]

It was Cambridge that provided the setting for his poetic imagination, which "burst out like a mountain cascade, rushing chaotically with no sense of direction . . . My life was shaken by a great force, and all kinds of half-mature and immature ideas were pouring out in split seconds like a rain of flowers. At that time I had nothing to rely upon, knew no discretions. Whatever pent-up feelings I had at heart were entrusted confusedly to my hands. The sense of urgency seemed as if I were trying to save my life . . . Thus I wrote a lot in a short period, but nearly all of it is not worth being shown to the public."[47] One of these unpublished poems, completed supposedly on November 23, 1921, included the following lines:

Oh, poet!
> You are the prophet of the spirit of the age!
> You are the consummation of intellect and art!
> You are the creator between heaven and man!

> . . . . .

> Your furnace is "Imagination";
> Your everlasting flame, "Inspiration,"
> Forges, poeticized and beautified, the
> > splendored firmament.[48]

In exalting the poet, Hsü was also celebrating his new role in life. As he finally discovered Cambridge, he had also discovered himself. A poet was born. For Hsü himself, it was also a spiritual rebirth—a new sense of identity after a long period of "moratorium" in China and the United States. The "tutorial record" of King's College registered his name as Hsü Ching-hsu (Hamilton); but in the column under the heading "college examinations" was entered a more fitting comment: "Looked at the world with intelligence and propriety."[49]

Love and Lu Hsiao-man

Hsü Chih-mo returned to China on October 15, 1922,[50] barely one year after he had, alone, "discovered" the real Cambridge. A possible explanation for his hasty return may again be related to his private life. As suggested by Hsü's recent Chinese biographer, he came back in order to find Lin Hui-yin, marry her, and bring her back to Cambridge.[51] The reality that confronted him upon his return was more complicated. The truth of the matter was that Lin Ch'ang-min had already agreed to marry his daughter to Liang Ssu-ch'eng, the eldest son of Liang Ch'i-ch'ao. The match had been made informally by the two families.[52]

It is very likely that as soon as Hsü returned to China he resumed contact with Lin Hui-yin and, with his disarming naiveté, persisted in his courtship despite the problems posed by personal relationships. But Liang Ch'i-ch'ao could not help becoming increasingly concerned over the intrusion by his free spirited favorite disciple upon his son's future happiness. On January 2, 1923, Liang wrote a long letter to Hsü nominally to reprimand Hsü for his divorce, but the undertones of warning might refer to a matter of immediate urgency. Near the end of the letter, Liang entered some personal pleas:

> You are a man of emotions; it is not easy to say such things. But as I reflect upon myself, my emotions are no poorer or weaker than yours. Thus I am qualified to talk to you . . . Chih-mo, you should know that it is difficult to establish but easy to dissipate oneself. Your age now is the most precious period in life, but also the most dangerous. If you indulge yourself in unattainable dreams, you will, after a few setbacks, lose your interest in life and die in dejection and anonymity. But death is all right compared to the most frightening prospect of neither life nor death, of helpless decadence . . . What I am worried about may not entirely reflect the facts, but I am greatly concerned over my Chih-mo . . . When I think about this deep in the night, I can no longer go back to sleep. Thus I . . . write these few pages. It may not be what you like to hear. But I do hope you know the depth of my sentiment toward you.[53]

The letter allows us an intimate glimpse of the private side of this formidable intellectual figure who prides himself on his emotion-laden prose style. Despite his reformist stance in politics and his titanic contributions in introducing Western culture, Liang Ch'i-ch'ao in private life was still very much a scholar of the traditional type. He would take comfort in the established ways of life with which he was familiar and in which he wanted to define the future happiness of his children. It was something of a great irony that this political reformer should have felt the urge to defend the sanctity of that most prevalent of old social conventions, the arranged marriage system, especially when the happiness of his own family was at stake. Written in his characteristically emotional yet elegant style, Liang's letter did not specifically mention Lin Hui-yin, although by all accounts the "practical" side of his intention was predominant; he attempted to discourage Hsü from pursuing Lin Hui-yin, for Hsü's irresponsible ways could only jeopardize the happiness of a third party—his eldest son who was already betrothed to Miss Lin. The emotional tone of the letter also indicated that Liang was extremely fond of not only Hsü Chih-mo but also Lin Hui-yin, whom the old man had treated like his own daughter. A few days later, Liang wrote another letter to his eldest daughter in which he stressed the pressing need to formalize the engagement of Liang Ssu-ch'eng and Lin Hui-yin.[54]

Hsü Chih-mo's answering letter demonstrated the inevitable generation gap between master and disciple. Avoiding likewise any reference to specific personalities, Hsü chose to reassert his ideal of love. But the very act of challenging his master's personal convictions with his own was evidently no less than an act of defiance. The letter was couched in equally emotional language:

I brave the adverse criticisms of society and struggle with my total energy, not to avoid the pains of a miserable lot but to seek the calm of my conscience, the firm establishment of my personality and the salvation of my soul.

Among men, who does not seek virtuous mediocrity? Who does not feel content with the status quo? Who does not fear difficulty and danger? Yet there are those who break loose and go beyond . . .

Alas, my teacher! I strive to exert the very kernel of my soul so as to crystallize it into a bright jewel of ideal. I nourish it with my warm and full heart and blood, so as to let it shine through the innermost recesses of my soul.[55]

To counter his master's worldly advice, Hsü made a resolution: "I shall search for my soul's companion in the sea of humanity: if I find her, it is my fortune; if not, it is my fate."[56]

Liang Ch'i-ch'ao's immediate reaction to Hsü's letter was not known. But Hsü's favorite-disciple status did not sem to be affected. Nor did the formal engagement seem to send Hsü into the abyss of despair. He was still a frequent guest at both the Liang and Lin households.[57] Despite their disagreements in outlook, Liang could not help being impressed by his young disciple, bristling with youthful energy and dedicated to Western literature. Knowing of Hsü's formidable command of English, Liang summoned Hsü to translate his *Hsien Ch'in cheng-chih ssu-hsiang shih* (History of political thought in the pre-Ch'in period)—a project which Hsü failed to finish—and presented, not without pride, his favorite disciple to his own mentor, K'ang Yu-wei.[58] When he decided to reorganize the format of his newspaper, *Shih-shih hsin-pao*, he put Hsü in charge of its literary supplement.[59] Again the project proved abortive. As Liang turned from politics to scholarship, Hsü had become Liang's constant companion in his lecture trips in Peking and Tientsin. When Liang was invited to lecture at Nan-k'ai University in Tientsin for the summer of 1923, Hsü also lectured there for two weeks on modern English literature.[60] His reputation was gradually established first through his teaching but, more important, through his poetry.

Since his return in 1922, Hsü had begun to contribute poems to the literary supplements of some of the leading newspapers, such as the *Shih-shih hsin-pao* in Shanghai, the *Ch'en-pao* in Peking, the *Ta-kung pao* in Tientsin, and Hu Shih's *Nu-li chou-pao* (Endeavor weekly). A great number of these poems, written in the new colloquial style, described his European experience. The freshness of both subject and form had at first baffled many printers. When his first "Farewell to Cambridge" appeared in the literary supplement of *Shih-shih hsin-pao*, the printer had mistaken poetry for prose and failed to separate one poetic line from another. At Hsü's request, the poem was printed again in the right order.[61]

In addition to writing poetry and giving occasional lectures, Hsü also managed to devote enough time to social activities and sightseeing. His first published diary, *Hsi-hu chi* (A record at West Lake), which covered the period from September 7 to October 28, 1923, described the activities of Hsü with a group of his friends, among whom were such eminent figures as Hu Shih, Chang Tung-sun, Car-sun Chang, Ch'ü Ch'iu-pai, and Wang Ching-wei. They invited each other for endless rounds of dinner parties. They cruised in the beautiful West Lake near Hangchow by moonlight. They hiked to the hills nearby to hear two hundred monks eerily chanting sutras in an incense-filled temple.[62] While their surface style may be reminiscent of that of traditional Chinese poets in an scenic excursion, the content of their conversations was concerned with such matters in Western literature as the poems of Thomas Hardy and the theories of Walter Pater.

Although Hsü's style of life upon returning to China still apparently carried traces of a lingering old tradition, the urban milieu along coastal China in the 1920s—the setting of Hsü's activities—was undergoing a modern transformation. Western fashions, customs, etiquette, and taste brought back by the returned students and imitated consciously by the increasingly Westernized compradors and intellectuals, began to set new trends in urban society. In Peking, one obvious social center of this new *étrangerie* was the Ministry of Foreign Affairs. Staffed by Western-educated diplomats, the ministry frequently gave dances for the social elite of Peking. One of the most admired socialites in these parties was a young married woman named Lu Hsiao-man.

Lu Hsiao-man was born in Shanghai but brought up in Peking, where her father held a high financial post in the warlord government. She was educated in a French missionary school where she learned French, and her father hired a private tutor to teach her English.[63] She grew up to be a beautiful woman, adept in both Western dancing and Peking opera. In 1920, Hsiao-man's family arranged for her marriage to a young Chinese officer fresh from Princeton and West Point. Hsiao-man seemed satisfied with her new husband, Wang Keng, who knew English, French, and German and had attended the Paris conference as military attaché to the Chinese delegation.[64] But the hard-working young man, as one of his close friends later recalled, had brought back the American way of planning and organizing his daily life. Only on weekends and Sundays did he manage to satisfy his wife's social vanity by taking her to parties and dances. From Monday to Saturday morning, he worked hard.[65] The stage was therefore set for the entrance of Hsü Chih-mo, and one of the most talked-about romances in twentieth century China unfolded.

Legend has it that Hsü and Lu met on stage when he played an old scholar and she a cute maid in a charity performance; no sooner was the play over than the hero and herone fell madly in love with each other.[66] A more plausible account indicated that Hsü had already been a good friend to both Wang Keng and Lu Hsiao-man and the three often went to parties and plays together. But during weekday evenings, Wang was not in the habit of combining work and pleasure; thus he often asked Hsü to accompany his wife. Little was he aware that Hsü's youthful passion knew no bounds. Soon Wang was appointed chief of police in Harbin. Rather than take his wife with him to Manchuria, he left her with her parents in Peking.[67] Thus the casual spark of romance between Chih-mo and Hsiao-man flared into passionate love.

Hsü's motive in pursuing Hsiao-man is hard to determine. He still maintained his close associations with Lin Hui-yin before she went to the University of Pennsylvania and married Liang Ssu-ch'eng.[68] Hsiao-man's initial appeal to him, we may surmise, was not so much her beauty or talent as her immense popularity in Peking society. In chasing her, as the young Scott Fitzgerald once courted his celebrated Southern belle, Zelda,[69] Hsü must have had an exhilarating feeling of playing an exciting game. The temptation of vanity in winning the heart of a popular socialite in Peking must have been irresistible to this young poet, editor of an esteemed journal, and above all debonair man of the world, who could hardly have been immune to some degree of narcissism.

The drama of Hsü's courtship of Lu Hsiao-man was amusingly heroic. He wrote her numerous love letters. He sent her imported Parisian perfume. When the servants of the house of Lu barred his entrance for a rendezvous with his beloved, he used his enviable affluence to bribe them. On Hsiao-man's part, the situation was more difficult. When Hsü's gifts and letters were confiscated by her mother, our amorous heroine had to write letters in English at midnight and sneak out to mail them herself. When her family moved to Shanghai in order to cut off their relationship, the indomitable Hsü followed her in the same train.[70]

These details provide an interesting kaleidoscope which mirrors both traditional and modern elements. The furtive encounters between a gifted young scholar (ts'ai-tzu) and a reigning beauty (chia-jen) seems to have been taken directly from traditional Chinese novels. But the language they used was not classical poetry, but colloquial prose sometimes reinforced with English. The channel of communication was not the lady's clever maid, but the modern postal system. Most significantly, this amusing story dramatized China's rapidly changing manners and morals. The mere fact that a married woman could set foot in public and be looked at and chased openly by men would have caused a traditional Confucian moralist to gasp in horror.

Hsü's courtship of Lu Hsiao-man created a great flurry of social gossip. It also left posterity a piece of confessional literature of unprecedented candor. The letters he wrote to Hsiao-man in the diary form, titled "Love Letters to May," provide easy access to his emotional "soul." They reflect his constantly changing moods of depression and elation, day after day, even hour after hour. The following is a most revealing example. (The italicized words were written in the original in English.)[71]

It's already twelve o'clock. Still no news from you. Let me lie in bed and think about you.

Three quarters past twelve. Still no news . . . Why are spasms of solitary sadness thronging in my heart? Tears—hanging down like threads! What to write? I had better go to bed.

It's one o'clock . . . My heart is beating; my heart is splitting into pieces . . . Ten minutes past one. Still so early. How slowly time passes!

Chih-mo, you are really unfortunate! You are pitiable! If you had known that this world would be like this, you should not have been born. Sooner or later this abundance of hot blood will all be poured out.

Twenty minutes past one!

141

Half past one—*Marvelous!*

Thirty-five minutes past one—*Life is too charming, too charming indeed, Haha! !*

Three quarters past one—*O is that the way woman love [sic]! Is that the way woman love!*

1:55—Heavens!

2:05—The blood in my soul is dripping drop by drop . . .

2:18—I am mad!

2:30—

2:40—*"The pity of it, the pity of it, Iago!"*
  Christ what a hell
  Is packed into that line! Each syllable
  Blessed when you say it . . .

2:50—Extremely quiet.

3:07—

3:25—No more fire!

3:40—My heart is at a loss!

4:45—Cough!

6:30—

7:27—

The agony and ecstasy exhibited in these passages may appear adolescent to a bemused reader of the 1970s. But these outbursts from a poet's heart exerted tremendous impact upon millions of Chinese youths. Together with Yü Ta-fu's *Nine Diaries*, the love letters of Hsü Chih-mo may be regarded as a milestone in the journey of sentiment which began at the turn of the century: in the diaries of these two men, the immediacy and intensity of private emotions reached the highest peak. Unlike Yü's diaries, which are permeated with the author's self-indulgent decadence, Hsü's letters were filled with exultant passion, intense yearning, and volcanic love. Witness, for instance, the following passage written entirely in English:

O May! love me; give me all your love, let us become one; try to live into my love for you, let my love fill you, nourish you, caress your daring body and hug your daring soul too; let me rest happy in your love and confident in your passion for me!

May, I miss your passionately appealing gazings and soul-communicating glances which once so overwhelmed and ingratiated me . . .[72]

Hsü's unbridled outburst of love drew the whole-hearted admiration of Yü Ta-fu himself, who was moved to comment that "when an honest and beautiful woman like Hsiao-man met a passionate and sincere man like Chih-mo, naturally it would set off sparks and flare into burning fire. How could they care about cardinal norms or ethical tenets? How could they care about clan laws or family conventions? When the affair was becoming the butt of social gossip in Peking, my admiration for the bravery of Hsiao-man and the sincerity of Chih-mo could not have been greater." [73]

As the social gossip intensified, Hsü was advised to take a second trip to Europe so as to avoid further scandals. To himself, this was a "sentimental journey" to test the lasting love between him and Hsiao-man. He left China in March 1925, took the Trans-Siberian Railway across Russia, traveled through Germany, Italy, France, England, and did not return until August. In his numerous letters to Hsiao-man he showered his beloved with his passionate yearnings: "You should know how I love you, how you have possessed my soul, my body, my entire being." "Do you know how your beloved is talking to you with two eyes filled with hot tears, now deep in the night? I miss you, cherish you, comfort you, love you." [74] He implored her not to indulge in her whims, to refrain from social engagements. He encouraged her to "fight on," and, citing the example of Nora, to "assert your personality." [75]

Hsiao-man's response, as described in her diary, was in clear contrast to Hsü's blinding intensity. She procrastinated in answering his letters, masking her uneasiness with various pretexts. There were her inimical mother and distrustful husband to appease, and numerous rumors to avoid or dispel. There were always social engagements. "Everyday I whiled away my time in social spots, either playing cards at one house or going out dancing." [76] She pretended that she was trying to forget herself and the sorrows of parting. But it seemed she was actually enjoying everything she did. She easily succumbed to the influence of her environment and lived in a world of aristocratic luxury. Again Fitzgerald's Zelda comes to mind: "She was as ambitious as he was . . . Though she was in love with him, she did not, for all her yielding, commit herself as he did." [77] Hsiao-man was finally moved by the sincerity of Hsü's sentiments: "The genuine feelings that he poured out from his heart made my life change its direction, and at the same time I also fell in love."[78] On October 3, 1926, they were married, after Hsiao-man had obtained her divorce. The wedding ceremony was held in the Pei-hai Garden of Peking and presided over by none other than Hsü's displeased mentor. With Hsü's prior consent, Liang Ch'i-ch'ao surprised the large crowd of friends and guests by delivering a scathing lecture on the moral inadequacies of his beloved disciple.[79]

As we now read the love diaries of Hsü and Lu, the rosy aura surrounding their romance seems to pale in historical perspective. Both were intoxicated by the wonder of uninhibited emotions. While Hsiao-man married Chih-mo out of gratitude for the profusion of emotions he had showered upon her, he poured out his love because she was for him the incarnation of love. He was chasing as much the phantom of love and beauty as a living human object. He was in love with love itself. With the acquisition of his love object, the discrepancy between ideal and reality became inevitably clear. Thus Hsü was uncharacteristically sparing in describing his "marital bliss" with an often bedridden wife. His diary written from 1926 to 1927 abounds rather in narratives of outings with friends and discussions of books. They became rather poor, and Hsü had to teach and write in order to support her luxurious tastes. One source even indicates that Hsiao-man became involved more and more with performances of Peking operas. At Christmas, when Hsü intended to go to a solitary church and enjoy the serenity of Christmas carols, he was dragged by his pampered wife to appear in the clamor and hubbub of the opera stage.[80] Hsiao-man went so far as to smoke opium and have an affair with an actor and playboy.[81] The sage warnings of Liang Ch'i-ch'ao proved prophetic.

Tagore and the "Crescent Moon"

Love and marriage seem to have preoccupied Hsü's life in the first three or four years after his return from England in 1922. For him, this private drama was as important as his many public activities. It is already reflected in his answering letter to Liang Ch'i-ch'ao: his ideals would be not only expounded in words but also exemplified in action. Thus his second marriage, albeit a private affair, was regarded by Hsü also as a gesture of dramatic defiance of social conventions. In his resolution to make himself a living embodiment of his ideals, his private acts thus assumed a public significance. And the public responded to him enthusiastically, on account of both his poetry and his personality.

Although he had contributed poems and articles to prominent magazines after his return to China, Hsü probably did not become nationally famous until 1924 when the famous Indian poet Rabindranath Tagore visited China. The story of Tagore's visit to China and Japan has been treated elsewhere.[82] It remains only for us to trace Hsü's connection with the Indian sage. When some time in 1922 the Chianghsüeh she (Lecture Society) in Peking, which was formed by a group of leading scholars, extended an invitation to Tagore to give a series of lectures in China, Tagore sent an Englishman, Mr. Leonard K. Elmhirst, to Peking to raise funds and arrange the itinerary of the visit. As business manager and secretary for Tagore's group, Elmhirst naturally met and made friends with the liaison man from the Chinese side, Hsü Chih-mo. Their friendship persisted through correspondence after Elmhirst returned to England. Elmhirst has recently recorded his reminiscences of the trip which provide some interesting clues to the personalities of both Tagore and Hsü.

Tagore had first planned to visit China in 1923 but the trip was postponed until the next year because of his illness. In addition to Elmhirst, Tagore brought with him three eminent Bengalis: a historian (Kalidas Nag), an artist (Nandalal Bose), and a scholar-philosopher (Kshitimohan Sen). The group was carefully selected, according to Elmhirst, so as to establish a cultural relationship between the Chinese and India.[83] Tagore himself also publicly announced that he came to China not as a tourist, nor as a preacher, but as "a pilgrim to pay respects to Chinese culture."[84] After landing in Shanghai on April 12, 1924, he was very eager to have members of his entourage meet their Chinese counterparts, especially younger men in the field of the arts.[85] Naturally, the Indian poet was immediately impressed by Hsü as his young Chinese translator. According to Elmhirst, "Tagore immediately recognized in him first of all a fellow poet, secondly a man with a sense of humor, thirdly a man through whom he felt he could get into touch with the spirit of the Chinese, especially the spirit of the younger Chinese."[86] The two poets spent a most memorable evening together in a boat on West Lake where they composed and talked about poetry till dawn.[87] Elmhirst was struck by the miraculous spiritual rapport between the two poets. On Hsü's part, what he sought and found in this great Indian poet was his "great harmonious and beautiful personality, through which one can find inspiration for the culture of India, both ancient and modern."[88]

After a brief stay in Shanghai, the group traveled to Nanking and Tsinan. At both places Tagore lectured to students and Hsü interpreted in his elegant, Chekiang-accented Mandarin.[89] They arrived in Peking on April 23 and were received by nearly all the leading members of the academic community. At a welcoming banquet Liang Ch'i-ch'ao presented a glowing tribute to Indian culture.[90] Tagore gave six public lectures; Hsü Chih-mo and Lin Hui-yin were his constant companions. The sight of a white-haired old sage flanked by this dashing young pair was turned into something of a legend.[91] On May 8, on the occasion of Tagore's sixty-fourth birthday, the Chinese scholars gave a grand party in his honor. Hu Shih presented him with several treasured Chinese paintings; Liang Ch'i-ch'ao presided over a ceremony of nomenclature at which Tagore formally received his Chinese name, "Chu Chen-tan"; and finally both Hsü and Lin Hui-yin participated in a performance of Tagore's short play, "Chita"—she in the role of a princess and he as the god of love.[92]

From Peking the visiting dignitaries journeyed to T'ai-yüan, in Shansi province, then turned south to Hankow, and returned to Shanghai where they departed for Japan. At every step Hsü worked closely with Elmhirst on details of itinerary and did "a lot of face-saving . . . in a whole series of international puzzles."[93] He also accompanied the Indian poet to Japan where he stayed until midsummer.

The prominent role Hsü played in Tagore's visit earned him the popular title, obviously inspired by Tagore, of "poet-philosopher." As Tagore's interpreter and Lu Hsiao-man's suitor, Hsü had become a national celebrity. In 1925 he was made editor of the literary supplement of the prestigious *Ch'en pao* of Peking. In addition to teaching at Peking University, he also lectured on Western literature at Kuang-hua University, Soochow University Law School, and Ta-hsia University in Shanghai. In 1926, Hsü established in the pages of the *Ch'en pao* two more supplements: a poetry journal, *Shih-k'an*, dedicated to the exploration of new poetic forms, and a drama section, *Chü-k'an*, for the introduction of Western-style plays. The former terminated after eleven issues but resumed its independent publication under the same title in 1931, with the assistance of Wen I-to, and lasted for five issues. The drama journal published fifteen issues. Despite their short durations, Hsü's two poetry journals were responsible for some daring experiments. Both Hsü and Wen attempted to break away from the rhyming patterns of traditional Chinese poetry and to substitute an essentially Western form of versification with rhyme.

The most important literary endeavor initiated by Hsü was the publication of the magazine *Hsin-yüeh*. The first issue bore the publishing date of March 10, 1928, and featured an eight-page manifesto supposedly written by Hsü Chih-mo. Titled "The Attitude of the Crescent Moon," it set forth the guide lines of the journal. Hsü explained his choice of the term "crescent moon" with a note of optimism: "We cannot forsake this name because, although it is not such a strong symbol, its frail crescent nevertheless denotes and embraces the fullness of the future." [94] To stress its promise, Hsü did not hesitate to preface the manifesto with two quotations in English: one from Genesis, "And God said, Let there by light: and there was light"; the other from Shelley, "If Winter comes, can Spring be far behind?" The shaft of light with which the Crescentists endeavored to penetrate the dark chaos of China's literary scene was what Hsü called "creative idealism," the two guilding principles of which were "health" and "dignity." "Dignity, because its voice can call back life which has wandered at the crossroads; health, because its power can destroy all the bacteria that erode life and thought." The combination of these two principles would provide an individual with a correct frame of thinking which is, according to Hsü, "the natural product

147

of the emancipation of our life energies." Therefore, he exhorted, "we should first of all release our life energies." While claiming health and dignity for themselves, Hsü and his group branded all other publications as bacteria, which he further divided into no less than thirteen categories: sentimentalism, decadentism, aestheticism, utilitarianism, didacticism, detracticism, extremism, fragilism, eroticism, fanaticism, venalism, sloganism, and "ism-ism."[95] This sweeping and scathing survey aroused the fury of nearly all the vociferous spokesmen on the left, from Lu Hsün to the younger members of the Creation and Sun societies.

In the context of Hsü's life and personality, the two principles are very much the hallmark of his idealized personality. Sentiments are "healthy" if they are genuine. A release of man's inner energies would result in a "healthy" man who would merit and justify the "dignity" of life. The two epithets seem both descriptive and exhortative for a more vitalistic and activistic philosophy of life. But in the eyes of leftist critics, however, Hsü's ideas were but ivory-towerish sputterings hardly relevant to the grave political situation. The younger members of the Creation and Sun societies countered Hsü's idealism with materialistic dialectics: "Spirit is a complicated function of matter and is controlled by matter."[96] Thus, Hsü's slogans of health and dignity were no more than high-sounding nonsense reflecting the ideology of the declining bourgeoisie. Lu Hsün, on the other hand, felt indignant at a group of self-styled "gentlemen" who championed the purity and sanctity of literature in a period in which the social and political demands on literature were becoming all the more urgent.[97] In retrospect Lu Hsün's criticism proved quite perceptive, for the *Crescent Moon* in fact turned political in late 1929. The force of circumstances had pressured the previously debonair and apolitical Crescentists to proclaim solemnly: "Yes, we are talking politics; we will continue to talk politics."[98] The dominance of Hsü Chih-mo was over. His name was dropped from the list of editors from Volume II, Number 2 of the journal. Although his energies might have been diverted to a new poetry journal, *Shih-k'an*, which formally began publication in January 1931, his own mood was hardly untouched by politics. The social and political realities of China since 1927 had wreaked more and more afflictions on his mind as he struggled through his literary endeavors.

The Darkling Plain

Hsü's public activities with Tagore and later with the *Crescent Moon* magazine had established him as one of the foremost men of letters in his day; his private romance with Lu Hsiao-man had also made him a social celebrity, a figure for rumors and gossip, but also for emulation. The convergence of the public and private realms of his life reached its culmination in 1926, when he married Lu Hsiao-man. But after 1926, the inevitable clash between ideal and reality also led to a gradual divergence of these two realms. His carefree, youthful exuberance seemed to be an established hallmark of his public image, reaffirmed repeatedly by the legendary accounts of his friends and admirers. "He came in a whirlwind, sweeping across his companions; he was also like a torch which enkindled everyone's heart." "His words are clear-cut, uttered amidst fits of shouting and jumping. He could be suddenly melancholy or joyous. When he was moody, the sky would fall and the earth splinter. When he was happy, he was high above, roving with wind and clouds, heaven and earth . . . This man liked excursions. He was sensitive to gods and ghosts. Once he jumped at the sound of a nightingale, exclaiming: 'This is Shelley's nightingale!' " [99] This fond portrait by Hsü's friend Lin Yutang bears a great deal of true insight into Hsü's personality. But, as one studies more carefully the last years of his life, this exhilarated image is shadowed by many darker moods.

Due to their close collaboration in managing Tagore's visit, Hsü formed a lasting friendship with Leonard Elmhirst. Their correspondence lasted for five years, from 1924 to 1929. Hsü's letters, numbering more than twenty, all written in elegant English and carefully preserved by Elmhirst, give a sense of his growing political consciousness and his increasingly tragic mood.

The series of letters began in 1925 when Hsü was traveling in Europe to forget about Lu Hsiao-man. In his letter dated June 18, 1925, from Paris, he lamented: "You know it? Well, well, everybody is realizing his share of happiness. As for myself, a lonely wanderer —and no more . . . Meanwhile China is in a terrible fix and I have no longer any peace of mind." [100] By this he must have been referring to the May Thirtieth incident in which the death of Chinese workers and students turned the whole nation into a whirlwind of anti-imperialist protests. He missed meeting Tagore in Paris in June and sent an apologetic letter to Elmhirst: "I hope you understand the situation and do feel sympathy for me which I need so badly. Never before have I found myself in such immensely difficult position; never before have I been so deeply worried; I hardly know what is going to happen next; it may be tragedy, it may be farce; it may be the end of everything, it may be the beginning of a new life." [101] "It" most likely meant his romance with Lu Hsiao-man, for on December 26, 1926, Elmhirst received a letter from Hu Shih informing him that Hsü was married. Hu Shih further suggested that it would be wonderful if Elmhirst could help the Hsü's to get away from China and spend two or three years in England and Europe.[102]

And on January 5, 1927, Hsü himself wrote to Elmhirst: "I have had a bitter struggle since, in which I suffered not the least, nearly everything except the sympathy of one or two friends (Hu Shih being one) being in my way. However I triumphed—triumphed against the deadly force of ignorance and prejudice in which all societies rest. I am not sure you had any recollection of my wife (her name is Siao-May) . . . She is rather weak of health, and I had desired to cure her by the health of great nature." [103]

Happy with his good friend's marriage, and in answer to Hu Shih's request, Elmhirst, who had become quite wealthy, wrote to Hsü on March 7, 1927 offering Hsü some money to cover travel expenses to Europe.[104] On April 1, 1927, Hsü wrote a long letter from Shanghai in which he acknowledged the receipt of Elmhirst's £250, but he was preoccupied with more despondent thoughts:

Leonard, how am I to thank you for such great kindness? Things here have turned so utterly dark that acts of true friendship strike one dumb with gratitude and wonder . . . The whole country is fast tumbling into a nightmare of hideous passion and bestiality. And what is there to save the situation? The soberer forces are fast giving way, being trodden down, and will soon disappear altogether. Who are the present masters? Simple workmen, regular knaves, and young boys and girls, mostly under twenty . . . The native soil is fertile and ready for revolution: that is the secret. A curious and wonderful performance indeed, the present upheaval in China: something like a parody of the Russian Revolution.

. . . If the Russian Revolution succeeded in terminating the aristocratic and bourgeois classes, the revolution here is also hastening things toward that end. The greatest achievement the Communists here have so far accomplished is to my mind the fact of having created not only class distinction, but class hatred as well . . . The intellectuals are absolutely helpless and powerless against the turbulent flood of catchwords and mob movements.

As for myself I have been dumb for half a year already. I am teaching in a college here, earning a little money to live on, having as I so decided not to depend any longer on my father, who, by the way, is himself in sore difficulties. (The rascals in our home town have started hell of trouble against him, and have actually taken possession of our newly built house.) Words, therefore, are quite inadequate to describe my present state of mind. My only hope is that we should be able to get out, to quit China, for some length of time . . . Then my wife is at the present too weak to travel. The Indian summer would half kill her. So we have to wait till summer is over before we can think of our visit to India. The best time for us to get to India is probably October.[105]

Hsü did leave China, without the company of his wife, on his third European tour via the United States sometime in the summer of 1928. He wrote a letter from New York to Elmhirst on July 20, 1928, registering the same despondent mood: "China as you know has suffered tremendously in spite of the Nationalist success and, as for myself, I have not been too happy altogether either, since for one thing my wife has been practically continuously ill since last summer."[106] He arrived in London in mid-August and went immediately to Totness, Devon, to visit Elmhirst's estate, Dartington Hall, an industrial-agricultral-educational community inspired by Tagore's ideas. Hsü praised it as "yet the nearest approach I have found on earth to the idea of an Utopia."[107] He also called upon Russell whom he found "as pungently witty and relentlessly humorous as ever," and later wrote an article on Russell's personal method of educating his children.[108]

Hsü's European tour this time was not meant merely to escape the chaos in China. The increasing awareness of the worsening political situation even made an almost apolitical person like Hsü eager to engage in some concrete action. At Dartington Hall, he seems to have consulted Elmhirst, himself an agricultural expert who had once helped Tagore in India, on an experimental rural project to be funded by Elmhirst and carried out by Hsü and his friends. For, in September, he wrote: "The first thing I will do when I get back to China in November will be to get P. C. Chang, S. Y. Chu, and a few others down to Shanghai and form a party to travel in the interior of Chekiang and Kiangsu and, having looked into the actual conditions there and found out the needs of the day, decide upon a tentative programme of an experimental scheme, which we shall submit to you for approval and further suggestion." [109] Elmhirst immediately mailed to him an initial sum of £300. He embarked upon his return journey via Germany, France, and India, where he again met his good friend "Goldie" [Tagore]. In his first letter after arriving in Shanghai, dated January 7, 1929, Hsü informed Elmhirst that he had contacted both P. C. Chang and S. Y. Chu, who had been working in the Mass Education Association. He also reported on the progress of his rural plan: "I have seen something of the interior of Kiangsu and Chekiang and so far decided in favor of the latter. For one thing the people are much more honest and still retain some beauty of character which comes from close contact with nature and is yet unspoilt by modern influences." [110]

Hsü never mentioned his rural project again in his subsequent letters. Possibly it was planned to be a model village after Tagore's project in India and Dartington Hall. But how could a man who still treated Chinese peasantry in Rousseauian images carry out successfully a project which was equally idealistic? Dartington Hall, supported by the private wealth of the Elmhirsts, became for Hsü more and more a nostalgic Utopia into which his sensitive mind sought temporary escape from the sordid realities of life in China. "I always look forward for news from Dartington for it looms on my mental horizon as a spot of unusual light and great beauty, which two things are too ruthlessly denied the present-day China," [111] he wrote on

March 5, 1929. The letter was further punctuated by sorrow and bitterness. His mentor Liang Ch'i-ch'ao had died on January 19. "It is an irretrievable loss for me . . . He is a much greater man than any of his contemporaries, not excepting Dr. Sun." [112] His grief over the loss of his teacher launched him into a bitter tirade about conditions in China:

Sordidness instead of nobility, hostility and mutual destructiveness rather than fellowship and co-operation, dead and infectious dogmas, not living principles, run wild, like stalking corpses, to plunge the whole nation into yet greater disaster and suppress the creative function of human spirit! Meanwhile whole provinces are dragging on in simply incredible conditions of existence. I myself have had some glimpses of the starving North and my blood chills with the mere thought of it. Children that look no longer human actually fight over lichen and mosses that their bony fingers scratch off from the crevices of rocks and stuff into their desperate effort of [sic] assuage excruciating hunger and cold! Lord, wherefore such were caused to be born!

Not all this, the unfeeling rulers on the one hand and the mute suffering masses on the other, are inevitably helping to pave the way for goodness knows what terrible catastrophe that's ahead of us. Even the so-called intelligentsia—what impotent lot!—appear to be possessed of an intolerable feeling of ennui and, lacking courage to sustain responsibilities, secretly crave a thorough reshaping of human nature.[113]

Thus near the end of the decade, the exuberant, optimistic "poet philosopher" was voicing nearly the same dark pessimism as his friend Yü Ta-fu. The muddled political situation was such that even his Crescent Moon colleagues, led by Hu Shih and Lo Lung-chi, turned political in 1929 and devoted numerous pages to their ineffectual liberal schemes of constitutionalism. But Hsü Chih-mo became awakened to politics too late. He had always been on the far fringes of China's social and political vicissitudes. He left Peking for America just in time to miss the May Fourth Incident. He was in England when the Chinese Communist Party was founded. After he returned to China, he first found his haven in Peking, while in Canton the power struggles between Chiang Kai-shek and his rival factions were gathering momentum. When the May Thirtieth Incident occurred, he was again traveling in Europe, learning about "China in

153

a terrible fix" possibly in the hills near Florence. In 1926, as Chiang moved his troops northward, Hsü was too involved with his new wife to hear the guns of war. When finally the warlords became alarmed by the advances of the Northern Expedition, Hsü sought asylum in the foreign concessions in Shanghai. He frankly confessed his own political ignorance: "I have never been a worker; I have not tasted the bitterness of life. I have not been in prison, nor have I ever joined any secret society, killed any man, undertaken any commercial enterprise, made any big money."[114] He was simply a good-natured man who passionately cherished "the creative function of the human spirit." On May 3, 1928, when the Tsinan Incident broke out (the Chinese envoy of the forces of the Northern Expedition was killed by the Japanese troops), Hsü's patriotism was aroused and he wrote in his diary: "This is the first time in my life that I grieve over national affairs."[115] In 1929, he gave a speech to the students of Tsinan University, in which he attempted to offer some prescriptions for the ills of China. He singled out three dangerous symptoms: "chaos," "abnormality," and "the reversal of all standards." Still, he endeavored to encourage himself and his students with a few positive words:

Hsü Chih-mo and Lu Hsiao-man

If we are not mistaken about the illness, there is always a way. My view is that we should be exposed to nature more often, because nature exerts healthy and pure influences, and it contains an inexhaustible source for the nourishment, enlightenment, and inspiration of the soul . . . This all depends upon the conscious self-cultivation of each one of us. We should be resolved first not to be the slaves of the times. We want to be masters of our thinking and fate. This temporary depression will not overcome our ideals . . . Just as I ended my Fallen Leaves speech two years ago with an exclamation of everlasting yea, today I still want you to exclaim with me the everlasting yea.[116]

The call for a return to nature and the final Nietzschean plea sounded, even for his own mood, pathetic if not totally anachronistic. In February 1931 the *Crescent Moon* published an unfinished story by Hsü in which appeared the following words:

What world is this, with the victories of death everywhere? What we hear are the cheers of death; what we see are the wild dances of death. All point toward death. What are the vicissitudes of time? What is reform? What is revolution? They are but the tower of death's victory built by imbecile mankind with their own bones and flesh. This tower, reaching high to the sky, brims with neither gold nor silver, but mankind's own blood, particularly the fresh blood of the innocent. Time is an immeasurable, voracious, and poisonous serpent addicted to sucking the flesh and blood of humanity.[117]

He did not stay long to confront this bloody Tower of Babel. Nine months later, on November 19, 1931, he found his own death in a plane crash. A friend who was with Hsü on the previous night recalled that Hsü "was especially alive, in an especially good mood."[118]

I have no other methods, I have only love; no
other talents, only love; no other abilities, only
love; no other energies, only love.
—Hsü Chih-mo

Chapter 8

Hsü Chih-mo: Exultations of Icarus

After returning to China in 1922, Hsü delivered one of his first lectures at Tsinghua University. Unfortunately, the important messages contained in the lecture, "Art and Life," escaped the attention of the young audience, because Hsü had chosen to flaunt his acquired British style by reading his paper in English with the pedantic air of an Oxford don.[1] For with this speech, Hsü had in fact taken the entire Chinese tradition to task in the light of what he had learned from the West.

He put forth a daring thesis: "We have no art precisely because we have no life." His elaboration on this thesis was no less daring:

With all our virtues and qualities, we Chinese as a race have never realized and expressed ourselves completely, as the Greeks and Romans did, through the medium of art—which is the consciousness of life . . .

With his soul unrecognized and senses denied, together with an ingenious device in operation by which his vital forces are directed, partly through repression, partly through sublimation into "safe" and practical channels, the Chinese has come to be a creature, human enough to be sure yet capable neither of religion nor of love, nor indeed of any spiritual adventures. We are admired, as by sincere friends like G. Lowes Dickinson, and Bertrand Russell, . . . for our dispassionate attitude towards life, love of moderation, reasonableness and compromising spirit and so forth, a compliment we assuredly deserve, yet I for one, in accepting it, can't help feeling the poignancy of the irony that is behind it. For what is a dispassionate attitude towards life but a patent negation of life by smothering the divine flame of passions almost to extinction? What is life for moderation but an amiable excuse for cowardice in thought and action, for shallowness and flatness in life-activities? And what is obsequiously called rationalistic and compromising spirit has produced nothing but a habit of laziness at large and that ridiculous monster which we are told to regard as the Chinese Republican Government![2]

The failure of this cultural tradition, according to Hsü, has stultified both human life and the artistic imagination, "and poverty of life necessarily begets poverty of art." He then brought to bear on this impoverished tradition his creative masters from the West:

Isn't it significant that none of our poets, with the only possible exception of Li Po, can be said to be of cosmic character? Isn't it striking that we look in vain in the scroll of our literary fames for even the least resemblance of a Goethe, a Shelley, a Wordsworth even not to say Dante and Shakespeare? And as for the other arts, who is there here to rank with the vast genius of men like Michelangelo, Leonardo da Vinci, Turner, Corregio, Velasquez, Wagner, Beethoven —to name but a few? . . . We possess an artistic heritage, essentially inferior to that of the West, in that it fails to comprehend life as a whole.[3]

Hsü's final exhortation to Chinese youth was: "Therefore, enrich, augment, multiply, intensify and above all spiritualize your life and art will come of itself."[4]

The Dynamism of Life and Love

Hsü's scathing onslaught on the Chinese tradition and his unrestrained admiration of the West could be regarded as typical products of the May Fourth mania of iconoclasm. But since he himself played no role in the initial movement, they seem more likely to have sprung from his own observations as a student in Europe. His impatience with dispassionateness, rationality, and moderation in Chinese culture is also reminiscent of Lin Shu's criticism of the vulgarized notion of the "golden mean." Yet, as Lin Shu admired the more vital West from the distance that separated the Western tradition from his own Confucian upbringing, Hsü took a giant step further by embracing what he considered to be the essence of the West. And he took it upon himself to activate and exemplify his own credo. It is in this perspective that his life, both public and private, became immensely meaningful. Rather than assume the more negative pose of a hero afflicted with a curse, like Su Man-shu and Yü Ta-fu, Hsü positively regarded himself as a man of mission.

This sense of mission was manifested as early as 1918 when he wrote his long letter to his friends and relatives. His schedule of daily life indicated even more the determination of a young man preparing himself for his goals. The problem is that these goals had not yet been sharply defined by him and remained in the hazy horizon of patriotism. Hsü was, in other words, echoing the prevalent sense of national consciousness of his generation. It was not until his years in Cambridge that he gradually brought into focus his own temper and capacities. The nationalistic framework in which he previously defined his own mission gradually gave way to a more individualistic focus; he would plunge himself into Chinese society as a living embodiment of those virtues and traits which he had learned to admire in the West. Unlike Yü Ta-fu, therefore, Hsü Chih-mo was the very image he presented to others; there existed no dichotomy between himself and the vision of himself, between his private life and his public life. It was only in the last years of his life, when his idealism began to be undermined by his darker moods of despair, that image and reality parted ways.

The life and art of Hsü Chih-mo can thus be seen as the presentation and elaboration of a new personality and a new philosophy of life which would replace those habits of thought and behavior attributed by him to the cultural tradition of China. Thus Hsü was never dispassionate, never moderate, never compromised his principles—even at the risk of offending his mentor Liang Ch'i-ch'ao. He pursued Lin Hui-yin and later Lu Hsiao-man with naive, yet passionate, persistence, because they were not merely figures in his life; they were, in those periods of his life, the totality of his life, the quintessence of his principles. His love letters to Lu Hsiao-man read more like self-justifications than endearments to win her over. In publishing his letters and diaries, Hsü was in fact trying to win over the entire reading public to his philosophy.

The theoretical aspects of Hsü's philosophy are best summarized in an essay titled "Word." Hsü acknowledged two "great professors": Life and Nature. From the myriad phenomena and movements of nature—the sunrise, the starry firmament of a summer's night, the waves in the ocean, the clouds on the mountain peaks, and even a "cheap wild flower, waving in the spring wind under the glorious sun" —can be derived the lesson that "all things exert the utmost of their nature." By analogy, therefore, one's life is but the manifestation of one's personality. Hsü admits the influence of environment on man, but he still asserts that "the possibility of the human mind holding sway over environment is at least equal to the possibility of environment holding sway over human life." Accordingly, "I am not doing justice to myself if I cannot realize in my life what makes man man; I am not doing justice to life if in my life as a man I cannot realize what makes me me." [5] Hsü's advice is therefore, echoing Yen Fu, the realization of the fullest human potential. The meaning of one's life lies in developing one's individual personality. But one's genuine personality cannot be achieved merely by one's idiosyncratic, external life style; it rather requires inner exertions. It is this inner life that provides man with a "conscious life" different from mere "mechanical existence." [6] The essence of this inner life, to Hsü Chih-mo, is love. Hsü's own life and personality are its perfect embodiment.

Hu Shih once characterized Hsü's *Weltanschauung* as consisting of "a simple faith on which were written three big words: love, freedom, and beauty . . . He dreamed of having these three ideal conditions merge into the life of one individual. This was his simple faith. The history of his life was the history of his seeking the realization of this simple faith." [7] Liang Shih-ch'iu interpreted Hsü's "simple faith" not as three separate ideals but as one central ideal which has already fused the three: "Chih-mo's simple faith, in other words, is romantic love," and it is realized "in the pursuit of a beautiful woman." [8] Hsü himself has also made numerous confessions about love as the hall-mark of his personality and the reigning theme in his mental universe: "I have no other methods, I have only love; no other talents, only love; no other capacities, only love; no other energies, only love." "Love is the central focus and crystallization of life; the success of love is the success of life; the failure of love is the failure of life. This is beyond doubt." [9] No doubt, his whole life hinged on his craving for love, as a human object, as a principle of life, and as an all-encompassing idealization. Hsü's pursuit of love as a human object and as a principle of life have been illustrated in his pursuit of Lu Hsiao-man. His explorations of love as a concept or ideal can be found in his poetry.

In Hsü's poetry, love is often related to death, which is the ultimate consummation of love's passion. This theme is powerfully exemplified in his famous poem, "A Night in Florence":

. . . Love, I cannot even breathe now,
Kiss me no more, this flame-like life I cannot bear.
My soul at this moment is like hot iron on an anvil,
Being struck, struck by the hammer of love, its sparks
Flying in all directions . . . Hold me, I am fainting.
Love, just let me, in this quiet garden,
Close my eyes and die in your embrace—how beautiful!
. . . . .
I follow the breeze with a smile; on my way again,
Letting it lead me anywhere—to heaven, or hell,
So long as I leave this hated human life to realize death
In love. This death in the heart of love, isn't it better
Than five hundred reincarnations? . . .[10]

The poem is in the form of a confessional monologue by a woman who is overpowered by the yearning and passion of love. Another longer monologue by another love-stricken girl can be found in "Love's Inspiration." One of Hsü's last poems and the longest of all, the piece is in many respects a summation of Hsü's tenets on love.

The long poem tells a vivid story by means of a flashback. Lying on her death-bed, holding the hands of her lover (who, like Armand, arrives too late), the heroine begins to confess: Having fallen in love

at first meeting, she feels, however, that her lover is unattainably re-
mote, and keeps her love a secret. She leaves her family to engage
herself in relief work in a stricken countryside, where she finally at-
tains peace and maturity through imaginative understanding of Nature. After three years of hardships she contracts a fever and is taken
home by her brother. Recovered somewhat but still too weak to resist
the pressure of her family, she submits to a conventional marriage
and gives birth to a child, who dies. Still she keeps the secret of her
great love, but at last, in a return of delirium, she inadvertently discloses it. The man she has loved through these years is summoned.
He holds her as she makes her final confession.[11] After she has made
the confession, the poem ends with the following lines:

> Now that I
> Really, really can die. I want you to
> Hold me until I pass away,
> Until my eyes can open no more,
> Until I fly, fly, fly into outer space,
> Disperse into sand, into light, into wind.
> Ah agony, but agony is short,
> Transitory; happiness is long,
> And love is immortal:
> I, I want to sleep . . .[12]

The story line brings back faint echoes of *La Dame aux Camélias*.
The prefiguring of immortality savors strongly, as Cyril Birch suggests, of Blake and Tagore.[13] The link between love and death seems
to be, as in the above-quoted "A Night in Florence," a refrain of that
favorite romantic cliché, "l'amour est la mort." The influence of Keats
can also be detected. As Birch has noted: "The basic concept of death
as transcendence is still there, but the means of deliverance into death
from 'the weariness, the fever, and the fret' is for Hsü's dying girl not
the ecstasy of bliss in the song of the nightingale, but that understanding and desire of the eternal to which love has opened her
eyes."[14] In the context of Hsü's writings as a whole, this metaphysical
theme is a minor strand. I would argue that Hsü's conceptualization
of love and its relationship with death and freedom is imbued precisely with "the ecstasy of bliss in the song of the nightingale." As

the girl in the poem contemplates the power of love, the imagery takes on the ebullience and ecstasy of positive affirmation:

I looked only for a more enduring
Measure of time to receive my breath,
When the glittering stars should be my eyes,
My hair, a sheen at the sky's edge,
The disarray of the tinted clouds,
And my arms, my breast, borne on the wind's
Whirling, free against my brow,
And the waves dashing my legs, from each
Surging, rising a mystic aura.
With these, the lightning for my thought,
Flashing its dragon-dance on the horizon,
My voice the thunder, suddenly breaking
To wake the spring, to wake new life.
Ah, beyond thought, beyond compare
Is the inspiration, the power of love.[15]

The use of grandiose naturalistic metaphors blends dynamically the power of love with the power of nature. The ultimate source of the above vision, springing from the imagination of a love-stricken girl, is, as Birch points out, that primordial, masculine image in Chinese mythology, P'an Ku.[16] The myth of P'an Ku opening up heaven and earth and the transformation of his body into elements of nature is one of the few dynamic myths in China. Whether Hsü may or may not have had P'an Ku in mind when conjuring up such imageries, the dominance of a dynamic ethos in his poetry on love is unmistakable. Thus even his apparently escapist and metaphysical poems on love may seem impregnated with positive meanings. To love is an act of supreme honesty and defiance—stripping oneself of civilized hypocrisy and renouncing all the external restraints of artificial society so as to merge ecstatically with nature. The consummation of love, which may lead inevitably to death, also brings ultimate freedom.

Let loose all your hair,
And lay bare your feet,
        Follow me, love,
Renounce this world
And die for our love!

I'll hold your hand,
Love, follow me;
> Let thorns pierce our feet,
> Let hailstones split our heads.
Come along with me
And I'll hold your hand
> To flee this cage, and once again be free.
> Come with me,
> Love!
The world of man is now behind us—
Look, isn't this the white boundless sea?

. . . . .

> The white boundless sea,
> The white boundless sea,
You and I, love, let's be forever free![17]

In short, Hsü's ultimate vision of love is dynamic, just as his ultimate vision of nature is dynamic. Love, like nature, is a source of inexhaustible energy. "I am fortunate, because I love, and because I have love. How great, how full is the word! With it my bosom evinces warmth, radiates light, and generates energy."[18]

Seen in our thematic perspective of sentiment, Hsü Chih-mo has indeed come a long way. He has not only persisted in glorifying sentiment ("I am a believer in sentiment; perhaps I was born a man of sentiment . . . true sentiment, true human sentiment, is precious, hard to acquire, and should be shared in common. We should not deny sentiment or suppress it, for that would be an act of crime"),[19] but also elevates love as the central manifestation and supreme consummation of sentiment. More than Yü Ta-fu, who has also alleged the centrality of love in life, Hsü has imbued it with a dynamic grandeur. While Lin Shu justifies love, Su Man-shu drifts in love, Yü Ta-fu creates his visions of love, Hsü Chih-mo embodies love itself.

The journey of sentiment has also been a journey of increasing Westernization. Lin Shu, Su Man-shu, and even Yü Ta-fu approach the West mainly through books. Hsü Chih-mo, having set foot in both America and Europe, learns by reading and personal experience. His personality and outlook on life contain few elements that can be clearly traced in Chinese tradition. His sense of mission germinates on his way to the West, and the message that he takes upon himself to spread by virtue of his life and works also comes largely from the West.

Heroes and Hero Worship

As a Western-oriented poet, Hsü could not claim to have followed his illustrious contemporaries in the West: Eliot, Yeats, or Auden, who led the way toward what is generally called "modernism" in poetry. Nor was he in any sense akin to Russian poets of his time. He was not revolutionary enough to be a Chinese Mayakovsky, nor did his experiments in poetic forms match the complexity of the formalists. A kindred spirit may be found in F. Scott Fitzgerald, but the similarities lie less in their literary craftsmanship than in their personalities. The comparison Lionel Trilling has drawn between Fitzgerald and Goethe seems also to apply to Hsü on a general level. They are all "so handsome . . . winning immediate and notorious success . . . rather more interested in life than art, each the spokesman and symbol of his own restless generation." [20] In addition, Fitzgerald and Hsü were involved in similar courtships.

But here the comparison ends. Hsü is an altogether different writer in matters of content. What has provided the major source for Hsü's poetic imagination and intellectual orientation can be found not in America, but in Europe, not the Europe of the postwar disillusionment, but a more ebullient Europe of the nineteenth century. His temperament and personal circumstances are the cause rather than his intellectual or academic grasp of Western literature.

According to his own confessions, his encounters with Western literature were ludicrously random and accidental: "I found Walter Pater one day when I looked for shelter from rain in an old bookstore. Goethe . . . was introduced to me by Stevenson. [In his *Art of Writing* he praised George Henry Lewes' book on Goethe . . .] I suddenly decided to visit Plato when I was taking a bath. Shelley was studied carefully only after I learned that he also had had a divorce. Dostoevsky, Tolstoy, d'Annunzio, Baudelaire, Rousseau—these men came to me each in his own way; none of them was introduced to me formally. It was encounter, not rendezvous." [21] Once he seized upon his Western masters, he worshiped those in whom he could find echoes of his own temperament. He liked Keats because the "low, tremulous undertone" in the "Ode to a Nightingale" gave rise to a sensation which reminded him of Beethoven's Pastoral Symphony.[22] (He gave a "fragrant" translation of the word "symphony" as *ch'in-fang-nan,* or literally "the south of distilled fragrance.") Byron was one of his favorite heroes. His admiration of Byron was similar to Su Man-shu's; he saw Byron as a man with tempestuous temper and superhuman bravery. "He stands on the crest of the waves, flaunting his flawless skin under the sunshine, with his pride, his strength, his grandeur, and his sorrow, which can come only from Zeus and Jupiter. He is a beautiful devil, a glorious rebel."[23] In his long article on Byron, Hsü in fact portrayed the English poet as a superhuman Greek god and mentioned nothing of his poetic achievements. The image of Byron that appealed to Hsü, as it had done to Su Man-shu, was that of a hero whose short life had made human history.

When he first read d'Annunzio's "The Dead City," he jotted down his impressions in his diary:

March 3—first read d'Annunzio, in Arthur Symons' translation of "The Dead City." An unmatched masterpiece. It is pure energy and heat; it is a concerto of the poetry of life and the hymn to death. Its harmonies float in the air; it's the apocalypse, incomparable phenomenon . . . It is like the stormy sea that howls infinite profundities in the solitude of space; it is like clouds, enveloping earth . . . like wind, wild wind, gushing blast, hurricane . . . Great passion which formlessly brews great, glorious tragedies! Life and death, victory and defeat, glory and sinking, sunshine and dark night, empire and nihilism, joy and sadness, absolute truth and beauty in the bottomless depths. Jump, brave seeker.[24]

The crescendo of hyperboles in Hsü's reaction to this Italian author of decadence and sensuality differs very little from his response to an earlier Romantic poet like Byron. The keynote of dynamism sets Hsü's hero worship far apart from the gentle, gloomy decadence in Yü Ta-fu's visions of Ernest Dowson. The contrast between Hsü's stormy adulation of d'Annunzio and Yü's sad and self-pitying invocation of Dowson reveals two different views about two writers who are generally regarded in the West as belonging to the same decadent Neo-romantic camp. And both of them came to their Chinese interpreters through the same literary agent, Arthur Symons.

It is apparent that Hsü approached his Western heroes "impressionistically," by seeking similarities in temper between his hero and himself. It is an emotional reaction lacking in intellectual depths, the same kind of reaction found in Su Man-shu and Yü Ta-fu and many of their contemporaries. On this "emotional" galaxy of heroes also stand Nietzsche, Goethe, Tolstoy, Dostoevsky, Tagore, Gandhi and Rolland: "This is Rolland, the brave fighter for humanity! . . . Love and sympathy, he believes, are forever the fierce weapons with which to crush hatred. He never doubts the ultimate victory of his ideals. Prior to him, there were Tolstoy and Dostoevsky . . . Contemporary with him, there are Tagore and Gandhi . . . They stand on the peaks of high mountains; their vista encompasses, in time, the totality of history and, in space, the whole of mankind." [25]

Hsü never denied his penchant for hero worship. "Of mountains we like the high ones," he once wrote, "so of men, why aren't we willing to approach the great ones?" [26] Accordingly, he worshiped particularly the two great writers whom he had personally visited: Katherine Mansfield and Thomas Hardy.

Hsü visited Katherine Mansfield and her husband, John Middleton Murry, one day in July 1922, six months before her death.[27] From reading his own accounts of the visit we can only conclude that the Murrys received him as a guest and Murry was nice enough to let Hsü chat with his ailing wife for twenty minutes. Their courteous attitude toward Hsü reflected nothing more than the decency and good manners of a highly educated couple, and Katherine Mansfield merely chatted about literature in general and nothing in particular. But the memory of this visit, as recaptured glowingly by Hsü, became a milestone in his life. "I have seen you only once—but those twenty immortal minutes!" [28] The image of Miss Mansfield became the very personification of beauty: "Of the purity, grace, and brightness of her brows, eyes, mouth, and nose I cannot convey one iota. It was as if you were confronted with a masterpiece of nature—be it the autumn moon, the clean, washed lake or mountain, the multilayered afterglow of the setting sun, or the clear, glittering skies above the South Seas

—or with a masterpiece of art: a Beethoven symphony, a Wagner opera, a sculpture of Michelangelo, a painting by Whistler or Corot.— You could only feel their total beauty, pure beauty, perfect beauty, unanalyzable, inexplicable beauty." [29] Miss Mansfield's tuberculosis-ridden voice sounded like a "miracle" to the ears of her Chinese admirer. She finally saw him to the door, her piercing gaze and "musical voice inundated my soul like thunderstorms. At that moment even if I had had self-consciousness, it could only have been like the case of Keats when he heard the nightingale:

My heart aches, and a drowsy numbness pains
My senses, as though of hemlock I had drunk

. . . . .

'Tis not through envy of thy happy lot,
But being too happy in thy happiness." [30]

In worshiping a Western writer as in worshiping nature or love, Hsü exuded the same heightened intensity of intoxication. His surging emotions invariably filled his mind with that ultimate trinity: beauty–goodness–truth. The madly ecstatic frenzy of his zeal blinded all his "intellectual" qualities. One wonders how the ailing and temperate Miss Mansfield would have borne the overpowering weight of Hsü's worship had the latter in those "immortal twenty minutes" conveyed one iota of his inner passion.

Hsü's impressions of Thomas Hardy were equally permeated with his own obsessive notions of heroism and hero worship. In his second tour of Europe in 1925, he obtained a letter of introduction from Dickinson and visited Hardy in July. The manner in which the old man treated him could at best be described as lukewarm. After a few minutes of random discussion on poetry, Hardy led our young poet to the garden, picked a flower for him as a souvenir and bade him good day! When Hardy died in 1928, Hsü wrote a long article of condolence, paying glowing tribute and recalling his visit with gratitude and respect.[31] It must have troubled him greatly to reconcile himself to Hardy's pessimistic outlook on the human condition; he was certainly not unaware of it but saw it as something positive, the wise warning of a clairvoyant, independent prophet. In his poem dedicated to Hardy's memory are found the following lines:

> To defend the dignity of his thought,
> A poet such as he cannot be idle.
> Holding high his ideals, opening wide his eyes,
> He plucks the errors of human life.[32]

To emphasize further Hardy's dignity of mind, Hsü wrote: "Hardy only wishes to preserve his freedom of thought, to preserve the everlasting privileges of his soul—to preserve his right of obstinate questionings."[33] The quotation of Hardy's famous phrase, "obstinate questionings" in its original English is noteworthy. It indicates, in the first place, that Hsü's justification of Hardy's pessimism was based on Hardy's own justification in his "Apology": "What is today, in allusions to the present author's pages, alleged to be 'pessimism" is, in truth, only such 'obstinate questionings' in the exploration of reality . . . (as) is the first step towards the soul's betterment, and the body's also."[34] Second, it indicates that Hsü had probably read few of Hardy's novels, which are heavy with a feeling of the "apparent helplessness of mankind."[35] In other words, his admiration was based almost entirely on Hardy's poetry.[36] It was the sense of intimate simplicity with an "accent of unmistakable sincerity"[37] in Hardy's poetry that inspired another paragraph of Hsü's Hardy poem:

> Not that he does not have love—
> He loves sincerity, he loves passion.
> Even if life is but a dream,
> It is not devoid of consolation.[38]

No doubt, it is "this deep, moving, and easily accessible humanity" in Hardy that unites Hsü with his master.[39] But Hsü seems to have missed the central message of Hardy's poetry, which obviously runs counter to his temperament. As one leading critic of Hardy remarks, his poetry as a whole conveys "the sense of life as a succession of small, undramatic defeats; the honest declarations of unfaith and 'unhope.' "[40] Surprisingly, Hsü saw fit to put this deeply grieved cynic at the end of an intellectual tradition which began with Rousseau: "His [Rousseau's] words and actions marked the formal birth of modern 'self-emancipation' and 'self-consciousness.' From the *Confessions* to the French Revolution, from the French Revolution to the Romantic movement, from the Romantic movement to Nietzsche (and Dostoevsky), from Nietzsche to Hardy—in those 170 years we have seen the bursting emotions of men break loose from the confines of reason and swoop down like flames from which various other movements and doctrines are mere offshoots." [41]

In depicting this tradition from Rousseau to Hardy, Hsü was in fact seeing it in the general perspective of European romanticism. Rousseau's *Confessions* indeed provided a "lengthy analysis of the manifestation of the individual personality, the *moi*, different from the personalities of other men." [42] It was also Rousseau who "proclaimed the natural goodness of the human emotions and their efficacy as a guide to human conduct." [43] Hsü's notions of "self-emancipation" and "self-consciousness" are but dynamic images which accentuate one of the Rousseauean legacies: the romantic creed of human emotions. He would have also included in this tradition Madame de Staël and George Sand who argued that "if virtue resides in the human emotions, the noblest of these emotions is unquestionably love; and to love must therefore be the supreme act of virtue." [44]

Many of Hsü's favorite Western authors in his pantheon of heroes belong in one way or another to this romantic tradition. Rousseau, Byron, Shelley, Keats, Baudelaire (whom Hsü regarded as "the confessor of the nineteenth century just as Rousseau had been in the eighteenth century and Dante in the medieval times"), d'Annunzio, Nietzsche, and Romain Rolland. [45] Those literary figures who do not fit into such a category are viewed through Hsü's own romantic lenses, thereby transformed into romantic heroes. Thus he found no difficulty in summing up Hardy, Tolstoy, Rolland, Tagore, and Russell by remarking that "their tender voices invariably called up the tender elements in human nature and awakened them, so as to sweep away all kinds of obstacles with love's boundless power and, with the power of our mutual love, to . . . destroy all kinds of ideologies and propaganda which restrict our freedom and degrade human dignity." [46]

The general range of Hsü's Western heroes and heroines can be gauged in the long list of names mentioned in connection with his second trip to Europe in 1925. The trip was described by himself as a "sentimental journey" at least on two accounts: emotionally, to test his own sentiments toward Hsiao-man and intellectually to seek his kindred spirits in Europe. He had intended chiefly to see Tagore again but also to visit Romain Rolland in France, d'Annunzio in Italy, and Hardy in England. Eventually he saw only Hardy.[47] He also diverted himself by attending performances of "La Traviata" in Berlin, Hamlet (with John Barrymore playing the lead) in London, and Wagner's "Tristan and Isolde" in Paris. He identified himself with Tristan and imagined Hsiao-man as Isolde paying her last visit; the idea and music in the famous love-death scene impressed him as earth-shaking.[48] He had also enough time to pay his tribute to the graves of Chekhov, Kropotkin, Mansfield, Marguerite Gautier (La Dame aux Camélias), Heine, Baudelaire, Voltaire, Rousseau, Hugo, Shelley, Keats, Elizabeth Browning, Michelangelo, the Medicis, Dante, St. Francis, Virgil, and his own son.[49] Hsü's personal propensities in Western literature revealed themselves clearly in this list; he was taking a sentimental journey through the history of romanticism. One can further accentuate this romantic list by recording the names of authors whose works Hsü has translated; predictably, one finds the poetry of Byron, Shelley, Keats, Rossetti, Tagore, Hardy, Elizabeth Browning, Coleridge, Swinburne, Schiller, Whitman, the short stories of d'Annunzio, and Mansfield; and somewhat unexpectedly, a *Charwoman's Daughter* by James Stephens, Voltaire's *Candide*, and *Undine*, a fairy tale by Friedrich Heinrich Karl, Baron de la Motte Fouqué.

Icarus Ascendant

Hsü's fascination with European romanticism is also psychologically revealing. From one entry in his diary we learn that he weighs 136 pounds.[50] The few blurred photos we find in the collections of his works present the profile of a gentle, suave, and somewhat effeminate man. Spectacles with dark, thin frames accentuate an oblong and pallid face with sensitive, piercing eyes. He often wore a long gown which curiously half-covered a pair of Western-style trousers. The profile is in many ways reminiscent of the familiar self-portrait of Yü

Ta-fu. But the impression Hsü conveys to his friends and in his works is almost the opposite of Yü's gentle melancholia and decadence. It is the disparity between Hsü's inner dynamism and his far from robust outer appearance that makes him so interesting.

Love in Hsü's poetry is often defined in dynamic terms. Moreover, love is personified in women, both real, such as Lu Hsiao-man and imaginary, such as the female narrators in the love monologues of "Love's Inspiration" and "A Night in Florence." In both cases, Hsü's heroines are possessors of consuming passion, hardly the fragile "persecuted" type in the fictional works of Yü Ta-fu or Su Man-shu. Yet Hsü's emotional identification with his heroines is never total. In two of his prose pieces, both bearing the same title, "Too Dense to Dissolve," Hsü provides a rare sample of his sexual fantasies. The two pieces describe two dreamy encounters. One presumably takes place in Hong Kong: the hero's erotic desires are aroused while following an enigmatic, voluptuous girl into a mysterious cave. When he finally re-emerges from the cave and loses sight of the girl, a sudden confrontation with the beauty of nature dissolves—and sublimates—his sexual desire.[51] In the second piece, the setting changes to hot and humid Singapore. The same hero dreams of meeting a voluptuous, prostitute-like "chocolate" girl who gradually and aggressively imposes her immense sensuality on his fragile and sweating body.[52] When one juxtaposes the two poems with these two prose pieces, a curious combination of craving and fear reveals itself. Hsü has once "psychoanalyzed" himself through the mouth of an imagined friend: "Precisely because you cannot find equilibrium in your life, precisely because you have desires which have not attained fulfillment, the *libido* [his own term in English] repressed inside you has produced the phenomenon of sublimation. As a result, you use literature to release your accumulated psychological knots."[53] Hence the imagined yearnings of the heroine in "A Night in Florence." In that memorable night when his fictional Florentine woman was supposedly consumed by passion, Hsü was in fact consumed by his own yearning for Hsiaoman. (We find in his letter to Hsiao-man written in Florence on May 27, 1925: "If I can't go to sleep once I am in bed, I call 'Man.' And as Man does not answer me, my heart is sour.")[54]

A similar theme can also be found in Hsü's hero worship. His images of heroes disclose a common feature of real or imagined strength and grandeur. One notices especially his portrait of Byron as a young pagan god flaunting his flawless skin under the sun, which calls to mind, among others, the young lad in Thomas Mann's "Death in Venice." Craving to be a Byronic hero yet lacking a massive, masculine stature, Hsü seems to find psychological compensation in adulation of essentially foreign and fiery heroes and heroines. His conscious, intellectual justification of European romanticism thus blends with a psychological need. It is from this angle that we could see him as approaching the true archetype of the artist in European romanticism, the image of Icarus.

Hsü Chih-mo had always wanted to fly. In his celebrated essay, "Wanting to Fly" he wrote: "Everybody wants to fly. It is so tiresome to be crawling on earth all the time, not to mention anything else. Let's fly away from this circle! To the clouds! To the clouds! Who does not dream of soaring up in the sky to watch the earth roll like a ball in infinite space? . . . That alone is the meaning of being man. If this fleshy carcass of ours is too heavy to be dragged along, throw it away. Whenever possible, fly away from this circle, fly away from this circle!" [55]

This metaphoric passage certainly describes more than his physical exhilaration for flying. We can find a revealing parallel in Theophile Gautier's famous summation of the 1830s, the high tide of French romanticism: "The fate of Icarus frightened no one. Wings! wings! wings! they cried from all sides, even if we should fall into the sea. To fall from the sky, one must climb there, even for but a moment, and that is more beautiful than to spend one's whole life crawling on the earth." [56]

Like the French romanticists who "hoped to soar above the *profanum vulgus* and the realities of nineteenth century life," [57] Hsü wanted to rise above all the "sorrow and joy, parting and reunion, strife and existence" of life in twentieth-century China.[58] For Hsü, to fly also means to attain total freedom, to go beyond the reaches of social convention. Moreover, the desire of soaring high up in the sky is for both Hsü and his French predecessors a symbolic assertion of the self-styled superiority of the *artiste*, being carried above other philistine mortals on the wings of artistic genius and sensitivity.

From a psychological perspective, both Hugo and Hsü can be regarded as good examples of the "ascensionist" personality in Dr. Henry A. Murray's Icarus syndrome, which is characterized by "passionate enthusiasm, rapid elevations of confidence, flights of imagination, exaltation, inflation of spirits, ecstatic mystical up-reachings." [59] Furthermore, Hsü has fully embodied what Dr. Murray has noted in an Icarian personality as "an unprecedented upsurge or excess of psychic energy (spontaneity, creative zest, self-confidence, and enthusiasm)." [60] All these Icarian elements did not merely produce, as Hsü once described in his self-anatomy, "the phenomenon of sublimation." Hsü was not content simply to "sublimate" his psychic energies in his writings. His boundless passion, his "whirlwind" behavior among his friends, his "fits of shouting and jumping," his vicissitudes of moods —"suddenly melancholy or joyous"—all seem to indicate that the excessive dynamism in his own life and personality has propelled him to be an Icarus. In searching for the ideal of love and in worshiping titanic heroes, he was indeed attempting to shake off his own "fleshy carcass." Thus in the ultimate act of flying are consummated all the dynamic traits in his personality, and the "up-reachings" of his dynamism seem to prompt him to go even beyond his own limits.

But the fate of Icarus, after ascending to the zenith of passion, is to be consumed in its flames. Hsü seemed to have such intimations. At the end of his essay on "Wanting to Fly," he wrote: "Suddenly the wings are slanting, and a ball of light swoops all the way down, clashing in a boom—and breaking up my imaginings while in flight." [61] And he died a truly Icarian death.

After 1929, owing to his teaching duties, Hsü often commuted by airplane, first between Nanking and Shanghai, then between Shanghai and Peking, at a time when commercial aviation in China was only in its beginning stage. Air travel was still a dangerous affair, but Hsü relished its speed and convenience. Moreover, a friend in the aviation company had given him a courtesy pass, so he could travel free. [62] On November 19, 1931, when he was flying from Shanghai to Peking to resume his teaching at Peking University, the plane which carried him along with two pilots crashed in dense fog against the peak of a hill near Tsinan in Shantung province.[63] Hsü died, like the young Icarus, in the flames of his "wings." As a romantic personality, Hsü alone had also re-enacted its archetypal myth.

In dying at the peak of his creative power before premonitions of despair had dragged him down, Hsü had avoided the second half of the Icarian sequence in European Romanticism—the fate of the "fallen Icarus"—the regression into narcissistic decadence as represented by Wilde or Baudelaire, by seeking a haven from life in art.[64] In the Chinese context, however, Hsü was fortunate to have escaped the fate of Yü Ta-fu: to compromise his art with his life, and his life with his society. Nor did Hsü have to face the increasingly ominous dilemma of the choice between artistic creativity or political conformity, a dilemma that crippled many of his contemporaries who drifted toward the left.

A great number of memorial poems were written by Hsü's friends after his death. Yet none seems more fitting to the memory of Hsü Chih-mo than the following lines from one of his own poems:

Waiting for her to sing, we watch silently,
Afraid of startling her. But she flutters her wings,
Penetrating the density and merging into a colored cloud;
Thither she has flown, gone, no more—
Like the light of Spring, like flames of fire, like passion.[65]

Part Three The Romantic Left

Three Creationists: Kuo Mo-jo (left),
Yü Ta-fu (center), Ch'eng Fang-wu (right)

I am a worshiper of idols.
I am I!
My ego is about to burst.
—Kuo Mo-jo

Chapter 9

Kuo Mo-jo

On May 30, 1925, several thousand people in Shanghai marched to the International Settlement in protest against the killing of a Chinese worker by a Japanese foreman. A panic-stricken British police officer shouted orders to fire. Ten demonstrators were killed and over fifty were wounded.[1] This famous May Thirtieth Incident sent tumultuous waves across the country: protests, demonstrations, strikes, boycotts, and militant anti-imperialism soon enveloped the entire nation. The burgeoning Chinese Communist Party profited by this nationwide indignation; its membership increased to 20,000 by 1925.[2]

The impact of the incident on the political sensibilities of literary men was immense. Cheng Chen-to, one of the leaders of the Association for Literary Studies, wrote in the *Hsiao-shuo yüeh-pao:* "Nothing surprised and frightened me more than the May Thirtieth Incident."[3] Yeh Shao-chün, another eminent member of the association and by no means politically radical, recounted angrily his experience of the day after the incident: "Hurrying to the front door of the police station, I wanted to pay a pilgrimage to my comrades' blood stains, I wanted to lick with my tongue all the blood stains and swallow them into my stomach. But there was nothing, not a tiny bit. They had been swept away by the water pumps of our foes, stamped away by the corrupted ones, cleaned away by the devilish, torrential rain." [4] Yeh's fury was echoed by the poet Chu Tzu-ch'ing in the following lines:

> Bloody mouths!
> Bloody mouths!
> Crying and cursing,
> Spit on him, you, and me!
>   Blood of the Chinese people!
> Blood of the Chinese people!
> All are our brothers,
> All are our brothers! [5]

Such indignant outbursts from these usually more sedate association members were clear indications of the increasingly heated political climate of the literary scene. When the sympathies of the literary intellectuals for the plight of the industrial workers in Shanghai were aroused, the way was paved for a general drift toward the left. Chiang Kai-shek's 1927 massacre of Communists further entrenched them in their leftism.

The leftward trend charted a new course for the development of New Literature. Slogans like "proletarian literature" and "revolutionary literature" began to appear in the late twenties. A series of heated debates between Lu Hsün and some younger enthusiasts of proletarian literature led to a series of translations from Soviet theoreticians. Most were done by Lu Hsün himself or under his sponsorship. The chief instigators and popularizers of this leftist trend, however, were some of the members of the Creation Society and its associate organ, the Sun Society. Kuo Mo-jo, one of the leaders of the Creation Society, was also the first and leading exponent of leftist literature, having declared his conversion to Marxism as early as 1924. Chiang Kuang-tz'u, one of the founders of the Sun Society, was one of its most fervent practitioners. His life can be regarded as the epitome of this urban leftist phenomenon. Hsiao Chün, the third figure included in this portion, adds a sequel to this trend by exemplifying in his life and works the fate of the leftist writer in changed circumstances since the 1930s.

Kuo Mo-jo as a Young Rebel

Born in Sha-wan, Szechwan province, on November 16, 1892, Kuo Mo-jo was four years Yü Ta-fu's senior.[6] He also had a similar educational background. Introduced to formal study when he was barely four, the young boy went through the popular ritual of kowtowing in front of the statue of Confucius. As in the case of all the youngsters of his age, his first book was the *Three Character Classic*. Later on he was taught to read the classics and T'ang poetry. He liked Li Po, but not Tu Fu; preferred Wang Wei, Meng Hao-jan, Liu Tsung-yüan, and hated Han Yü.[7] At the age of eleven or twelve, Kuo was attracted, as was Yü Ta-fu, to works of traditional fiction: the *Romance of the Western Chamber, Interesting Tales of West Lake*, and *Scars of Romance*. While these pieces of fiction aroused Yü's sentimentality, the precocious Kuo found them sexually stimulating and began to indulge in masturbation at the age of eleven.[8] The impression one might gather from this bold revelation is that, unlike Yü Ta-fu, young Kuo took great pride in his budding energies. He believed that the rumor of his breech birth signified "the first step in my life toward becoming a rebel."[9] Brought up in an area where bandits were numerous, he developed a fascination for these grass-roots heroes. His grandfather supposedly had had connections with banditry; his father, in addition to being a "medium landlord" and a local magnate, was also engaged in trading tobacco and liquor,[10] an enterprise that might interest smugglers and bandits. It was said that the young Kuo loved guns and enjoyed participating in armed clashes between the rival Kuo and Yang clans; he even beat up a youngster from the Yang family.[11]

When the examination system was abolished and new-style schools opened in the provinces, Kuo, like Yü, enrolled in one of them at Chia-ting. His rebellious spirit was further developed by his activism in student movements. After confronting the school principal and receiving a "big demerit," Kuo found himself one of the student leaders. Again the pattern was typical, but Kuo emerged from these experiences a different man from Yü. Instead of becoming an introvert, Kuo began drinking and smoking, and with his "sworn brothers," frequented theaters of Peking opera, flirted with the performers, and got involved in fist-fighting. He followed the school fashion of homo-sexuality. When he graduated from the elementary school in 1907, he ranked third in the entire graduating class for his academic achievements.[12]

In the fall of 1907, Kuo entered the Chia-ting Middle School and continued his misconduct. His homosexual activities included occasional visits to male prostitutes. His dominant role in student strikes soon earned him the title of one of the school's "eight big stars."[13] In 1909, he was ejected from Chia-ting Middle School; he went to Chengtu and enrolled in another school there. On November 25, 1911, following in the wake of the Wuchang uprising, Chengtu declared independence. On the eve of the previous day, Kuo had already cut his queue.[14]

Kuo's early intellectual development, like that of Yü Ta-fu and Hsü Chih-mo, was dominated by the journalistic writings of Liang Ch'i-ch'ao. He immersed himself in Liang's *Ch'ing-i pao*, and Liang's description of the three national heroes of Italy captivated Kuo in Sze-chwan as much as it engrossed Hsü Chih-mo in Worcester, Massa-chusetts. Cavour, Garibaldi, and Mazzini became his heroes, fervently worshiped together with Napoleon and Bismarck.[15] Kuo's admiration of these statesmen-heroes reflected the general nationalistic mood among young students. The slogans of "enriching the country and strengthening the military" still resounded in their youthful minds. Yen Fu's translations of Montesquieu, Spencer, and Huxley were read avidly. New schools of politics and law (*cheng-fa*) mushroomed; in the provincial capital of Chengtu itself there were no fewer than forty to fifty such schools.[16] To study "practical" subjects—practical for building the new republic—was the fashion of the day. "Almost every young man could be said to be a nationalist . . . All those who had even a slight ambition wanted to learn something practical so as to make the country strong."[17] Under the impact of the new tides, Kuo purposefully curbed his literary inclinations and took up medicine, a compromise choice, since he avoided law and economics for lack of interest and forsook natural sciences because of his fear of mathe-matics.[18]

In 1913 he left home for Tientsin in order to enter the army medical school there. During the entrance examination he was asked to write a Chinese composition on the brand-new topic of "total and unit," that is, society and individual.[19] Although he passed the examination, he failed to register. Instead, he followed the more "prestigious" trend and went to Japan in January 1914, shortly after Yü Ta-fu arrived there with his brother.

Pantheism

In Japan, Kuo was admitted to the preparatory class of the First Higher School in Tokyo in the fall of 1914, where he met Yü Ta-fu. He was then assigned to the Sixth Higher School in Akayama. Upon graduation in 1918, he entered the medical school of Kyushu Imperial University at Fukuoka.

While Yü was attracted to Japanese women and vented his sexual frustrations in his first stories, Kuo did much better by actually falling in love—first "platonically" and then physically—with a Japanese girl, Sato Tomiko, who in fact became his common-law wife and bore him five children. Yü's sexuality was awakened in Japan; Kuo's was fulfilled. While Yü vacillated between social sciences and medicine, Kuo persisted in his medical studies. Yü's sense of quandary and superfluity is noticeably absent in Kuo's reminiscences of his Japanese years. His complaints about the humiliations inflicted upon him by the Japanese people, unlike Yü's, do not seem to be motivated by deep psychological disturbances, although Kuo, too, often indulges in self-pity. Perhaps the fact that in childhood he was often at the center of action kept him from feeling left out in Japan. Confronted with similar environmental stimuli, Kuo was able to react more positively than Yü. This can be seen most vividly in their intellectual preoccupations and literary creations.

Kuo Mo-jo was first exposed to Western literature through the translations of Lin Shu. In his autobiography, he singled out three works as having left an indelible impression on his youthful mind: Haggard's *Joan Haste*, Scott's *Ivanhoe*, and *Tales from Shakespeare* by Lamb.[20] While the last work appealed to the boy's fancy for stories and storytelling, the two novels by Haggard and Scott in fact epitomized two major strands in Kuo's personality: his sentimentalism and his hero-worshiping tendencies, two omnipresent traits among his contemporaries.

With regard to *Joan Haste,* Kuo recalled: "How that herone elicited my deep-felt sympathies and induced large quantities of my tears! I pitied her and I admired her lover, Henry . . . I imagined that should I have such a charming girl as Joan who loved me, I would die content for her by falling from the top of a tower on Ling-yun mountain." [21] Kuo's maudlin response and the sentimental images he indulged in can be readily compared with Yü Ta-fu's reminiscences of his youth. Although Lin Shu's translations were noticeably absent in Yü's intellectual development, emotionally both were nourished by the same "talent-beauty" type of traditional Chinese sentimental novels. Kuo has repeatedly admitted the lachrymose quality of his personality: "I am a man with highly developed lachrymal glands, always overflowing with tears." [22] This personal trait has led him to assert that "those who can shed tears are invariably good men; those poems which can move people to tears are always good poetry." [23]

But Kuo's sentimentalism seems to lose its luster against the two supreme examples of Yü Ta-fu and Hsü Chih-mo. His youthful dream of finding a charming girl like Joan Haste who would love him seemed to come true in the person of Anna, his Japanese mistress and common-law wife. But in his letters to T'ien Han, Kuo described the whole affair as if it were the ruthless defloration of a pure Christian virgin.[24] The affair in fact lost the last bit of its sentimental attraction with the birth of their children. The former Japanese nurse became simply another housewife and our poet was burdened more and more by the trifling chores of family life. The trilogy of family life which Kuo wrote in 1924,[25] obviously inspired by a similar account by Yü Ta-fu, pales in comparison with the sincerity and the depth of feeling with which Yü wrote of his first wife. Nor can one find in Kuo's autobiographical works the kind of genuine passion which characterized Hsü Chih-mo's attitude toward his women. Neither Hsü nor Yü would be able, as Kuo did with a total lack of compassion, to write a mocking account of his arranged marriage to his childhood fiancée.[26]

Kuo's sentimentalism, therefore, is more apparent than real, more for public display than as private emotion. The dominant trait in Kuo's personality has to be sought elsewhere. In addition to Haggard's *Joan Haste*, Kuo described Sir Walter Scott's *Ivanhoe* as exerting a "decisive" impact on him in "visibly bringing to me that romantic spirit."[27] Thus, in his mind, the reigning "romantic spirit" consisted not so much of sentimental love as of chivalry and heroism, a theme that was well in line with his youthful role as a self-appointed rebel. It also paved the way for his fervent espousal of "pantheism" in Japan.

When Kuo was a student of medicine in Japan, a classmate at the First Higher School introduced him to the works of Tagore, whose "light and fresh flavor" enlivened him. For students of medicine, German was taught as the first foreign language requirement, which led Kuo to read such works as Goethe's autobiographical *Dichtung und Wahrheit* and Mörike's *Mozart auf Reise nach Prague*. Thus, through Tagore he came to know Kabir and the Upanishads of ancient India, and through Goethe he approached the works of Spinoza. These Western works revived his interest in Chuang Tzu.[28] He had also become engrossed in the philosophy of Wang Yang-ming. From his reading of these Chinese and Western masterpieces, he proclaimed himself an ardent believer in pantheism, which he found to be the common thread running through all these works, and which "led him almost inevitably to Western romanticism."[29]

What, then, is Kuo's conception of pantheism? He revealed the true nature of his propensities by giving the following exuberant summary: "Pantheism means atheism. All nature is the manifestation of God; I am also a manifestation of God. Therefore I am God; all nature is a manifestation of myself."[30] Thus, to become selfless or to merge the self with God or nature meant for Kuo not the negative sense of losing oneself in nature but positively identifying oneself with the basic dynamic force of the universe which "is the source of the myriad beings, the will of the universe, the *Ding an sich* of things."[31] In short, one might argue that Kuo Mo-jo's conception of pantheism comes very close to Hsü Chih-mo's theory of love and nature: both represent a kind of reductionist dynamism which betrays more an impetuous inclination to act than profound philosophic speculation. Accordingly, Kuo's notion of pantheism should never be interpreted apart from the heroic streak in his personality and the theme of the "rebel" in his thought: underlying both is an activistic ethos which asserts and imposes his personality on his general outlook of life and society. The numerous other traits in Kuo's later intellectual development, it seems to me, all spring from this fundamental source.

As Kuo was immersed in pantheistic works, once during his second year at Kyushu Imperial University he bought a Japanese book by Arishima Takeo (1878–1923) entitled *Hangyakusha* (Rebels), which discussed three "rebel" artists: Rodin, Millet, and Whitman.[32] The book led him to Whitman's *Leaves of Grass* just as he was beginning to write poems and send them to the literary supplement of *Shih-shih hsin-pao* in Shanghai. The editor, Tsung Pai-hua, "who seemed also to be inclined toward a fondness for pantheism,"[33] became Kuo's friend through correspondence. Kuo's "pride in seeing his poems in print for the first time produced an explosion of poetic activity."[34] Thus began the Whitman period of his poetic development (from 1919 to 1921)—the most memorable period in his own assessment and also his most productive and successful period. In one poem written in this period, under the revealing title, "Hymn to the Bandits," Kuo sang unstinting praises of Cromwell, Washington, José Rizal, Marx, Engels, Lenin, Sakyamuni, Mo Tzu, Luther, Copernicus, Darwin, Nietzsche, Rodin, Whitman, Tolstoy, Rousseau, Pestalozzi, and Tagore.[35]

Kuo's mania of hero worship not only penetrated his works but also pervaded his life style in Japan. On the walls of his house in Japan were hung a portrait of Beethoven and a painting by Millet. His three sons became the owners of three domesticated rabbits in the house: one which limped was named Byron, the other two were naturally called Shelley and Keats.[36] He regretted that at his Japanese abode he could find no stools in the pine woods, for otherwise he could imagine himself to be the Goethe of Giekelhahn; and no boats on the sea, thus depriving him of a chance to roam on starry nights and to be drowned in water like Shelley. His aspiration to re-enact Keats was only partially fulfilled by his sitting in a Japanese fishing vessel and addressing to his friends a letter "writ in water."[37] When

T'ien Han visited him and the two men went out for a scenic trip, they reminded themselves constantly of their favorite poets and artists. A bird's chirrup would find confirmation in Shelley's ode "To a Skylark"; a walk in the moonlight would invoke the legend of Beethoven's "Moonlight Sonata"; the clouds on mountain peaks were compared to the sculpture of Rodin; resting in the pine woods, Kuo recalled a poem by Li Po; after a drink in a roadside inn, the two poets chatted about Maeterlinck's *Blue Bird;* and finally, totally drunk, they went into a Japanese temple in order to find a sculptor to carve two bronze statues of Goethe and Schiller.[38] Returning at dusk, T'ien Han told Mo-jo: "In fact you resemble Shelley." "Why?" "Because Shelley once studied medicine, and you, too, study medicine . . . But in other relationships you resemble Goethe." "What relationships?" "Female relationships!"[39]

It is only too apparent that the heroes they conjured up come predominantly from European romanticism. This romantic aura also envelops Kuo's idiosyncratic interpretation of his favorite figures in the Chinese tradition. Ch'ü Yüan, the solitary genius and poet-statesman of the ancient Ch'u state, topped his list of Chinese heroes. Kuo wrote a play on Ch'ü Yüan in which he used his hero to bring out his own miseries. Ch'ü Yüan's pride, his impetuosity, the nobility of his frustrated ambitions became a model of tragic greatness which Kuo pathetically attempted to relate to his own parasitic existence as an exile in Japan.[40] He would later deny his identification with Goethe but proudly acknowledge himself as Ch'ü Yüan's modern avatar, for, after all, Goethe's feudal allegiances made him less heroic than Ch'ü Yüan.

Nor did Kuo hesitate to impose his own *Weltanschauung* on other ancient Chinese philosophers. Hui Shih, the "logician" of the Warring States period, was regarded as "a thorough human being . . . a thoroughly human individual who embodied all the human virtues and vices."[41] Kuo compared Lao Tzu to Nietzsche by stressing their rebellious spirits: "Both of them rebelled against theistic religious thought, against the established morality which confined individual personality. Both based themselves on individuality and endeavored to develop themselves positively."[42] And most amazingly, Kuo reinterpreted Confucius in the same light, thereby instilling the much needed dynamic element into his conception of traditional Chinese culture. The lack of such a dynamism, we recall, is the central theme of Hsü Chih-mo's sweeping attack on Chinese tradition. Kuo declared that he worshiped Confucius because the sage Master had "exerted his personality to the fullest possible extent—in depth as well as in breadth . . . His real life was a piece of beautiful poetry. His physique could never be matched by that of those neurotic modern poets. The harmony and perfection of his body and mind complemented each other. He had the strength of a Samson." [43] At the end of his eulogy, Kuo summarized his fascination with pre-Ch'in philosophers: "Whether in Lao Tzu or in Confucius or in ancient thought before them we can find the following two messages from the heart:

—to see all existence as the actual realization of dynamism!
—to embark upon all endeavors as the free realization of the self.[44]

One may debate, academically, the validity of Kuo's interpretation, but one cannot but be overwhelmed by the shattering exuberance of Kuo's feverish visions, which for their grandeur and dynamism even surpassed those of his contemporary, Hsü Chih-mo. And like Hsü Chih-mo, Kuo's *Weltanschauung* was deeply imbedded in his personality.

The Hero as Poet

While Kuo's pantheistic-heroic philosophy could be seen as a projection of his own personality, it also contributed to the shaping of this personality. Chronologically, the important fact is that Kuo's initial immersion in pantheism coincided with the genesis of his literary creativity. He became interested in Goethe and Spinoza in 1918–1919. In the fall of 1918, his first short story began to take shape, the product of his idle reveries in the anatomy lab sessions. The story, entitled "Skull," was "reminiscent of the worst excesses of European romanticism or the Gothic horror tales of 'Monk Lewis' and Charles Robert Maturin." [45] In the early autumn of the next year, some of his poems were first published. His published correspondence with Tsung Pai-hua was in fact a series of vivid accounts of the transformation of his identity from that of a medical student to that of a poet. The familiar symptoms of identity confusion—quandary, depression, self-indulgent decadence, sense of humiliation at the hands of the Japanese —were all acknowledged by Kuo Mo-jo. On January 18, 1920, he wrote to Tsung Pai-hua: "My own personality is really rotten to the core. I feel more depraved than Goldsmith, more piqued than Heine, more decadent than Baudelaire . . . Now I want very much to be like the phoenix . . . to burn my present body . . . and to be reborn a new 'I' from its cold ashes."[46] In another letter dated February 16, 1920, he made the following confession:

I often regret that I lack the genius of an Augustine, a Rousseau or a Tolstoy, that I might write a naked "confession," and thus reveal myself to the world. Unless I rid myself completely of my past, my future will be enveloped in dark shadows, without any hope of development. If I do not rid myself completely of my burden of guilt, my pitiful soul will remain embroiled in a sea of tears, with no prospect of escape. In the past, the only solution I could see to my problems was death; but now I have adopted a different approach, and want to move in the direction of life. In the past I lived as a devil in darkest hell; from now on I want to live as a man in the world of light.[47]

His correspondence with Tsung Pai-hua and T'ien Han "had apparently helped him recover from the mood of depression into which he had fallen in medical school."[48] But it was the pantheistic writers that provided the backdrop of affirmation. If Goethe had taught him to be weary of the weakening of his vital energies by the excesses of the intellect, it was Whitman who revived his rebellious tendencies by providing him with a kind of "rebel-prophetic" vision.[49] David Roy perceptively comments that "it was Whitman's consuming sense of mission and the feeling he conveys of being driven to create by some compelling force that probably had the greatest influence on Kuo Mo-jo."[50] To Kuo, this compelling force can be no other than the vital energies of a human individual, which, in Kuo's pantheistic scheme, reflect the more metaphysical source of cosmic energies.

In 1919, he read Carlyle's "Of Heroes and Hero-Worship" and wrote a poem in which he proclaimed at the end: "Oh Hero-poet!/Oh proletarian poet!" [51] From 1919 to 1920, he wrote poetry feverishly. "During these months, I was intoxicated by poetry almost every day. Whenever I was attacked by poetic inspiration, I acted as if I had contracted a fever . . . I shivered as I picked up the pen and sometimes could hardly write. I have since said: 'Poetry is written, not wrought.' " [52] Thus, poetry becomes for Kuo "a strain flowing from the well of life, a melody played on the lute strings of the heart, a tremor of life, a cry of the soul." [53] Poetic creation becomes the process of releasing the potentialities of man; and by virtue of his creative act a poet becomes a hero. Kuo Mo-jo had finally found his own heroic role as a poet. In April of 1921, as he suddenly left Japan for his homeland, he "actually had the feeling of 'new Birth,' and everything in front of my eyes seemed to be singing the paeans of life." [54]

The period from 1921 to 1924 witnessed Kuo's immense power and volume of literary creativity. In addition to traveling back and forth between China and Japan, he also translated the first book of Nietzsche's *Thus Spoke Zarathustra*, Fitzgerald's *The Rubaiyat of Omar Khayyam*, Theodor Storm's *Immensee*, part of Goethe's *Faust*, a number of poems by English and German Romantic poets—Shelley, Grey, Heine—and a work which became the bible of modern Chinese youth, *The Sorrows of Young Werther*.

Besides his translation activities, Kuo was instrumental in founding, in July 1921, the Creation Society with friends he had known in Japan. Together they published *Creation Quarterly*, *Creation Weekly*, and *Creation Day*. While the founding members were together responsible for the format and content of these publications, the initial conception and ideology may have been supplied by Kuo himself. In the first issue of the *Creation Quarterly* appeared his poem, "The Creator," which served as a manifesto of the Society.

More than an ecstatic proclamation of the founding of a literary journal, the poem signified the consummation of a spectacular process which led Kuo to assume the new role of hero-poet. References to his favorite authors, invocations of cosmic forces, hyperbolic tributes to the creative act—in short, all of his pantheistic-heroic attributes converge in the poem to evoke that ultimate dynamic hero of Chinese mythology, P'an Ku.

I conjure the first God of man,
I conjure P'an Ku, founder of Heaven and Earth.
He is the Spirit of Creation,
He is the pain of birth;
Listen, his voice is like majestic thunder,
Listen, his breath is the wind;
Look, his eyes flash like lightning,
Look, his tears are the streaming waters.
Reality is He, God is He;
He was before the Infinite
He is exterior to the Senses;
From his own corporeal being
He created a glorious world.
His eyes became the Sun and Moon,
His hair became the trees and grasses,
His flesh the rivers and seas.
O joy, joy, joy,
From the dark primal chaos,
Suddenly emerged the light.
O laurel, for whom do you sway? [55]

Kuo's explicit evocation of P'an Ku is couched in images of dynamism similar to those in Hsü Chih-mo's poem, "Love's Inspiration." The ultimate realm for the ebullient poetic imagination of both men lies in mythology. And Kuo asserted further that only poets are capable of creating the world of myth, for "the world of myth is born from man's faculty of feeling, not from his faculty of reason." [56]

In addition to editing the Creation Society journals, Kuo also wrote and published his own poetry. The most significant testimony to Kuo's stature as a poet is his first collection of poetry published in 1921. "Goddesses" was a collage of all the ideas and emotions which had dominated him in the past three or four years. Some of his heroes —Ch'ü Yüan, Beethoven, and Carlyle—received fervid tributes. But the most lavish and pretentious eulogies he reserved for himself. In a poem titled, "Heavenly Hound," Kuo presents a typically pantheistic and "egotistical view of the universe":

I am a Heavenly Hound!
I have swallowed the moon,
I have swallowed the sun,

I have swallowed the myriad stars,
I have swallowed the entire universe.
I am I!

I am the splendor of the moon,
I am the splendor of the sun,
I am the splendor of the myriad stars,
I am the total energy of the universe.

I run swiftly,
I cry wildly,
I burn fiercely.

. . . . .

I am I!
My ego is about to burst.[57]

Never in the history of Chinese poetry has the word "I" appeared
with such persistent frequency as in the above poem. Its presence
accentuates the omnipotence of the subjective ego in Kuo's frame of
thinking. In both form and content, the poetry of Kuo Mo-jo is far
more Western than Chinese in its original source of inspiration. The
indebtedness of most poems cited here to Walt Whitman in terms of
poetics has been convincingly demonstrated by Achilles Fang.[58] Their
underlying pantheistic ethos, which Kuo attributed to both Chinese
and Western sources, proclaims in fact the ultimate view of European
romanticism—the notion of the free individual spirit of man struggling against and holding sway over nature and society. Following
Spinoza, romantic pantheism hinges on the concept of the monism
of man: God is man, and the artist as free creator creates God in his
own image.

This romantic vision not only justifies Kuo's new heroic role and
inflates his personality but is also projected far beyond his individual
ego. Kuo wrote a highly mythological and architectonic poem, "The
Rebirth of the Goddesses" to symbolize the war between the northern
warlords and the Kuomintang in the south. And out of the strife between the two, Kuo attempted in this poem to construct a "third
China—a beautiful China."[59] By his own admission, the poem was
a failure. But his vision of a new China can also be seen in a more

successful piece, "The Nirvana of the Phoenixes." In the final apocalyptic scene of the resurrection of *feng* and *huang* (male and female phoenixes), amidst the refrains of "fire," Kuo piled up words of glory to symbolize shining vistas of the future—his own future and the future of his new China: light, freshness, beauty, fragrance, harmony, joy, enthusiasm, heroism, vividness, freedom, mystery, and eternity.

One is reminded of his earlier remark in Japan that he wished to be reborn like the phoenix. Magnifying this private drama to the national level, Kuo argued, both in poetry and prose, that his country, like himself, needed a total destruction of the past in order to bring about the birth of new China: "Alas, in order to save China, to save the Chinese, unless there is a thoroughgoing war, unless all the ugly garbage is burned out, the phoenix in nirvana cannot be reborn." [60] Kuo was also echoing Hsü Chih-mo's famous appeal to youth: "We demand a thorough overhaul . . . We demand a 'total rebirth.' " [61] And Chinese youth, fresh from the cataclysm of the May Fourth Movement, responded with wild adulation. Wen I-to, himself a poet, praised *Goddesses* as the only work which captured the "essential spirit of the twentieth century"—dynamism and rebelliousness.[62] Ch'ien Hsing-ts'un considered Kuo's passion and energy very "healthy" elements which were seldom found in Chinese poetry.[63] Wang I-jen, another young novelist, wrote: "I have read and reread *Goddesses* many times. I think it is the crystallization of the pent-up passions of modern life; at the same time it raises the bright banner of rebellion against society." [64]

Conversion to Marxism

As the poetry and translations of Kuo Mo-jo elevated him to new heights of prestige and popularity, as admirers were exhilarated by his poetic imagery and critics were carping at his "art for art's sake," Kuo Mo-jo suddenly, in 1924, before most writers turned left, announced his total conversion to Marxism.

In April 1924, Kuo returned to Japan and brought with him only three books: *The Complete Works of Goethe*, *Virgin Soil* by Turgenev, and *Social Organization and Social Revolution* by the Japanese

Marxist Kawakami Hajime.[65] In a letter to Ch'eng Fang-wu, dated August 9, 1924, Kuo declared: "Oh, Fang-wu! we are living in a most meaningful age! The age of mankind's revolution! The age of the great revolution in human history! I have now become a thorough convert to Marxism!"[66] He acknowledged the influence of two of the three books on his sudden conversion. Turgenev's *Virgin Soil*, which he had read with Ch'eng in the previous year, made him aware of the similarity between Turgenev's superfluous heroes and Chinese literary men like him. "We are all fond of literature, but we also disdain literature. We all want to be close to the masses but we still retain some aristocratic spirit. We are lazy; we are skeptical; we all lack the courage to act. We are the 'Hamlets' of China."[67] This view of the intellectuals' superfluity seems identical with Yü Ta-fu's image of himself, which is also partially inspired by Turgenev. But unlike Yü, who indulged himself in embellishing his self-styled superfluous role with intentional decadence, Kuo looked for and found in Turgenev more positive messages. Although the work portrayed superfluous intellectuals, was it not also impregnated with prophesies of the coming of radicalism? "Wasn't the Russia of the 1870s after the emancipation of the serfs exactly like the China of the 1920s after the overthrow of the Manchus?"[68] On the eve of a Marxian dawn, men in a transitional age should act as "midwives" who would help bring about the birth of a new world—a world where "everyone can develop his abilities in accordance with his personality, everyone can dedicate himself to truth so as to make some contributions, everyone can find release, and everyone can attain nirvana. This is truly the most ideal and most perfect world." "Is this world a dreamer's Utopia?" Kuo asked and answered, "No! no! it can definitely be realized on our earth . . . If it cannot be realized in our lifetime . . . we must strive to further its realization, so that our compatriots can benefit from its natural rewards, so that our posterity may soon be free of life's material bonds and thus permitted free and complete development of their individualities."[69]

This personal manifesto of a self-styled Marxist convert bristles with interesting implications. First, it reveals none of the essential theoretical doctrines of either Marx or the Marxists, except an emotion-tinged description of that favorite slogan: from each according to his ability, to each according to his need. Kuo acknowledged Hajime's book and in fact translated it, but in the letter he complained that he was dissatisfied with the book's contents, especially Hajime's disapproval of Marx's "early intent of political revolution." [70] One is led to wonder whether by 1924 Kuo had read anything by Marx aside from the *Communist Manifesto*. Although he publicized his intention to translate at least part of *Das Kapital*, the project was never begun. In one of Kuo's few theoretical pieces on Marxism, entitled "The Building of a New Nation," he attempted to defend Marxism against the attack from the followers of the "Nationists" (Kuo-chia chu-i p'ai), who held that Marx denied the role of the nation. In the political temper of the 1920s when nationalism was perhaps the overwhelming concern of all Chinese intellectuals, criticism on the issue of the nation is not difficult to understand. Nor was Kuo willing to give up his apocalyptic vision of "a third China—a beautiful China" reborn from the ashes of the old tradition. Thus he cited clause by clause (including its German original) the second chapter of *The Communist Manifesto* to prove that Marx had indeed assigned to the state major functions. [71] But he did not admit—or did not know enough to admit—that the state played a functional role primarily in the transitional stage of "the dictatorship of the proletariat." The overriding problem of the "withering of the state" was never mentioned in the article.

When Kuo felt the need to justify the international implications of Marxism in other articles, he would resort to such tactics as blaming the contemporary state system as the "prison of humanity" or recalling the cosmopolitanism of imperial China. [72] But the ultimate recourse was simply to overshadow nationalism with humanism by invoking the grandiose image of "humanity" or "mankind." In the 1920s, pan-humanists, like Romain Rolland and Henri Barbusse, were received by many Chinese intellectuals on the same footing as Marx or Lenin.

One is therefore tempted to argue that Kuo's Marxism, insofar as it can be pinned down theoretically, is much more akin to the theories of the "young Marx"—the more voluntaristic and revolutionary Marx from the *Philosophical and Economic Manuscripts* to the *Communist Manifesto*—than to those of the "old Marx" of *Das Kapital*. The central thrust of Kuo's own Marxist manifesto is contained in his apocalyptic exhortation that a future Communist utopia will come into existence where "our posterity may soon be free of life's material bonds and thus permitted free and complete development of their individualities." The humanistic ethos is apparent in this argument. Kuo was not concerned with the historical problem of dehumanization or alienation in terms of the relations of production. He was more preoccupied with the prospects of human life in a future Communist utopia and the role human action could play in bringing it about. He conceded that it was "pretentious on the part of a minority to assert their individuality and freedom" when "the majority had involuntarily lost their freedom and individuality." Therefore, "in order for the individual to develop his personality, all should likewise develop their personalities; in order for the individual to lead his life freely, all should likewise lead their lives freely." [73] He would even go so far as to construct an imaginary dialogue between Marx and Confucius so as to vindicate Marx not as a materialist but as an idealist whose envisioned Utopia would receive Confucius' own approval as a close facsimile of the world of "great harmony" (*ta-t'ung*) in the Confucian classics.[74] The responsibility to "reclaim the collective personality and freedom of the people" by realizing on earth the Communist utopia falls, according to Kuo, on "those who are far-sighted" and who "should sacrifice their own personality and freedom." [75] By the far-sighted elite Kuo is no doubt referring to intellectuals like himself and Ch'eng Fang-wu. The voluntaristic and activistic ethos exhibited here is reminiscent of that of Li Ta-chao, Kuo's senior contemporary and China's first Marxist theoretician.[76]

But did Kuo really give up his own freedom? As one probes the wealth of his writings both before and after 1924, one finds that his avowed transformation from romanticism to Marxism is more apparent than real.[77] One finds, for instance, that Marx, Engels, and Lenin had already appeared in his pantheon of his "bandit heroes." Lenin was worshiped especially as "a dynamic individual." [78] Kuo recalled that "when Lenin died in early 1924, I really felt sad as if I had lost the sun."[79] In a poem written in memory of Lenin, entitled "The Sun Has Set," we find the following lines:

Ah! the sun has set—on the northwestern horizons.

. . . . .

His burning light waves are sweeping away the heavenly devils,
His flowing hot torrents are storming through the piles of ice.
Unclothed, jobless people of poverty
Receive the glittering sacred fire that he has stolen from heaven.[80]

The Promethean image of Lenin is not only typical of Kuo's pantheism-heroism but is also noteworthy for its romantic connotations. As will be shown in a later chapter, Prometheus was in fact the key mythical figure, constantly invoked by Kuo's generation of hero worshipers. To glorify Lenin as essentially a heroic figure rather than an important theoretician of Marxism was another shared practice among most leftist intellectuals. In Kuo's expansive mood, it was easy to broaden his focus on Lenin to cover a collective image of heroism, Soviet Russia. Before he turned to Marxism, he was eager to hail Russia: "Ah! ah! Oh Russia, to which I stand in awe!/Good morning! Oh Pioneer, of whom I stand in awe!"[81] In honoring Russia, he would readily identify himself with the proletariat. His *Goddesses* collection begins with a "preface poem" in which he declared:

I am a member of the proletariat,
For besides my naked body,
I have no property whatsoever.[82]

It is apparent that Kuo saw no problem in freely employing Marxian terms to enrich his heroic vocabulary. His Marxist heroes in his pre-Marxist period were worshiped more as heroes than as Marxists. Kuo himself openly admitted that, because of his ignorance of Marxist theory, the Marxist terms in his poems were no more than "word games."[83] But even after he became more knowledgable, we find that this heroic trait persisted. The hyperbolic tone remained the same; only his heroic vista was enlarged to be renamed the Communist utopia. "It did not prove a difficult step for him to move from Whitman's prophetic eloquence to the Communist vision of world revolution."[84] The phoenix of China would be reborn to bring about a Communist state, and far-sighted men like Kuo himself would assume the heroic role of facilitating this "rebirth." He remained his own hero.

A more crucial problem posed by Kuo's conversion concerned his gloriously inflated image of himself as a poet. Should he sacrifice his identity of poet-hero in order to assume the new role of a revolutionary activist? The problem of literature and revolution, of art and politics, became the key issue that besieged an entire generation of literary intellectuals. Despite the fact that Kuo later joined the Northern Expedition as a political commissar, he was obviously reluctant to give up his literary endeavors. He zealously attempted to solve the possible contradiction, first by linking literature with revolution and, second, by stressing the influential role of the literary intellectuals on the eve of revolution.

In his celebrated article, "Revolution and Literature," Kuo presented the following argument:

We know that the essence of literature begins and ends with emotions. The aim of a literary man in expressing his emotions—whether consciously or unconsciously—always lies in eliciting the same emotional response from the readers. Thus the stronger and more pervasive the author's emotions, the stronger and more pervasive the effect of his work. This kind of work is certainly the best work. The greater number of good literary works in an age is the manifestation of the greater prosperity of literature in that age. What a revolutionary age demands is the strongest and most pervasive kind of collective emotions. For the literature produced by this kind of emotion, there are inexhaustible sources and myriad different ways of expression. Therefore, a revolutionary age always contains a golden age of literature.[85]

This theory of revolutionary emotions and revolutionary literature evinces the same apocalyptic optimism as his espousal of the Marxist doctrines. Just as he broadened the horizons of hero worship from individual personalities to the amorphous mass of the proletariat, he expanded individual emotions into collective emotions, which he defined *ipso facto* as revolutionary. Rather than justify his Marxist position, his theories served in fact to reinforce his earlier romanticism. While proclaiming the passing of individualism and romanticism, Kuo was groping toward the formation of a broader type of collective romanticism which would prove its relevance forty years later.

After having established the link between literature and revolution, it was but another step for Kuo to assert that "since literature is always revolutionary and true literature can consist only of revolutionary literature, true literature is always at the vanguard of the revolution"[86] by expressing the mass emotions of discontent with the status quo. Therefore, the practitioners of literature naturally belonged to the revolutionary vanguard. For historical proof, Kuo was only too ready to cite the example of Rousseau and Voltaire, among others, as forerunners of the French Revolution.[87] The impact of Russian radical writers of the nineteenth century on the 1917 Revolution was another obvious example of immediate significance. Thus, Kuo's attempts to justify literature in revolutionary terms also served to maintain intact, if not to elevate further, his previous status as a literary man. But behind the façade of his fervent conversion to Marxism lurked the familiar face of romanticism.

The combination of fortuitous circumstances and personal ingenuity made it possible for Kuo Mo-jo to realize some of his ideals to his own satisfaction. Through his writings and the journals of the Creation Society, Kuo was able to establish himself as one of the most popular literary men by the time he announced his conversion to Marxism in 1924. The problem of literature and revolution which he had raised theoretically in his articles was provided a happy solution in real life when, in July 1926, he was appointed to the propaganda staff in the political department of the Northern Expedition forces, and promoted in November to vice-chairman of the department.[88] His personal record of this revolutionary experience, *Pei-fa t'u-tz'u* (On the journey of the Northern Expedition), shows that he was thoroughly enjoying his prestige as a high-ranking officer acting in the company of KMT generals and Russian advisers. As the chasm of discord gradually widened between the CCP and the KMT, Kuo managed to ride another revolutionary tide by associating his name first with the Wuhan leaders and then with the Communist insurrectionists in the Nanchang uprising in August and the Swatow uprising in

September 1927. He was the only literary figure who went through this complicated process of a revolution within a revolution. Forced into hiding in the International Settlement of Shanghai after October 1927, he plunged into the literary arena by planning to revive the Creation Society. When his efforts to seek Lu Hsün's cooperation failed owing to the return of a group of young radicals from Japan, Kuo again managed to put himself in the company of his younger colleagues to publish the *Deluge* and other new radical magazines, while Yü Ta-fu was ousted from the society altogether. Unable to live long in China with a price on his head, Kuo went to Japan in February 1928 and for the next ten years led the life of a poet in exile—à la Ch'ü Yüan—while immersing himself in ancient Chinese history and archaeology. "During his ten years in Japan he wrote about fifteen scholarly works, seven autobiographical works, a number of scholarly articles, short stories, and comments on topical issues. He translated three novels by Upton Sinclair, a German history of archaeology, Marx's *A Contribution to the Critique of Political Economy* and *The German Ideology*, and part of Tolstoy's *War and Peace*." [89] When in August 1937 his name was finally removed from the list of enemies of the National Government, Kuo resumed his political activities back in his homeland, this time to head the literary propaganda section in the political department of the Military Affairs Commission. His tenure in this position came to an end in the autumn of 1940, when the National Government decided to remove radicals from important posts. In his second "slump" period from 1940 to 1945, while holding a sinecure post as head of a cultural works committee, Kuo again turned his attention to his literary interests and wrote five historical plays, including the most popular one, *Ch'ü Yüan*. In May 1945 he was invited to the anniversary celebrations of the Russian Academy of Sciences in Moscow and Leningrad. In January 1946 he participated in the Political Consultative Conference as one of the nine non-partisan delegates. After the founding of the People's Republic, Kuo was promoted to the post which commanded the highest academic prestige, the Presidency of the Academy of Sciences.

This brief sketch of Kuo's major activities since 1924 shows that Kuo has moved with apparent ease between the realms of literary creation, academic scholarship, and political activity. In spite of charges of cunning duplicity,[90] this impressive record would at least vindicate some of his theories about the role of a revolutionary writer. He could indeed claim that he had performed the role of a "midwife" in bringing about the birth of a New China. Perhaps because of this apparent consistency of theory and practice, one is justified in looking for more continuities of his romantic stance. It is not surprising, therefore, to find Kuo Mo-jo praising Stalin with the same pantheistic imageries he had once employed in eulogizing Lenin. It is altogether fitting to have a former hero worshiper as the official commentator on Mao's own highly heroic poems. The cult of Mao's personality, to which Kuo had contributed his share through his poetic panegyrics, could only represent a new peak in Kuo's almost endless galaxy of heroes. Perhaps the most significant piece of evidence is to be found in the pages of the official party journal, Red Flag (Hung ch'i). In issue number 3 of 1958, one finds an article by Kuo which helped to launch the nationwide campaign for "the merger of revolutionary realism and revolutionary romanticism."[91] Even in justifying official policy, Kuo has not forgotten to insert a paragraph in praise of his personal hero, Ch'ü Yüan. But Mao, instead of Ch'ü Yüan, became "the greatest romanticist."[92] The "Age of the Great Leap Forward" is characterized by Kuo as "the age of genius . . . of the emancipation of the people's productivity and the people's realization of their potentialities."[93] The collective hero image has finally been elevated from the illusions of an individual mind to form a part of a state ideology.

Kuo should have rejoiced at the realization of his Communist utopia. But in 1966, the news media relayed the following "confession" from Kuo Mo-jo: "I am afraid I have written several million words. However, if I value it according to the standard of today all I have written should strictly speaking be burned. It has no value at all."[94] The confession could be interpreted as a preemptive measure taken by Kuo to clear himself of possible charges by the younger radicals of the Cultural Revolution. Understandably he would feel the need to deny his pre-Marxist writings. But to sweep his post-1924 works into the dustbin of history implies a clash between his individual visions and the official line. If we believe that Kuo's confession was sincerely made, we shall also have to accept the gloomy fact that this most successful of romantics turned Communist has belatedly acknowledged errors which were present all along. The fate of most other leftist writers who had shared Kuo's early heroism and hero worship was different. The collision between their individual visions and social reality or party policy often resulted in disillusionment or in purges and "thought reform," whereby the individual writer was made to reject his previous visions and achieve, in a sense, "rebirth." Two individuals could be singled out as representatives of this pattern: Chiang Kuang-tz'u imposed his heroic vision on socio-political reality and ended in disillusionment; Hsiao Chün pitted his ego against party policy and became a victim to purges.

Romantic? I myself am romantic.
All revolutionaries are romantic.
—Chiang Kuang-tz'u

Chapter 10

Chiang Kuang-tz'u

Chiang Kuang-tz'u was one of the first Communists to establish a reputation as a poet and novelist.[1] While Kuo Mo-jo was dramatically transformed from a romantic to a Marxist, Chiang Kuang-tz'u had declared himself a Communist before his emergence on the literary scene. Born in 1901 in Liu-an, Anhwei, the son of a small shopkeeper, he took part in student activities related to the May Fourth movement. In 1921, he was sent to Russia as a member of the Communist Youth League.[2] He was probably among the first group of some thirty Chinese students—Liu Shao-ch'i among them—who studied at the International Toilers' University in Moscow.[3] He returned to China in 1924, equipped with the rudiments of Marxism–Leninism and a reading knowledge of Russian. At Shanghai College, he was appointed to teach sociology, which was but a euphemism for Marxism–Leninism. Many of the students and faculty at Shanghai College were involved in working for the then united Kuomintang–Communist revolutionary cause. Bored with teaching, he accepted a job as an interpreter for the Russian advisers in Marshal Feng Yü-hsiang's army in North China. He was in Kalgan at the time of the May Thirtieth

Incident, in which his former students at Shanghai College took an active part.[4] In November 1925 he returned to Shanghai where he continued to teach until 1927.

After Chiang Kai-shek's massacre of Communists, he had to flee Shanghai in order to avoid arrest, but he soon found himself facing another anti-Communist purge in Wuhan. Again he escaped safely and returned to Shanghai where, under the protection of the foreign settlements, he was able to live a largely unmolested life, and to apply himself diligently to writing poetry and fiction.[5] He associated himself with the younger members of the Creation Society and, together with Ch'ien Hsing-ts'un and Meng Ch'ao, founded the Sun Society in 1928. From 1928 to 1931, he edited successively a number of leftist literary journals such as *T'ai-yang yüeh-k'an* (Sun monthly), *Shih-tai wen-i* (Literature of the time), *Hsin-liu* (New current), and *T'o-huang che* (Pioneer). On June 30, 1931, he died of cancer of the intestine at the age of thirty.

From the above brief sketch it would appear that Chiang Kuang-tz'u's career is similar to those of many leftist writers in China in the 1920s and 1930s. His literary accomplishments, in the judgment of one eminent literary critic, are nothing but a succession of glaring deficiencies.[6] The paucity of his literary imagination has led another scholar, T. A. Hsia, to raise the rhetorical question at the end of his lengthy and scathing critique of Chiang Kuang-tz'u's works: "Who will read Chiang Kuang-tz'u?"[7]

The literary historian springs eagerly to the fore. In historical perspective, Chiang's humdrum typicality is transformed into a significant "phenomenon." In our thematic framework, that significance lies in the crucial problem raised by the case of Kuo Mo-jo: what happened when the journey of sentiment drifted toward the left, when literature became increasingly and inevitably embroiled in politics? The story of Kuo Mo-jo provides the "happier" side of this phenomenon: his persistent personal romanticism blended with his revolutionary activities, and he lived long enough to reap the harvest of both. Chiang Kuang-tz'u epitomizes the other—and more pathetic— side of the same phenomenon.

A portrait of Chiang Kuang-tz'u

Russia: Byron and Blok

Chiang Kuang-tz'u wrote nothing about his childhood. The story of his life, as can be sketchily reconstructed from his writings, begins with Russia. As a student in the Far Eastern section of the International Toilers' University, Chiang was expected to equip himself with the principles of Marxism—Leninism and the art of political propaganda. For a young man of barely twenty, life in Moscow might not consist entirely of classroom discussions of theory. Chiang's study of the Russian language, like Kuo Mo-jo's assimilation of German literature through learning German, initiated him into Russian and European literature. But we know little, for the only records existent of Chiang's Moscow years are a collection of poetry and a portrait by a Russian lady artist.

Although the revolutionary élan of the October days had long subsided, and Lenin's temperate New Economic Policy was under way, to a young activist from China, the Russian landscape still resonated from the Bolshevik Revolution. The following are portions of his poem, "Hymn to Moscow":

The snows of Moscow are white,
The flags of Moscow are red;
Flags which are as bright and intoxicating as the morning glow,
Snows which transform Moscow into a crystal palace.
I lie in the morning glow,
I roam in the crystal palace;
I sing when I like to sing,
I dream when I like to dream.

．　．　．　．　．

This morning I stand on the clouds of dawn.
As I look out:
Wonderful! wonderful!
Mankind is beginning to wear bright red garb.
The October Revolution,
Like cannon,
In a roaring boom,
Has frightened wild wolves and evil tigers,
Has alarmed ox ghosts and serpent gods.
The October Revolution,

Like a pillar of fire reaching the skies,
Behind it is the burning debris of the past,
In front of it is shining the new path of future.
Ah! the October Revolution,
Let me dedicate my soul to you.
Mankind is reborn because you are born.[8]

Despite the crudities of craftsmanship, Chiang's poetic homage to Moscow and the October Revolution breathes heroic exultations reminiscent of Kuo Mo-jo. His political convictions are conveyed rather in the dynamic images of cannon fire, flaming pillar, gushing torrents and the rebirth of humanity. Chiang's emotional proximity to Kuo Mo-jo is even more striking in his poem bemoaning the death of Lenin:

My Lenin!
Lenin of the Russian proletariat!
Lenin of the proletarian revolutions of the whole world!
Lenin of the emancipation movements of mankind!
Ay! Lenin, you are dead!
You are really dead!

. . . . .

How can I not cry bitterly and howl with sorrow!
There have been many great men in history,
Who also deserve the poet's paens and adulation.
But you Lenin!
You are an unprecedented great personality:
You have donated to mankind unforgettable gifts;
Your legacies will shine with the sun and moon![9]

Chiang Kuang-tz'u wrote the poem on January 23, 1924, the very day he heard the news of Lenin's death. Some time later, a sonorous echo came from another poet in China: "Ah, the sun has set—on the northwestern horizon."[10] It is very unlikely that Chiang and Kuo had read each other's poems, and yet the same heaving hymns of hero worship issued from a self-styled pantheist in China and a dedicated Marxist in Russia. It could almost be said that the collection of poetry which resulted from Chiang's experience in Russia was a minor replica of *Goddesses*, though tinged with political hues. As in Kuo's preface to *Goddesses*, Chiang declared that he was a member of the proletariat in the same vein: "Friends!/I am a member of the proletariat,/For besides a pair of bare hands, and a bare mouth,/I have nothing else." [11] As Kuo poeticized on the top of Mount Fudetate near the city of Moji in Japan and looked down upon the "unfolding vision" of the "pulse of a great city!/Oh, throb of life! striking, blowing, calling . . ." [12] Chiang Kuang-tz'u, while in the Ural mountains in central Russia, commanded an even broader vista:

> Straddling Europe and Asia,
> I stand on the highest peak of the Ural mountains.
> Look! Isn't that the Pacific Ocean?
>
> . . . . .
>
> Barely visible, isn't that
> The American banner of false humanitarianism,
> The shuttling battleship of English capitalism,
> The wild demon-king of Japanese imperialism?
>
> . . . . .
>
> Hear!
> The roaring waves
> Aiding the beating of the battle drums
> Is it the sound of striking?
> > the sound of crying?
> > the sound of calling? [13]

While Kuo praised the city of Moji as the "famed flower of the twentieth century" and "stern mother of modern civilization," [14] Chiang in another poem, again on top of the Urals, looked to the city of Moscow as the "mistress I have dreamed about for so many years." [15] The grandeur of the naturalistic and anthropomorphic imagery of Kuo Mo-jo was used by a lesser poet to arouse anti-imperialist and anti-capitalist sentiments. Even a sophisticated Marxist critic would find Chiang's "political" poems more naively heroic than political. Yet the sincerity and dedication of this young Chinese Communist can hardly be doubted. The dilemma of the poet as political worker or the political activist as poet plagued Chiang Kuang-tz'u from the time he returned from Russia, but it had already been planted in Russian soil. He had come to Moscow to learn the Marxist–Leninist tenets of political action, but his exposure to Russian and European literature stimulated his poetic creativity. The root of

Chiang's petit bourgeois individualism was a kind of heroic and emotional craving that he shared with Kuo Mo-jo and many other budding "poets" in the early 1920s. Obviously Chiang had not sensed the latent conflict and confusion between his two roles. In fact he blissfully meshed poetry with politics and declared his self-appointed new status as "a young poet from the East" in a poem praising the "Pioneers," the Soviet counterpart of the Chinese Communist Youth League.[16] The most significant piece of Chiang's poetic output in Russia, a glowing tribute to the hero as "political poet," was a long poem written in April 1923 on Byron.

Ah, Bryon!
You are the rebel against darkness,
You are God's prodigal son,
You are the singer of freedom,
You are the fierce enemy of tyranny.
Wandering, calumny—
Was this your fate,
Or the tribute paid by society to genius?

. . . . .

I!
I was born in an oppressed country in the East.
My soul is filled with the fury of humiliation!
A hundred years ago you mourned the weakened Greece,
A hundred years later I bemoan the sinking of my native land.

. . . . .

We are both friends of the oppressed.
We are both men who love justice and righteousness:
In those years, in the solemn House of Lords,
You step forward to protect the workers who broke up
            the machines;
Today, in the red proletarian country,
I sing of the world's proletarian revolution.

. . . . .

Ah, Byron!
You of the nineteenth century,
And I of the twentieth . . .[17]

Chiang Kuang-tz'u might have intended to draw political lessons from Byron's life as a fighter for freedom and the oppressed, so that his own ambitions as a political fighter against foreign oppression in China could be justified by a glorious precedent. But the reader can easily detect our poet's own heroic pretensions that protrude through the ideological surface. Chiang's personal identification with Byron is obvious and readily recalls a similar posture of a far from revolutionary poet, Su Man-shu: "Alone, I bewail Byron's fate/as I pore over his poetic remains./You, poet, and I are wanderers, fluttering like reeds in the storm./May I beckon to your soul from across a strange land?" [18] In fact, this similarity has been noticed by a perceptive Communist critic as one of Chiang's grave ideological deficiencies.[19]

More important in a biographical perspective is Chiang's definition of the poet—and himself—not only as a hero but also as one who "wanders" and whose poetic genius dooms him to a life of suffering —a familiar and highly romantic pose. Thus the symptoms of romanticism in Chiang's personality are already amply apparent in his poetic works written in his Russian period. His self-image as a hero-poet was evolved essentially in the same pattern of Kuo Mo-jo. While Kuo Mo-jo arrived at his *Weltanschauung* of heroism–pantheism mainly through his immersion in ancient Chinese and German romantic literature, Chiang must have gradually groped toward his heroic pose via Russian literature. Although he again wrote nothing concerning Russian literature before 1925, a long article which was subsequently serialized in *Creation Monthly* in 1927 provides abundant evidence.

If Chiang's favorite hero in European literature was Byron, his idol in Russian literature was Alexander Blok, the colorful Jewish poet turned revolutionary during the October Revolution. The second installment of his long article, "The October Revolution and Russian Literature" is devoted entirely to Blok and bears the subtitle: "The Revolutionary and the Romantic—Blok." In praising the romanticism of Blok, Chiang first noted what he considered to be the crucial difference between Blok's true romanticism and the pre-Blok brand of romanticism. The latter failed to "link imagination with real life, to link romanticism with revolution, thereby causing many great tragedies." [20] Blok, however, realized the true meaning behind the principle that "revolution is art; a true poet cannot but feel what he shares in common with the revolution. A poet—a romantic poet—has an even keener feeling toward the revolution than other poets."[21] But how can revolution be art? Chiang's explanation hinges on his definition of romanticism: "A romantic soul always craves to reach beyond the limits of mundane life, craves to merge with the whole universe. The more violent is the revolution, the more boundless is its scope, and the more can it grasp a poet's soul. For what a poet's soul craves can only be the great, interesting, and romantic things."[22]

This facile explanation demonstrates Chiang's own conviction that the true spirit of a poet and a revolution has to be, by definition, romantic. It is the romantic animus that underlies a revolution's dynamism and a poet's creativity: "In the sweeping actions of the revolution, there is a kind of boundless, onrushing trend which stirs the human passion for emancipation. And a poet, amidst its waves, can hear the exhilarating music and see through the soul of the revolution."[23] On the basis of this logic Chiang asserts that "revolution is the greatest romanticism" and since by revolution Chiang obviously had in mind the October Revolution, Blok is "the last, the greatest" poet in "this century of historical transformations."[24] Blok's chef-d'oeuvre, The Twelve, becomes, in Chiang's mind, "a testimonial of revolution, the key to the transformation of the romantic soul in the past one hundred years, and to what made Blok a great poet, a poet worshiped by the laboring masses of workers and peasants."[25]

Chiang's adulation of Blok in this lengthy article was obviously not for academic purposes but was indicative of his efforts at self-justification. The central themes which he found represented by Blok in fact became the central themes of his own life and work after he returned to China in 1924.

Love and Revolution

Chiang's activities in China unfolded again a typical pattern among literary intellectuals returning from abroad. Having been trained in mostly non-literary disciplines but nevertheless exposed to literature, they found themselves upon landing on their native soil at a crossroads: to find the kind of position for which their specialized training equipped them or to continue to develop their newly discovered literary interests? The conflicts and wanderings at the crossroads had been most movingly illustrated in Yü Ta-fu. But similar fates also befell Hsü Chih-mo and Kuo Mo-jo. The problem of choice for Chiang Kuang-tz'u was even more harrowing, owing to the fact that he had been sent by a specific political organization for specific political purposes. One could well imagine Chiang's conflict when he found teaching sociology "boring" both as a channel to extend his political activities and a financial source to subsidize his literary endeavor. Like most literary intellectuals Chiang had chosen to put priority on his literary work, but as a political worker he was either under pressure from the Party or stricken by his own conscience to make his literary work serviceable for his political goals. The sad result was a series of stories and novels which proved unsatisfactory by either standard.

T. A. Hsia has discussed thoroughly Chiang's creative output from a literary point of view and has come to the following conclusion: "Chiang Kuang-tz'u had a predilection for generalizations which overpowered his imagination, while he tried very hard, almost to the point of breathlessness, to express rage and sorrow at the abstractions which seemed to have deep emotional meaning for him." [26] These "generalizations" are without exception political and derived from an immersion in Marxism–Leninism. Mr. Hsia noticed that Chiang in all his works had "two commodities to sell: communism and sentimentalism," [27] but in neither was he able to demonstrate enough eloquence. Thus his literary works become patchworks which combine intense but inept descriptions of people's suffering with general abstractions that degenerate into mere slogans—"fascism," "landlord class," "capitalists," "society," "world." All these defects we could easily accept as the natural earmarks of a slipshod, albeit sincere and dedicated, writer. What seems more intriguing in his works, viewed from a biographical standpoint, is that his inability to convey successfully the emotional depth of his communism is coupled with an unwillingness to unveil the breadth of his sentimentalism. Before Chiang could confront the ambiguities and ambivalences involved in his subject matters, he was already convinced that love would inevitably conflict with revolution and would sooner or later be sacrificed for revolution. A few examples will suffice.

Chiang's first novel, *The Youthful Tramp*, was written in the form of a confessional letter. The hero, seeking "compassion" from the recipient of the letter, an established literary man, recounted the death of his parents at the hands of an evil landlord and his subsequent experiences as "in turn a beggar, a grocer's apprentice, a worker in a cotton mill, and an assistant at the railroad workers' union during a strike." [28] Chiang inserted a love story between the hero and the grocer's daughter, which could have provided more spice in the picaresque structure of the novel; but after a few scanty passages filled with emotional hyperboles like "I love you! I love you," the heroine was allowed to die of self-induced illness. [29] Another novelette, "The Sorrows of Lisa" tells the story, again in the first person, confessional form, of a White Russian lady in Shanghai, whose gradual degeneration ends in prostitution. [30] The work elicited much criticism and displeasure from leftist circles on account of Chiang's sympathies with the "reactionary" heroine. A better writer might have concentrated on the emotional elements, playing them off against the background of a dim and decaying society.

Chiang, on the contrary, seemed constrained to stress the social and political setting—revolution and civil war, crime and sin in the "capitalist" dominated Shanghai—and again sent his heroine to death. A famous short story, "On the Yalu," presumes to be a Korean revolutionary's account of the only girl he loves in life, his cousin. [31] She dies in prison. In "The Broken Heart," a kind-hearted nurse falls in love with a wounded revolutionary; after he is cured, he is killed in underground activity and she commits suicide. [32] In another short story, we are finally enlivened to find the following declaration: "Can't it be that you love me because you have discovered that I am a revolutionary, because you have noticed that I have great spirit, rebellious energy, and a pure soul? . . . If you love me because of this, my sister, how fortunate I am! How happy I am!" [33]

The letter written by this love-yearning revolutionary, for some reason, is never sent to his beloved in this story appropriately titled, "An Unmailed Letter." The revolutionary activist is the hero of another story, "Wind across the Fields," in which he wins the hearts of two heroines but in the end marries neither.[34] Moreover, the hero, who is a landlord's son turned revolutionary, agrees to set fire to his own home. A poignant moment comes when the revolutionary admits: "Alas! Comrade Chin-teh! A man after all has his sentiments. You know how distressed I am! I love my innocent, little sister."[35] But this precious outcry from the heart is quickly inundated in the heroic chorus of peasants singing a revolutionary song that the hero has taught them.

Only in two or three stories did Chiang assign a positive function to romantic love as an aid to revolution. In "Sansculottes," a panorama of workers' strikes in Shanghai, we do find a happy couple both working for the strikes, but another couple are made martyrs of the struggle.[36] The heroine in *The Moon Forces Its Way through the Clouds* "goes through the stages of enthusiasm and dejection (when she became a streetwalker after the 1927 debacle) and revived hope (when she goes to work in a factory and reunites with her lover)."[37] Thus the revolutionary finds love and wins love, and love even seems to aid revolution. But this forced glimmer of hope also marks the end of the novel.

Why must love hinder revolution? Why did Chiang Kuang-tz'u find it necessary to fill his fiction with females and then hastily send them to death? Why, for a revolutionary writer like Chiang Kuang-tz'u, is there a relative lack of "positive heroines" in his works? Communist critics have noted that many of Chiang's heroines are old-fashioned girls and his love stories smack of the traditional "talent–beauty" stories.[38] T. A. Hsia remarked, in a similar vein, that "his insistence on the inclusion of 'love' in his books about revolution was to satisfy his own emotional needs" and that "the ideal woman whose love, no less than the revolutionary ideal, was an object of pursuit throughout Chiang's life" was really "an old-fashioned housewife, one who should bear a closer resemblance to his mother than did the revolutionary type."[39] Granting Chiang's petit-bourgeois and even feudal tastes in matters of love and women, I suspect that his reluctance to give love its posititve role in revolution reflects, rather than his total allegiance to the latter, his preoccupation with the former. Behind the façade of revolution in his fiction there lurks a sort of dual anxiety; he was, in truth, unwilling to do the type of political work assigned to him, and yet he wanted to prove his worth as a revolutionary; he yearned for love, human warmth, and a decent home, but was ashamed of their petit-bourgeois connotations. Accordingly, he was over-eager to portray revolution and emphasize its priority over romantic love and filial piety. He was prompted by a kind of guilty conscience to cry out against "the darkness of the world, the cruelty of humanity, the injustice of society, the destruction of reason," when in fact he was leading a reasonably comfortable life in the foreign concessions of Shanghai on the royalties of his books.[40] He had become more a romantic than a revolutionary, although he wanted to bridge the gap by exalting Alexander Blok. The evidence is to be found not so much in his works as in his life.

Chiang Kuang-tz'u and Sung Jo-yü

Yü Ta-fu met Chiang Kuang-tz'u in Shanghai in the spring of 1925, shortly after Chiang had returned from Russia. Yü's first impressions of this self-styled revolutionary poet were not entirely favorable: "At that time he had just returned from Russia. He wore a foreign suit of good quality . . . He was tall, and not bad looking, with a pair of thin-rimmed glasses which made his gentlemanly manner even more lively . . . Kuang-tz'u's attitude and conversation were perhaps influenced by the examples of certain Western European writers. When he talked he showed an extremely high ambition, and his tone was arrogant. But at that time he had not yet published a serious work. Therefore, the younger writers at the Creation Society publications department did not hide their contempt for him."[41] Yang Ts'un-jen, who first met Chiang in 1927 and with him later founded the Sun Society, remembered him as "of slender build, with a slender face, and with a particularly long lower jaw which slightly tilted upward. The glimmer of his eyes, as reflected through his glasses, was not terribly bright."[42] Although by 1926 he had published a collection of poetry, *New*

Dreams, and his first novel, *The Youthful Tramp,* they had "had no effect on the literary scene" and he often grumbled about his unappreciated talent.[43]

It was in this depressive period that Chiang met Miss Sung Jo-yü, a teacher at a girls' normal school in Hsin-yang, Honan. They fell madly in love, and Chiang married her one month before she died of tuberculosis in November 1926. This tragic affair was immortalized by Chiang when, in 1927, he published their correspondence under the title of "Monument"—a monument, indeed, in Chiang's life.

We do not know how the romance first began. One of Miss Sung's letters indicated that Chiang wrote his first letter to her as early as June 4, 1920.[44] They must have kept up the correspondence throughout the years when Chiang was in Russia and despite his romance with a Russian girl, whom he called Anna in a poem.[45] By the time the story unfolded in the printed pages of *The Monument,* they were undergoing the climactic transition from friendship to love. She wrote him offering her sympathies and admiration. He accepted them while still heaving the sighs of a solitary genius: "I feel that in the boundless sea of humanity there is no single person who loves me . . . You address me as a beloved friend—this, honestly, I doubt somewhat, because I feel in the present world no one loves me." She declared her love: "Hsia-sheng! Dear Hsia-sheng! I have now developed a passionate, irresistible energy of love toward you! Emotion has defeated will! My friend! Do you know?" To this he reacted with gratitude: "Jo-yü! my Jo-yü! You love me so, you love me so passionately . . . How can I not feel boundless gratitude? I decide to accept your love . . . Good! I am now yours, I am now yours!" She repeated her love: "Hsia-sheng! How grateful I am to you! . . . My Hsia-sheng! Why can't I stop loving you? I wish I could sincerely and everlastingly love only you! . . . My Hsia-sheng, can you love me forever? Now I really believe that will can never triumph over emotion." He responded with equal fervor: "My heart is burning with the flames of passionate love . . . My present joy is indescribable. I have never experienced such a heightened degree of happiness in my life. My Jo-yü! My love!" But he did not forget to warn her: "I have told you repeatedly that I am a revolutionary poet, that I am a rebel . . . Dear

Jo-yü! Aren't you afraid that in the future I may cause you to suffer?"[46]

The distinct feature in this otherwise typical exchange of youthful love is that in the midst of emotional outbursts Chiang was constantly reasserting his self-image as a solitary, suffering hero. To Chiang, there is a tragic grandeur in the role of a poet: "I am a poet. Poets—both ancient and modern, and especially those with a revolutionary nature—are all known for their solitary, wandering existence. For humanity, for society, I cherish limitless hope; but at the same time I know that I am doomed to a destiny of rugged uncertainties."[47] The background against which these narcissistic lamentations were registered certainly augured many uncertainties. Chiang was confronted with the same problem which pestered Yü Ta-fu and many others—to find a vocation in China's "boundless sea of humanity." The fantasies in which they had indulged themselves while abroad now crashed on the hard-rock of social reality. In contrast to Yü Ta-fu, whose glamorous decadence soon gathered a band of loyal followers, Chiang attempted to camouflage his quandaries by a heroic pose around which revolved the two major themes of his life: love and revolution. It was on the basis of this ideal that he managed to win the heart of Miss Sung Jo-yü: feminine adulation embellishes a poet's life and inspires his poetic imagination; love springs from his own self-love. "You love me, you love me madly,/Only because I am a poet, and you are the Muse of Art and Literature."[48] Chiang Kuang-tz'u has employed the same device as did Yü Ta-fu and Su Man-shu to build up a vision of himself; he has merely revised Kuo Mo-jo's ebullient vision of the Carlylian hero as poet with a few gloomier touches. The unique contribution of Chiang to this familiar picture lies in his efforts to justify on the basis of this romantic pose not merely his art but also his revolutionary activities.

Chiang was said to have compared himself to Pushkin,[49] in addition to Byron and Blok. Obviously he was convinced by his glorious predecessors that the poet could perform a rebellious, and hence revolutionary, role vis-à-vis his society. Byron's last years in Greece and Blok's involvement in the whirlwind of the October Revolution must have further encouraged him to think that a poet was able to combine writing with political action. The last years of Chiang Kuang-tz'u witnessed again a series of worsening disillusionments as his heroic ideals proved unsuitable to the harsh political reality of China.

Following Chiang Kai-shek's anti-Communist coups which resulted in the dissolution of the KMT–Communist alliance, Communist activities were forced underground. Chiang Kuang-tz'u, as a prominent proletarian writer and a party member, found himself in genuine "uncertainties." The spectre of "white terror" began to haunt him, and he had to keep his abodes in Shanghai secret and changed his name from Chiang Kuang-ch'ih (red) to Chiang Kuang-tz'u (kind), which elicited Lu Hsün's bemused reference to him as Chiang Kuang-X.[50] The atmosphere in Shanghai for the urban underground activists under the Li Li-san line appeared ripe for revolution. But instead of plunging himself into helping the workers' strikes or planning for insurrections, as both the Li Li-san line and Chiang's own novels suggested, he turned to editing literary journals. The Sun Society, which later published a series of proletarian journals, was founded in 1927 by Chiang and his friends in a typically personal fashion. The title Sun was adopted while the founders were walking in the streets of Hankow one day in June. Yang Ts'un-jen complained about the unbearable heat of the sun, and the term immediately stuck in Chiang's mind.[51]

Although Chiang's journals were in the forefront of the leftist line and the young members of the society were bold enough to challenge both the Creation Society and Lu Hsün, it seemed that the party authorities were far from satisfied with Chiang's contribution. In 1929, Chiang published The Sorrows of Lisa, which provoked more displeasure among his comrades. He was forced to seek escape from both the KMT police and his own co-workers in the party in Japan. The diary he kept from August 25 to November 9, 1929, while nursing his "illness" in Tokyo, affords us another precious firsthand record of his mental tribulations.

Diary in Japan

Physically, Chiang was indeed ill, with the stomach ailment which eventually caused his death. Mentally, he was smarting under the very unfavorable reception of his new work. The White Russian heroine in *The Sorrows of Lisa* seems to have won sympathy only from Chiang himself. That he should have written a book on the sad fate of a White Russian lady at such a critical juncture, when the backlash of white terror made revolutionary work even more urgent, was a problem which Chiang himself had failed to explain. It may serve as an indication of a certain sense of escapist nostalgia for a haven of comfort of which both Lisa and her author were deprived. Tokyo may have provided for him such a haven. Yet he was haunted by his homeland. "Ay! I am a Chinese, an unfortunate Chinese! Even if I stay in a foreign country, there isn't any freedom to talk about. How can this be compared to Heine of those past years when he was detained in Paris, or to Byron when he was wandering in Italy?"[52] Even on the verge of his downfall, Chiang had not forgotten his poet-heroes.

The diary also records his plans for a new novel, *The Moon Forces Its Way through The Clouds*, his visits to the famous Japanese leftist writer Kurahara Korehito and his immersion in Russian literature and Marxist literary criticism. He read Dostoevsky's "Poor People," perhaps the Russian master's most sentimental work. He read Gorky's "Malfa" and was impressed by the "firm life outlook of Gorky's early 'tramp' hero." Somewhat humbled by the Russian masters, he nevertheless reasserted his heroic estimation of himself: "Do I have some literary talent? It seems I have some . . . But when I think of Dostoevsky, Tolstoy, Gorky . . . I feel that my talent is so infinitesimal, so indescribably infinitesimal! But should I despair? Should I escape? No, no, absolutely not! I should strive to bring out whatever I have!"[53] He read the literary criticism of Belinsky, Plekhanov, and Lunacharsky. After having completed the translation of Lebedinsky's "One Week," he registered the following thoughts: "When the readers read this work, they will realize that the so-called real revolutionaries are not simple, fierce animals, but rather men with true intellect, true emotions, who can truly sacrifice themselves for a great endeavor."[54]

He liked reading Fadeyev, Ehrenberg, Fedin, Esenin, Ida Axelrod. The list of Soviet authors would convince every Marxist critic of Chiang's firm belief in Socialist Realism and proletarian lierature.

But the motive behind his apparent attraction to Soviet literature was intriguingly personal. Rather than elaborate on their ideological significance, Chiang was seeking to justify his own past life as a writer, to find historical precedents for the relevance of literature to revolution. Thwarted by his fellow revolutionaries, he wanted to heal and buttress his own ego. He had to convince himself that a writer could be a revolutionary and true revolutionaries could have literary tastes and inclinations. In short, Chiang attempted to justify an essentially Carlylian posture of the hero as poet in the Marxian framework. He took great pains to point out, for himself and for his critics, that "Marx and Heine had developed close friendships, and Lenin had paid special attention to Gorky," that Lassale once wrote a play which had received warm praise from Marx and Engels, that Rosa Luxembourg "had practically read all the works of famous Russian masters." The lessons he had drawn from Marxism was that "great revolutionary leaders like Marx, Lassalle, Mehring, Lafargue, Plekhanov, Luxembourg, Lenin, Lunacharsky—they had had such an interest and deep understanding of art and literature." Why was it so? Why was it that one could find "on Lenin's desk the works of Pushkin, Nekrasov, and Tolstoy?" Why, in fact, is literature so important to revolutionaries? "Because great social reformers [that is, revolutionaries] want not only to find sociological material in art but also to acquire esthetic feeling in art so as to enrich their own spirit." [55] Chiang seemed to imply in this final argument that even if his political work had proved unsatisfactory to the party, his literary works would still be relevant and important to the revolutionary cause. This rationalization might be sufficient for him to justify his past life, but the party thought otherwise. For, on October 20, 1930, the party underground paper *Red Flag Daily News* (*Hung-ch'i jih-pao*) announced the expulsion of Chiang Kuang-tz'u from the Chinese Communist Party. The reasons for the party's decision were given as follows:

In spite of his membership in the CCP for several years, Chiang Kuang-ch'ih was originally a student of the petit-bourgeois class. He has never engaged himself in any hard task, nor made any attempt to approach the masses. He maintains a comfortable and luxurious way of life, supposedly proper to his position as a writer. He showed vacillation in the recent upsurge of revolutionary struggles because there was at the same time an increase in white terror by the reactionary regime. As a cultural worker, he was among those who were ordered by the Central Committee, CCP, to start actual work among the masses. Having been a waverer for some time, however, he was afraid of the hard work involved in such a move. He made a request in writing to resign his membership in the party but to remain "a member of the active revolutionary masses" for the reason that the romantic, luxurious life he was accustomed to rendered him unfit for the iron discipline of the party. The party cell to which he belonged judged his case with a view to the duty of every Communist of regularly doing hard work under iron discipline—a duty which has become more demanding on the vanguard of the proletariat . . . The party cell looked upon his application as the most dastardly act of a petit-bourgeois, motivated as it was by fear of sacrifice and hard work in the face of the sharpening crisis of class struggle. With a view to purging the party of opportunists and cowards and strengthening its organization, the cell reached a decision at a meeting to read him out of the party. The decision was ratified by the Kiangsu Provincial Committee.[56]

The human drama that led to Chiang's downfall, however, was much more complex and interesting than what appeared in this official defamation.

The Last Years

Chiang returned to Shanghai from Tokyo in late November 1929, not having reformed his thought as the party might have expected, but rather with a reinforced ideal of the poet as hero. In the spring of 1930, at T'ien Han's house in the French Concession, he met Miss Wu Ssu-hung, a young student of art and an actress of T'ien Han's Nan-kuo (Southern country) dramatic club. In their first conversations, Chiang scribbled the titles of his own works and asked Miss Wu whether she had read any of them. He was disappointed to learn that she had read none. For one of their early dates, Chiang took her to a Russian restaurant. As she struggled with the famous "Lo-sung" (Russian) soup, our writer condescendingly remarked: "When Dostoevsky married his [second] wife, he was more than forty years of age, but his wife was only a young girl reaching twenty."[57] Chiang was then twenty-nine. But Miss Wu already found that he looked

old, his back was somewhat "hunched," his fingers "white and slender." [58] When he proposed, he put his arms around her "like a kind
father" and said: "I hope you can help me as Mrs. Dostoevsky helped
her husband and become my life companion." [59] She regarded herself
as a bohemian, and registered her feelings in these lines when she
decided to live with him and move to his flat:

> You are a Bolshevik, a political figure;
> I am an art student, a bohemian,
> But who says that we cannot live together? [60]

She did not really love him, but like the second wife of Hsü Chih-
mo or Yü Ta-fu, she might have been flattered by his literary fame.
Chiang had seen fit to gild his image by confessing to his second wife
that he had fallen in love with a Russian girl and Sung Jo-yü and
after Sung's death, "many girl friends lived with me, but I never
thought of marrying them." [61] He also attempted to enlighten her
mind with the literary theories of Plekhanov and Trotsky. [62]

It was perhaps under the influence of his vivacious wife that Chiang
finally reached a decision to resign his membership from the party.
She felt lonely and bored when he often had to go to his party meetings. One day, as Miss Wu later recalled, she asked him with displeasure: "Why do you go to meetings?" Chiang answered, "You
should know I am a political writer, and politics requires that I go to
meetings." [63] On May Day 1930, Chiang returned home from a dem-
onstration and looked extremely tired. He explained: "I cannot stand
it." Wu wrote in her memoirs:

> I stood by him, stupefied. Then he continued:
> "They (his comrades in the party and the league) think that revolu-
> tion means to go with them to smash glass windows and to stage riots.
> But I am a writer! I can only struggle with words—literature is my
> revolutionary tool."
> "Then why must you go? If I were you, I go if I am willing; I don't
> go if I am not willing!" I said.
> "This is not the question whether you are or you are not willing,
> you don't understand." When he said this, his whole face looked as
> if it were about to explode." [64]

Sometime later, he finally made a decision: "Since I cannot do practical work, why should I assume my membership? Since writing is

not considered work, then I quit." [65] He sent out his letter of resignation. Three days later, the *Red Flag Daily News* announced his expulsion from the party. The irony of Chiang's tragedy was that, according to Miss Wu, after he was expelled from the party, he was hunted by the KMT police. One day in the summer of 1930, as he went to a bookstore to get some Russian books he had ordered, he was arrested and jailed. [66] When he was released, Wu Ssu-hung decided to leave him. In a letter written to her on June 7, 1931, after they had separated, Chiang wrote: "I have been lying sick in bed for several days . . . Ay! Ah-hung! . . . What is my consolation? Who gives me passion? My passion, I am afraid, has been exhausted. But what rewards have I got? The concern of friends? The consoling caresses of my love? The sympathies of society? . . . Ay! How can I not feel cold? How can I excite my passion? Heavens! I can only cry!" [67]

Chiang had moved into a hospital in May. In the morning of June 20, 1931, about three weeks after he had written the above letter, he died. [68]

Since 1949, Chiang Kuang-tz'u's name has been slowly reestablished in the People's Republic of China. The official reinstatement of Chiang Kuang-tz'u took place in 1953 when his remains were removed to the Hung-ch'iao Cemetery in Shanghai on the eve of the twenty-second anniversary of his death. The monument on the new grave carried the legend, "Here lies Chiang Kuang-tz'u, the writer," in the calligraphy of Ch'en Yi, then mayor of Shanghai. [69] Literary historians also heaped praise on this "revolutionary poet" who had once been ousted from the party. Ting Yi's opinion is typical of the re-estimation. "As his novels contain analyses of the main motive forces of revolution and descriptions of important revolutionary events, they won warm approval among the younger people of those days . . . These big circulations [of his works] spread the influence of the revolution and won many new readers to revolutionary literature. His contribution to the revolution should therefore never be forgotten . . . In propagating the revolutionary ideas of the proletariat, in rousing the revolutionary ardour of the masses, and in taking a lead in writing revolutionary literature Chiang Kuang-tzu [tz'u] did excellent service." [70]

All is force; all is struggle.
My ambition was to become a regular in the
mounted bandit corps.
—Hsiao Chün

Chapter 11

Hsiao Chün

The death of Chiang Kuang-tz'u in 1931 marked the end of the urban romantic drama of an entire decade. On September 18, 1931, the Mukden Incident heralded the Japanese invasion of Manchuria. The gathering clouds of the impending war cast long shadows on the literary scene. The May Thirtieth Incident, moreover, had shocked many literary intellectuals and ushered in a general drift toward the left. With Kuo Mo-jo's melodramatic proclamation of his conversion to Marxism, with a proliferation of leftist journals published by the young Creationists and their associates, the so-called proletarian literature swept the literary market. The phenomenon, as represented by Chiang Kuang-tz'u and his fictional writings, first enraged Lu Hsün and then forced this literary doyen in Shanghai into an excruciating study of Soviet literary theories. In 1930, the League of Left-wing Writers was formally established with Lu Hsün delivering the inaugural address. The decade of the 1930s, therefore, witnessed the unfolding of two trends: patriotism, which was directed mainly against Japan, and leftism, which under its general anti-imperialist posture encompassed such variegated doctrines as Marxism—Leninism (that is, the official Soviet line), Trotskyism, and anarchism. The merger of these two trends was represented in 1936 with the dissolution of the Left-wing League and the beginning of the United Front proclaimed both internationally and on the home front by the CCP. On the literary scene, the two trends were combined to the great advantage of the leftist writers. The apparent reluctance of the Nanking government to declare war against Japan provided these writers with a convincing argument that the "fascist" KMT government had betrayed China to the imperialists and thus abetted the oppression of the Chinese proletariat by foreign capitalism and imperialism. The persecution of the "Five Martyrs" by the KMT police was portrayed by Communist critics and historians as an example of this glaring double-oppression. By the time the Nationalist government formally declared war following the Marco Polo Bridge incident on July 7, 1937, the CCP and the leftist writers had already established a firm ideological front on the literary scene. Since to be anti-Japanese meant also to be anti-imperialist, patriotism became part of the leftist stance. The muddled inner story of the leftist camp remains to be fully explored. On the surface, however, both the CCP and the leftist writers, employing their tactics of the United Front to their great advantage, proclaimed themselves as the vanguard of the anti-Japanese struggle. And the less politically oriented writers such as Lin Yutang and Yü Ta-fu, who grouped around Lin's two magazines, *Jen-chien-shih* and *Yü-chou-feng*, were regarded by their leftist colleagues as not only petit-bourgeois but also unpatriotic. A new temper had set in, and new faces began to replace the old to enjoy the popular acclaim of a patriotically awakened public.

Shortly after the Mukden Incident, a group of young writers from the Manchurian provinces escaped to the Chinese mainland. In the vortex of patriotism that soon devoured the entire population of China, these young "refugee" writers, who were the first witnesses of Japanese aggression, became famous almost overnight. Their works enjoyed immediate popularity and distinction. The content and style of their works began to replace the short-lived "proletarian literature" as models of war literature, of which there ensued a profusion of imitations. The leader of this group was Hsiao Chün, whose novel *Pa-yüeh ti hsiang-ts'un* (Village in August) had the honor of being the

Hsiao Chün and Hsiao Hung

first contemporary Chinese novel to be translated into English, in addition to being the first specimen of war fiction.[1] Ideologically, Hsiao Chün was also one of the most famous leftist writers. He occupies a notorious page in the history of Chinese Communist literature as one of the first "poisonous weeds" to be purged by the party. The case of Hsiao Chün, therefore, supplies a fitting sequel to the drama of transition from romanticism to leftism as represented by Kuo Mo-jo and Chiang Kuang-tz'u, as he himself typifies another transition from the urban Shanghai phase to the rural Yenan phase in Communist literary historiography.

A Hero from the Grassroots

There is no better description of Hsiao Chün's early life than his own autobiographical account:

I was born in Manchuria in 1908, in a not-too-small village separated by some seventy li of mountain paths from the nearest city. The population consisted of peasants, craftsmen, hunters, soldiers, and mounted highway men—i.e., bandits.

My grandfather was a peasant and my uncles and my father were at first farmers, then carpenters, and later on merchants, army officers, and "mounted bandits." At times my family had property, at times we owned nothing at all. After the Mukden Incident . . . my father and three of his brothers . . . enlisted in the Volunteer Army against the Japanese.

I received no systematic education, was invariably expelled by the authorities of every school I attended, and in all studied in school only six or seven years.

In 1925 I joined the army, and remained a soldier for about six years. I was in the cavalry, infantry, gendarmery, artillery, and the cadet corps, and later became a junior officer. I joined the Volunteers in 1931 also, but after a while I began my literary career in a Manchurian city. I came to Shanghai in 1934.

Besides my career in the army I have been a vagabond-tramp, a secretary, an apprentice to a professional boxer—one of those stunt-doers in open-air markets—a waiter, a millstone pusher in a bean-shop, and what-not. My ambition was to become a regular in the mounted bandit corps, and though I did not succeed and am now writing novels, I still cherish that hope, and perhaps some day it will be realized.[2]

225

This autobiographical sketch, which Hsiao wrote at the request of Edgar Snow as a short self-introduction to the English-speaking readers of his first novel, itself reads like a highly picaresque story which is even more colorful than Chiang Kuang-tzu's *Youthful Tramp*. Moreover, Hsiao's background resembles that of Kuo Mo-jo especially through the "bandit" connections of their family members. In both men a sense of dare-devil heroism was injected into their personalities. This heroic and rebellious trait is all the more blatant in Hsiao Chün, as can be seen in his own description of his childhood environment: "They encouraged small children to be bold, to defy any set regulations and principles . . . They worshiped strength . . . They all cherished the hope that their sons would someday become extraordinary, heaven-resounding 'heroes' who rise above a multitude of people—no matter at what expense this hero status could be acquired."[3]

The way was paved for Hsiao Chün to become a grassroots hero. His various roles early in life—vagabond-tramp, secretary, professional boxer's apprentice, waiter, millstone pusher—served as the necessary training ground for his ultimate goals: to be a *hu-tzu*, a mounted bandit hero. As he later confessed: "I was fond of fighting from early childhood. When I grew a little older, I became enthralled with the 'art of fighting,' under the influence of 'chivalry tales.' I paid homage to various masters, called upon various 'friends,' and engaged in various competitions of strength."[4] That he later joined the army can also be viewed as an extension of this life ambition to be a hero of action. What he called the "bandit spirit" remained the hallmark of his life and, as he later gave up the gun and took up the pen, of his literary work.

The genesis of Hsiao Chün's bandit image is also inextricably related to the physical landscape of Manchuria, a secluded region rich in natural resources and naturally clement, yet profuse in natural beauty. Hsiao Chün's reminiscences of his early years were full of nostalgia for this lost landscape: "I love the endless depths of her blue sky, her ink-dark forests of pines and cypresses, her straight branches and maples thrusting into the clouds, shining with silver; I love the herds of cattle wandering over the plains like the waves of a sea; and above all I love her fearless honest people. The whirring snow-flakes and roaring winds may cut my face like knives, but I love them all."[5]

For Hsiao Chün, the "fearless honest" people are woven into that vast expanse of rugged nature which is "Tung-pei" (Northeast), or Manchuria. Against this background are to be found the follies and cruelties of his people, which are the dominant themes of his early stories. Looming on the horizons is the landlord's castle, solidly entrenched and heavily guarded. Under those gloomy shadows the peasants have toiled, suffered, rebelled in vain, and returned to their rugged lives.[6] The only way to break away from this tragic pattern and to assert the dignity of man is to become a mounted bandit. For only among the bandits does one find real brotherhood and real heroes. The leader of the bandits, in particular, exemplifies for Hsiao the prototype of the grassroots hero who leads his brothers with benevolence, fights against the landlords with courage, and dies with heroism and honor. One is easily reminded of the famous one hundred and eight "tough guys" (hao-han) of the Water Margin, whose heroic deeds filled the youthful imaginations of Hsiao Chün, Kuo Mo-jo, and Mao Tse-tung. In Hsiao's case, however, the heroes of historical fiction found their closest avatars in real life.

The loss of Manchuria to the Japanese forces meant also the end of the heroic idyll, of Hsiao Chün's youthful dream to become a bandit. When he began to write his first novel, reality could only be recaptured but not relived. Literary creation was for him a compensatory endeavor so that what he had failed to attain in real life would be fulfilled fictionally, with the aid of imagination. But to write fictionalized memoirs for a would-be bandit-hero involves more problems than simple wish fulfillment. Literary creation, which attaches more importance to the ingenuity of the mind than the strength of the body, seems hardly a fitting vocation for a man who is enthralled with "the art of fighting" and who has "engaged in various competitions of strength." Writing, therefore, never served to tame his fighting spirit. But the prestige attached to being a popular writer carries with it other possibilities. A writer could be a different kind of hero, one who fights social injustice with his pen rather than his fists. The writer's rebellious spirit could be expressed through words which might goad others to action. The story of Hsiao Chün as a writer reveals this interesting process of redefining heroism. He sought to perpetuate another heroic role by transporting his bandit spirit from the Manchurian steppes to the literary arenas of Shanghai and Yenan—a process that totally victimized him at the end.

Village in August

Hsiao Chün began the writing of his most important novel, *Village in August*, in the spring of 1934 when he was still in Japanese-occupied Harbin. In May he escaped with Hsiao Hung to Tsingtao where, with a heart laden with bitter memories, he finally completed it.[7] In November he took the finished draft to Shanghai where it was shown to Lu Hsün and published under the latter's auspices as one of the Slave Series. In his preface to Hsiao Chün's novel, Lu Hsün revealed the temper of the work, which also goes far to explain its popularity: "Although it is like a succession of short stories, and its structure and characterization cannot be compared with Fadeyev's *The Rout*, it is serious and tense. The emotions of the author, the lost skies, earth, the suffering people, and even the deserted grass, *kao-liang*, frogs, mosquitos—all are muddled together, spreading in gory-red color before the very eyes of the reader, and revealing both part and whole of China, both the present and the future, both the way to death and the way to life."[8]

Lu Hsün's enthusiastic introduction points to the interesting fact that the success of Hsiao Chün's novel was due not so much to its artistic merit, which is scanty, as to the muddled and heightened emotions of its author. It reflected both Hsiao Chün's own patriotic emotionalism and the ferment of patriotism among most young intellectuals in the 1930s. Since Hsiao Chün joined the volunteer army to fight the Japanese, the work is avowedly autobiographical. It is significant that Hsiao Chün represented another facet of the transitional phenomenon in which the autobiographical impulse was expressed in the shifting focus from personal emotions of love to political feelings.

The loose plot of *Village in August* centers around a roving band of Communist guerrillas in Manchuria. Led by their intellectual captain, Hsiao Ming, they exemplify in one episode after another their admirable valor in fighting against the overwhelming force of the Japanese army. The significance of this guerrilla band is that they were not only patriotic fighters against Japan but also Communist guerrillas. *Village in August* is supposedly "the first nationally successful communist novel to embody the theme of Anti-Japanese resistance." [9]

There is nothing in Hsiao Chün's autobiographical accounts which may give any clue to the origin and genesis of his Communist ideology. And the "Communist" tinges in his novel betray a somewhat superficial knowledge. Terms such as "the toiling masses," "bourgeoisie," and "revolution" are profusely used, and there are occasional, vaguely Marxist lines such as, "Only when the revolution of the proletariat of the whole world breaks into the open can our own country be saved." [10] But Hsiao Chün characterized the guerrillas both as a "people's army" and as Communists, the proletariat. He also attempted to envelop all the possible ambiguities in sweeping "red" imageries—red flags, red star, red light—all crowned in an aura of superstitious idealism. ("May heaven guard me! May the Red Light of our revolution guard me!" [11])

The superficiality of Hsiao Chün's communism is compounded in the novel by a total neglect of guerrilla warfare tactics, thus forfeiting a potential comparison with Mao's celebrated theories of guerrilla warfare. On the contrary, in the ranks of the "revolutionary army" we find the majority to be rugged and dogged Manchurian peasants to whom Hsiao Chün was personally attached. The peasants found it hard to renounce their private affections for their wives, children, their land, and their pipes. And Hsiao Chün invariably found himself on their side. The novel is therefore an imperfect example of Socialist Realism which results from an unresolved conflict on the part of its author: his patriotism demands unstinted heroism from his characters, but his sense of realism can only bring him to the many human flaws which detract from pure heroism. The humanity of his peasant heroes, whom he has come to know so well, made it impossible for him to paint all his heroes as positive prototypes imbued with Communist virtues and armed with correct ideology.

The typical image of a peasant hero in the novel is represented by Boil T'ang. A member of this Communist guerrilla force, he was also a peasant with unbridled passions. In one episode, the Japanese troops are approaching and the guerrillas have to retreat for the safety of the entire company. Boil T'ang's mistress has been raped and severely wounded by a Japanese soldier. At this crucial moment, Boil T'ang's personal sentiment gains the upper hand: he renounces the revolution and insists on staying behind with his mistress. Iron Eagle, commander of the guerrilla force, decides reluctantly to execute Boil Tang to ensure discipline and safety for the whole group: "Iron Eagle's face had become even darker than its usual color, and the corners of his mouth were drawn even further down. The pistol strapped to his wrist was in his hand now, his arm half raised." [12]

This episode was written when Hsiao Chün was in Tsingtao in 1934. He later recalled: "Down to this point I could write no more. I didn't know how to handle the situation. I looked out at the sea—I was then in Tsingtao—at the mountains . . . I went out, walked in the streets, and returned . . . pondering upon it for two whole nights and two whole days, until finally I resolved to let the stray Japanese bullet kill him." [13]

Hsiao Chün's own reason for this solution, *deus ex machina*, is: "I do not wish to see, nor let the readers see, bullets fired by one comrade penetrate the chest of another." [14] But it reveals more than what he confesses. One can easily sense Hsiao Chün's admiration for Boil T'ang's "guts," a personality trait acknowledged to be one of the chief features of the Manchurian character. But, on the other hand, Iron Eagle is obviously Hsiao Chün's apotheosis of a positive revolutionary hero who can do no wrong. With a kind of naiveté Hsiao Chün let the two men clash in the battleground of his own heart so as to resolve his emotional dilemma. It is interesting, therefore, that the high degree of realism of this novel is derived not so much from penetrating characterization as from the sincere revelation of the author's real feelings. The novel is a mirror in which we can see the rather awkward attempts of Hsiao Chün to recreate the conflicts of his own experience. We know from the very imperfections of craftsmanship which character is fictional and which character still has flesh and bones.

The one character with whom Hsiao Chün personally identified is Hsiao Ming, the intellectual leader of the guerrilla band under the general commander, Iron Eagle. Like Hsiao Chün, Hsiao Ming is not only a guerrilla fighter but also an intellectual. More important, Hsiao Chün has chosen to use Hsiao Ming to dramatize a central conflict which lurks behind Boil T'ang's intransigence: the conflict between romantic love and revolutionary duty which has also obsessed Chiang Kuang-tz'u. The decline of this brave intellectual from a beloved revolutionary leader to a position of political impotence is due to his love affair with Anna, a Korean girl who is also a member of the guerrilla force. The final solution—to sacrifice love for revolution—is not reached before a passionate, maudlin breakdown between the two lovers. Hsiao Chün put the following words in the mouth of his tearful hero: "Anna . . . you should at least let me cry just once more in front of you. Only once! Even if we had not loved each other, let me then cry once more as a comrade . . . Let me disgrace just once more the dignity of the revolution tonight! . . . I will buy back its honor with my own blood." [15]

The character of Anna may be fictitious and the episode itself suggests contrivance. But one cannot help noticing in Hsiao Ming's confessional outburst a high degree of genuine feeling on the part of the author. Again Hsiao Chün resorts to the same device of letting two currents of his emotions battle it out in his novel. Hsiao Ming is defeated at the end but not without a last dramatic attempt to apologize for harboring private emotions. Moreover, in spite of Hsiao Ming's defeat, the novel ends with a glimmer of hope: left behind with a small detachment to take care of the sick and wounded, Hsiao Ming has shown signs of ideological recuperation.

Hsiao Chün's treatment of his characters invites immediate comparison with a Soviet work after which Village in August is modeled —Fadeyev's The Rout (Razgrom).[16] Both novels deal with the wanderings and struggles of a band of guerrillas against a setting of the northeastern countryside. (In Fadeyev's novel the story took place during the civil war period in the Far Eastern Maritime provinces of Russia.) And in both novels we find three chief characters: Boil T'ang and Morozka, Hsiao Ming and Matchik, Iron Eagle and Levenson.

Hsiao Chün is more emotionally committed to Boil T'ang than Fadeyev to Morozka. As described earlier, Boil T'ang serves as an eruptive outer manifestation of Hsiao Chün's attachment to his rustic countrymen in Manchuria, while Morozka is described as crude, passionate, and prankish. Fadeyev's detached treatment of this Russian peasant reveals that his major concern lies elsewhere—in the two intellectuals, Matchik and Levenson. Writing in the grand nineteenth century tradition of Russian fiction, albeit with Marxist embellishments, Fadeyev assigns to Matchik from the very beginning the hallmark of the Russian intelligentsia: their alienation. Matchik is "never able to become a part of the unit, never perceives its inner human 'mechanism,' and expresses his intellectual's selfishness in a final moment of cowardice that destroys the entire company."[17] Hsiao Ming, on the other hand, is not afflicted with this stigma, and his partial alienation near the end of the novel does not derive from either social or philosophic sources, as in the case of the Russian intelligentsia, but rather from romantic love. Moreover, his love of Anna does not entirely disgrace the revolution. The differences between these two parallel characters illustrate the authors' different conceptions of the intellectual. Unlike Yü Ta-fu, Hsiao Chün was too enamored of his new status as a writer to consider an intellectual character totally superfluous. An intellectual, to Hsiao Chün, is identical with a literary man, an educated "new style" radical who writes in order to defy his society. His only weakness, from an ideological viewpoint, is that he may be too sensitive to his private emotions. Accordingly, Hsiao Ming is in every aspect a typical intellectual in the May Fourth tradition, although Hsiao Chün has seen fit to transform him into a guerrilla fighter.

It may be said that Hsiao Ming represents the "intellectual" side of Hsiao Chün—a figure who serves to bridge the transition of Hsiao Chün's own roles in life from a man with a gun to a man with a pen. But his self-image as a hero from the grassroots still remains with him. Thus he creates another hero to supplement Hsiao Ming. Iron Eagle is conceived not merely as the prototype of the positive hero, as prescribed in the canons of Socialist Realism, but also to serve as Hsiao Chün's personal type of positive hero. Iron Eagle has been a peasant, a soldier, and a bandit. He is also a man of vision and valor, self-disciplined, correct in thought, and devoted to his official duties. Thus, for Hsiao Chün, he combines the character traits of an ideal Communist and an ideal grassroots bandit-hero. Unlike Fadeyev's Levenson, the hunched, "gnome-like" Jewish Communist who is gradually alienated even from his own comrades, Iron Eagle is always beloved by his men and by peasants. Levenson is Fadeyev's "interim man" who feels that "he is keeping alive the strain that will issue in the higher human type he dreams of"—the positive hero.[18] Iron Eagle, on the other hand, is Hsiao Chün's ideal self-image in that he embodies the virtues and qualities which Hsiao Chün does not, but wishes, to possess. It was this essentially individualistic vision of a positive hero that later landed Hsiao Chün in trouble with the party.

Hsiao Chün, Hsiao Hung, and Lu Hsün

Village in August marked Hsiao Chün's debut as a literary man. His personal life while in the process of writing this novel also added more credentials to his new role as a *wen-jen*. In the autumn of 1932, Hsiao Chün met a fellow refugee writer, a young girl named Hsiao Hung (Chang Nai-ying). Their romance and the later complications became something of a minor legend. As they retreated to Shanghai, they met Lu Hsün. Hsiao Hung immediately endeared herself to the old master and Hsiao Chün became in fact his protégé. Both Hsiao Hung and Lu Hsün thenceforth played decisive roles in Hsiao Chün's life.

Hsiao Hung was born in 1911 to a landlord family in the Amur (Heilungkiang) province of Manchuria. Like most "new style" girls, Hsiao Hung migrated from her rural environment to the city of Harbin. In 1929, as a student of the First Girls' School in Harbin, Hsiao Hung was already a celebrity among her classmates. She organized a painters' outing club and began reading the new literature of Mao

Tun, Ping Hsin, and Hsü Chih-mo. In 1930, she was forced to return home from the school to be married to a general's son. Already a rebel, she escaped to Peking with her lover, a law student she had met in Harbin, only to find that her lover was already married.[19] She went back to Harbin alone, stricken with poverty and illness.

It was at this critical juncture in her life that a friend at a Harbin newspaper brought another wandering writer, Hsiao Chün, to visit her. Hsiao Chün's sympathy for her deplorable lot soon turned into love. Despite the fact that she was pregnant with her lover's child, the equally impoverished Hsiao Chün put her up in a dingy hotel owned by a White Russian and the two of them began their strictly bohemian life together. They called each other "my lover" and lived on bread, salt, and water, bought with the small sum Hsiao Chün earned as a private tutor.[20] As Hsiao Chün later recalled: "Like the swallows in spring . . . I and my love have finally built our home . . . My duty was to fly . . . in order to find edible stuff and make my sick partner in the nest become strong again!"[21] Their new home was located in the corner of a street lined with artisans and pedlars. Every morning, Hsiao Chün went out to find work and borrow money while Hsiao Hung waited. Thus they passed the first winter of their life together. The next year, Hsiao Hung gave birth to a girl. She was ill and penniless and could not leave the hospital because the medical expenses could not be met. The doctors refused to treat her, and Hsiao Chün had to resort to bandit methods by threatening to kill the doctors and their entire families.[22]

In the spring of 1933 the Hsiaos gave away their child, sold everything they had, and borrowed enough money to make their trip to Tsingtao. There he completed *Village in August* and she finished her first novel, *Sheng-ssu ch'ang* (Fields of life and death). In October 1934 they brought their works to Shanghai and paid their first visit to Lu Hsün on November 27 in a coffee house. On November 30 they again met in Lu Hsün's favorite Japanese bookstore. On December 17 Lu Hsün invited the Hsiaos to dinner.[23] Thereafter, the Hsiaos became frequent visitors to Lu Hsün's residence and kept up a correspondence with him for almost two years.[24] As young refugee writers from Japanese-occupied Manchuria, the Hsiaos may have had a stronger appeal to Lu Hsün who had become embittered by leftist writers in Shanghai. From Hsiao Hung's reminiscence of Lu Hsün and from Hsiao Chün's correspondence with him, it is clear that the saddened and suspicious old master harbored a particular loving regard for these two newcomers. He warned them against the wiles of other literary men in Shanghai. He assisted them with money, corrected and praised their works, and sought various channels to publish them. He even advised Hsiao Hung on the color and styles of her dresses.[25]

It was from Lu Hsün that Hsiao Chün learned a few rudiments of writing. The influence of Lu Hsün can readily be seen in Hsiao Chün's short stories from his Shanghai period. Somewhat dispirited by the urban sophistication and debauchery he felt around him, Hsiao Chün began to describe the dispossessed and displaced Manchurians who came to Shanghai after many narrow escapes from the Japanese-controlled territories—only to find their doom in debauchery and degradation.[26] But the outcry of a tormented voice is often muffled by a sense of restraint, and Manchurian pastoralism is accompanied by an intensity of atmospheric touches—obviously under the influence of Lu Hsün.

The master's praise of his protégé's stories was profuse in his letters. Elsewhere he also mentioned Hsiao Chün as one of the seven best writers who had appeared since the New Literature movement.[27] The imprint of the master is equally indelible in the process of Hsiao Chün's intellectual maturation. Hsiao Chün had approached Lu Hsün with great expectations. The haggard appearance and the plain attire of the master might have distressed him at first. But in Lu Hsün's mind he apparently found an inexhaustible spring of ideas which enlightened, refreshed, and to some extent even justified his own thoughts and outlook.

Hsiao Chün summarized Lu Hsün's ideals as follows: "The ideal he has left us is how to raise our own nation from her slavish position to the status of true humanity, to elevate mankind from the half-animal position to the status of human beings."[28] Lu Hsün's "basic spirit," according to Hsiao Chün, is therefore "to fight for the existence, the liberation and the development of the Chinese nation; to fight, like all the other great men, for the justice, righteousness, well-being, and liberty of mankind."[29] This heroic portrait of Lu Hsün as a fighter for the oppressed also has elements of Hsiao Chün's own self-image. Karl Marx once in play with his daughters named two heroes he admired most: Spartacus and Kepler.[30] The soldier–artist complex in Hsiao Chün's mentality also prompts him to seek a dual image of a heroic leader. In *Village in August* the characterization of its two major protagonists—Hsiao Ming and Iron Eagle—certainly reflects this Spartacus-Kepler denominator. In real life, Hsiao Chün appears to have granted Lu Hsün the role of a Chinese Kepler, a prophet of wisdom endowed with a depth of vision and indomitable courage. But where could he find a true Spartacus, a grassroots hero with both courage and physical prowess to lead the oppressed in regaining their human status? Evidently, he found his Spartacus in himself. His activities and writings in Yenan showed that he was also eager to assume the patriarchic status of his master.

Yenan

Lu Hsün died on October 19, 1936. On July 7, 1937, the Marco Polo Incident led to the formal declaration of war by China against Japan. In October, Hsiao Chün and Hsiao Hung were among the new refugees who left Shanghai for Wuhan. As the war raged on from northern China to the plains of the Yangtze area, the Hsiaos were also involved in a series of domestic wars which finally terminated their relationship. A friend's sympathetic account of their life reveals that Hsiao Chün became more and more dominant over his often bedridden mistress. Their physical incompatibility may have sown the seed of discord. But the more plausible reason may have been his vanity. He considered her work as inferior to his and even humiliated her in front of a friend's wife with whom he was having an affair in Shanghai.[31] Hsiao Hung had reportedly said: "He is too self-confident!"[32]

The cleavage between the two lovers was widened when they moved from Wuhan to Hsian in Shensi where she made friends with Ting Ling and another young writer from Manchuria, Tuan-mu Hung-liang. The efforts of Ting Ling and other friends to help salvage their relationship proved futile, especially in view of a vaguely developed triangular relationship with the intrusion of Tuan-mu.[33] Hsiao Chün finally forsook his mistress and went to Yenan while Hsiao Hung, after a period of cohabitation with her new lover, was left to die of tuberculosis on January 22, 1942, in a hospital in Japanese-occupied Hong Kong.[34]

When Hsiao Chün first arrived in Yenan in 1940 he was invited to lodge in the special hostel for literary celebrities, the Literary Association of the Border Regions, and he was said to have occasionally heaved a sigh for the "lack of social life" in this revolutionary base.[35] By November 1941 he had become one of the "invited senators" in the Second Congress of the Senate of the Border Regions of Shensi-Kansu-Ninghsia.[36] Earlier in October, the first edition of the Series on the Study of Lu Hsün was published by the Yenan Research Council under the chairmanship of Hsiao Chün.

Although he enjoyed high prestige in the literary circles of Yenan, Hsiao Chün was not content. Like most intellectuals who went to Yenan in search of personal heroism, he found that the revolutionary reality, hemmed in as Yenan was by both the Japanese and the Nationalist armies, fell far short of his preconceived ideals. Wang Shih-wei led the attack in a series of articles published in the *Liberation Daily* under the title "Wild Lilies." Ting Ling deplored the fate of women in Yenan in an article commemorating March 8, Women's Day. Hsiao Chün soon followed suit. In an essay titled "On 'Love' and 'Patience' among Comrades" he unleashed his personal grudges in a patriarchic manner. He praised the true fighters "who crawled from blood and iron, bruised all over, but still fought on with untiring determination," and extended his sympathies also to those "who occasionally became weak and did something detrimental to the honor of revolution." In the conclusion he stated: "I respect them [true fighters who had erred] more than I do those 'heroes' who have never seen blood and iron while still flaunting their 'heroism' in a 'safe closet.' For after all, they [the erring true fighters] have gone through the ordeal. Isn't it a precious thing to welcome 'the return of the prodigal son?' "[37]

The target of his attack lies mainly in those inexperienced cadres in the higher strata of the party bureaucracy in Yenan. In satirizing the false heroes, Hsiao Chün also implied that he himself was a true veteran hero who had gone through the crucible of "blood and iron." The authoritarian tone reveals clearly that he had assumed his master's role as the literary doyen in Yenan. He even took up Lu Hsün's patronizing attitude toward new authors in another article titled "The 'Bulba Spirit' on the Literary Scene." According to his reading of Gogol's novel, old Taras Bulba welcomes his two sons home with joy, which he conveys by exchanging fist blows with them. When he is struck down by his sons he sheds tears of satisfaction.[38] In Bulba's attitude toward his sons, Hsiao Chün found an analogy to what he thought to be the correct attitude toward new writers: "In our literary movements, we should also put in a degree of Bulba spirit—that is, not to be afraid of being struck down by newcomers. You should encourage them by competing with them and you should feel all the more pleased when you get beaten. Only thus can there be hope for humanity and hope in our literary circles."[39]

The Bulba spirit, to Hsiao Chün, was essentially Lu Hsün's help and encouragement of new writers. But his selection of a rustic Cossack hero easily leads one to another analogy, his celebrated bandit spirit. Years later, his Communist critics, citing it out of context, were able to see the connection between the Bulba spirit and the bandit spirit, which they regarded as the root of his anti-party stance.

Hsiao Chün's self-aggrandizement was not curbed even when the *Liberation Daily* printed a large number of articles criticizing Wang Shih-wei. He continued to write his *tsa-wen*, an essay form he had learned from Lu Hsün, but the themes of his essays invariably revolved around himself. In one of them, casually titled "Also to Try My Pen," he blatantly declared: "I am an advocate of new heroism. Its principles are: for mankind, strengthening oneself, and striving to be the first."[40] This declaration of principles was followed by a long list of his favorite personalities and what he considered to be the great moments in their lives: the spirit of "If I don't go to hell, who would?" in Mahayana Buddhism; Moses, who led the Exodus; Jesus, when he asserted "eye for an eye"; Socrates who, at the moment of his death, did not forget to return a chicken to his neighbor; Hsiang Yü, the aristocrat—rebel defeated by the Han founder, and Huang Ch'ao, the bandit—rebel at the end of the Han, both of whom had executed a grand finale of heroic suicide; Ts'ao Ts'ao, the famous statesman—hero of the Three Kingdoms period, as he composed that tragic piece of poetry aboard his battleship and sensed premonitions of his defeat; Ssu-ma Ch'ien, the great Han historian who suffered castration but continued writing his *Shih-chi*; Marx and Lenin ("They are lovable because they are truly poets"); Homer, the blind poet; Tolstoy at his final desertion of his aristocratic family; Caesar's proclamation: "Not only do I create history but I also write history"; Napoleon; Byron in Greece; Beethoven, whose very deafness helped him silently accomplish "mankind's heroic feat"; and finally, Michelangelo and Rodin: "I can't name the reasons, for they are like mountains and oceans that 'naturally' exist." [41]

This vast gallery of great personages in history, as seen through the lens of Hsiao Chün's prejudiced and often erroneous interpretations, represents a summary of not only his own heroic outlook but also all the perennial favorites of his predecessors from Lin Shu to Kuo Mo-jo. But Hsiao Chün was daring enough, long before Kuo Mo-jo began to sing his hymns to the New China, to include Lu Hsün, Mao Tse-tung and Chu Teh in this pantheon of heroes: "In China, I have seen three great 'Realists.' They are Lu Hsün, Chu Teh, and Mao Tse-tung. The years of their birth were close to each other. The historical mission they carry on their shoulders is the same. But what is the most important is their common goal—for our nation and for mankind—[which is pursued with] the realistic, 'flexible' method of struggle." [42]

When Mao Tse-tung convened the famous Yenan Forum on Literature and Art on May 2, 1942, Hsiao Chün was one of the more than 200 participants. Afterwards he wrote a resume of his viewpoints which he had presented in the forum. The article, "My Viewpoints Concerning Current Problems in Literature and Art," yields many interesting points for comparison with the Maoist line.

With regard to the writer's standpoint, Mao stated clearly: "We take the standpoint of the proletariat, and the mass of people. For members of the Communist Party, this means that they should adopt the standpoint of the party, abide by the spirit and policy of the party." [43] Hsiao Chün, on the other hand, blurred Mao's clear-cut picture with his universalistic hues: "What standpoint should we—Chinese people of the present age—take in order to write? This is obvious. First, it is to achieve the liberation of our nation. Second, it is to achieve the liberation of mankind. All should be in the service of this liberation." [44] Concerning the subject-matter and sources for literary creation, Mao's worker–peasant–soldier focus was not observed; instead, Hsiao Chün maintained that materials could be gathered everywhere: villages, cities, war front, and the immediate environment of the writer himself. He made only one compromise with the Maoist guideline. In maintaining the merits of realism, he also stressed that "one should write more about the progressive aspect and that which contains more typicality." [45]

On May 23, nine days after the publication of Hsiao Chün's article, Mao delivered his final "Summing Up" to officially close the forum. Among the well-remembered sentences can be found the following ones: "There has not been any such all-embracing love of mankind since the division of mankind into classes. All the ruling classes in the past liked to advocate this love, and so did many of the so-called sages and wise men, but nobody has ever put it into practice for the very good reason that it is impracticable in a class society." [46]

Despite Hsiao Chün's obviously unorthodox and tangential views, no criticism against him appeared in print in 1942. He apparently survived the Rectification campaign without any open harassment. It was only after the termination of the war when he returned to Manchuria that cases against him were finally initiated by the party.

The Cultural Gazette

Hsiao Chün returned to Manchuria with the Communist armed forces and arrived in Harbin in September 1946.[47] Under the auspices of the party authorities, he founded *Wen-hua pao* (The cultural gazette), a periodical which, beginning with May 4, 1947, appeared once every five days.[48]

The return of a native son should have been an occasion for joy. But Hsiao Chün felt otherwise. "In Shanghai, I sometimes felt depressed and rootless . . . This was because we were strangers in Shanghai. Now that I have finally returned to my own native land, I should not have this sense of desolation any more. But it still exists and seems to have become somewhat more intense . . . and I still feel rootless." [49]

To feel uprooted on his beloved native soil was certainly something Hsiao Chün had not anticipated. The social reality of the Communist-occupied areas, which emerged from the turmoil of a disastrous war only to be engulfed in a new one, apparently failed to coalesce with Hsiao Chün's cherished images. Moreover, his return was not simply the return of a native son but also the triumphant homecoming of a hero from the revolutionary base. The sense of self-importance that he had developed in Yenan rendered him restless when confronting the chaotic bureaucratic structure of the Communists. And he took up the only weapon at his command. His cutting essays in *The Cultural Gazette* achieved a vehemence and bold pungency hitherto unsurpassed.

He directed his attacks against many targets: the Russians in Manchuria,[50] both sides in the Chinese civil war, and especially party administration in the Communist-occupied areas. The rank and file of the local bureaucracy was crowned with 124 "isms" ranging from "Ah Qism," "Don Quixoteism," to "so-so-ism," and "well-fed-and-doing-nothing-ism." [51] About the Communist land reform programs launched in Manchuria, he wrote: "The idea of redividing other people's land and taking away their property . . . this is an unprecedented act of robbery indeed." [52]

The manner in which Hsiao Chün dealt with his enemies bespeaks the consistency of another facet of his mentality. His self-assertive and self-aggrandizing tendencies, which gradually took shape and manifested themselves in his Yenan articles, now poured forth unbridled and pitted against the party itself. Behind his sweeping diatribes was a reassertion of self-importance: if the party line of coping with social reality was wrong, he as a true Communist fighter was right. His autobiography, "My Life" was serialized in *The Cultural Gazette*. Time and again he reminisced about the turbulent years of his early youth, which had inculcated in him a sense of "grand defiance" and a conviction that "all is 'force,' all is 'struggle,' " that "one should therefore take revenge, be indomitable, and invest one's life as a last bullet—one should triumph over all." [53] The ghost of Lu Hsün as a great fighter was invoked and Lu Hsün's letters were reprinted with copious notes, in which accounts about Hsiao Chün far surpassed those about his master. His house was named "Truthseeking Tower" in which our wearied veteran hero wrote poems in the classical style:

Years of bloody war have brought chaos in the four seas.
Who will, single-handed, save the masses? [54]

All these heroic effusions prove beyond doubt that the campaigns and reforms in Yenan did not at all affect Hsiao Chün's personality or his self-image as a grassroots hero. Nor was his attitude toward communism changed much from that manifested in *Village in August*: his individual heroism dominated his communism. And this preconceived vision finally brought him disaster. The purge of Hsiao Chün began at last.

The process was heralded by a series of articles in the Harbin *Sheng-huo pao* (Life news) by such party authors as Sung Chih-ti and Chou Li-po. Discussion meetings on Hsiao Chün's reactionary thought were soon held in factories and schools in Harbin and Kirin. Hsiao Chün gallantly defended himself in *The Cultural Gazette*. On February 13, 1949, Liu Chih-ming, Deputy Director of the Propaganda Department of the CCP Northeastern Bureau, issued an over-all criticism of Hsiao Chün in the *Tung-pei jih-pao* (Northeastern daily). Finally a joint meeting was convened by fifteen civic organs in Harbin, headed by the Northeastern Federation of Literature and Art, to prosecute Hsiao Chün. The party's Northeastern Bureau made public the text of a resolution on the "Problem of Hsiao Chün," in which it was announced that "no further material support will be given to Hsiao Chün to assist his literary activities." [55] *The Cultural Gazette* was suspended. Hsiao Chün disappeared. According to most non-Communist sources, he was sent to the coal mines in Fushun for labor reform. [56]

About half a year later, on October 1, Mao Tse-tung read a proclamation before a cheering crowd of more than 200,000 in Peking announcing the establishment of the Central Government of the People's Republic of China.

Epilogue: Coal Mines in May

In January 1951 Hsiao Chün emerged in Peking. In June he set out to write a spectacular new novel based on his own experience in the Manchurian coal mines. On April 16, 1952, he completed the first draft. In November 1954 the 550-page novel, entitled *Wu-yüeh ti k'uang-shan* (Coal mines in May) was published by the Writers' Press in Peking.[57] But in December 1955 the leading party literary organ, *Wen-i pao* (The literary gazette), published a critical article condemning this new work as poisonous.[58] In early 1958, following the liquidation of the Ting Ling–Ch'en Ch'i-hsia clique, *The Literary Gazette* initiated a re-criticism movement in which Hsiao Chün again became one of the main targets. "Hsiao Chün's attempt to vindicate his new orthodoxy had only boomeranged."[59]

Obviously the novel was intended not merely to vindicate his new orthodoxy but also to restore his previous position as a writer. It is a painstakingly elaborate piece fraught with enthusiastic eulogies to the bravery and dedication of miners under the guidance of the party cadres. In contrast to his previous careless attitude toward ideology, Hsiao Chün manifested a studied seriousness in meeting all the demands of Socialist Realism and the guidelines as set forth in Mao's *Talks at the Yenan Forum*.

But in fervently embracing his new proletarian outlook and consciously denigrating his own ego, Hsiao Chün has unconsciously apotheosized his worker-heroes in his new novel. Ironically, it is in his over-enthusiastic portrayal of proletarian heroes that the official critics find the root of the work's poison. One critic wrote: "The 'hero' determines all—this is the argument Hsiao Chün posits in this novel with all his demoniac passions . . . He has magnified his 'heroes' to such fantastic proportions as to hold them aloof from the masses."[60] Another found in it a resurgence of his Bulba spirit.[61] Hsiao Chün was therefore charged for his distortion of the real image of the people and his calumny of the party. Hsiao Chün was again silent.

The life of Hsiao Chün has epitomized the fate of the romantic-leftist writer through a period of cataclysmic permutations. He may have suffered more than others, but the pattern he represents is typical —the pattern of an impulsive individualism seasoned into resignation, of a rosy, all-embracing idealism lacerated into silence, and of an effusion of overpowering emotionalism shattered into powerlessness. The transition from romanticism to leftism and communism may have been facile enough, but writers, to paraphrase Chiang Kuang-tz'u, are doomed to be solitary and unhappy, their visions never realized. Hsiao Chün and his older contemporaries sufficiently exemplified the case. The larger issues—literary, social, political, and intellectual— which loom behind the lives of these individuals will be discussed in the concluding chapters.

Of Life immense in passion, pulse, and power,
Cheerful, for freest action form'd under the laws
    divine,
The Modern Man I sing.
—Whitman

I want a hero: an uncommon want,
    When every year and month sends forth a
      new one,
Till, after cloying the gazettes with cant,
    The age discovers he is not the true one.
—Byron

Part Four   The Romantic Generation: Reflections on a Theme

Chapter 12

The Modern *Wen-jen* and Chinese Society

The phenomenon of the modern Chinese *wen-jen* may be likened to a tragicomic drama enacted on the urban setting of the literary scene. The prelude can be dated at the turn of the century. The Literary Revolution of 1917 raised the curtain and a host of protagonists rushed onto the stage. The climax was reached in the mid-twenties, followed by a leftist *dénouement* after the May Thirtieth Incident of 1925, and the furor gradually waned in the early 1930s. The drama may be said to have come to an end in 1937 when the stage itself was destroyed by Japanese cannon fire. The Sino-Japanese War began a new saga of national experience and the Yenan interlude a new chapter in the history of Communist literature. But the *wen-jen* was no longer the unchallenged hero, as can be seen in Hsiao Chün's tragic fate.

Identity and Alienation

The immense "gossip" literature written by friends and admirers in the twenties and thirties demonstrates clearly that the contemporary audience was most impressed by what they believed to be the scintillating personalities of the literary men. What mattered to them was neither the expertise of craftsmanship nor the vigor or exuberance of creative imagination but rather the intensity of the author's own emotional experience. This exaltation of the writer's personality and life experience, for the audience of later generations, yields a few important lessons.

The *wen-jen* in traditional China—from Ssu-ma Hsiang-ju of the Han dynasty, Li Po of the T'ang, to Huang Chung-tse of the Ch'ing —was also renowned for his life and personality as much as for his work. But since literature was never an established vocation in traditional China, the *wen-jen* never became a self-conscious status group in traditional Chinese society. The peculiarities of personality or of life experience remained individual idiosyncracies rather than hallmarks of a group. Moreover, the status of a *wen-jen* in traditional China was seldom clearly demarcated from that of a scholar-official; often the epithet *wen-jen* indicated merely the literary side of a scholar-official. The emergence of *wen-jen* as a social group with literature as a vocation is a modern phenomenon which is obviously related to the changed socio-political circumstances.

The practice of literature as an independent vocation was, in part, the result of the increasing prosperity of journalism and publishing after the turn of the century. This commercial factor, however, was not decisive in the evolution of the modern men of letters as an esteemed status group. Their group consciousness stems from other sources. The modern men of letters shared a common pattern of life experience. Born at the turn of the century in a traditional milieu already in decline, they grew up witnessing the rapid decomposition of the old regime. Reaching maturity in the first decades of the twentieth century, they were caught in the current of institutional change in which the established prospects of life in a traditional society were replaced by an uncertain future. For these budding intellectuals the most dramatic example of this institutional change was found in education. As the new-style schools sprang up and foreign, specialized subjects were offered in the curriculum, they were seized at once with wonder and apprehension.

It was also in these modern schools, most of which were situated in provincial urban centers, that these impressionable adolescents felt released for the first time in their lives. The departure from home to enter a new school in a big city represented an initial dual emancipation: first, from the physical milieu of traditional society; second, from the whole ritualistic complex of traditional ethics and conventions. The splintering of ties with the traditional milieu—their childhood world—was evidenced in a few personal and melodramatic acts, notably the breaking up of parental arrangements of marriages. The acts and feelings of liberation from the past led to a sense of jubilation toward the future: once the paraphernalia of an established environment had been rejected, the future held a vista of infinite possibilities. It was now up to the individual to determine his own fate. The discovery of the self, therefore, became the first step toward the formation of a new identity. The manifestations of self-assertiveness can be seen in acts of defiant protest against old-style teachers or administrators, in the formation of groups or societies to discuss "new subjects," and in the exchange of letters of mutual admiration. As their minds leaped into a brave new world through reading Liang Ch'i-ch'ao's essays and Yen Fu's translations, their hearts felt the stirrings of emotion—perhaps a psychological facet of a physiological stage of puberty, now freed from restraint.

The beginning attempts at literature reflected the second stage in the process of their identity formation. Why literature? In his celebrated account of watching a newsreel in which Japanese soldiers beheaded Chinese peasants, Lu Hsün explained his decision to give up medicine for literature by asserting that "the first important task was to change their spirit"[1]—the pervasive ethos and mode of thinking among the Chinese people. Lu Hsün's primary concern to transform people's minds through literature reflected, in a sense, a traditional mode of thinking which regarded literature as a vehicle of moral instruction (wen i tsai tao). But what he in fact wanted to convey, as can be seen in the iconoclastic mania of the May Fourth movement, was nothing less than a total rejection of the Chinese tradition. The phenomenon of the New Youth, in which Lu Hsün played an important role, clearly indicates a significant irony in the execution of their mission. While May Fourth intellectuals downgraded the content of

Chinese tradition, their mode of thinking still reflected the predominant concern of traditional intellectuals with the problem of commitment: an intellectual in traditional China who is almost ipso facto a scholar-official either in or out of office, should be, as the famous Sung statesman Fan Chung-yen put it, "the first to worry and the last to rejoice." Political service for the state and moral responsibility in society are the two inseparable elements which comprise the Confucian tenet of commitment. But with the termination of the examination system in 1905, the institutional channel—whereby the intellectual's commitments to both state and society had been combined—was severed forever. And modern Chinese intellectuals, disillusioned by the muddle of warlord politics, became intelligentsia en masse, in that the majority of them were alienated from political power. In a short note on a collection of essays, Yü Ta-fu makes this feeling poignant:

Since last winter my emotional frame of mind has been a continuous series of depressions. I have harbored the idea of going to Russia in order to become a worker there, but I was stopped by my brother in Peking. I have also embraced the nihilist idea and once wandered along the banks of the Yangtze River, seeking death, but my docile and unintelligent woman persuaded me to stop it. That day—the day of Spring Festival—after I sent my woman home to Chekiang, I thought about having a big meal and getting drunk in the moonlit night and seeking a pleasant suicide, but some friends entangled themselves in pleading with me to wait for a while. I have since been waiting for half a year, and now in my heart I feel as depressed as I did half a year ago.

Living in this world, one has to do something. But for such a superfluous man like me, castrated by advanced education, what can I do?[2]

Whether intentionally or unintentionally, Yü Ta-fu hit upon the celebrated prototype of the nineteenth-century Russian intelligentsia, the "superfluous man."[3] Chinese intellectuals had cut themselves off from the state. Advanced education now became castration: having been deprived of the traditional channel to political power, a modern Chinese intellectual therefore became politically impotent unless he wished to prostitute himself to the indignities of the warlords or later the high-handed measures of Chiang Kai-shek's Nanking government. Thus the source of Yü's frustration lies deeper than is reflected by his decadent surface. Behind the façade of studied depravity is perhaps a conscience-ridden mind seeking a proper milieu for commitment: "Living in this world, one has to do something." The literary scene, therefore, provided such a milieu and offered an attractive alternative to political service for a sizable portion of modern Chinese intellectuals. It was also a change of focus from the state to society. In his pioneer essay on the "Relationship between Fiction and People's Sovereignty," Liang Ch'i-ch'ao presented new guidelines concerning the function of literature in society which Lu Hsün echoed: to sway and change social mores, to cleanse China of old values and habits and to bring in new ones from the West. The Association for Literary Studies formally established literary endeavor as a serious practice. The alienated intelligentsia thus found a new arena in which to rechannel their commitment, to exert their influence, and to make a living. The *wen-jen* became a new status group in modern Chinese society, maintaining their alienated existence in the big urban centers with their gilded manners and glamorized morals.

In the eyes of the modern *wen-jen* themselves, the problem of identity and alienation can be turned into a personal asset. As Su Man-shu has demonstrated, a life doomed to "unutterable sorrows" can take on a certain irresistible glamor. Being alienated, the typical modern *wen-jen* considers himself different from the mundane crowd. This sense of difference is derived also from a discovery of the preciousness and uniqueness of his own life experience—the feeling that the vicissitudes of his life and the emotional sufferings he has gone through have not been adequately understood and appreciated by his fellow countrymen. Rather than look at himself from without, in the larger socio-political perspective, he searches within, indulges in self-pity, and assumes an inflated posture of self-importance which he glorifies in his autobiographical works. His rationale for this narcissistic pose is, in other words, not socio-political but romantic: a *wen-jen* in twentieth-century China, like an *artiste* in nineteenth century France, *feels* himself different because he is more "capable of heightened emotional responses than are ordinary men."[4] His hypersensitivity, which dooms him to suffering for life, can also be a blessing, a gift of feeling that average mortals do not possess. Thus this romantic pose of a genius misunderstood or unreceived *(huai-ts'ai pu-yü)* becomes, for the modern Chinese man of letters, a gesture of self-deception in order to ease the anxieties over his alienated existence.

The autobiographical literature produced in the 1920s was studded with references to such a rationale. "A literary man's feeling of love is stronger and his feeling of hatred greater than those of other men," Ch'eng Fang-wu proclaimed.[5] "His senses are twice as sharp as those of ordinary men and his sensitivity twice as strong." Yü Ta-fu echoed, "Therefore, often he cannot escape the excruciating reprimands of self-consciousness."[6] Another literary critic remarked: "For every literary man, his senses are most susceptible to stimulation, his feeling of sympathy broad and profound, his sensitivity sharp. Where the average people do not feel pain, he feels very painful; where average people can tolerate, he cannot tolerate; where average people do not consider themselves worthy of sympathy, he bursts with sparks of sympathy."[7] Therefore, a true literary man, as Ch'eng Fang-wu asserted, "is a superman, a man and deity."[8]

By virtue of this superhuman endowment of sensitivity and feeling, a literary man considers himself superior. Since he is different, he is accursed with loneliness; but because he is also superior, he deserves and demands attention and adulation. This seeming contradiction is characteristic of the self-images of Su Man-shu, Yü Ta-fu, Kuo Mo-jo, Chiang Kuang-tz'u and their many colleagues. These men were able to turn this essentially romantic pose to great advantage. As T. A. Hsia perceptively sees Chiang Kuang-tz'u, "If he was under attack, it meant that he was misjudged and alienated . . . Since every great romanticist in the past was known to have been misjudged and alienated from society in at least some period of his life, he derived comfort from the thought that he was in distinguished company."[9] On the other hand, if a literary man was not under attack, his loneliness and suffering, plaintively and profusely confessed, could elicit enough sympathy from young and receptive readers to make him a celebrity. Thus what began as perhaps genuine "unutterable sorrows," after having been uttered *ad infinitum,* ended as glamorized legends. Personal problems became public poses; a quality of feeling degenerated into a qualification for fame.

Politics and Personality

The problem of the political alienation of literary men became more acute when a general drift toward the left took place after 1925, partially as a result of the impact of the May Thirtieth Incident. The political context from 1925 to 1937 brought into relief the dilemma of the leftist writers. The Northern Expedition of 1926, which provided a brief interlude of political commitment for some literary intellectuals to a "revolutionary" cause, ceased to be revolutionary from a leftist point of view after Chiang Kai-shek's Shanghai massacre of Communists in April 1927. When the leftist writers began to clamor for revolutionary literature, revolution itself was at its lowest ebb. For leftist writers, the ironic fact was that the term revolution no longer possessed any practical substance except in the loosely organized labor movement in the urban factories. Thus the leftist writers seized upon the catchy phrase, proletarian literature, in order to reorient themselves toward this new revolutionary camp. As the debates on proletarian literature raged in 1928, a further irony was noted at once by Lu Hsün: the leftist writers were, in fact, hopelessly out of touch with the realities of proletarian life, and the few samples of proletarian literature they produced were spurious and deceptive escapism. For, although all literature may be propaganda, as Upton Sinclair proposed and Lu Hsün agreed, not all propaganda is literature— certainly not those borrowed slogans from other countries to be applied to a native situation which was not yet fully revolutionary.[10]

The leftist rebuttal of this realistic argument is found in a positive reworking of the romantic pose. The gift of sensitivity, they argued, makes a man capable not only of heightened emotions but also of a deeper perception of social malaise. According to the Creationist theoretician, Ch'eng Fang-wu, since the literary man is endowed with stronger feelings of love and hatred, "literature is the conscience of an age; the literary men must be fighters for conscience."[11] Their works are therefore true reflections of the state of their society. The role of the writer as confessor is extended to that of prophet, seer, and ultimately revolutionary by the messianic Kuo Mo-jo:

The practitioner of literature belongs in temperament to the sensitive type. His sensitivity is sharper than that of ordinary men. Accordingly, when a society is about to change—that is, when the oppressor-classes have afflicted the oppressed classes to the point of action, when the kind of latent class struggle is about to be concretely realized—the sensitive literary man has already felt, before average mortals do, its urgency. Thus he is the first to cry out for the sufferings of the people, the necessity of revolution. Therefore literature has often been the vanguard of revolution, and the streams of revolutionary thought in every revolutionary age originate mainly among literary men or men with literary tastes.[12]

Did the meagre output of leftist literature from 1925 to 1937 become the vanguard of the Communist revolution? Mao's *Talks at the Yenan Forum* in 1942, directed mainly against these urban leftist writers, indicated clearly that Kuo Mo-jo's argument was premature. Viewed in the political context of the late twenties and early thirties, this messianic interpretation of the writer's role is but another retreat into self-deception. The example of Chiang Kuang-tz'u demonstrated that leftist writers were neither in close contact with the urban proletariat nor in a harmonious working relationship with the underground agents of the Chinese Communist Party. Chiang Kuang-tz'u was expelled from the party for his petit-bourgeois tastes and life style. Even an esteemed writer like Lu Hsün, who had turned left in his last years, was driven to his death by a series of painful entanglements with some of his leftist colleagues and underground workers of the CCP.[13] Although both Lu Hsün and Chiang Kuang-tz'u have been lionized in Communist China, their political plight during this leftist interlude epitomized the central dilemma of the leftist writer: eager to commit himself to a revolutionary cause, he endeavored to identify himself with a rising group—the urban proletariat—of whom he knew practically nothing; eager to escape his political impotence by some political action, he found himself at odds with the real practitioners of proletarian revolution, the party underground workers.

Alienated from both, he resorted to wish-fulfillment by redefining his self-importance in a mirage of self-heroism. Commenting on this leftist drama on the literary scene, T. A. Hsia remarked: "The May Fourth Movement brought forth a number of rebellious youths who pitted their egos against society; and when they found their individual strength too puny for the contest, they extolled one class of society —the mythified proletariat with whose interest they identified their own."[14] It was obvious that their act of identification with the mythified proletariat was itself mythified by themselves.

The urban leftist interlude came to an end with the outbreak of the Sino-Japanese War in 1937. The political atmosphere changed to patriotism. The proletarian cause was submerged by the overriding national purpose of anti-Japanese struggle. As most literary men evacuated the coastal urban centers and plunged into the nationwide war effort, their two decades of political impotence and alienation seemed to be over. But this changed political temper did not make life easier for leftist writers. The experience of Hsiao Chün provided a typical case.

Hsiao Chün's "patriotic leftism" can be seen as a sequel to Chiang Kuang-tz'u's "romantic leftism." In spite of the change of setting from urban Shanghai to rural Yenan, Hsiao Chün's life and thought revealed amazing continuities from such urban leftists as Kuo Mo-jo and Chiang Kuang-tz'u. Central to his *Weltanschauung* is what may be called a heroic vitalism which is also evident in both Kuo Mo-jo and Chiang Kuang-tz'u. The theme of heroism and hero worship is obviously an important legacy of the 1920s bequeathed to newcomers like Hsiao Chün who first emerged in the 1930s. All three share a long list of foreign heroes—especially dynamic personalities like Byron and Romain Rolland—and native political figures are also readily included in their heroic pantheon. In his reminiscence of Chiang Kuang-tz'u, Kuo recalled that on the desk of Chiang's study were once found the photos of Wang Ching-wei and Chiang Kai-shek, whom our young hero worshiper considered "China's Lenin and Trotsky."[15] Kuo himself described his audience with Chiang Kai-shek in 1937 with comparable awe and admiration.[16] Hsiao Chün, in Communist-occupied Yenan, fervently grouped Lu Hsün with Chu Teh and Mao Tse-tung as China's three giant realists. And amidst their hero-worshiping mania all three writers found ample justification in worshiping themselves—Kuo as bandit, Chiang as revolutionary poet, and Hsiao as bandit–writer–revolutionary.

The fad of heroism and hero worship could not have direct political consequences in a period of political alienation, for if served merely to glamorize the writers' own narcissicism. But once the writers became politicized and involved themselves in political action, subjective heroism and hero worship sometimes clashed with the more objective demands of politics. With regard to leftist literature, the new setting —Yenan—witnessed a series of such clashes. Mao's Yenan *Talks* defined a new relationship which had not existed in the urban literary scene: literature as a vocation must serve specific political purposes to be prescribed, not by the writers themselves, but by the party. The independence of the *wen-jen* as a group was destroyed forever. The example of Hsiao Chün shows that Kuo Mo-jo's exaltation of the writer as a far-sighted member of the revolutionary vanguard is in direct conflict with the Leninist–Maoist conception of the party. Hsiao Chün's continuous self-glorification on the basis of the former finally made him a victim of the latter. For no matter how sensitive, conscientious, or far-sighted, a *wen-jen* can never be more prophetic than the real vanguard of the proletariat, the party. Hsiao Chün's victimization under the party spelled the triumph of politics over personality and the final resolution of the writers' political alienation in China: once a writer ceased to be alienated, he ceased to be a modern *wen-jen*.

Chapter 13

The Journey of Sentiment

In his famous essay, "Some Suggestions on Literary Reform," which unleashed the literary revolution, Hu Shih posed eight general guidelines for New Literature. While the first five are concerned exclusively with the form of New Literature, the last three deal with matters of content:

What you write should reflect your personality.

Do not write that you are sick or sad when you do not feel sick or sad.

What you write should have meaning and real substance.[1]

Were these three principles fulfilled by the New Literature created in the 1920s? Few scholars have seen fit to tackle the vague generality of Hu Shih's suggestions and to attempt to answer. Obviously Hu Shih's eight suggestions, which were originally put in the form of "eight don'ts," represented his personal reaction to certain dominant trends in traditional Chinese literature. Did the New Literature, then, bring about a clean break from traditional literature? What are some of the major themes and trends that one can find in traditional and modern Chinese literature? The works of our seven literary men have supplied sufficient material for more than a case study.

257

Hu Shih's contemporary and fellow student at Columbia, Liang Shih-ch'iu, viewed the anti-traditional New Literature movement in the following way:

In Chinese life, rites and law are most heavily emphasized. Sages in the past ruled with rites and music. For thousands of years, the tradition of music was lost; what was left became the trivial sounds of Cheng and Wei. The rites (li) have also lost their original meaning and become merely surface etiquette. As a result, the emotional side of Chinese life seems to have dried up. In recent times, because of foreign influences, the so-called New Literature movement came into being, which everywhere clamored for expansion, liberation, freedom. Emotion, at this time, is like a fierce tiger let loose from an iron cage that not only breaks open the shackles of convention but also crushes reason which controls emotion.[2]

The New Literature movement, in Liang's analysis, represented an emotional reaction against what may be called a formalization or ritualization of Confucian norms, which had governed Chinese life and society in the past millennium. To substantiate this argument, one must, first of all, assess the problem of emotion and the role of literature in the Chinese tradition.

The Tradition of Sentiment

Emotion was, of course, not totally lacking in Chinese life in the past. But sentiment (ch'ing), for Confucius, must reflect and reciprocate propriety (li). Behind this ideal, however, lurks one of the central polarities of Confucian thought, the problem of the "inner" versus the "outer."[3] Sentiment, which springs from within, could be regarded as one manifestation of man's innate humanity. The problem arises when the outburst of ch'ing no longer conforms to the confines of li. Should one opt for the former or the latter? Neither Confucius nor Mencius seems to have tackled the problem adequately. With Hsün Tzu, who emphasizes the regulating and educational functions of li, sentiment thus is subject to the check of correct rites. In the general Confucian tradition that developed after the Han dynasty, the problem of ch'ing was often discussed, but not fully resolved.

Inheriting mainly the Mencian legacy most Neo-Confucianists of the Sung period tended to imbue the innate "good" nature of man with a heavily moral connotation. Sentiment was regarded as peripheral to, if not divorced from, the core of this innate morality.[4] Perhaps under the influence of Buddhism, *ch'ing* was relegated to the lower realm of *ch'i* as differentiated from the realm of *li* (principle) which infuses man's moral nature. Thus *ch'ing* was put in the same category as *yü* or desire, the result of mutations of the impure *ch'i*. Hence the implications of evil in both sentiments and desires. It was not until the late Ming period that the problem of *ch'ing* became a matter of serious moral concern and the subject of extensive intellectual debate.

Concurrent with the increasing emphasis on the problem of *ch'ing* in the Confucian tradition was the emergence of a "counter tradition" in literature which opposed the orthodox view that literature has no value unless it is the vehicle of moral instructions *(wen i tsai tao)*. According to Arthur Waley, "the counter claim that literature has rights of its own dates from at least as early as the thirteenth century; but it has generally been the view of a small, sporadic opposition. This opposition had indeed some influence at the turn of the sixteenth and seventeenth centuries and maintained a footing down to Yüan Mei's time."[5]

The opposition Waley referred to may be found in the so-called Kung-an and Ching-ling schools in the late sixteenth and early seventeenth centuries. According to Chou Tso-jen, this minor tradition in Chinese literature as represented by these two schools advocated, as opposed to the orthodox tradition of moral instruction *(tsai-tao)*, personal expression *(yen-chih)*.[6] The slogan of the Kung-an school demanded "individual expression of personality, unhampered by formulas and conventions."[7] Thus Chou Tso-jen considered the two schools as the true precursors of the Literary Revolution.

It is in this general context of traditional Chinese culture that the two precursors—Lin Shu and Su Man-shu—assume historical significance. When Lin Shu, an avowed Confucian scholar, described his fainting spells and tormented wailings on account of his deceased emperor and beloved family members, he might well have justified his behavior by a Confucian conviction that this was correct conduct,

that genuine sentiments, springing from within, should be fully manifested without, as Confucius himself behaved while bewailing the
death of his favorite disciple, Yen Hui. But when Lin was heard weep-
ing for a foreign "lady of the camellias," he was well on his way
beyond Confucian bounds toward the notion that personal sentiments,
if genuinely expressed, can be the central *Weltanschauung* of a man,
whether or not they reflect the established ethical norms of Chinese
society. The contribution of Lin Shu in a transitional age lay in bridg-
ing the gap between morality and emotions by seeking an emotional
basis for his morality and justifying his emotions in moral terms.
Moreover, he has chosen to express his personal sentiments through
the medium of prose, which he wrote with admirable ease and elegance. Hu Shih, despite his otherwise severe criticism, lauded Lin's
unprecedented use of classical prose in his translations and fictional
writings: no other Chinese novel of considerable length had ever been
written in the classical style.[8]

Struggling with the same problem of emotional expression, Su Man-
shu sought a different realm of Chinese tradition. Not as totally at
home as Lin Shu with the Confucian classics, Su cleverly managed
to weave his life into the matrix of Buddhism and Taoism. In his individual way Su was reminiscent of the Seven Sages of the Bamboo
Grove in the Six Dynasties period. Like these neo-Taoist sages, Su
flaunted a bohemian life style which he attempted to justify in Buddhism. But his monastic veneer served less as justification than as
decoration, to gild his personality with the glamor of a legend. The
Taoist–Buddhist legacy in Chinese life, which supplements the increasingly moralistic Confucian orthodoxy, has been regarded as offering a romantic side of Chinese tradition, which has been glorified
again in poetry, in such works as those of the famous Chin poet T'ao
Ch'ien (Yüan-ming). Su Man-shu inherited from this tradition two
basic modes of personal behavior: naturalness (*tzu-jan*) and bohe-
mianism (*feng-liu*). The Confucian inner and outer polarity becomes
almost irrelevant in this framework, for a Taoist denies the shackles
of external convention and lets loose the natural flow of his sentiments and instincts. His inner self is his outer self. In Su's case, his
inner self finds an outer manifestation in his individual life-style and

it becomes an end in itself, divorced from conventional morality. In consciously glamorizing this traditional romantic stance Su has gone beyond his predecessors in establishing an untraditional precedent, that a man's emotional nature not only needs no moral justification but also, when externalized into a unique life-style, should be the only earmark of his personality and the proper index to his creative output. While Su flaunted his emotional personality and life-style alongside the established social conventions of his time, the May Fourth men of letters employed them to defy and destroy these established conventions.

In their different ways, both Lin Shu and Su Man-shu established the centrality of sentiment and heralded the emergence of a prototypical personality based on it. The popularization of sentiment as the central mode of existence can be found in their contemporaries, the treaty-port journalist-littérateurs. In their fictional works for mass consumption these journalist-littérateurs created a world of sentiment permeated with both Confucian and Buddhist, Chinese and Western elements. This new popular genre of fiction, written in semi-vernacular prose, was called *hsieh-ch'ing hsiao-shuo* or novels depicting sentiment. The trend was begun, according to one Chinese authority on late Ch'ing fiction, with Wu Wo-yao's novel, *Hen-hai* (Sea of sorrow). To justify the "novel of sentiment," Wu had the following to say: "I commonly hold the opinion that man is born with sentiment. By this I mean that sentiment, born with the human heart, is applied everywhere as the human being grows up . . . Between heaven and hell is but a large puppet stage and the general thread which pulls and moves the puppets is sentiment. From the noble concerns of ancient sages with people and things, their selfless sympathies with the starved and the drowned, to such petty matters of individual tastes for a thing or item—all are encompassed in the confines of the word sentiment." [9]

Concomitant with this emphasis on sentiment in late Ch'ing literature was a tendency toward an awareness of the individual personality. Jaroslav Průšek was among the first to note the trend of subjectivism in such late Ch'ing masterpieces as Liu Ê's (T'ieh-yun) *Lao Ts'an yu-chi* (The travels of Lao Ts'an), Shen Fu's *Fu-sheng liu-chi*

261

(Six chapters of a floating life), Li Pao-chia's *Kuan-ch'ang hsien-hsing chi*, and Wu Wo-yao's *Erh-shih nien mu-tu chih kuai hsien-chuang*. All these works pointed to an "orientation toward the writer's own fate and own life." In some cases the author would "set his own person and character in opposition to the whole society." [10] This subjective tendency which gave prominence to the author's personality was given formal notice in Hu Shih's seventh credo of literary reform: "What you write should reflect your own personality."

This subjective tendency coupled with an emphasis on personal sentiment, was also shared by Lin Shu and Su Man-shu. The important point which Lin strove to justify and Su to embody is that personal sentiments, subjectively presented, should be genuine in order to assume any positive value. This may also be what Hu Shih had in mind when he offered the other two of the three guiding principles in matters of content. Reacting against the excess of embellished self-pity in some late Ch'ing sentimental novels and possibly in classical lyrical poetry, Hu Shih cautioned the practitioner of New Literature: "Do not write that you are sick or sad when you do not feel sick or sad," and "What you write should have meaning and real substance."

Love in the May Fourth Era

Hu Shih's dictum of writing with meaning and substance was indeed the modern credo of *wen i tsai tao*. The new literary medium, however, was neither classical prose nor poetry but the vernacular language. The new "way," moreover, no longer meant Confucian orthodoxy but rather individual personality and its unadorned and uninhibited expression. The May Fourth movement broke the dam and a torrent of individual emotions poured out in profusion. Yü Ta-fu's autobiographical fiction unleashed a welter of confessions—an intensification, so to speak, of the subjectivist trend which had been gathering momentum since the late Ch'ing period. The literary market in the 1920s was congested with autobiographies (by Yü Ta-fu, Kuo Mo-jo, Wang Tu-ch'ing, Huang Lu-yin, and many others), personal biographies (for instance, Shen Ts'ung-wen on Ting Ling and Hu Yeh-p'in), diaries (Yü Ta-fu, Hsü Chih-mo, Chang I-p'ing), letters and love letters (*Three Leaves* by Kuo Mo-jo, Tsung Pai-hua, and T'ien Han; Hsü Chih-mo's *Love Letters to May*, Chang I-p'ing's *A Batch of Love Letters*). Numerous fictional works also assumed the format of diary, letter, or monologue, not to mention the frequent use of the subjective "I." Under the lead of Yü Ta-fu, Kuo Mo-jo, and Hsü Chih-mo, the vogue of self-exposé—laying bare the author's innermost secrets, emotional and sexual—all but carried the day. Yü Ta-fu summed up the whole trend by asserting that "the greatest success of the May Fourth movement lay, first of all, in the discovery of individual personality." [11]

The ferociousness of this outburst of personal emotions was such that the new vernacular medium was often found inadequate to convey sufficient intensity. Supplementary devices were used which paved the way for exaggerations. A bemused contemporary observer noted that the modern Chinese poets were six times more emotional than their Western colleagues because "in the current vernacular poetry in China there appears on the average one exclamation mark in every four lines or 232 exclamation marks in every thousand lines, whereas acknowledged good poetry in foreign countries average about one exclamation mark in every 25 lines." [12]

What is the nature of this emotional outburst? What are its basic components? The journey of sentiment illustrated by the lives and works of representative literary figures covered in the previous chapters have pointed to a thematic line of progression. The two precursors, in their pioneering explorations of sentiment in human life, seized upon its central importance but have neither pinpointed its focus nor delimited its boundary. Lin Shu perhaps put more premium on the three cardinal relationships—emperor and subject, father and son, husband and wife; the genuine interplay of emotions between them represents the crystallization of human sentiment. But this essentially Confucian canvas has been broadened to encompass more personal portraits: his mother, grandmother, daughters, uncle, his concubine, a fallen woman, and a filial girl. Out of this maze of human relations a familial axis seems to have emerged toward which his personal sentiments were directed. Su Man-shu, on the other hand, went beyond his family circle and plunged into the expansive "sea of sentiment," a term popularized by the treaty-port littérateurs. Despite his Buddhist outlook in which this sea of sentiment presents merely the irridescent but ephemeral "red dust," Su lavishes his personal emotions on young and amorous women. Sentiment is, therefore, closely related to women, and the relations between the sexes have become his central axis. Yü Ta-fu, in his relentless confessionalism, supplied this axis with an explicit sexual basis—a daring feat which Su Man-shu either consciously or subconsciously avoided. But what Yü Ta-fu yearns for, at the end of a depraved sexual experience, is love.

What I want is love!
If there is a beautiful woman who can understand my suffering and who wants me to die, I am willing to die.
If there is a woman—whether she is beautiful or ugly, who can love me wholeheartedly, I am willing to die for her.
What I want is the love of the opposite sex.[13]

But throughout Yü's various emotional entanglements with women, love as personified by an understanding woman remained an unfulfilled wish, in spite of his scandalous affair with Wang Ying-hsia. Life, for a self-styled "superfluous" loner, was a darkening plain of melancholia on which our sentimental soul roamed in a style of self-indulgent decadence.

It is left for Yü's contemporary, Hsü Chih-mo, to embody and justify the centrality of romantic love in sentiment. All the ramifications of sentiment are overshadowed by a persistent outlook founded on passion and faith: "I have no other methods but love; no other talents but love; no other potentialities but love; no other energies but love."[14] And a host of other writers reciprocated Hsü's exultations. A young novelist, after reading one of Hsü's short stories, proclaimed: "Now I know the mystery of sentiment and the greatness of love. Now I admit that I am born for sentiment and live for love. A man's inner self, if not burning with sentiment and love, is nothing but a soulless carcass. What hope is there for a carcass without soul?"[15] Another literary man, enthusiastic about a translation of Rostand's *Cyrano de Bergerac*, stated: "That love has assumed such overwhelming importance in literary works is due to the fact that a life of love consists in the expansion of the human soul to the largest extent."[16] Chang I-p'ing, author of the best seller *A Batch of Love Letters*, asserted forthright: "I believe that love is better than life . . . Love is the greatest thing on earth."[17]

All these eulogies of love were symptomatic of a larger phenomenon in the 1920s. The May Fourth movement had unleashed not only a literary and an intellectual revolution; it had also propelled an emotional one. Hu Shih, introducing Ibsenism into China via *A Doll's House* in 1918, affirmed a new notion of marriage as a spiritual communion between two people rather than an alliance based on external forms. What would be the basis of this spiritual communion if it were not love? Soon after Hu Shih's clarion call, Chou Tso-jen argued that New Literature should stress the equality of women and marriage based on love, taking for models such works as *A Doll's House, Anna Karenina*, and *Tess of the D'Urbervilles*.[18] A set of data, compiled by Mao Tun and covering three months in 1921, showed that more than 70 out of a total of 115 literary works were focused on love between the sexes.[19] What this capsule survey suggests is that the torrent of subjective emotions was flowing into the whirlpool of love, particularly love between the emancipated young men and women themselves.

The *wen-jen* themselves were leaders of this trend. In fact, the popular image of *wen-jen* in the twenties and thirties was often that of a couple or even triangle bound and complicated by love: Hsü Chih-mo and Lu Hsiao-man, Yü Ta-fu and Wang Ying-hsia, Chiang Kuang-tz'u and Sung Jo-yü, Hu Yeh-p'in–Ting Ling–Shen Ts'ung-wen, Hsiao Chün–Hsiao Hung-Tuan-mu Hung-liang, to name but a few. The importance of the individual personality was given wide recognition by the amorous acts and styles of these love-torn figures on the literary scene. Love had become an over-all symbol of new morality, an easy substitute for the traditional ethos of propriety which was now equated with external restraint. In the general temper of emancipation, love was identified with freedom, in the sense that by loving and by releasing one's passions and energies the individual could become truly a full and free man. To love was also considered an act of defiance and sincerity, of renouncing all the artificial restraints of hypocritical society so as to find one's true self and expose it to one's beloved. Thus true love cannot but be good and beautiful. The prevalent trinity of new faith, truth–goodness–beauty in the 1920s, as expounded by Hsü Chih-mo and the early Creationists, was inescapably inspired and infused by the reigning spirit of love.

This effusion of love in the context of social rebellion and intellectual iconoclasm can only betray its theoretical paucity. For Hsü Chih-mo and the May Fourth generation, love is defined invariably in dynamic and activistic terms, as "method," "talent," "potentiality," "energy." It is founded, not on a fixed idea, but on a flux of emotion; it represents not a category of thought, but a cataclysm of personal experience. The many high-sounding abstractions such as freedom, beauty, and truth are but emotional ideals springing from ebullient minds seized in the delirium of action. Thus Plato was brushed aside except in terms of "Platonic love," which, as a May Fourth cliché shorn of any philosophic underpinnings, meant simply love between the sexes without the acts or emotions of sex. The possible philosophical and theological implications of love have seldom occurred to the fervid minds of modern Chinese intellectuals.

Women and Sex

The central issue concerning love in the 1920s, both in theory and in practice, hinges on the relationship between love and sex or the polarity of spirituality versus physicality in love. The role of sex is, in turn, related to the traditional and modern conceptions of women.

Although classical Chinese literature is never lacking in descriptions of love and women, love is never elevated to a dominant philosophy of life, nor are women assigned by the great tradition to an exalted position. Thus in translating the chivalric romances of Sir Walter Scott, Lin Shu found Scott's attitude toward women, "respecting them like goddesses—even to the extent of worshiping them," simply ridiculous.[20] In the realm of traditional popular literature, however, the function of women borders on the physical—as delicate dreams of wish-fulfillment, where the beautiful and obliging fox-fairy would step out from the pages of a lonely scholar's book, for instance, or

266

suddenly appear from the peony garden in his secluded mountain retreat.[21] In fact, the *femmes fatales* in traditional literature are almost invariably conceived as physical predators of the masculine essence who would drain their men to death: the "Golden Lotus" is the most celebrated example. This sexual connotation is further reinforced by popular Taoism which treats women as no more than a vehicle for sex or sexual magic. Su Man-shu's stories reflect the dominance of this tradition. After presenting two types of women he cringes under the shattering passion of his aggressive heroines but ultimately sets his preference on the more docile and devoted weaker type. Following Su Man-shu, Yü Ta-fu also vacillates between the afflictive and the afflicted. Sympathetic to the latter but physically drawn to the former, Yü differs from Su in finally settling for a *femme fatale* even in real life. The choice may have been a wrong one in view of Yü's traditional predilections; his testimony about his traditional first wife is much more moving than the account of his mistress and second wife in his diaries.

With Yü's contemporary, Hsü Chih-mo, tradition is cast to the winds. Hsü comes closest to the Western tradition by idealizing woman as the embodiment of love and by making the pursuit of love the reigning purpose of his life. Thus Hsü has gone a long way from Lin Shu and Su Man-shu, who would allow women only a share of sentiment and partially salvage them from pure physicality. But unlike Blake and other religious poets in the West, Hsü, although idealizing women, stops short of imparting any sense of godhood in his idealization. Nowhere in his poetry can one find the images of the Virgin Mary; and the invocations of Dante's Beatrice in Hsü and Yü Ta-fu are not meant to equate her with the search for divine wisdom. What Hsü has taken from the Western romantic tradition seems to be a dynamic, Dionysian concept in which love is invested with a vital, life-giving force; the fullest possible realization of the self is identified with the attainment of the maximum frenzy of love's passion, beyond which are found total freedom, death, and transcendence. This dynamic interpretation of love poses a dramatic contrast with Su Man-shu's Buddhist-flavored nirvana of love, an ideal mental state of distilled, condensed spirituality.

The two divergent images of love between Su Man-shu and Hsü Chih-mo point also to the implications of the spirituality and sexuality of love. Su's works still reflect the dichotomy between the upper realm of pure and spiritual sentiments and the lower realm of carnal desires and sexuality in traditional Chinese thinking. In his devotion to his spiritual ideal of love Su has generally avoided the issue of sexuality in his works; the rumor concerning his relegation of sex to a subordinate role in his life betrays the dominance of this traditional view toward sex in his frame of thinking rather than his possible impotence. With the publication of Yü Ta-fu's "Sinking," however, a radical step is made toward obliterating this dichotomy. Sex in Yü's works is treated with all seriousness as one of the major symptoms of spiritual affliction. What Yü himself interpreted as hypochondria, which is manifested in both his indulgence in and his inability to resist sex, is itself an indication of his perpetual feeling of loneliness and superfluity. Therefore, Yü's frank exposure of his sexual life was never meant for purposes of commercial exploitation but for accentuating in an unprecedentedly daring manner the reality of his own modes of feeling. As Lin Shu sanctifies sentiment, Yü Ta-fu salvages sex; their original intentions are similar—to strive toward a genuine expression of their individual personalities and to exalt an outlook toward human life founded on emotions.

Hsü Chih-mo's Dionysian treatment of love represents a further radical break with tradition. Spiritual purity and physical intensity of love, he implies, are but two sides of love which are ultimately inseparable. He is, therefore, equally attracted to Dante's Beatrice and Wagner's Isolde, Wordsworth's highland lass and d'Annunzio's heroines of passion. All these are manifested in his works. But one cannot help venturing a psychological query: whether his yearnings for this essentially Western concept of love have not betrayed a familiar trait he may have shared with Yü Ta-fu and even Su Man-shu. For a man whose physical appearance is more reminiscent of the traditional Chinese prototype of "pale-faced" scholar, this kind of Dionysian craving may be less a fulfillment than a wish-fulfillment. Although passion and sexuality are freely discussed in his poems and diaries, Hsü in real life was not known for excessive indulgence in sexual activity.

His two exotic dreams seem to indicate, on the contrary, that in confronting a real *femme fatale* (Lu Hsiao-man, with her ill health, was not) he may be as overwhelmed as Yü and Su. The facts underlying Hsü Chih-mo's love, as in Su Man-shu's women, remain an enigma. And despite his earnest self-exposure, Yü Ta-fu has demonstrated that sexuality is but a way of expressing himself and not an aim in itself.

These personal explorations of love and sex on the part of a few leading literary men offer an index to the confused obsessions of a whole generation, all under the name of love. The inherent attraction of love and sex certainly would not pass unnoticed by the commercially minded publishers and writers. The most notorious exploiter, a master of triangular or multi-angular sex, was Yü's one-time colleague in the Creation Society, Chang Tzu-p'ing. Interestingly enough, Chang was perhaps the only literary man in the 1920s who attempted to justify his commercialism of sex by invoking the divine-love mysticism of William Blake![22] Chang I-p'ing, another exploiter, reaped immense popularity through his diaries and letters of love, which depicted his amorous encounters with various emancipated heroines, including his wife, Wu Shu-t'ien, to whom he devoted a whole volume of his diaries, *I-chen jih-chi* (Diary on the pillow), describing their boudoir bliss together while he was ill! His *A Batch of Love Letters* sold three thousand copies in the first two months after it was published in 1926 and was translated into Russian.[23] A friend told Chang that nearly every girl student in Amoy had read it.[24]

The popularity of Chang Tzu-p'ing and Chang I-p'ing reflected a crescendo of preoccupation with love and sex in the publishing establishment. Women's journals devoted special issues to sex, love, and marriage. The *New Woman* magazine even showered on their new subscribers as a half-price bonus a precious copy of *Sexual Knowledge* translated from the original authoritative work of Dr. William J. Robinson, head of the "Pu-lun-k'e-ssu" (Bronx?) Hospital in America![25] Books by Havelock Ellis were massively translated into Chinese under such alluring titles as *The Sexual Impulse of Women* and *Instincts for Sexual Games*. A volume of essays appeared under the title of *Discussions on New Sexual Morality*. The enterprising Pei-hsin Bookstore published a new Sexual Love Series of eleven titles. A famous literary historian noted near the end of the decade that the New Literature was filled with descriptions of homosexuality—male and especially female (Huang Lu-yin, Yeh Shao-chün, Chang I-p'ing, Chang Tzu-p'ing, Yeh Ting-lo)—sadism and masochism (Yü Ta-fu, Chang Tzu-p'ing, T'ien Han), autoeroticism (Yü Ta-fu, P'an Han-nien), the Oedipus complex (Yü Ta-fu, Huang Lu-yin, Yeh Ling-feng), the Electra complex (Ping Hsin), and sexual dreams (T'ien Han, Kuo Mo-jo).[26] The list of authors cited by him included all the leading Creationists and some eminent members of the Association for Literary Studies.

For an extremist and vitalistic exaltation of sex none could surpass "Dr. Sex," Chang Ching-sheng. The author of the most notorious book on sex in the 1920s, Hsing shih (History of sex), Chang took a totally positive view of sex and advocated an unprecedented radicalism in his journal, Hsin wen-hua (New culture). Each issue of his journal presented a host of articles concerning sexual hygiene, anatomy of genital organs, sexual techniques, and the creation of a utopian society founded on the beauty of sex. More than an exploiter and a Westernizer in thought, Chang was a visionary who advocated a total Westernization of the human body. Arguing on the heretical premise that "the Chinese are born ugly" with "the males not masculine and females not feminine enough," Chang took great pains to chisel out his new Pygmalions: the new male should have a big nose, whiskers, wide shoulders, strong muscles; the new female, big nose, rosy cheeks, big breasts, big hips, strong legs, and a fully developed sexual organ—all to be products of the maximum release of energies in sexual intercourse.[27] In another series of articles written for the Ching-pao of Tientsin he openly advocated interracial marriage of Chinese with Caucasians and Japanese—but not with Indians and Negroes—and envisioned a future utopia at once prophetic and fantastic.[28] In this new society, which is to be called "a society of love, beauty, and fun," free sexual relationships between full-blooded and able-bodied lovers will finally replace the conventional marriage system. The governmental bureaucracy in this utopian China will be headed by the Ministry of National Prowess, whose function is to produce beautiful citizens by the following means: (1) to limit and control marriage by careful selection; (2) to implement nationwide contraception and to take care of newborn children and their mothers; (3) to keep the Chinese population to the 400,000,000 figure or possibly to reduce it to 300,000,000; (4) to manage public hygiene by establishing nationwide hospitals and bath pools for mixed bathing.[29]

Chang Ching-sheng's sexual mirage should not be dismissed simply as the weird product of a deranged mind. His theories, in fact, have carried some of the seminal ideals of Liang Ch'i-ch'ao, Yen Fu, Lin Shu, and Hsü Chih-mo to an extreme frontier that borders on the absurd. Liang Ch'i-ch'ao's "New Citizens," characterized by a total release of human energies as advocated by Yen Fu, are envisioned by Chang to be Caucasian-looking "beautiful people" with strong, uninhibited sexual appetites. Lin Shu's ambivalent feelings toward Rider Haggard's predatory "White Hero" are recast in Chang's mind as all-out racial admiration. Hsü Chih-mo's longing for "that sense of Dionysian madness" with pagan-like youth "singing and dancing in the vineyards"[30] cannot be more vividly realized than in Chang's young males and females fresh from the public baths and hospitals of the Ministry of National Prowess! The notoriety of Chang Ching-sheng testified most dramatically to the permeation of a vitalistic ethos which underlined the transition of an essentially traditional mode of sentimentalism into dynamic outpourings of love and sexuality drawn, more and more, from Western sources.

From Love to Revolution

The intensity and vitality of this emotional avalanche of love and sex continued until the late 1920s. With the death of Hsü Chih-mo in 1931, whose life was a moving testimony to incessant up-reachings toward the ultimate dynamism of love, an extraordinary decade of emotional commotion came to an end. In a story appropriately titled "Shanghai in the Spring of 1930," Ting Ling offered the following valedictory to this heady decade of literary activity:

I sometimes feel that it would not be a serious loss if we gave it up entirely. We write, and a handful of people read. Time passes and there is no influence whatsoever. What is the meaning of all this except that we get paid for it? It is possible that some readers may be moved by a turn in the plot or by certain passages of writing, but who are these readers? Students of the petit-bourgeois class above the middle-school level, who have just reached adolescence and are subject to melancholy. They feel that this kind of writing just fits their temper and expresses some melancholy which they feel but cannot personally experience. Or they feel that some passages present their own ideals. The characters depicted therein they find only too lovable and partly resembling themselves. Thus they believe that this is probably the embodiment of the author . . . Now I realize that we have done something harmful: we are dragging these young people onto our old path. Some sentimentalism, individualism, grumblings or sorrows with no way out! . . . Where is the way out? They will only sink deeper, day by day, into their raging moroseness, not seeing the relation between society and their sufferings. Even if they could improve their language and produce some good essays and poems that win praise from some old writers, what good, tell me, is that to them? And what good to society? Therefore, with regard to writing, personally I am willing to give it up.[31]

Ting Ling did not, however, give up writing. The above valedictory registered simply the passing of a "silver age of lyricism" for her and many of her colleagues. The general temper on the literary scene indeed indicated "a swing from passive sentimentality to revolutionary frenzy."[32] But did "sentimentalism, individualism, grumblings or sorrows" in fact give way to revolution? Should a writer sacrifice love for the sake of revolution? The problem became the subject of heated debates among leftist writers. In Mao Tun's trilogy, *Eclipse*, the revolutionary hero, after a brief period of self-indulgence in love's bliss, had to forsake his girl for his revolutionary work in the Northern Expedition.[33] Chiang Kuang-tz'u's novels also posed the same problem and derived the same answer, although the revolutionary setting was changed mainly to the labor strikes of Shanghai. In Hsiao Chün's *Village in August* the guerrilla intellectual, Hsiao Ming, confessed his love to the Korean heroine Anna in a fit of self-indulgence, as if their love affair would be terminated forever the next day.

In the context of the changed political temper in the late twenties and early thirties, it seemed as if love had become the lingering vestige of a gilded and irresponsible world of the past. That romantic world, according to Ting Ling, was passé, and the poet Chu Tzu-ch'ing issued a similar comment in 1928: " 'Romantic' used to be a good term, but now its meaning is reduced to slander and a curse. 'romanticism' was to release to the utmost one's animated emotions, thereby expanding oneself. But now what is needed is work and the animated emotions, undisciplined, cannot produce practical effects. Now is the time of urgency and such unimportant matters are not necessary." [34]

Both Ting Ling and Chu Tzu-ch'ing had correctly sensed that the temper of their age had changed. And a similar realization made Chiang Kuang-tz'u embarrassed and Hsiao Chün apologetic about their preoccupation with love. While they advocated the primacy of revolution in their fictional works, in real life both Chiang and Hsiao were entangled in love affairs with women. "Animated emotions" continued to envelop their lives and works and suffused leftist litera-ture in general.

The two trilogies of Pa Chin—*Turbulent Stream* and *Love*—present perhaps the best summary of a generation's obsession with love and revolution. The heroes in the earlier novels deny themselves love. But Pa Chin soon changed his attitude. The hero in *Lightning*, for in-stance, "tells his young friends that revolutionaries have the same right to love as other people" and resolves his own conflict by finding a girl who is herself a revolutionary.[35] For Pa Chin, as for Turgenev, love more than politics is the leading motive of all his novels. Chiang Kuang-tz'u would broaden the scope of love further by announcing forthright: "Romantic? I myself am romantic. All revolutionaries are romantic. Without being romantic, who would come to start a revolu-tion? . . . Idealism, passion, discontent with the status quo and a desire to create something better—here you have the spirit of roman-ticism. A romantic is one possessed of such a spirit." [36] Reportedly Kuo Mo-jo liked the idea so much that he urged the reader to take these lines as if they were Kuo's own words put into Chiang's mouth.[37]

Chiang Kuang-tz'u received Kuo's endorsement because he had revolutionized emotions. Idealism and passion, which for Hsü Chih-mo culminated in love, took on a political aura in Chiang's revolu-tionary-romantic manifesto. This politicization of emotions was the predominant feature of the leftist men of letters. Although most of them embroiled themselves in repeated debates in order to separate love from revolution, it was obvious to the more perceptive Yü Ta-fu that the two in fact are inextricably linked by the same emotional denominator: the passion of love springs from the same source as the passion for revolution.

I think it would not really matter if poets were socialized. A truly revolutionary poem is not one which rattles with pistols and grenades or contains the word "revolution" repeated hundreds of times. But speak out your genuine sentiments under no disguise, emit your passion as if it were a lava from a volcano—this is the paramount duty of a poet. The emergence of a revolutionary career is possible only for that little passion, the cultivation of which is inseparable from the tender and pure love of a woman. That passion, if extended, is ardent enough to burn down the palaces of a despot and powerful enough to destroy the Bastille.[38]

What Yü Ta-fu extolled as "that little passion" was, indeed, the stuff that fired the revolutionary zeal of Kuo Mo-jo, Chiang Kuang-tz'u, Hsiao Chün, and a host of other leftist writers. This revolutionary passion sprang from the very volcano of subjectivism which had emitted earlier the lava of love and sex in the early twenties. That our journey of subjective sentiment should end with a political twist is certainly the result of changes in the political environment. But political conditions had not affected the persistence of this subjectivist trend until the Yenan era. Mao was ingenious enough to realize that while romantic passion might aid the destructive mob to storm the Bastille, it could only be destructive when the Communist revolution, at its low ebb in Yenan, was in a stage of retrenchment and construction. After Mao delivered his famous *Talks*, individualism and subjectivism, which had been exalted in the twenties, began to take on purely negative connotations in the eyes of the party. The fall of Hsiao Chün illustrated the severance of the last link between the May Fourth legacy of subjectivism and the emergent literature of Socialist Realism.

Chapter 14

The Romantic Heritage

The trend of subjective sentiment in modern Chinese literature is partially of Chinese origin; the inspiration for its modern quality, however, is derived from the West. As noted in an earlier chapter, the urban literary scene in China in the 1920s was enveloped in the general phenomenon of *étrangerie*; even the term "modern" in its Chinese transliteration *(mo-teng)* conveys a thickly foreign flavor. The impact of Western literature on modern China will have to be gauged in this framework.

The Literary *Étrangerie*

The vogue of *étrangerie* in the May Fourth era may be compared to the "Western craze" of Meiji Japan in the 1870s. For both countries, the models came entirely from the West—predominantly Europe (including Russia) and to a lesser extent America. Japan served further as a go-between in this cultural borrowing, as many of the Chinese literary men were educated in Japan and many Western works were translated into Chinese from Japanese translations. Returned students from Japan, Europe, and America acted as the chief heralds of this Western cult and the increasingly lucrative task of translation became its main channel. Aided by a thriving publishing industry, translations from Western literary works reached immense proportions within one decade after the Literary Revolution. The section on translations in Volume X of *Chung-kuo hsin wen-hsüeh ta-hsi* (A comprehensive compendium of modern Chinese literature) lists a grand total of 451 titles of individual works and collections which were published in the period from 1917 to 1927.[1] Translated poems, short stories, plays, and articles which appeared in the literary journals were too numerous to count. Tremendous energies were unleashed to introduce Western literature, which was received generally with tremendous enthusiasm.

The lists of translations in the 1920s readily reveal that the overwhelming majority of Western works introduced into China belong mainly to nineteenth century literature, with Russian, French, English, and German authors preponderant. The popularity of a Western author in China is hard to gauge. Sometimes the works of an author were extensively translated but his name did not become a household word: Haggard, Andreyev, Galsworthy, and Hauptmann belong to this category. Sometimes an author enjoyed immense popularity on the basis of a single work, such as Dumas fils and his *La Dame aux Camélias*. In most cases, however, the popularity of a Western author rested on a combination of his translations and his personal appeal. In general, it may be said that two major trends in nineteenth century Western literature held sway in China: realism and romanticism.

It might be argued that since a dominant number of Western works translated into Chinese belong to the tradition of nineteenth century realism, the keynote of this literary *étrangerie* in May Fourth China was realism *(hsieh-shih chu-i)*. But this argument bears further examination. A recent study of the introduction of Western literary theories into China has demonstrated that the May Fourth writers were strongly influenced by a concept of literary evolutionism, which they borrowed from a host of secondary books in English and Japanese on Western literary history. European literature was seen as developing organically and deterministically through the stages of classicism, romanticism, realism, naturalism, and neo-romanticism.

This belief in the forward progress of literature led many Chinese followers not only to a general lack of interest in the classical, medieval, and neo-classical literature of the West but also to an over-eagerness to fit modern Chinese literature into these evolutionary categories.[2] Convinced that traditional Chinese literature stopped somewhere between the stages of classicism and romanticism, they decided that modern Chinese literature had to go through the stages of realism and naturalism, whether or not they might be personally attracted to neo-romanticism. Accordingly, Western works of realism and naturalism would be introduced in great quantities.

But a closer look at the Chinese reception of Western "realists" reveals some interesting phenomena. Two European favorites—Sienkiewicz and Tolstoy—were regarded as both realists and romanticists.[3] Other realists like Turgenev, Gorky, and Anatole France have their romantic sides. Even the works of the most orthodox realists or naturalists like Maupassant, Flaubert, and Zola were often revered as "products of a crusading idealism."[4] The emotional fervor with which these realistic authors were received in China in fact rendered them indistinguishable from such "neo-romantics" as Baudelaire and Rolland. They were all worshiped as heroes of humanity. It seems that despite their theoretical espousal of realism or naturalism the Chinese writers were motivated by an emotional ethos more akin to romanticism. Their evolutionary uses of the word "neo-romanticism" served only to cause terminological confusion.

This emotional reaction to Western literature was best exemplified by the fetish of personal identification among Chinese literary men with their Western counterparts. Su Man-shu initiated the whole trend by consciously imitating Byron, although his admirers later likened him to Verlaine.[5] Yü Ta-fu found a kindred soul in Ernest Dowson while professing his profound admiration for Rousseau. Hsü Chih-mo earned the title of poet–philosopher, an epithet which was applied also to Tagore. Kuo Mo-jo was identified with Shelley and Goethe. Chiang Kuang-tz'u compared himself to Byron in his poetry while assuming the role of Dostoevsky in his personal life. Kuo's friend T'ien Han claimed himself to be "a budding Ibsen in China."[6] Another eminent Creationist, Wang Tu-ch'ing, was rumored to be the second Hugo, but he preferred to call himself Armand, in memory of a French girl with whom he had fallen in love in France and whose name, naturally, was Marguerite.[7] Dumas *fils* would have been pleased.

The imitation of and identification with one's favorite Western authors was the central facet of this vogue of *étrangérie*. The result was to aggrandize both oneself and one's favorite Western counterparts into heroic proportions. The decade of the 1920s was certainly an unprecedented epoch of heroes and hero worship in modern Chinese intellectual and literary history. To be modern on the literary scene required that a man of letters not only flaunt his new poem or short story but also display a pantheon of his masters. On Hsü Chih-mo's pantheon stand Byron, Shelley, Keats, Rolland, Mansfield, and Hardy. Kuo Mo-jo's gallery of heroes includes Whitman, Tagore, Goethe, Tolstoy, and Nietzsche, among many others. Yü Ta-fu would single out Turgenev, Dowson, and Rousseau. A list of common top favorites drawn from the individual favorites among the seven literary men of this study would at least include: Byron, Shelley, Goethe, Rolland, Rousseau, Tolstoy, Nietzsche, Tagore, and Dumas *fils*. Most of these heroes are outstanding figures of European romanticism; even those who do not summarily fit into the romantic category—Tolstoy, Nietzsche, and Hardy, for instance—were worshiped by their adulators in a romantic perspective: as towering figures of superhuman love and vitality.

This panorama of nineteenth century European literature with a romantic gloss provided the background of modernity in Chinese literature. Few Chinese writers in the 1920s were aware of the beginning of a new trend in Europe. There were no significant traces of expressionism, futurism, formalism, or other forms of the avant-garde in the May Fourth literary scene.[8] The influence of Eliot, Auden, Rilke, and Valéry was not felt until the thirties and forties among small circles of modern Chinese poets. Some major writers of Western fiction of the early twentieth century—James Joyce, Thomas Mann, Franz Kafka, and Ernest Hemingway—were barely noticed by their Chinese contemporaries. Even a colorful figure like F. Scott Fitzgerald —a dandy of the Roaring Twenties in America and certainly a kindred spirit of Hsü Chih-mo—escaped Hsü's attention. It may not be too far-fetched to remark that the Western craze in China represented a zestful effort to squeeze the entire nineteenth century into one decade and to embrace the entire romantic legacy in one volcanic outburst of youthful emotion and energy.

The seven literary men discussed in this study have been chosen to illustrate not only the development of a subjectivist trend in modern Chinese literature but also the impact of Western romanticism, which, I am convinced on the basis of extensive evidence, provided the prevalent ethos and dominated at least a decade of literary development in China. The general themes of this study, therefore, must be presented in a romantic framework. For our purposes, the personalities of the seven men could be recast in the two prototypical models of the romantic personality; the impact of their favorite Western heroes on them and their generation could also be summarized in the light of a case study of two popular Western novels and a leading romantic hero whom they all admired, Byron.

Two Romantic Prototypes

It has been shown in the analysis of Lin Shu's translations that he was enamored of two modes of Western fiction: the world of sentiment and ethics and the world of adventure. The heroines of the former are represented by the virtuous lady of the camellias and the filial girls in Dickens' novels, both of whom evince a profusion of human sentiments and emotions, which Lin attempted to justify in Confucian terms. The world of adventure is represented by the heroes of Haggard and Scott with their dominant features of energy, dynamism, struggle, and self-assertion. Lin's contemporary, Su Man-shu, was attracted to a similar duality in Western literature: he admired the "enthusiasm and straight-forwardness" of Byron who "sought action for love and in love," but he was equally impressed by the more pensive Shelley, the philosopher—lover who "sought nirvana in love." These two general hero-types, as introduced by our two precursors, may be regarded as the two dominant modes of the Western romantic legacy on the Chinese literary scene. The names of two most popular protagonists of Western romanticism may be used to designate these two types: Wertherian (passive-sentimental) and Promethean (dynamic-heroic).

In European romanticism, the Wertherian type of personality has been defined as a man of feeling or a hero of sensibility who is "deepened, perhaps, by a greater sense of fatality and of impending doom." He is often "passive and submissive, with a singularly feminine nature." [9] He is characterized by his capacities for feeling, mostly tender emotions—gentle and tearful love, nostalgia, and a pervasive melancholy. He is also called a passive romanticist in that he seeks refuge in the realm of his inner life: the nuances of his emotion, the mysteries of his unconscious self, or the subjective world of imaginary passions. [10] The other model type, the Promethean man or the active-romanticist, is not without sensibility; but the emphasis is not on his delicacy and sensitivity. He is the enthusiast, the passionate and dominant man whose ultimate desire is "to impose his personality on the world, to shape the world—even to create it, to be a new Prometheus." [11] This active romanticist does not take refuge from life and society in his inner self. "Instead of trying to escape from life, he goes back to it; only he does so not in order to come to terms with it, but in order to assert himself against it, to expose it by showing all its drabness, injustice and ugliness; to prove, in short, that it is unworthy to be accepted." [12] The interplay of these two types is also visible in the five outstanding men of letters covered in this study.

The Wertherian type easily suggests the Chinese literary prototype, *ts'ai-tzu*, although the surface elegance and bohemian abandon *(feng-liu)* of a *ts'ai-tzu* often overshadow his probings into the inner self. In Yü Ta-fu's search for the visions of the self, the Wertherian type seemed to loom constantly on his mental horizon. His two favorite heroes—Huang Chung-tse and Ernest Dowson—are both men of feeling and sensibility with a melancholy and fatalistic bent. His autobiographical works register the poignancy of his uprootedness and introspective egotism which recalls the more pensive side of Rousseau. In his *Rêveries du Promeneur Solitaire* which Yü admired and translated in part into Chinese, this spiritual father of European romanticism wrote the following: "Whatever I notice in the external world brings to my heart only pain and affliction; whenever I cast my eyes upon things which surround me and are connected with me I always find in them some aspect or other which arouses my spite and indignation, or else gives me pain. Alone for the rest of my life—since I find the only solace, hope and peace within myself, I must not, and no longer want to, occupy myself with anything else except my own ego." [13]

While Rousseau's exaggerated sensitiveness rendered him "more and more helpless and morbid," [14] the sorrows and afflications of Yü's "superfluous" existence seemed to be contagious to his contemporaries. Their emotional reception of Yü's works succeeded in stultifying Yü's power of introspection and in pampering his ego. A passive romanticist endowed with a moving Wertherian mentality thus degenerated into a pallid modern replica of the traditional *ts'ai-tzu*. Still, in his most creative years, Yü Ta-fu came closest to the Wertherian type of personality with a Rousseauian touch of sensitivity and sincerity.

From his physical appearance and demeanor, Hsü Chih-mo could easily be seen as another Wertherian type. But his works and activities exhibited more Promethean aspirations. He openly declared himself to be an incorrigible individualist [15] in the sense that he asserted his individual personality and advocated personal experience. Never a cynic even in his last years, he called for positive action with frenzied enthusiasm so as to effect "a total overhaul" of his environment. But the measures he contemplated to reshape the social and political environment around him readily betrayed his naiveté as a social reformer and his impotence as a political activist. The hazy blueprint he drew from an isolated experiment in a chosen county of his home province—inspired by Tagore and supported financially by Elmhirst—was doomed to failure in the light of another illustrious case, the rural reconstruction programs of James Yen. Hsü's political credo lay in a self-defined notion of democracy which he equated with pan-individualism and which was imbedded in "self-consciousness and self-exertions of each individual." [16] His ebullient vision of a future utopia with able-bodied youth singing and dancing in the vineyards —all permeated with that sense of Dionysian madness—gradually gave way to a darkened plain of total despair on which he found only "the wild dances of death" and a "tower of death's victory built by imbecile mankind with their own bones and flesh."[17] Hsü Chih-mo can therefore be regarded as a Promethean type who failed and who substituted the unreality of his exuberant imagination for the reality of his immediate environment.

Hsü Chih-mo is not fully qualified as what may be regarded as the active romanticist. For, although Hsü was "thirsting for the fullness of life through activity,"[18] he did not become either a social outcast or a rebel. The pose of rebel was assumed by all three leftist writers discussed in this study, especially Kuo Mo-jo and Hsiao Chün. Fascinated with banditry as a boy, becoming a student leader in his adolescent years, Kuo Mo-jo represented the early spirit of the Creationists in viewing both the emerging literary scene and Chinese society as his enemies. His rejection of social reality was also projected into his pantheism. Although it does not manifest itself in a kind of "cosmic uprootedness" which culminates in "a spiritual rebellion against both the Universe and its Creator,"[19] it aims at fashioning God in the human image. "Therefore I am God," Kuo proclaimed, "All nature is a manifestation of myself."[20] The act of literary creation, as Kuo conceived it and put it in the manifesto of the *Creation Quarterly*, is impregnated with Promethean aspirations: to impose the personality of the poet on the world and to shape it in his own image. The heroic and cosmic imageries of his poetry lead one to expect a degree of Satanic grandeur in Kuo's personality, but whatever traces of Satanism there may have been in Kuo proved ephemeral, chiefly because of his volatile mentality, which betrays the lack of sustained sincerity in his convictions. Especially after he had managed to ascend the ladder of prestige in Communist China, even his rebellious pose was gradually replaced by that of blind hero-worship—no longer of himself, but of the political masters above him. The voluntary servitude of a self-styled poet–hero thus divested Kuo of any true stature as a romantic hero.

Both Chiang Kuang-tz'u and Hsiao Chün suffered a more tragic fate than Kuo Mo-jo because they were not willing to subject themselves to a higher order whose ultimate goals they shared. For a true romantic can never feel comfortable in any status quo, any established system; he aspires to, but can never realize, a utopia. The destiny of romantic genius, as Howard Hugo remarks, is that of a messiah who ultimately "becomes the outlaw, the scapegoat, the outsider." [21] The really doomed aspect of his nature is that he will inevitably be annihilated by the very society whose goals he has helped achieve and whose hopes he has articulated. Although neither Chiang nor Hsiao is a writer of greater talents than Kuo, both can be viewed as truer active romanticists in that they posed their assertive and combative egos against their society, be it under the tutelage of the KMT or the CCP. Like Hsü Chih-mo, Chiang Kuang-tz'u died opportunely, whereas Hsiao Chün, who outlived them, had to go through a painful rebirth in order to emerge as a new positive man in Socialist Realism instead of a romantic rebel.

Werther and Jean-Christophe

The dominance of the two major prototypes of the romantic personality on the Chinese literary men is also reflected in their enthusiastic response to two of the most popular romantic novels: *The Sorrows of Young Werther* by Goethe and *Jean-Christophe* by Romain Rolland. *The Sorrows of Young Werther* was first translated by Kuo Mo-jo in 1921. In his preface to this work, Kuo summarized Goethe's merits as revealed in this novel: 1. his emotionalism, 2. his pantheism, 3. his praise of nature, 4. his admiration of primitive life, and 5. his respect for the infant.[22] It is obvious that, to Kuo Mo-jo, this novel represented the quintessence of all the virtues and values he had found in the best works of Western literature.

Soon after Kuo's translated version was published, *Young Werther* reaped such popularity as to become almost the bible of modern Chinese youth. Their emotional identification with this young German hero can be illustrated by a few examples. Hsieh Ping-ying, author of the best-selling autobiography, *I-ke nü-ping ti tzu-chuan* (Autobiography of a girl soldier), confessed that she had read Goethe's novel five times. As a girl soldier serving in an army medical unit during the Sino-Japanese War, she had a lover whose name was Wei-t'e, a Chinese transliteration of Werther.[23] In Chang I-p'ing's best seller, *A Batch of Love Letters*, a young girl writes to her lover: "My dearest, to read that you have compared yourself to Werther in your last letter fills my eyes with bitter and hot tears. How pitiable is Werther's end! . . . Please be assured that I will never act like Charlotte in her devotion to Albert."[24] In Mao Tun's novel, *Tzu-yeh* (Midnight), Captain Lei, a former student and later a cadet of the Whampoa Academy, meets Mrs. Wu, his former love in student days and now the wife of a Shanghai industrialist: "Captain Lei lifted his head and drew out a book from his pocket. Opening it quickly, he extended it towards Mrs. Wu with both hands. It was an old, well-worn copy of *Die Leiden des jungen Werther*. The place at which it was open was marked with a pressed white rose . . . 'This book and this white rose are dearer to me than all else . . . I made my way over thousands, indeed tens of thousands of corpses. Innumerable times I escaped death by a hair's breadth, I lost everything. Only from this rose and book I never parted.' "[25]

The pervasive appeal of young Werther to Chinese youth is obvious. He is a well-educated German *ts'ai-tzu* with a charming affliction, unrequited love. His sorrows of love are expressed in the intensity of his emotions—a perfect source of inspiration to the emancipated love-hungry youth who had recently emerged on the literary scene by means of the cataclysmic Literary Revolution. But one important aspect of Werther was neglected by his Chinese worshipers. His sorrows are not only attributed simply to unrequited love but also contain some philosophic significance. Werther is a victim of the so-called romantic *Weltschmerz*, a passive and often pessimistic state of mind which arises from a disparity between a man's ideals and the reality of his environment.[26] In his "Reflections on Werther," Goethe himself described it as something close to a weariness of life under the most peaceful conditions. The culmination of *Weltschmerz* is often suicide, and Goethe himself once came very close to it early in his life. The novel can be read, therefore, as a study of suicide. In order to register faithfully the stages of his hero's mental disintegration, Goethe hit upon a most effective literary form—personal letters. Thus the rationale for the letter form is closely linked with the psychological build-up of the hero: "He is thrust upon by the very things that should serve to take him out of himself. If he ever does want to discuss it, then, surely only in letters, for a written effusion, whether it be joyous or morose, does not antagonize anyone directly." [27]

In their effusion of subjective emotions, the May Fourth youth entirely ignored this pessimistic note and wept over Werther's suicide in the same way they bewailed the death of La Dame aux Camélias. They received the work just as the German youth in the 1770s had received it when it first appeared—as a sentimental sob story. Although the Chinese youth had not, like their German counterparts, "made a fad of wearing his blue frock coat and yellow waistcoat, and in many cases found in the hero's fate an invitation to suicide," [28] some of them adopted the name of Werther and Charlotte, just as others had called themselves Armand. One also wonders whether the widespread use of the letter form as a fictional device was not due, at least partially, to the same influence. The sentimental and confessional temper in the early twenties was such that Goethe's Chinese readers would readily applaud the other side of Goethe's intention to write this book: "The decision to let my inner self rule me at will." [29] It was the plot—drawn from Goethe's personal experience—that appealed to the autobiographical mania of the Chinese audience. It was the profusion of emotions which the young Werther poured out in his letters, rather than the underlying *Weltschmerz*, which was reciprocated by a whole generation equally teeming with emotions.

In spite of Werther's overwhelming sentimentality, something was lacking in his personality. Liu Wu-chi noted perceptively that "although Werther was the embodiment of youth, he lacked an element of dynamism that youth should have. Accordingly, he could not but follow the inclinations of his heart and seek the path of self-destruction." [30] Liu made these comments in America in 1929, when a large number of his fellow literary men in China were already drifting toward the left. A sensitive writer like Mao Tun was able to observe that Werther's sentimentality and his lack of dynamism were no longer praiseworthy values. Mao Tun's usage of two images—"an old well-worn copy" of this novel and "a pressed white rose"—is both naturalistic and symbolic. He testified to the immense popularity of the novel but suggested, by implication, that this bible of youthful love had been trampled by war and revolution. By 1930, when the story of *Tzu Yeh* supposedly took place, the book, like love itself, had become cherished memory. The appearance of other translations served to perpetuate this memory, but its immediate relevance was lost.

In January 1926, the *Hsiao-shuo yüeh-pao* began to serialize a partial translation of *Jean-Christophe*. A letter from Romain Rolland himself under the title, "Jean-Christophe to his brethren in China" was reproduced in the same issue together with a translated Chinese text:

I know neither Europe nor Asia; I only know two races in the world: the race of the ascending soul and the race of the descending soul.

On the one hand, the patient, ardent, tenacious and intrepid impulse of men toward light—all the light: science, beauty, love of men, common progress.

On the other, oppressive forces: darkness, ignorance, apathy, fanatical prejudices and brutality.

I am with the former. Wherever they might come from, they are all my friends, my allies, and my brethren. My fatherland is a free humanity. The great people are its provinces and the common well-being is its Sun King.

January, 1925   Romain Rolland [31]

The letter, which was used as a kind of preface to the Chinese translation of *Jean-Christophe*, also sheds some light on Rolland's original intention in writing his *chef d'oeuvre*. Jean-Christophe Krafft was a German musician, a "Beethoven in the world of today." He was not Rolland himself but a projection of what he would like to have been: a great musician. The religious symbolism in his name ("Jean" from John the Baptist and "Christophe" from Christ) carries with it Rolland's own religious message. The function of Jean, the Precursor, is "to cry in the wilderness, to denounce the generation of vipers, to lay the axe to the root of the tree." [32] But after the theme of revolt in the first part of the novel—*La Révolte*—is concluded, the hero embarks upon a new journey (*Nouvelle Journée*) and here justifies his second name. "When at the end Christophe emerges from the river, like Christ after his baptism, he leaves the Precursor behind and goes forward to preach the gospel of the New Day: Primal Energy, or

'Krafft.' " [33] The river Rhine, one of the key sources of inspiration for Rolland in this novel, has a symbolic and structural significance in linking, first of all, Jean-Christophe's own life journey and, second, the two cultures on both sides of the river: the civil restraint of French culture and the primitive force of Germanic culture. The river is enriched from both banks just as Rolland, through Jean-Christophe Krafft, draws his nature and the quality of his thought from both cultures. His final message is clear: "Brothers, let us draw close together, let us forget what separates us, let us think only of our common misery! There are no enemies, there are no evil men, there are only unfortunates, and the only lasting happiness is to understand each other in order to love one another." [34]

This is the message that Rolland offered to his Chinese brethren. But in the heat of their nationalism the Chinese Rollandists conveniently overlooked the pacifist internationalism behind his advocation of French-German cooperation and the brotherhood of men.[35] Kuo Mo-jo, in a memorial article on Rolland written in 1948, simply identified the people of the light with the Allies and the oppressive forces with the Nazis and Fascists.[36] Nor did Rolland's Chinese admirers pay enough attention to the symbolic, allegorical, and musical elements in the novel. They passed over Jean and Christophe and went straight to the final message of Krafft—force. The first Chinese translator of *Jean-Christophe*, Ching Yin-yü, who was also Rolland's friend by correspondence, summarized the French master's entire *Weltanschauung* in one word, "dynamism," which was imparted to his hero, Jean-Christophe.[37] Ching may indeed have read the most heroic biography of Rolland by Stefan Zweig, who asserted that "Jean-Christophe is an apostle of force." [38]

The appeal of Romain Rolland to his Chinese brethren, like the appeal of Michelangelo and Beethoven to Rolland himself, lies in his larger-than-life heroic stature. The heroic streak in Rolland's mentality has been glowingly described by himself. "Our first duty," he declared, "is to be great, and to defend greatness on earth." [39] He shares a kindred spirit with Carlyle concerning heroes and hero worship. While Carlyle presents the hero as poet, Rolland exalts the hero as artist who, like himself, "aspires towards eternal forms" and "strives to fashion the monumental." [40] In their mania of hero worship the Chinese men of letters at once seized upon Rolland's heroic aspirations by showering upon him all kinds of titanic epithets. Hsü Chih-mo called Rolland "the brave fighter for mankind," "the spiritual and intellectual leader of the whole of Europe," and "the fountain spring of inspiration for the entire world." [41] Kuo Mo-jo eulogized him as "the great son of France, the navigator of truth," and "the great fighter for democracy." [42] Hsiao Chün regarded Rolland, together with Gorky and Lu Hsün, as the three greatest "spiritual engines" of the modern age: "With his crystal soul, his golden heart, his sun-like light and warmth . . . he fights with sword or pen for human progress until he sheds his last drop of blood, and exhales his last whiff of breath." [43]

It is interesting that Rolland's most fervent worshipers in China were also among the most dynamic personalities. The case of Kuo Mo-jo and Hsiao Chün is especially relevant. For Rolland's heroic philosophy sometimes does reach what Kuo Mo-jo would view as pantheistic proportions. One finds the following proclamation by Rolland which indicates clearly that he in fact joins hands with another of Kuo's favorite heroes, Walt Whitman: "What do you suppose that I would intimate to you in a hundred ways, but that man or woman is as good as God? and that there is no God any more divine than yourself?" [44] For Hsiao Chün, there could be no better apostle of force than Rolland and his *Jean-Christophe*, a work Hsiao Chün loved as much as he did *Taras Bulba*.

Hsiao Chün's admiration for Rolland and *Jean-Christophe* was representative of the general reception of this French giant in China. The emphasis on force, energy, suffering and the triumph over suffering puts Rolland's hero in sharp contrast with Goethe's young Werther. Jean-Christophe and Werther are kindred spirits only in the exuberance of their emotionalism. Aside from this, they are miles apart. While Werther is slender, pensive, almost effeminate, Jean-Christophe is "tall and massive, almost uncouth, with large hands and brawny arms . . . liable to outbursts of turbulent passion." [45] While Werther is "cultivated, well-to-do, generous, talented, sensitive, observant but more inclined to reverie," [46] one discerns in Jean-Christophe "some-

thing barbaric and elemental, the power of a storm or of a torrent . . .
His outward aspect is that of a fighter." [47] The contrast between the
two heroes, I suggest, reveals the general polarity between the Wertherian and the Promethean prototypes. The popularity of Rolland's
work reflected a gradual process of dynamization in the romantic
temper in China.[48] The appeal of Rolland even to the avowedly Marxist
writers like Kuo Mo-jo and Hsiao Chün is another indication that the
leftist tendency on the literary scene was due to the impact more of
romanticism than of theoretical Marxism. A Rollandist sense of heroism and humanitarianism lay at the root of the leftist writers' social
conscience and political stance.

Byron and the Byronic Hero

Whether the Chinese literary men preferred Werther or Jean-Christophe, they were uniform in their adulation of the epitome of Western
romanticism: Byron. Ever since Su Man-shu had introduced this English romantic poet and initiated the fad of Byroniana by consciously
modeling himself after his hero, Byron has become perhaps the most
glorified author of Western romanticism in China, towering even
above Rousseau, the father of European romanticism. Some consciously identified themselves with Byron, while others sang praises
and carved heroic images of Byron in their works.

What the Chinese admired most in Byron—the central feature of
the Chinese Byronic image—was that Byron was a great rebel. In a
special issue of *Hsiao-shuo yüeh-pao* devoted to Byron and published
in 1924 (the centennial year of Byron's death), some of the leading
members of the Association for Literary Studies propounded their
variations on the theme of Byron as a rebel. Cheng Chen-to, founder
of the association and editor of the magazine, wrote: "We love talented writers, particularly great rebels. Hence our adulation of Byron . . . His passionate actions of rebellion move us much more than
his poetry." [49] Cheng followed his assertion with four lines of panegyrics which appeared on the front page of the special issue:

He is an extraordinarily great rebel in the modern age!
He rebels against the evil devils that oppress freedom;

He rebels against all false and hypocritical societies.
The immortality of poets rests with their works, but
    Byron is a singular exception.[50]

The novelist Wang T'ung-chao admired Byron's "fiery passion, intense and exuberant energy"[51] and considered Byron second only to Shakespeare in literary achievements. The otherwise sedate Mao Tun registered an impassioned plea for Byron although warning against imitations of Byron's sensual indulgence: "What China needs now is exactly the kind of thunderous and stormy literature suffused with Byron's rebellious spirit."[52] In similar "Byron special" issues of the *Creation Quarterly*, Liang Shih-ch'iu made a rare appearance before his Babbittian legacies overcame his youthful romanticism. "The kernel of Byronism," Liang wrote, "is his rebellious spirit."[53] This rebellious spirit, Liang asserted, was the prerequisite for any movement of "emancipation," which he regarded as "the kernel of romanticism." "The romantic spirit of rebellion can be found in every romantic poet, but it can be said to have reached the peak with Byron."[54] Another Creationist writer announced forcefully: "What is the Byronic spirit? It is the spirit of revolution."[55] It is needless to recapitulate the even more grandiloquent visions of Byron in the works of Hsü Chih-mo, Kuo Mo-jo, and Chiang Kuang-tz'u.

This Chinese reading of Byron yields some interesting contrasts with the Byronic images in the West. The Chinese adulators make little differentiation between Byron and his works; therefore, the Byronic hero is mainly represented by Byron himself. The Western image of the Byronic hero, however, presents a composite picture— a blending of Byron and the heroes in his works—which encompasses all the major hero-types of European romanticism: the child of nature, the hero of sensibility, the Gothic villain, the intellectual rebel like Faust, the moral outcast like Cain, or simply the rebel against society and even God, like Prometheus and Satan.[56] The Chinese writers paint their Byronic images in more positive colors. Thus they have overlooked both Don Juan and Cain, and stripped Prometheus of his Satanic aspects. In short, they have not observed the more devilish side of the Western image of Byron which presents him as an erotic, sadistic, and satanic dandy.[57] Moreover, in glorifying Byron's "rebellious spirit," the Chinese Byronians also neglect the more Wertherian aspects: Byron as a tender lover and a man of sensitivity and sentimentality. Nor does the Chinese epithet of "rebellion" refer as much to the spiritual or cosmic rebellion of Faust or Prometheus as to the personal, social, and political rebellion of Byron himself, especially in his last years in Greece. This less intellectual but more emotional and positive interpretation of the Byronic image reveals the influence of the socio-political context of the May Fourth era. The growing nationalism which culminated in the student and worker demonstrations against foreign imperialism in the twenties and thirties prompted the Chinese men of letters to compare the plight of their homeland with that of Greece. Byron's last heroic act to help the Greek people regain their independence was regarded not only as an act of romantic rebellion but also a nationalistic act. The fact that Byron became an outcast from English society was received by his Chinese followers as another indication of Byron's rebellious heroism—a defiance of social conventions which fitted well into the iconoclastic and emancipational temper of the May Fourth generation.

A more subtle factor of Byron's popularity in China was psychological, in the context of the romantic personality. The Byronic hero in European romanticism represented in fact a combination of both the Wertherian and Promethean prototypes. Insofar as both types of the romantic personality had their equivalents in China, Byron's multifaceted glamor was obvious. But the dynamic interpretation of Byron reflected a general mood of exhilaration and increasing activism on the literary scene. The Wertherian type, which smacked more of the traditional *ts'ai-tzu*, became gradually outmoded as the sentimental trend turned political and leftist after the second half of the 1920s. The Wertherian temper of Yü Ta-fu had given way to the more Promethean aspirations of Kuo Mo-jo. The politicization of the Chinese men of letters had transformed Prometheus from a cosmic rebel into a social and political one. Even Lu Hsün had chosen this mythological figure as his alter ego while adding a cultural note: "I have stolen fire from other countries, intending to cook my own flesh. I think that if the taste is good, the other chewers on their part may get something out of it, and I shall not sacrifice my body in vain." [58] To be a Promethean martyr, for Lu Hsün, was to attain the true stature of a revolutionary.

It can be concluded, therefore, that in the romantic framework the shift from Literary Revolution to Revolutionary Literature is epitomized by the dynamizing view of Byron—a progression from sentiment to force, from love to revolution, from Werther to Prometheus.

The Romantic Generation

Lecturing at the University of Chicago some thirty years ago, Hu Shih compared the Literary Revolution in China to the Renaissance in Europe.[59] Perhaps it would be more appropriate, if analogies are needed, to substitute the Romantic Movement for the Renaissance. Both the Romantic Movement in nineteenth century Europe (in spite of the wealth of scholastic debates on the exact nature and definition of Romanticism)[60] and the Literary Revolution in twentieth-century China represented a reaction against the classic tradition of order, reason, schematization, ritualization, and structuring of life. Both ushered in a new emphasis on sincerity, spontaneity, passion, imagination, and the release of individual energies—in short, the primacy of subjective human sentiments and energies.

It can be argued that much of this new tendency in both cases can be traced back to the sentimental tradition in classical literature, which may have predisposed some modern men of letters toward these romantic values. What distinguishes this romantic tendency inspired by the West from the sentimental strains in traditional Chinese literature —a distinction that renders the word "sentimental" insufficient as a keynote to the temper of this era—is a marked and increasing degree of dynamism, which, I suggest, is primarily the legacy of nineteenth-century European Romanticism. Two mythological concepts can be regarded as its dynamic manifestations: Prometheanism, as seen through Chinese lenses, glorifies individual bravery, self-conscious and self-assertive efforts at the realization of human potentialities in rebellion against past orthodoxy or tradition; and Dionysianism, with its motive force in both spiritual and physical love, demands total release from the restrictions of convention and plunges the individual into the throes of subjective life experience in order to attain the state of frenzied, ecstatic abandon. The application of these two types of romantic ethos to the historical environment is found in Kuo Mo-jo's celebrated poem, "The Resurrection of the Phoenixes": the fire of individual and collective passion would burn up all the remnants of the past and, out of their ashes, the phoenix of New China would be reborn.

It is this dynamic ethos that overshadows the sentimental and Wertherian side of the modern Chinese man of letters, giving him a more positive stature and marking him off from the frail, effete *wen-jen* prototype of traditional times. One of the intriguing aspects of the personality of a modern Chinese man of letters lies in his inner dynamic cravings to transform his far from robust appearance. Hsü Chih-mo, with his old-style long gown and his dark-rimmed glasses framing a delicate face, would often come "in a whirlwind, sweeping across his companions," and utter words "amidst fits of shouting and jumping."[61] Even an otherwise mature and restrained man like Mao Tun could not resist naming the hero in one part of his trilogy, *Eclipse*, Ch'iang Meng (strong and fierce), alias Wei-li (sole force). It is also in this dynamic context that the word romantic may be applied to describe the personalities and life-styles of some prominent members of the May Fourth literary intelligentsia. We would have to distinguish, with Jacques Barzun, "Romanticism as a historical movement and romanticism as a characteristic of human beings."[62] In the latter category, Barzun has also noted that sentimentality, though commonly alleged to be a major facet of the romantic personality, is more of "a regrettable hangover from the past"[63] (as exemplified, in Europe, by the sentimental novels of Lawrence Sterne and Henry Fielding at the end of the neo-classical period and, in China, by the masters of *hsieh-ch'ing hsiao-shuo* and Butterfly fiction). In addition to sentiment, "energy is the distinguishing mark of romantic life."[64]

Was there a conscious Romantic Movement in twentieth century China? The answer, on the superficial level, has to be negative, although a few extremists in the twenties were determined to unleash a conscious Romantic Movement following entirely the European example. Chang Ching-sheng, that notorious "Dr. Sex" and one-time professor at Peking University, declared in his own journals: "I wish to publish a 'Romantic Series' by my 'Beautiful Bookstore' which will contain Chinese works and translations from the West; I really hope that generations of classicists in our country will be shattered into pieces, to be replaced by the free, heroic, and emotional Romantic School." [65]

Although Chang's promises were never realized, it was apparent, even to contemporary observers in the early twenties, that there indeed existed "a romantic trend with a tendency toward practically enveloping the youth of the entire country." [66] In a long article written in 1926 and titled, "The Romantic Tendencies in Modern Chinese Literature," Liang Shih-ch'iu discerned the following features in the New Literature Movement:[67]

(1) It is fundamentally under foreign influences.

(2) It upholds emotion and disdains reason.

(3) The general outlook it adopts toward life is "impressionistic" (that is, subjectivistic).

(4) It advocates a return to nature and emphasizes originality.

These four traits are, according to Liang, characteristically romantic and, for a self-styled follower of Irving Babbitt, excessive. For Liang's contemporaries on the literary scene, however, the epithet romantic was often acknowledged with conscious pride, especially in the early twenties. The analogy with European romanticism was often invoked consciously. A group of young poets who gathered at West Lake near Hangchow and published a collection of love poetry christened themselves with the charming title—like the famous group of early English romanticists composed of Wordsworth, Coleridge, Southey, and Leigh Hunt—the Lake Poets.[68] As if aware of the evolutionary sequence in French romanticism, another group of poets active in the late thirties —notably Li Chin-fa and Tai Wang-shu—began to write symbolist poetry by consciously imitating the French model.[69] A whole century of European romanticism—especially its French and English varieties —was swallowed up enthusiastically by one generation of Chinese literary men in one decade.[70] One is tempted, while cognizant of many exceptions, to brand the entire May Fourth generation of Chinese men of letters as a romantic generation and the decade of the 1920s as a romantic decade.

To define romanticism in China in the 1920s runs the risk of over-simplification. The various categories and characteristics of Western romanticism proposed by Western scholars can be combined into an interminable list. What unites most of these artificially categorized romantic features is a fundamental outlook which our major protago-nists also share. This outlook views life not as a given scheme reveal-ing itself objectively in a rational order but rather as a process of individual and subjective experiences. Reality is conceived not as a pre-established structure or schema to be grasped by systematically applying the human intellect, but rather as a fragmented flow, never static, never totally comprehensible, only to be felt and glimpsed through intuition and intimation. Thus what is emphasized in this out-look is impulse, not result; motive, not objective; creative will, not retrospective analysis; feeling and sensitivity, not reason and ritualiza-tion. Society is seen as chaotic, to be destroyed or overhauled *in toto*, but not remedied piecemeal. Utopia, a haven of the shining future, is ultimately indescribable, though craved for. Thus the visions and images of a romantic utopia are often couched in such vague, albeit exuberant, terms as "total rebirth," "the whole of mankind," "eman-cipation," truth, beauty, goodness, freedom, happiness.

From a historical viewpoint, this kind of outlook often reflects a period of transition. "What is known as romanticism was, above all, an inner reaction to that transitional period which dislocated all for-mer ways and values, mixed up all classes, destroyed all faith, all proper orientation." [71] Such a period often produces a number of indi-viduals who do not organically belong to any established class of society. Lacking an organic contact with life as a whole, this type of individual is compelled to fall back upon himself, and to oppose the value of his own ego to the rest of his society. His uprootedness and alienation become in his eyes a proof of his imaginary greatness. It is in this transitional context that the life stories of our romantic men of letters end in tragedy. In eulogizing love, glorifying individuality, celebrating emancipation, they seemed to have neither time nor mood for analyzing the complexities of their time and their changed role as alienated intelligentsia. After having swept away tradition, they have left a cultural vacuum which they attempted to fill up with Western panaceas—science, democracy, anarchism, socialism, romanticism. Intoxicated with themselves and possessed with the wonders from the West, they never seriously pondered the problem of modern China's cultural identity. Their basic outlook, emerging perhaps in a historical context of transition and uncertainty, was anything but realistic. The clash between their idealized images and the increasingly somber realities incurred not a re-evaluation of the self but a reassertion of the self: thus a host of leftist heroes and heroines since the 1940s, from Wang Shih-wei, Hsiao Chün, Ting Ling, to Feng Hsüeh-feng and Ai Ch'ing, have fallen under the rigors of party discipline.[72]

Has romanticism ceased to be the temper of post-1949 China? One finds, as late as 1958, in the pages of the official CCP journal, *Red Flag*, a slogan initiated by Kuo Mo-jo and Chou Yang advocating "revolutionary romanticism."[73] One also wonders whether the recent Cultural Revolution cannot be regarded as the resurgence of a kind of collective romantic spirit against the routinization of an established order and whether the release of human energies of a younger generation cannot be seen as the frenzied outburst of a collective will, guided by the thought of Mao Tse-tung, to destroy the old phoenix in order to hasten the rebirth of a new one. The problem of romanticism in a socialist setting will certainly be a most intriguing theme for another act in the drama. But the curtain for this act of our romantic drama has fallen.

Notes, Bibliography, Glossary, and Index

Notes

Abbreviations used in the notes

TH   Chao Chia-pi, ed., *Chung-kuo hsin wen-hsüeh ta-hsi* (A comprehensive compendium of modern Chinese literature; Shanghai, 1935–36), 10 vols.

CPSL   Chang Ching-lu, ed., *Chung-kuo hsien-tai ch'u-pan shih-liao* (Historical materials concerning contemporary Chinese publications; Peking, 1954–57), 4 vols. (1, 2, 3, and Addenda).

1. The Emergence of the Literary Scene

1. Chow Tse-tsung, *The May Fourth Movement* (Cambridge, Mass., 1960), chap. 11.

2. Lin Yutang, *A History of the Press and Public Opinion in China* (Shanghai, 1936), p. 11.

3. Yüan Yung-ch'ao, *Chung-kuo pao-yeh hsiao-shih* (Hong Kong, 1957), p. 13. For an account in English, see Roswell S. Britton, *The Chinese Periodical Press* (Shanghai, 1933).

4. Yüan Yung-ch'ao, p. 14.

5. Ibid., p. 26; Britton, p. 63.

6. See Lai Kuang-lin, *Liang Ch'i-ch'ao yü chin-tai pao-yeh* (Taipei, 1968). For Liang's life and thought, see Hao Chang, *Liang Ch'i-ch'ao and Intellectual Transition in China* (Cambridge, Mass., 1971); and Philip Huang, *Liang Ch'i-ch'ao and Modern Chinese Liberalism* (Seattle, 1972).

7. Pao T'ien-hsiao, "Hsin-hai ke-ming ch'ien-hou ti Shanghai hsin-wen chieh," in *Hsin-hai ke-ming hui-i lu, iv*, 8.

8. Yuan Yung-ch'ao, p. 43.

9. Ibid., p. 34.

10. *CPSL*, Addenda, p. 106.

11. A Ying (Ch'ien Hsing-ts'un), *Wan-ch'ing wen-hsüeh pao-k'an shu-lüeh* (Shanghai, 1958), pp. 14—16.

12. Yang Shih-chi, *Wen-yüan t'an-wang* (Chungking, 1945), p. 11.

13. The term was taken from the title of a magazine, *Li-pai liu* (Saturday), founded by Chou Shou-chüan. It featured "light fiction and other prose of no value" (Chow Tse-tsung, *The May Fourth Movement*, p. 284), and attracted its readers by printing photos of famous actresses in theater and cinema, society beauties, and fashion models. The themes of its amorous fiction usually centered upon the trials and tribulations of a pair of sentimental lovers—the pale, tuberculosis-ridden scholar (*ts'ai-tzu*) falling hopelessly in love with a glamorous but weathered sing-song girl or fallen beauty. Hu Shih satirically presented a typical formula of these stories: "One day, a dashing young man made excursions to an amusement garden. He saw a girl, gazed at her, and found her very pretty. The girl dropped her handkerchief on purpose, and the young man carried it home. Thinking about her day and night, he fell ill!" The critics from the New Literature camp branded this type of fiction, written in literary or semi-vernacular style, as *Yüan-yang hu-tieh p'ai* (Butterfly school). But in spite of their criticism, *Li pai-liu* enjoyed the largest circulation in sales in the first three decades of this century. Other magazines grouped in the same school included *Tzu-lo-lan* (Violet), *Hung tsa-chih* (Red Magazine), *Pan-yüeh* (half month), *Hung mei-kuei* (Red rose) as well as many literary supplements attached to newspapers, all published in Shanghai. No scholarly studies in Western languages have ever appeared in print concerning this significant social and literary phenomenon. For a bibliographical guide in Chinese, see Wei Shao-ch'ang, ed., *Yüan-yang hu-tieh p'ai yen-chiu tzu-liao* (Shanghai, 1962).

14. For more details see A Ying, *Wan-ch'ing wen-i pao-k'an shu-lüeh*, and his other work, *Wan-Ch'ing hsiao-shuo shih* (Hong Kong, reprint, 1966), p. 2.

15. For a sample, see Ts'ao Chü-jen, *Wen-t'an san-i* (Hong Kong, 1954), p. 25.

16. Chow Tse-tsung, *Research Guide to the May Fourth Movement* (Cambridge, Mass., 1963), p. 128.

17. Fang Ch'ing, *Hsien-tai wen-t'an pai-hsiang* (Hong Kong, 1953), p. 95.

18. Sun Fu-yüan, "Ts'ung Ch'en-pao fu-chüan tao Ching-pao fu-k'an" (From the literary supplement of *Ch'en-pao* to the literary supplement of *Ching-pao*), in *CPSL*, I, 223—229.

19. Chow Tse-tung compiled a list of 587 periodicals for the period 1915–1923, of which at least one third are literary or partially literary journals. Chow, *Research Guide to the May Fourth Movement*, pp. 26–124. Another list shows 641 titles of periodicals published from 1919 to 1927, of which perhaps one third or one fourth were essentially literary journals. *CPSL*, I, 86–102. A third list of purely literary periodicals presumably for the period 1917–1927 records a total of 284 titles, *TH*, X, 381–388. A later list compiled in 1935 showed that in Shanghai alone there were more than 70 literary periodicals; Hu Tao-ching, *Shanghai ti ting-ch'i k'an-wu* (Shanghai, 1935), pp. 41–48. Finally, a list of literary periodicals in 1919–1927 compiled by another research guide, with detailed information about publication, has 104 titles; *Chung-kuo hsien-tai wen-hsüeh ch'i-k'an mu-lu* (Shanghai, 1961), I, 6–14.

20. Mao Tun, "Tao-yen" (Introduction), *Hsiao-shuo i-chi* (Fiction, first series), *TH*, III, 5–7.

21. Chow Tse-tsung, *The May Fourth Movement*, pp. 44, 55.

22. Wang P'ing-ling, *San-shih nien wen-t'an ts'ang-sang lu* (Taipei, 1965), p. 88.

23. "Yü-ssu fa-k'an tz'u" (Inaugural manifesto at the publication of *Thread-of-Talk*), *TH*, X, 116.

24. Lu Hsün, "Wo yü yü-ssu ti shih-chung" (My associations with Yü-ssu from beginning to end), in *Chung-kuo hsien-tai wen-hsüeh shih ts'an-k'ao tzu-liao* (Peking, 1959), I, 172–178. A sharp difference of opinion developed between the Chou brothers after the May 30th Incident. Lu Hsün wanted to protest against Japanese brutality whereas Chou Tso-jen wished to avoid political controversies. See Amitendranath Tagore, *Literary Debates in Modern China, 1918–1937* (Tokyo, 1967), p. 61.

25. See, for instance, Wang Yao, *Chung-kuo hsin wen-hsüeh shih-kao* (Shanghai, 1951), I, 46–47.

26. Lu Hsün, "Tao-yen" (Introduction), *Hsiao-shuo erh-chi* (Fiction, second series), *TH*, IV, 12.

27. Li Chi-yeh, "Chi Wei-ming she" (Note on Wei-ming society), in *CPSL*, I, 171. For more details, see Tagore, pp. 64–66.

28. William Ayers, "The Society for Literary Studies, 1921–1930," *Papers on China* 7:39–40 (February 1953).

29. Ayers, p. 41; *CPSL*, I, 173–174.

30. According to Chao Ching-shen, the association had 172 registered members. A membership list had been printed which, however, showed a total of 131 persons. *CPSL*, I, 177.

31. Ayers, p. 43.

32. A preliminary list of publications in the period 1919–1923 registers six titles of fiction, three titles of poetry, one essay collection, one historical study of Western literature, and seventeen translated works as belonging to the as-

sociation series. Of the seventeen translations, Tagore claims three, Andreyev, Maeterlinck have two each; Tolstoy, Wilde, de Maupassant, Storm, Shaw, Galsworthy, Molière, and Schnitzler, each claims one title. *TH*, I 107–120.

33. Kuo Mo-jo, "Ch'uang-tsao shih-nien" included in *Ke-ming ch'un-ch'iu* (Shanghai, 1951), pp. 113–114.

34. Clarence Moy, "Kuo Mo-jo and the Creation Society," *Papers on China* 4:132 (April 1950).

35. T'ao Ching-sun, "Chi Ch'uang-tsao she" (Note on the Creation Society), in Yang Chih-hua, ed., *Wen-t'an shih-liao* (Shanghai, 1944), p. 408.

36. Moy, pp. 135–138.

37. Editorial note, *Hung-shui* 2.10:491 (Feb. 5, 1926).

38. Kuo Mo-jo, *Ch'uang-tsao shih-nien hsü-pien* (Shanghai, 1928), pp. 188–189.

39. Wang Tu-ch'ing, "Ch'uang-tsao she—wo ho t'a ti shih-chung yü t'a ti tsung-chang" (The Creation Society—my relations with it from beginning to end and its full accounting), in Huang Jen-ying, ed., *Ch'uang-tsao she lun*, 2d ed. (Shanghai, 1936), p. 17.

40. See Chapter 5.

41. *CPSL*, I, 190.

42. For a collection of polemical articles written by Lu Hsün and others, see Li Ho-lin, ed., *Chung-kuo wen-i lun-chan* (Shanghai, 1929).

43. Liang Shih-ch'iu, "I Hsin-yüeh" (Reminiscences of the Crescent Moon), in his *Wen-hsüeh yin-yüan* (Taipei, 1964), p. 294.

44. Wang Che-fu, *Chung-kuo hsin wen-hsüeh yun-tung shih* (Hong Kong, 1965), p. 68.

45. The whole spate of personal letters from Ch'en to Hsü and Chou Tso-jen, together with Hsü's reluctant, self-explanatory introduction, which originally appeared in *Ch'en-pao fu-chüan*, can be found in Juan Chi-ming, *Chung-kuo hsin wen-t'an pi-lu* (Shanghai, 1933), pp. 110–140.

46. Liang Shih-ch'iu, "I Hsin-yüeh," pp. 292, 299.

47. Ibid., p. 294.

48. For a forceful example, see Li Ho-lin, *Chin erh-shih-nien Chung-kuo wen-i ssu-ch'ao lun* (Shanghai, 1945), chap. 5.

49. Mao Tun, "Kuan-yü Wen-hsüeh yen-chiu hui" (Concerning the Association for Literary Studies), *TH*, X, 89–90.

50. *Hsin ch'ing-nien* 5.6 (Dec. 15, 1918), quoted in *TH*, 2:144.

51. Quoted in Li Ho-lin, *Chin erh-shih nien Chung-kuo wen-i ssu-ch'ao lun*, p. 89.

52. The second principle on Ch'en's banner reads: "To overthrow the stereotyped and over-ornamental literature of classicism, and to create the fresh and sincere literature of realism." Chow Tse-tsung, *The May Fourth Movement*, p. 276.

53. See his most important exposition on "naturalism," "Tzu-jan chu-i yü Chung-kuo hsien-tai hsiao-shuo" (Naturalism and contemporary Chinese fiction), *Hsiao-shuo yüeh-pao* 13.7 (July 10, 1922).

54. *Hsiao-shuo yüeh-pao* 15.2 (Feb. 10, 1924), front page.

55. Kuo Mo-jo, "Pien-chi yü-t'an" (editorial note), *Ch'uang-tsao chi-k'an* 1.2:21 (Winter 1922); Ch'eng Fang-wu, "Ch'uang-tsao she yü Wen-hsüeh yen-chiu hui," *Ch'uang-tsao chi-k'an* 1.4:13 (Feb. 28, 1924).

56. Quoted in Li Ho-lin, *Chin erh-shih nien Chung-kuo wen-i ssu-ch'ao lun*, pp. 97–98.

57. Kuo Mo-jo, "Ch'uang-tsao shih-nien," p. 133. Mme Doleželová shares the same view; see Milena Dolezelová-Velingerová, "Kuo Mo-Jo's Autobiographical Works," in J. Průšek, ed., *Studies in Modern Chinese Literature* (Berlin, 1964), p. 63.

58. Kuo Mo-jo, "Ch'uang-tsao shih-nien," pp. 92–93.

59. Ibid., pp. 133–136.

60. Wang Che-fu, p. 62.

61. Ch'eng Fang-wu, "Shih chih fang-yü chan" (The defensive battle of poetry), *Ch'uang-tsao chou-pao* 1:1 (May 13, 1923).

62. See *Ch'uang-tsao chou-pao*, Nos. 4, 13, and 15.

63. Kuo Mo-jo, "Ch'uang-tsao shih-nien," p. 156.

64. *Ch'uang-tsao chou-pao* 4:15 (June 3, 1923).

65. Ts'ao Chü-jen stated that Lu Hsün and Kuo had never seen each other; see his *Wen-t'an wu-shih nien* (Hong Kong, 1955), p. 166.

66. Lu Hsün, *Lu Hsün ch'üan-chi* (Peking, 1957), IV, 229, 234.

67. Ibid., IV, 96.

68. Ts'ao Chü-jen, *Shan-shui ssu-hsiang jen-wu* (Hong Kong, 1956), p. 136.

69. The phrase was coined by Liu Fu (Pan-nung) with specific reference to Kuo Mo-jo: "the poet on the Shanghai beach who compares himself to Goethe." Kuo was obviously smarting under this title. See Kuo, "Ch'uang-tsao shih-nien," pp. 73–74.

70. The evaluation and phraseology are from Shen Ts'ung-wen, another Peking School writer, as quoted in Ts'ao Chü-jen, *Shan-shui ssu-hsiang jen-wu*, pp. 136–137.

2. *The Phenomenon of* Wen-t'an *and* Wen-jen

1. Wang Che-fu, p. 7.

2. Ts'ao Chü-jen, *Wen-t'an san-i*, p. 34.

3. C. T. Hsia, *A History of Modern Chinese Fiction, 1917–1957* (New Haven, 1961), p. 93.

4. Wang Tu-ch'ing, *Wo tsai Ou-chou ti sheng-huo* (Shanghai, 1932).

5. *Hsin-yüeh* 1.1:60 (March 1928).

6. *Hsin-yüeh* 1.2:17 (April 1928).

7. Wang P'ing-ling, p. 86.

8. Liang Shih-ch'iu, *T'an Hsü Chih-mo* (Taipei, 1958), p. 17.

9. Yen-to, "Shih-tai ch'ao-liu chung ti i-ke nü-tzu" (A girl in the trend of time), *Hsin nü-hsing* 1.7:483–484 (July 1, 1926).

10. Henry McAleavy, *The Modern History of China* (New York, 1967), p. 275.

11. Chiang Mon-lin, *Tides from the West* (New Haven, 1947), p. 94.

12. Yü Mu-hsia, *Shanghai lin-chao* (Shanghai, 1935), I, 78–79.

13. Yen-to, p. 485.

14. Ching-feng, "Chien fa" (Cutting hair), *Hsiao-shuo shih-chieh* (Fiction world) 10.9:2 (May 29, 1925).

15. Ch'un-ying hung-yü, "Wen-kai chieh-chi lun," *Wan-jen tsa-chih* 1.1:1–23 (April 1, 1930).

16. Jen Pi-ming, "Man-t'an wen-jen" (Random discourse on literary men), *Lien-ho pao* (United Daily; Taipei, Sept. 1, 1969), p. 4.

17. "I-ke wen-hsüeh ch'ing-nien ti meng," (A literary young man's dream), editorial, *Wen-hsüeh* (Literature) 1.3:347 (Sept. 1, 1933).

18. See Lu Hsün, "Na-han tzu-hsü" (Preface to outcry), quoted in Huang Sung-k'ang, *Lu Hsün and the New Culture Movement of Modern China* (Amsterdam, 1957), p. 32.

19. Ts'ao Chü-jen, "Wen-jen hsiang ch'ing" (Mutual depreciation of the literary men), in his *Shan-shui ssu-hsiang jen-wu*, pp. 84–85.

20. Wang Jen-shu, "Tso-chia yü jen-sheng" (Writers and life), *Kung-hsien* 2.5:48 (April 15, 1928).

21. Chang K'e-piao, *Wen-t'an teng-lung shu* (Hong Kong, reprint, 1966), chaps. 1–9.

3. Lin Shu

1. My biographical account of Lin Shu is based mainly on the following sources: Chu Hsi-chou, "Cheng-wen hsien-sheng nien-p'u," *Lin Ch'in-nan hsien-sheng hsüeh-hsing p'u-chi ssu-chung*, ed. Chu Hsi-chou (Taipei, reprint, 1961); Chow Tse-tsung, "Lin Shu," in Howard Boorman, ed., *Men and Politics in Republican China* (New York, 1968), pp. 88–94; and a similar account in Howard Boorman, ed., *Biographical Dictionary of Republican China* (New York, 1968), II, 382–386. See also, Cheng Chen-to, "Lin Ch'in-nan hsien-sheng," *Hsiao-shuo yüeh-pao* 15.11 (Nov. 10, 1924).

2. Lin Shu, *Wei-lu san-chi* (Shanghai, 1924), p. 30b.

3. Chu Hsi-chou, "Nien-p'u," 1:26–27.

4. Chiang Shu-ko, *T'ung-ch'eng wen-p'ai p'ing-shu* (Shanghai, 1930), p. 76.

5. Lin Shu, *Wei-lu hsü-chi* (Shanghai, 1924), p. 49b.

6. Lin Shu, *Wei-lu san-chi*, pp. 2a–b.

7. Lin Shu, *Wei-lu hsü-chi*, p. 78b.

8. Ibid., p. 44a.

9. Tso Shun-sheng, *Chung-kuo hsien-tai ming-jen i-shih* (Hong Kong, 1951), p. 12.

10. Lin Shu, *Wei-lu wen-chi* (Shanghai, 1910), p. 25a–b.

11. Chu Hsi-chou, ed., "Ch'un-chüeh-chai chu-shu chi," in *Lin Ch'in-nan hsien-sheng hsüeh-hsing p'u-chi ssu-chung*, 3:40.

12. "Nien-p'u," 2:62–64.

13. "Chu-shu chi," 3:6.

14. Ibid., 3:56.

15. Aldous Huxley, "The Vulgarity of Little Nell," in George H. Ford and L. Lane, Jr., eds., *The Dickens Critics* (Ithaca, 1961), p. 154.

16. Louis Cazamian, *Le Roman Social en Angleterre, 1830–1850* (Paris, 1903), chap. 4.

17. Edgar Johnson, "The World of Dombeyism," in A. Wright, ed., *Victorian Literature* (New York, 1961), p. 140.

18. Charles Dickens, *Dombey and Son* (New York, 1963).

19. Lin Shu, trans., *Ping-hsüeh yin-yüan* 4:12 in *Shuo-pu ts'ung-shu* (Shanghai, 1915), 2d collection, No. 6.

20. Ibid., 6:89.

21. Ibid., 5:31.

22. Ibid., 5:27.

23. Humphrey House, *The Dickens World* (London, 1941), p. 130.

24. Lionel Trilling, *A Gathering of Fugitives* (Boston: Beacon paperback, 1956), p. 43.

25. Edgar Johnson, *Introduction to Dombey and Son*, p. 26.

26. Nancy Lee Swann, *Pan Chao: Foremost Woman-Scholar of China* (New York, 1932), p. 83.

27. "Chu-shu chi," 3:4. Chu Hsi-chou mistakenly attributed it to *Maiwa's Revenge*.

28. See Benjamin Schwartz, *In Search of Wealth and Power: Yen Fu and the West* (Cambridge, Mass., 1964), p. 40.

29. "Chu-shu chi," 3:4.

30. "Nien-p'u," 1:12.

31. Ibid., 1:21. Chow Tse-tsung, "Lin Shu," p. 91.

32. Entitled "Min-chung hsin-yüeh-fu" (New songs from Central Fukien). For selections, see "Nien-p'u," 1:19–20; for analysis, see Chow Tse-tsung, "Lin Shu," p. 90.

33. Morton Cohen, *Rider Haggard: His Life and Works* (London, 1960), p. 220.

34. Ibid.

35. Robert Kiely, *Robert Louis Stevenson and the Fiction of Adventure* (Cambridge, Mass., 1964), p. 152.

36. Lin Shu, Preface to *Wu-chung jen* (People in the Mist), in "Chu-shu chi," 3:27.

37. Ibid., 3:35.

38. Lin Shu, *Wei-lu hsü-chi*, p. 3.

39. Schwartz, p. 56.

40. Lin Shu mentioned the importance of Herbert Spencer in Western thought as "almost overshadowing his predecessors." See his preface to *Aesop's Fables,* "Chu-shu chi," 3:57.

41. Ibid., 3:28.

42. Lin Shu, Preface to *Kuei-shan lang-hsia chuan* (*Cetywayo and His White Neighbours*), in "Chu-shu chi," 3:33.

43. Ibid., 3:27.

44. Schwartz, pp. 55–56.

45. See Chow Tse-tsung, *The May Fourth Movement* (Cambridge, Mass., 1961), pp. 64–69.

46. Lin Shu, *Wei-lu hsü-chi*, p. 59.

4. Su Man-shu

1. My biographical sketch of Su Man-shu is entirely based on Liu Wu-chi, *Su Man-shu* (New York, 1972). Page references are given in accordance with the page numbers in this book.

2. See Liu Wu-chi, *Su Man-shu,* p. 17.

3. Ibid., p. 21.

4. Ibid.

5. Feng Tzu-yu, *Ke-ming i-shih* (Anecdotal history of the revolution; 3d edition, Shanghai, 1947), I, 241; translated in Liu Wu-chi, manuscript, p. 31.

6. Su Man-shu, "Yü Teng Meng-she shu" (Letter to Teng Meng-she) in Liu Wu-chi, ed., *Man-shu ta-shih chi-nien chi,* 2d ed. (Shanghai, 1949), pp. 70–71.

7. Chang Ping-lin (Chang T'ai-yen), "Man-shu i-hua i-yen" (Notes on Man-shu's posthumous paintings), *Man-shu ch'üan-chi,* ed. Liu Ya-tzu (Shanghai, 1929), IV, 77.

8. Liu Ya-tzu, "Chi Ch'en Chung-p'u hsien-sheng kuan-yü Su Man-shu ti t'an-hua" (A transcript of an interview with Mr. Ch'en Tu-hsiu concerning Su Man-shu) in Liu Wu-chi, ed., *Su Man-shu nien-p'u chi ch'i-t'a* (Shanghai, 1927), p. 284.

9. Chang Shih-chao, "Yü Liu Wu-chi lun Man-shu chu-tso han" (A letter to Liu Wu-chi on the works of Su Man-shu), in ibid., appendix, p. 17.

10. Su Man-shu, "Yü mo-chün shu" (Letter to Mr. X), in *Man-shu ta-shih chi-nien chi*, p. 60.

11. Su Man-shu, "Yü Yeh Ch'u-ts'ang Liu Ya-tzu Chu Shao-p'in shu" (Letter to Yeh Ch'u-ts'ang Liu Ya-tzu and Chu Shao-p'in), in ibid., p. 58.

12. Liu Wu-chi, *Su Man-shu*, p. 126.

13. Liu Ya-tzu, "Su ho-shang tsa-t'an" (Miscellaneous remarks on the monk Su), in *Su Man-shu ch'üan-chi*, V, 217.

14. Liu Wu-chi, "Su Man-shu chi ch'i yu-jen" (Su Man-shu and his friends), in ibid., V, 50.

15. Ts'ai Shou, "Man-shu hua pa" (Postscript to a painting by Man-shu), in ibid., IV, 26.

16. Shih-ming, "Chi Man-shu shang-jen" (On Reverend Man-shu), ibid., IV, 137.

17. Translated in Liu Wu-chi, *Su Man-shu*, pp. 92–93.

18. Su Man-shu, "Tuan-hung ling-yen chi" (The lone swan), in *Man-shu ta-shih chi-nien chi*, p. 225.

19. Ho-ho shih (Kawai-sen), "Man-shu hua-p'u hsü" (Preface to Collection of Man-shu's paintings), in *Man-shu ch'üan chi*. IV, 16–18; translated into Chinese by Chou Tso-jen in ibid., pp. 19–20.

20. Su Man-shu, "Sui tsan chi" (Tale of a broken hairpin), in *Man-shu ta-shih chi-nien chi*, pp. 276–277.

21. Su Man-shu, "Hua yang i-chen hui kuan" (Visit to Sino-Western charity sale), in ibid., p. 154.

22. *Man-shu ta-shih chi-nien chi*, p. 441.

23. Henry McAleavy, *Su Man-shu: A Sino-Japanese Genius* (London, 1960), p. 14.

24. Shih Ming, "Chi Man-shu shang-jen," *Man-shu ch'üan-chi*, IV, 142.

25. Chu P'in, "Shuo-wan chen-wen" (Precious accounts in the literary world), *Man-shu ch'üan-chi*, V, 261.

26. Quoted in Huang Ming-ch'i, *Su Man-shu p'ing-chuan* (Shanghai, 1949), p. 16.

27. Translated in Liu Wu-chi, *Su Man-shu*, p. 112.

28. Ibid., p. 57.

29. Ibid., pp. 75–76.

30. Ibid., p. 76.

31. Chang Ting-huang, "Su Man-shu yü Byron chi Shelley" (Su Man-shu and Byron and Shelley), in *Man-shu ch'üan-chi*, IV, 228.

32. Translated in Liu Wu-chi, *Su Man-shu*, p. 63.

33. *Man-shu ch'üan-chi*, I, 130–131.

34. Su Man-shu, "Yü Kao T'ien-mei shu" (Letter to Kao T'ien-mei), in *Man-shu ta-shih chi-nien chi*, p. 47.

35. For a discussion of the work, see Liu Ya-tzu, "Ts'an she-hui yü ts'an shih-chieh," in *Man-shu ch'üan-chi*, IV, 422—431.

36. Su Man-shu, "Yü Kao T'ien-mei shu," in *Man-shu ta-shih chi-nien chi*, p. 48.

37. Quoted in Liu Wu-chi, "Su Man-shu nien-p'u" (Yearly record of Su Man-shu), in *Man-shu ch'üan-chi*, IV, 336.

38. Liu Wu-chi, *Su Man-shu*, p. 120.

39. Su Man-shu, "Yü Liu Pan-nung shu" (Letter to Liu Pan-nung), in *Man-shu ta-shih chi-nien chi*, p. 77.

40. Lin Shu, *Wei-lu wen-chi*, p. 27b.

41. Su Man-shu, "Sui tsan chi," *Man-shu ta-shih chi-nien chi*, p. 265.

42. Perhaps too self-righteously, Hu Shih considers Man-shu's novels as bad nonsense, full of "bestial sensuality." See Hu Shih, "Ta Ch'ien Hsüan-t'ung shu" (Letter in response to Ch'ien Hsüan-t'ung), *Hu Shih wen-ts'un* (Shanghai, 1926), I, 54.

43. Lo Fang-chou, "Su Man-shu ti sheng-p'ing chi ch'i tso-p'in" (The life and works of Su Man-shu), in *Man-shu ta-shih chi-nien chi*, p. 461.

44. Huang Ming-ch'i, pp. 61—62.

45. Yü Ta-fu, "Tsa-p'ing Man-shu ti tso-p'in" (Random comments on the works of Man-shu), in *Man-shu ch'üan-chi*, V, 115.

46. Liu Wu-chi, *Su Man-shu*, p. 143.

5. Yü Ta-fu: Driftings of a Loner

1. Yü Ta-fu, "Pei-chü ti ch'u-sheng," *Jen-chien-shih* 17:11 (Dec. 5, 1934).

2. Ibid.

3. Ibid., p. 13.

4. Ibid.

5. Yü Ta-fu, "Ssu-shu yü hsüeh-t'ang," *Jen-chien-shih* 19:29 (Jan. 5, 1935).

6. Ibid.

7. Yü, "Shui-yang-ti ch'un-ch'ou," *Jen-chien-shih* 20:31 (Jan. 20, 1935).

8. Ibid.

9. Yü Ta-fu, "Wu-liu nien-lai ch'uang-tso sheng-huo ti hui-ku," *Kuo-ch'ü chi* (Shanghai, 1931), pp. 5—6.

10. Yü Ta-fu, "Ku-tu che," *Jen-chien-shih*, 23:33 (March 5, 1935).

11. Ibid., pp. 34—35.

12. Yü Ta-fu, "Ta-feng ch'üan-wai," *Jen-chien-shih* 26:25 (April 20, 1935).

13. Ibid., p. 27.

14. Yü Ta-fu, "Ch'uang-tso hui-ku," p. 6.

15. Yü Ta-fu, "Ta-feng ch'üan-wai," p. 28.

16. Ibid., p. 28.

17. Yü Ta-fu, "Ch'uang-tso hui-ku," p. 5.

18. Ito Toramaru, "Nempu" (Yearly record), in Itō Toramaru, Inaba Shoji, Suzuki Masao ed., *Iku Tappu shiryō* (Tokyo, 1969), p. 63. First drafts of this chronology and materials about Yü appeared originally in *Chūgoku bungaku kenkyū* 1:93–121 (April 1961). See also Anna Doležalová, "Remarks on the Life and Work of Yü Ta-fu up to 1930," *Asian and African Studies* 1:54 (1965).

19. Kuo Mo-jo, "Lun Yü Ta-fu," in his *Li-shih jen-wu* (Shanghai, 1947), p. 174.

20. Itō, "Nempu," p. 64.

21. Yü Ta-fu, "Hsüeh yeh," *Yü-chou-feng* Vol. I collection (May 1936), 520.

22. Yü Ta-fu, "Ch'uang-tso hui-ku," p. 7.

23. Itō, "Nempu," p. 64.

24. Erik H. Erikson, *Childhood and Society* (New York, 1963), chap. 7.

25. Yü Ta-fu, "Ch'an yü tu-pai" (Monologue after the confession), *Ch'an yü chi* (Shanghai, 1933), p. 5.

26. Yü Ta-fu, "Hsüeh-yeh," pp. 520–521.

27. Ibid., p. 521.

28. Ibid., p. 522.

29. C. T. Hsia, *A History of Modern Chinese Fiction*, p. 109.

30. Yü Ta-fu, "Hsüeh yeh," p. 520.

31. Tseng Hua-p'eng, Fan Po-ch'ün, "Yü Ta-fu lun" (On Yü Ta-fu), *Jen-min wen-hsüeh* 91:185 (May–June 1957).

32. Yü Ta-fu, "Hsüeh-yeh," p. 521.

33. Itō, "Chinrin ron" (On "Sinking"), *Chūgoku bungaku kenkyū* 1:52 (1961).

34. Yü Ta-fu, "Chung-t'u" (Mid-way), in *Kuo-ch'ü chi*, p. 92.

35. Ibid., p. 98.

36. Ibid., p. 105.

37. Itō, "Nempu," p. 67.

38. Kuo Mo-jo, "Ch'uang-tso shih-nien," p. 134.

39. Ibid., pp. 134–135.

40. Yü Ta-fu, "Niao-lo hsing" (Wisteria and dodder), in *Niao-lo chi* (Shanghai, 1923), p. 13.

41. Ibid., p. 17.

42. Yü Ta-fu, *Niao-lo chi*, pp. 192–193.

43. Yü Ta-fu, "Hai-shang t'ung-hsün" (Correspondence on the sea), *Kuo-ch'ü chi*, p. 207.

44. Ibid., pp. 207–208.

45. Yü Ta-fu, "Pei-kuo ti wei-yin" (Faint voices from the northern country), in *Kuo-ch'ü chi*, p. 266.

46. Ibid., p. 227.

47. Yü Ta-fu, "Ch'uang-tsao hui ku," p. 9.

48. Yü Ta-fu, Foreword to *Chi-chin chi* (Shanghai, 1928), p. 4.

49. Yü Ta-fu, *Jih-chi chiu-chung* (Shanghai, 1933), p. 1.

50. Ibid., p. 2.

51. Ibid.

52. Yü himself valued very highly diary as a genre of literature. See his essay titled "Jih-chi wen-hsüeh" (Diary literature) in *Ch'i-ling chi* (Shanghai, 1930), pp. 113–123; and another essay, "Tsai-t'an jih-chi" (More on diary), in *Yü Ta-fu jih-chi* (Hong Kong, 1961), pp. 9–14.

53. Yü Ta-fu, *Jih-chi chiu-chung*, p. 18.

54. Ibid., p. 19.

55. Yü Ta-fu, *Jih-chi chiu-chung*, p. 53.

56. Yü Ta-fu, "Tui-yü she-hui ti t'ai-tu" (My attitude toward society), *Pei-hsin*, 2.19:43.

57. "Kuang-chou shih-ch'ing" (Affairs in Canton), *Hung-shui* 3:25 (January 1927); "Tsai fang-hsiang chuan-huan ti t'u-chung" (En route to changed directions), *Hung-shui* 3:29 (April 1927).

58. Yü Ta-fu, *Jih-chi chiu-chung*, p. 93.

59. Ibid., p. 122.

60. Tseng Hua-p'eng and Fan Po-ch'ün, p. 196.

61. Yü Ta-fu, *Jih-chi chiu-chung*, p. 162.

62. Ibid., p. 171.

63. Ibid., p. 59.

64. Yü Ta-fu, "Tui-yü she-hui ti t'ai-tu," p. 44.

65. Yü Ta-fu, *Han-hui chi* (Shanghai, 1931), p. 11.

66. Liu Hsin-huang, *Yü Ta-fu yü Wang Ying-hsia* (Taipei, 1962), pp. 24–25.

67. Ibid., p. 22.

68. Sun Pai-kang, *Yü Ta-fu yü Wang Ying-hsia* (Hong Kong, 1962), p. 16.

69. Yü Ta-fu, *Jih-chi chiu-chung*, p. 56.

70. Sun Pai-kang, p. 28.

71. Ibid.

72. Yü Ta-fu, *Jih-chi chiu-chung*, p. 109.

73. Yü Ta-fu, *Ch'en-lun chi ch'i-t'a* (Shanghai, 1947), pp. 16–17. English translation by Joseph S. M. Lau and C. T. Hsia in C. T. Hsia ed., *Twentieth Century Chinese Stories* (New York, 1971), p. 9.

74. For a sample collection of Yü's classical poetry, see Liu Hsin-huang ed., *Yü Ta-fu shih-tz'u hui pien* (Taipei, 1970).

75. Yü Ta-fu, *Jih-chi chiu-chung*, pp. 164–165.

76. Ibid., p. 207.

77. Sun Pai-kang, pp. 33–34.

78. Yü Ta-fu, *Chi-chin chi*, p. 5.

79. Tseng Hua-p'eng and Fan Po-ch'un, p. 198.

80. Yü Ta-fu, "Wang Erh-nan hsien-sheng chuan" (Biography of Mr. Wang Erh-nan), in *Ta-fu san-wen chi* (Taipei, reprint, 1965), p. 184.

81. Ibid., p. 193.

82. *Yü Ta-fu jih-chi*, pp. 208, 215.

83. C. T. Hsia, *A History of Modern Chinese Fiction*, p. 110.

84. Yü Ta-fu, "Chi Feng-yü mao-lu" (Note on thatched hut from wind and rain), in *Hsien-shu* (Shanghai, 1936), p. 60.

85. Yü Ta-fu, "I-chia so-chi" (Scattered notes on moving my house), in *Tuan-ts'an chi* (Shanghai, 1933), p. 204.

86. Sun Pai-kang, p. 52.

87. Hsü Hsüeh-hsüeh, "Yü Ta-fu hsien-sheng fang-wen chi" (Interview with Mr. Yü Ta-fu), in Yao Nai-lin, ed., *Chung-kuo wen-hsüeh-chia chuan-chi* (Shanghai, 1937), pp. 44–45.

88. Yü Ta-fu, *Hsien-shu*, pp. 53–54.

89. Sun Pai-kang, p. 58.

90. Yü Ta-fu, *Hsien-shu*, pp. 211–212.

91. Ibid., p. 224.

92. Ibid., p. 265.

93. Liu Hsin-huang, *Yü Ta-fu yü Wang Ying-hsia*, pp. 131–133.

94. Ibid., pp. 120, 125.

95. Ibid., p. 116.

96. Ibid., p. 110.

97. Wen Tzu-ch'uan, *Yü Ta-fu nan-yu chi* (Hong Kong, 1950), p. 2. A collection of memorial essays on Yü has been published by Yü's friends in Malaya. See Li Ping-jen, Hsieh Yün-sheng, eds., *Yü Ta-fu chi-nien chi* (Singapore, 1958).

98. Ibid., p. 4.

99. Hu Yü-chih, *Yü Ta-fu ti liu-wang yü shih-tsung* (Hong Hong, 1946), pp. 20–22.

100. Liu Hsin-huang, *Yü Ta-fu yü Wang Ying-hsia*, p. 197.

101. Ibid., p. 234.

102. Wong Yoon-wah, "A Study of Yü Ta-fu's life in Singapore, Malaya, and Sumatra, 1939–1945," (unpublished seminar paper, University of Wisconsin, 1969), p. 50.

103. Mei Ch'i-jui (Gary G. Melyan), "Yü Ta-fu yü-hai chih mi," *Ming-pao yüeh-k'an* 5.12:60 (December 1970). Melyan's article is based on information obtained by Suzuki Masao who recently interviewed more than 100 Japanese connected with Yü's case. Suzuki's findings are included in *Iku Tappu shiryō*, pp. 91–110.

6. Yü Ta-fu: Visions of the Self

1. Anna Dolezalová, "Quelques Remarques sur la Question de l'Autodescription chez Yü Ta-fu," *Asian and African Studies* 2:57 (1966).

2. Yü Ta-fu, *Ch'en-lun chi ch'i-t'a*, p. 1.

3. Ito, "Chinrin ron," *Chugoku bungaku kenkyu*, Nos. 1 and 3 (1961).

4. C. T. Hsia, *A History of Modern Chinese Fiction*, p. 104.

5. Yü Ta-fu, *Ch'en-lun chi ch'i-t'a*, p. 28.

6. Ibid., p. 29.

7. Mark Longaker, *Ernest Dowson* (Philadelphia, 1945), p. 148.

8. Yü Ta-fu, "Ch'uang-tso hui-ku," p. 3.

9. Yü Ta-fu, "Chi-chung yü Huang-mien-chih ti jen-wu" (Personalities who gathered around *The Yellow Book* magazine), in his *Pi-chou chi* (Shanghai, 1928), p. 93.

10. Arthur Symons, "Memoir of Ernest Dowson," in *Poems of Ernest Dowson* (London, 1909), p. x.

11. Mark Longaker, p. 156.

12. Arthur Hummel, *Eminent Chinese of the Ch'ing Period* (Washington, D.C., 1943), I, 337. Unless otherwise noted, my biographical sketch of Huang is based on this source.

13. Hung Liang-chi, "Hsing-chuang" (Exemplary record), in Huang Chung-tse, *Liang-tang-hsüan shih-chao* (1833), 1:1.

14. Chang I-p'ing, "Ch'ing-tai shih-jen Huang Chung-tse p'ing-chuan," *Hsüeh-lin tsa-chih* 1.12:14.

15. Hung Liang-chi, 1:2b.

16. Huang Chung-tse, "Tzu-hsü" (Self-account), *Liang-tang-hsüan shih-ch'ao*, 1:1.

17. Ch'iu Chu-shih, "Huang Ching-jen chi ch'i lien-ai shih-ko," *Hsin-yüeh*, (December 10, 1929), 3.1:9–10.

18. Chang I-p'ing, p. 8.

19. Yü Ta-fu, "Ts'ai-shih chi" (The cliff of colored rock), in his *Han-hui chi* (Shanghai, 1930), p. 3.

20. Ibid., p. 4.

21. Ibid. p. 5.

22. Ibid., p. 8.

23. Ibid., p. 18.

24. Ibid., p. 21.

25. Ibid., p. 29.

26. Ibid., p. 30.

27. For an analysis of Yü's style, see Jaroslav Prusek, *Three Sketches of Chinese Literature* (Prague, 1969), pp. 44–98. See also, Anna Dolezalová, *Yü Ta-fu: Specific Traits of His Literary Creation* (New York, 1971).

28. Yü Ta-fu, "Kuan-yü Huang Chung-tse" (About Huang Chung-tse), in his *Wen-hsüeh man-t'an* (Hong Kong, n.d.), p. 99.

29. Ibid.

30. Yü Ta-fu, "Shui-yang ti ch'un-ch'ou," p. 38.

31. Chao Ts'ung, *Wu-ssu wen-t'an tien-ti* (Hong Kong, 1964), p. 185.

32. Kuo Mo-jo, "Ch'uang-tsao shih-nien," p. 148.

33. Shih Chien, *Kuo Mo-jo p'i-p'an* (Hong Kong, 1954), p. 84. Kuo himself bluntly asserted that Hu Shih was the chief cause for Yü's writing this story. Kuo, "Lun Yü Ta-fu," p. 177.

34. Yü Ta-fu, "T'u-ke-nieh-fu ti 'Lo-t'ing' wen-shih i-ch'ien" (Before the appearance of Turgenev's 'Rodin'), in his *Hsien-shu*, p. 85.

35. In Yü's "Mang-mang yeh" (Boundless nights), the two heroes—both alter egos of Yü—shook hands and one of them pondered: "The 21-year-old young poet Arthur Rimbaud, and Paul Verlaine of 1872, the pastoral landscape of Belgium, and the pure love between the two of them . . . ," see *Han-hui chi*, p. 6.

36. Yü Ta-fu, "Ch'uang-tso hui-ku," p. 3.

37. Yü Ta-fu, "Tzu-wo-k'uang-che Hsü-ti-erh-na" (Egomaniac Stirner), in his *Pi-chou chi*, p. 73.

38. Yü Ta-fu, "Ho-erh-ts'an" (Herzen), in his *Pi-chou chi*, p. 71.

39. Yü Ta-fu, "Wen-hsüeh shang ti chieh-chi tou-cheng" (The class struggle in literature), *Ch'uang-tsao chou-pao*, 3:4 (May 27, 1923).

40. Ibid.

41. Yü Ta-fu, "Lu-sao chuan" (Biography of Rousseau), *Pei-hsin*, 2.6:650 (Jan. 6, 1928).

42. Itō Toramaru, "Iku Tappu ni okeru josei," in *Kindai chugoku no shiso to bungaku* (Tokyo, 1967), pp. 310–311.

43. Ho Yü-po, *Yü Ta-fu lun* (Shanghai, 1936), p. 136.

44. Yü's addiction to smoking was as notorious as his drinking. He smoked "at least fifty cigarettes everyday," regardless of their quality. Fang Mu, "Yü Ta-fu liang-mi" (Two addictions of Yü Ta-fu), in Li Ping-jen and Hsieh Yün-sheng, p. 4.

45. Quoted in ibid., p. 25.

46. Ch'ien Hsing-ts'un, "Yü Ta-fu tai-piao-tso hou-hsü" (Preface at the end of Yü Ta-fu's Representative Works), in Su Ya, ed., *Yü Ta-fu p'ing-chuan* (Shanghai, 1931), p. 37.

47. Lu Hsün, "Fu-ch'in ti ping" (Father's illness) in *Lu Hsün ch'üan-chi*, II, 261–262.

48. See Erik H. Erikson, *Young Man Luther* (New York, 1958) and his new book, *Gandhi's Truth* (New York, 1969), pp. 123–133.

7. Hsü Chih-mo: A Life of Emotion

1. Yü Ta-fu, "Chih-mo tsai hui-i li" (Chih-mo in memory), in Chiang Fu-ts'ung and Liang Shih-ch'iu, eds., *Hsü Chih-mo ch'üan-chi* (Taipei, 1969), I, 377.

2. "Hsü Chih-mo," in Howard Boorman, ed., *Men and Politics in Modern China*, p. 59. A similar account of Hsü's life in English can also be found in Boorman, ed., *Dictionary of Republican China*, II, 122–124.

3. "Hsü Chih-mo nien-p'u" (Yearly record of Hsü Chi-mo), in *Ch'üan-chi*, I, 549.

4. Chang Chün-ku, *Hsü Chih-mo chuan* (Taipei, 1970), pp. 14–15.

5. "Nien-p'u," *Ch'üan-chi*, I, 552.

6. Ibid., pp. 553–554.

7. Ibid., pp. 558–559.

8. Chang Chün-ku, p. 4.

9. "Nien-p'u," *Ch'üan-chi*, I, 561.

10. Chang Chün-ku, p. 31.

11. "Nien-p'u," *Ch'üan-chi*, I, 563.

12. Quoted in Liang Shih-ch'iu, *T'an Hsü Chih-mo*, p. 22.

13. Hsü Chih-mo, "Hsü-wen" (Preface), *Meng-hu chi* (Fierce tiger), in *Ch'üan-chi*, II, 340.

14. Clark University Bulletin (1969–70), pp. 10–11.

15. "Nien-p'u," *Ch'üan-chi*, I, 564–565.

16. Ibid., p. 565.

17. Ibid., p. 564.

18. Chang Chün-ku, p. 63.

19. Hsü Chih-mo, "Nan-hsing tsa-chi" (Random notes written in my southern journey), *Ch'en-pao fu-k'an*, 1434:37 (Aug. 23, 1926).

20. Hsü Chih-mo, Preface to *Meng-hu chi*, in *Ch'üan-chi*, II, 340.

21. Hsü Chih-mo, "Wo so chih-tao ti K'ang-ch'iao" (The Cambridge I know) in *Ch'üan-chi*, III, 243.

22. "Hsü Chih-mo nien-p'u," I, 568.

23. Hsü Chih-mo, "Wo so chih-tao ti K'ang-ch'iao," *Ch'üan-chi*, III, 244.

24. E. M. Forster, *Goldsworthy Lowes Dickinson* (New York, 1934), p. 142.

25. Ibid.

26. Ibid., p. 143.

27. Ibid., p. 154.

28. Recounted by Professor I. A. Richards during an interview on March 27, 1969.

29. Robert Payne, ed., *Contemporary Chinese Poetry* (London, 1947), p. 35.

30. See note 28.

31. "Nien-p'u," *Ch'üan-chi*, I, 569.

32. Hsü Chih-mo, "Hsi-yen yü wen-hua" (Smoking and culture), in *Ch'üan-chi*, III, 239.

33. Hsü Chih-mo, "Wo so chih-tao ti K'ang-ch'iao," *Ch'üan-chi*, III, 244–245.

34. The story was titled "Ch'un-hen" (Traces of spring). When Lin died in 1926, Hsü wrote a moving memorial essay, "Shang Shuang-kua lao-jen" (Mourning the old gentleman Shuang-kua), see *Ch'üan-chi*, III, 493–499.

35. See Hsü's introductory note to Lin Tsung-meng (Lin Ch'ang-min), "I-feng ch'ing-shu" (A love letter), *Ch'en-pao fu-k'an*, 1437:13 (Feb. 6, 1926).

36. Chang Chün-ku, pp. 107–133.

37. Ibid., pp. 118–120.

38. Disclosed first by Hu Shih in his memorial essay, "Chui-tao Chih-mo" (Mourning for Chih-mo), in *Ch'üan-chi*, I, 359.

39. Ibid., pp. 359–360.

40. "Nien-p'u," *Ch'üan-chi*, I, 753.

41. Hsü Chih-mo, "Wo so chih-tao ti K'ang-ch'iao," *Ch'üan-chi*, III, 245.

42. Ibid., p. 248.

43. Ibid., p. 252.

44. Ibid., pp. 246–247.

45. Ibid., p. 250.

46. Hsü Chih-mo, "Fei-leng-ts'ui shan-chü hsien-hua" (Random words on my sojourn in the hills at Florence), *Ch'üan-chi*, III, 232.

47. Hsü Chih-mo, preface to "Meng-hu chi," *Ch'üan-chi*, II, 343.

48. Hsü Chih-mo, "Ts'ao-shang ti lu-chu-erh" (Drops of dew on the grass), *Ch'üan-chi*, I, 143–147.

49. King's College, *Tutorial Record*, Vol. II (1918–1938).

50. "Nien-p'u," *Ch'üan-chi*, I, 577.

51. Chang Chün-ku, p. 212.

52. Ibid., p. 135.

53. *Ch'üan-chi*, I, 135–136. Liang's letter was first disclosed to the public by Hu Shih in his memorial essay already cited.

54. Chang Chün-ku, p. 234.

55. Quoted first in Hu Shih, "Chui-tao Chih-mo," *Ch'üan-chi*, I, 362.

56. Ibid.

57. Chang Chün-ku, p. 251.

58. "Nien-p'u," *Ch'üan-chi*, I, 584. The translation, unfortunately, was left unfinished.

59. Chang Chün-ku, p. 259.

60. Ibid., p. 273.

61. "Nien-p'u," *Ch'üan-chi*, I, 581.

62. Hsü Chih-mo, *Hsi-hu chi* (A record at West Lake) in *Ch'üan-chi*, IV, 495.

63. Liu Hsin-huang, *Hsü Chih-mo yü Lu Hsiao-man* (Taipei, 1965), pp. 48–49.

64. Ibid., pp. 179–180.

65. Ibid., p. 183.

66. Liang Shih-ch'iu, *T'an Hsü Chih-mo*, p. 11.

67. Liu Hsin-huang, p. 183–184.

68. They were married in 1927, according to Ch'en Ts'ung-chou in his *Hsü Chih-mo nien-p'u* (Shanghai, 1949), p. 71.

69. See Arthur Mizener, *The Far Side of Paradise: A Biography of F. Scott Fitzgerald*, 2d ed. (Boston, 1965), p. 81.

70. Liu Hsin-huang, p. 73.

71. *Ch'üan-chi*, IV, 284–287.

72. Ibid., pp. 293–294.

73. Yü Ta-fu, "Huai ssu-shih-sui ti Chih-mo," *Yü-chou-feng*, Vol. I collection (May, 1936), p. 364.

74. "Chih-mo shu-hsin" (The letters of Chih-mo), in *Ch'üan-chi*, IV, 357–358.

75. Ibid., pp. 349, 350, 360.

76. Lu Hsiao-man, "Hsiao-man jih-chi" (The diary of Hsiao-man) in *Ch'üan-chi*, IV, 422.

77. Mizener, p. 83.

78. Lu Hsiao-man, preface to "Ai Mei hsiao-cha" (Love letters to May), in *Ch'üan-chi*, IV, 251.

79. "Nien-p'u," *Ch'üan-chi*, I, 623.

80. Hsü Chih-mo, "Mei-hsüan so-yü" (Trifling words at May's balcony) in *Ch'üan-chi*, IV, 528.

81. Liu Hsin-huang, p. 153.

82. See Stephen N. Hay, *Asian Ideas of East and West: Tagore and His Critics in Japan, China, and India* (Cambridge, Mass., 1970), chaps. 5–6.

83. Transcript of Leonard K. Elmhirst's "Recollections of Tagore in China" (taped on March 3, 1959), p. 9.

84. Quoted in "Nien-p'u," *Ch'üan-chi*, I, 594.

85. Elmhirst, p. 11.

86. Ibid.

87. "Nien-p'u," *Ch'üan-chi*, I, 594. Liang Ch'i-ch'ao wrote one of his own favorite poems dedicated to Hsü in which he also mentioned this incident. See Ch'en Ts'ung-chou's "Hsü Chih-mo nien-p'u," p. 42. Elmhirst also remembered this incident with great excitement in an interview with the present author on June 24, 1969.

88. Hsü Chih-mo, "T'ai-ke-erh lai-hua ti ch'üeh-ch'i" (The exact date of Tagore's arrival in China), *Hsiao-shuo yüeh-pao*, 14.10:2 (Oct. 10, 1923).

89. "Nien-p'u," *Ch'üan-chi*, I, 595.

90. Liang's speech was published in *Ch'en-pao fu-k'an* (May 3, 1924), pp. 1–3.

91. "Nien-p'u," *Ch'üan-chi*, I, 595.

92. Ibid.

93. Elmhirst, p. 14.

94. Hsin-yüeh, 1.1:3 (March 10, 1928).

95. Ibid., 5–6, 9.

96. P'eng K'ang, "Shen-mo shih 'chien-k'ang' yü 'tsun-yen'?" (What are 'health' and 'dignity'?), in *Chung-kuo hsien-tai wen-hsüeh shih ts'an-k'ao tzu-liao*, I, 365.

97. Lu Hsün unleashed his pent-up fury in a long article of more than twenty pages titled, "Ying-i yü wen-hsüeh ti chieh-chi hsing" (Forced translation and the class nature of literature), included in his *Erh-hsin chi* (Two hearts).

98. *Hsin-yüeh*, 2.6/7 (September, 1929), specially attached page.

99. Liang Shih-ch'iu, *T'an Hsü Chih-mo*, pp. 30, 32–33.

100. Leonard K. Elmhirst, ed., "Letters from Hsu Tsemou," p. 1.

101. Letter dated July 13, 1925, in ibid., p. 3.

102. Ibid., pp. 7–8.

103. Ibid., p. 10.

104. Ibid., p. 12.

105. Ibid., pp. 13–15.

106. Ibid., p. 16.

107. Ibid., p. 20.

108. Hsü Chih-mo, "Lo-su yü yu-chih chiao-yü" (Russell and the education of children), *Ch'en-pao fu-k'an*, Nos. 1389–1390 (May 10 and 12, 1926).

109. "Letters from Hsu Tsemou," p. 19. P. C. Chang is brother of Chang Po-lin, president of Nankai University.

110. Ibid., p. 32.

111. Ibid., p. 34.

112. Ibid., p. 36.

113. Ibid., pp. 34–35.

114. Hsü Chih-mo, "Ying-shang ch'ien-ch'ü" (Coming forward), *Ch'üan-chi*, III, 438.

115. "Nien-p'u," *Ch'üan-chi*, I, 639.

116. Hsü Chih-mo, "Ch'iu" (Autumn), *Ch'üan-chi*, III, 688–689.

117. Hsü Chih-mo, "Tang nü-shih" (Miss Tang), *Hsin-yüeh*, 3.11:12 (February, 1931).

118. Han Hsiang-mei, "Chih-mo tsui-ho ti i-yeh" (Chih-mo's last night), *Ch'üan-chi*, I, 398.

8. Hsü Chih-mo: Exultations of Icarus

1. Liang Shih-ch'iu, *T'an Hsü Chih-mo*, p. 6.
2. Hsü Chih-mo, "Art and Life," *Ch'uang-tsao chi-k'an*, 2.1:3–5.
3. Ibid., p. 7.
4. Ibid., p. 8.
5. Hsü Chih-mo, "Hua" (Words), *Ch'üan-chi*, III, 74–77.
6. Ibid., p. 74.
7. Hu Shih, "Chui-tao Chih-mo," *Ch'üan-chi*, I, 358.
8. Liang Shih-ch'iu, *T'an Hsü Chih-mo*, p. 35.
9. Hsü Chih-mo, "Ai Mei hsiao-cha," *Ch'üan-chi*, IV, 273, 308–309.
10. *Ch'üan-chi*, II, 191–193; see also Kai-yu Hsü, *Twenty Century Chinese Poetry: An Anthology* (Garden City, N.Y., 1963), pp. 75–76.
11. Cyril Birch, "English and Chinese Meters in Hsü Chih-mo," *Asia Major*, new series, Vol. 8, Pt. 2 (1961), p. 280.
12. Hsü Chih-mo, "Ai ti ling-kan" (Inspiration of love), *Ch'üan-chi*, II, 573.
13. Cyril Birch, p. 289.
14. Ibid., p. 288. This interpretation is inspired by Hsü's own interpretation of Keats' ode "To a Nightingale," in which he wrote: "Death is limitless, a transcendence, an intimate union with the endless flow of the spirit . . . For in the utter freedom of the realm of death, all that was in accord is given accord, all that was incomplete is given completion." Quoted in ibid., p. 288.
15. Hsü Chih-mo, "Ai ti ling-kan," *Ch'üan-chi*, II, 547–549; English translation by Cyril Birch, in ibid., p. 285.
16. Ibid., p. 289.
17. Hsü Chih-mo, "Che-shih i-ko no-ch'üeh ti shih-chieh" (This is a coward's world), *Ch'üan-chi*, II, 40–42; see also Hsü, Kai-lu, p. 74.
18. Hsü Chih-mo, "Ssu-ch'eng" (Dead city), *Ch'üan-chi*, V, 119.
19. Hsü Chih-mo, "Lo-yeh" (Fallen leaves), *Ch'üan-chi*, III, 16–18.
20. Lionel Trilling, "F. Scott Fitzgerald," in Arthur Mizener, ed., *F. Scott Fitzgerald: A Collection of Critical Essays* (Englewood Cliffs, N.J., 1963), p. 16.
21. Hsü Chih-mo, "Chi-tz'u ti Yeh-ying-ko" (Keats' ode *To a Nightingale*), *Ch'üan-chi*, III, 315–316.
22. Ibid., p. 317.
23. Hsü Chih-mo, "Pai-lun" (Byron), *Ch'üan-chi*, III, 266.
24. Hsü Chih-mo, "Tan-nung-hsüeh-wu" (d'Annunzio), *Ch'en-pao fu-k'an*, 102:51 (May 8, 1925).
25. Hsü Chih-mo, "Lo-man lo-lan" (Romain Rolland), in *Ch'üan-chi*, III, 286.
26. Hsü Chih-mo, "Ha-t'i" (Hardy), in *Shih-k'an* (Poetry journal of *Ch'en-pao*), No. 9 (May 27, 1926), p. 61.

27. "Nien-p'u," *Ch'üan-chi*, I, 576.

28. Hsü Chih-mo, "Ha-t'i," p. 61.

29. Hsü Chih-mo, "Man-shu-fei-erh" (Mansfield), *Hsiao-shuo yüeh-pao*, 14.5:7 (May 10, 1923).

30. Quoted in ibid., p. 8.

31. Hsü Chih-mo, "Chieh-chien Ha-tai ti i-ko hsia-wu" (The afternoon I visited Hardy), *Ch'üan-chi*, VI, 303–312.

32. Hsü Chih-mo, "Ha-tai" (Hardy), *Ch'üan-chi*, II, 469–470.

33. Hsü Chih-mo, "Ha-tai ti pei-kuan" (Hardy's pessimism), *Ch'üan-chi*, VI, 317.

34. Quoted in Harvey C. Webster, *On a Darkling Plain: The Art and Thought of Thomas Hardy* (Hamden, Conn., 1964), p. 213.

35. Patrick Braybroke, *Thomas Hardy and His Philosophy* (Philadelphia, 1927), p. 159.

36. Hsü may have read Hardy's *Jude the Obscure*, as he once advised Lu Hsiao-man to read it. See "Ai-Mei hsiao-cha," *Ch'üan-chi*, IV, 346.

37. Albert Guerard, *Thomas Hardy* (New York: New Directions, 1964), p. 188.

38. Hsü Chih-mo, "Ha-tai," *Ch'üan chi*, II, 468.

39. Albert Guerard, p. 189.

40. Ibid., p. 163.

41. Hsü Chih-mo, "T'ang-mai-shih Ha-tai" (Thomas Hardy), *Ch'üan-chi*, VI, 295–296.

42. Maurice Z. Shroder, *Icarus: The Image of the Artist in French Romanticism* (Cambridge, Mass., 1961), p. 26.

43. E. H. Carr, *Romantic Exiles* (Boston, 1961), p. 63.

44. Ibid.

45. Hsü Chih-mo, "P'o-t'e-lai ti san-wen-shih" (The prose poems of Baudeliare), *Ch'üan-chi*, VI, 406.

46. Hsü Chih-mo, "T'ang-mai shih Ha-tai," *Ch'üan-chi*, VI, 301.

47. "Nien-p'u," *Ch'üan-chi*, I, 602.

48. "Chih-mo shu-hsin," *Ch'üan-chi*, IV, 382, 384, 392.

49. Hsü Chih-mo, "Ou-yu man-lu" (General notes on the European journey), *Ch'üan-chi*, III, 576.

50. Hsü Chih-mo, "Mei-hsüan so-yü," *Ch'üan-chi*, IV, 532.

51. Included in *Ch'üan-chi*, IV, 101–107.

52. Ibid., pp. 91–99.

53. Hsü Chih-mo, "Tzu-p'ou" (Self-anatomy), *Ch'üan-chi*, III, 398.

54. "Chih-mo shu-hsin," *Ch'üan-chi*, IV, 395.

55. Hsü Chih-mo, "Hsiang-fei" (Wanting to fly), *Ch'üan-chi*, III, 430–431; English translation in Kai-yu Hsü, pp. 72–73.

56. Quoted in Shroder, p. 217.

57. Ibid.

58. Quoted by Chao Chia-pi in his introduction to Hsü's essay collection, "Ch'iu" (Autumn), in *Ch'üan-chi*, IV, 652.

59. Henry A. Murray, "American Icarus," in Arthur Burton and Robert E. Harris, eds., *Clinical Studies of Personality* (New York, 1955), p. 639.

60. Ibid.

61. Hsü Chih-mo, "Hsiang-fei," *Ch'üan-chi*, III, 433.

62. "Nien-p'u," *Ch'üan-chi*, I, 663; Kai-yu Hsü, p. 77.

63. "Nien-p'u," *Ch'üan-chi*, I, 665.

64. See Shroder, chap. 7.

65. Hsü Chih-mo, "Huang-li" (Golden oriole), *Ch'üan-chi*, III, 424–425.

9. Kuo Mo-jo

1. Jean Chesneaux, *The Chinese Labor Movement, 1919–1927*, trans. H. M. Wright (Stanford, 1968), p. 263.

2. John K. Fairbank, Edwin O. Reischauer, Albert Craig, *East Asia: The Modern Transformation* (Boston, 1965), p. 685.

3. Hsi-ti (Cheng Chen-to), "Chieh-hsüeh hsi ch'ü hou" (After the blood is washed off the streets), *Hsiao-shuo yüeh-pao*, 16.7:3 (July 10, 1925).

4. Yeh Sheng-t'ao (Yeh Shao-chün), "Wu-yüeh san-shih-i jih chi-yü chung" (May 31, amidst torrential rain), *Hsiao-shuo yüeh-pao*, 16.7:5.

5. Chu Tzu-ch'ing, "Hsüeh ko" (Song of blood), *Hsiao-shuo yüeh-pao*, 16.7:1.

6. David Roy's meticulous biography, *Kuo Mo-jo: The Early Years*, has eliminated the necessity to recount Kuo's life in detail. This study, therefore, focuses on an intrepretation of Kuo's transition from early rebelliousness and pantheism to self-styled Marxism.

7. Kuo Mo-jo, "Wo ti t'ung-nien" (My childhood), in his *Shao-nien shih-tai* (Shanghai, 1948), pp. 33, 38.

8. Ibid., p. 53.

9. Ibid., p. 13.

10. Ibid., p. 21.

11. Shih Chien, *Kuo Mo-jo p'i-p'an*, p. 33.

12. Kuo Mo-jo, *Shao-nien shih-tai*, pp. 75–102.

13. Ibid., pp. 113–116.

14. Ibid., p. 278.

15. Ibid., p. 125.

16. Ibid., p. 385.

17. Kuo Mo-jo, "Ch'uang-tsao shih-nien," p. 62.

18. Ibid.

19. Kuo Mo-jo, *Shao-nien shih-tai*, p. 369.

20. Kuo Mo-jo, *Shao-nien shih-tai*, pp. 126–127.

21. Ibid., p. 126.

22. Kuo Mo-jo, *Ch'uang-tsao shih-nien* (Chungking, 1943), p. 6.

23. Kuo Mo-jo, *Nü-shen* (Shanghai, 1929), p. 30.

24. Kuo Mo-jo, "Chih T'ien Han shu" (Letter to T'ien Han), in *Kuo Mo-jo shu-hsin chi* (Sanghai, 1937), p. 22.

25. *P'iao-liu san-pu ch'ü* (Shanghai, 1931).

26. Titled "Hei-mao" (Black cat), included in *Shao-nien shih-tai*.

27. Kuo Mo-jo, *Shao-nien shih-tai*, p. 127.

28. Kuo Mo-jo, *Ke-ming ch'un-ch'iu*, pp. 62–63.

29. Roy, p. 70.

30. Kuo Mo-jo, "Hsü-yin" (Preface), *Shao-nien Wei-t'e chih fan-nao* (Hong Kong, reprint, 1949), p. 3.

31. Ibid.

32. Kuo Mo-jo, *Ke-ming ch'un-ch'iu*, p. 63.

33. Ibid., p. 64.

34. "Kuo Mo-jo," in Howard Boorman, ed., *Dictionary of Republican China*, II, 272.

35. Achilles Fang, "From Imagism to Whitmanism in Recent Chinese Poetry: A Search for Poetics That Failed," in Horst Frenz and G. A. Anderson, eds., *Indiana University Conference on Oriental-Western Literary Relations* (Chapel Hill, N.C., 1955), p. 187.

36. Kuo Mo-jo, "P'u-t'i-shu hsia" (Under the linden tree), in his *Pao-chien chi* (Shanghai, 1948), p. 77.

37. Kuo Mo-jo, "Hai-wai kuei-hung" (A letter from abroad), *Ch'uang-tsao chi-k'an*, 1.1:10–11.

38. Kuo Mo-jo, "Yü Tsung Pai-hua shu" (Letter to Tsung Pai-hua), in *Kuo Mo-jo shu-hsin chi*, pp. 84–93.

39. Ibid., p. 96.

40. Kuo Mo-jo, *Ke-ming ch'un-ch'iu*, p. 74.

41. Kuo Mo-jo, "Hui Shih ti hsing-ke yü ssu-hsiang" (The character and thought of Hui Shih), *Ch'uang-tsao chou-pao* 32:3 (June 16, 1923).

42. Kuo Mo-jo, "Lun Chung-Te wen-hua shu" (A letter on Chinese and German culture), *Ch'uang-tsao chou-pao* 5:16 (June 10, 1923).

43. Kuo Mo-jo, "Chung-kuo wen-hua chih ch'uan-t'ung ching-shen" (The traditional spirit of Chinese culture), *Ch'uang-tsao chou-pao* 2:13 (May 20, 1923).

44. Ibid., p. 15.

45. Roy, p. 74.

46. *Kuo Mo-jo shu-hsin chi*, pp. 5–7.

47. Quoted in Roy, p. 87.

48. Ibid.

49. Ibid., pp. 81–82.

50. Ibid., p. 83.

51. Kuo Mo-jo, *Nü-shen*, p. 121.

52. Kuo Mo-jo, *Ke-ming ch'un-ch'iu*, p. 64.

53. Roy, p. 87.

54. Kuo Mo-jo, *Ke-ming ch'un-ch'iu*, p. 82.

55. English translation, with my minor revisions, by William R. Schultz, "Kuo Mo-jo and the Romantic Aesthetic: 1918–1925," *Journal of Oriental Literature* 6.2:59–61 (April 1955).

56. Kuo Mo-jo, "Shen-hua ti shih-chieh" (The world of myth), *Ch'uang-tsao chou-pao* 27:4 (Nov. 11, 1923).

57. Schultz, p. 58.

58. See Achilles Fang, "From Imagism to Whitmanism in Recent Chinese Poetry," pp. 185–189.

59. Kuo Mo-jo, *Ke-ming ch'un-ch'iu*, p. 75.

60. Kuo Mo-jo, "Hu-hsin t'ing" (Pavilion in the center of the lake), in his *T'ien-ti hsüan-huang* (Shanghai, 1951), p. 195.

61. Hsü Chih-mo, "Ch'ing-nien yün-tung" (Youth movement), *Ch'üan-chi*, III, 54.

62. Wen I-to, "Nü-shen ti shih-tai ching-shen" (The spirit of the time in *Goddesses*), in Li Lin, ed., *Kuo Mo-jo p'ing-chuan* (Shanghai, 1932), pp. 61–62.

63. Ch'ien Hsing-ts'un, "Shih-jen Kuo Mo-jo" (The poet Kuo Mo-jo), in ibid., 14.

64. Wang I-jen, "Mo-jo ti hsi-chü" (The plays of Mo-jo), in ibid., p. 167.

65. Kuo Mo-jo, "Ku hung" (Solitary letter), *Ch'uang-tsao yüeh-k'an* 1.2:127 (August 1927).

66. Ibid., p. 129.

67. Ibid., p. 136.

68. Ibid., p. 137.

69. Ibid., p. 128; Roy, p. 166.

70. Ibid., p. 130.

71. Kuo Mo-jo, "Hsin kuo-chia ti ch'uang-tsao" (The building of a new nation), *Hung-shui*, Vol. I collection (June 1926), pp. 228–229.

72. Kuo Mo-jo, "Kuo-chia ti yü ch'ao kuo-chia ti" (National and supernational), *Ch'uang-tsao chou-pao* 24:1–2 (Oct. 20, 1923).

73. Kuo Mo-jo, "Wen-i lun-chi hsü" (Preface to *Essays on Literature*), *Hung-shui*, Vol. I collection, pp. 197–198.

74. Kuo Mo-jo, "Ma-k'e-ssu chin wen-miao" (Marx enters the Confucian temple), *Hung-shui*, Vol. I collection, p. 215.

75. Kuo Mo-jo, "Wen-i lun chi hsü," p. 198.

76. See Maurice Meisner, *Li Ta-chao and the Origins of Chinese Marxism*

(Cambridge, Mass., 1967).

77. This view has been gradually accepted by most scholars. See, for instance, David Roy's book cited above and Akiyoshi Kukio, "Koku Motsuyaku no romanchishizumu no seikaku," in *Kindai Chūgoku no shiso tō bungaku,* p. 236.

78. Roy, p. 99.

79. Kuo Mo-jo, *Ke-ming ch'un-ch'iu,* p. 174.

80. Kuo Mo-jo, "T'ai-yang mo-liao" (The sun is set), *Ch'uang-tsao choupao* 38:7 (Jan. 13, 1924). The poem was written about three months before his conversion.

81. Quoted in Roy, p. 98.

82. Kuo Mo-jo, "Hsü shih" (Preface poem), *Nü-shen,* p. 2.

83. Kuo Mo-jo, *Ke-ming ch'un-ch'iu,* p. 140.

84. Roy, p. 82.

85. Kuo Mo-jo, "Ke-ming yü wen-hsüeh" (Revolution and literature), *Ch'uang-tsao yüeh-k'an* 1.3:6–7 (September 1927).

86. Ibid., p. 5.

87. Ibid., p. 8.

88. "Kuo Mo-jo," *Dictionary of Republican China* II, 273. My sketch of the latter part of Kuo's life is entirely based on this source.

89. Ibid., p. 274.

90. The most typical of right-wing critical works on Kuo is Shih Chien, *Kuo Mo-jo p'i-p'an.*

91. Kuo Mo-jo, "Lang-man chu-i ho hsien-shih chu-i" (Romanticism and realism), reprinted in *Chung-kuo hsien-tai wen-hsüeh-shih ts'an-k'ao tzu-liao,* III, 703–715.

92. Ibid., pp. 705–706.

93. Ibid., p. 712.

94. *New York Times* (May 2, 1966), p. 5.

10. Chiang Kuang-tz'u

1. T. A. Hsia, "The Phenomenon of Chiang Kuang-tz'u," in his *Gate of Darkness: Studies on the Leftist Literary Movement in China* (Seattle, 1968), p. 84.

2. Huang Yao-mien, "Chiang Kuang-tz'u hsiao chuan" (A Short biography of Chiang Kuang-tz'u), in *Chiang Kuang-tz'u shih-wen hsüan-chi* (Peking, 1955), p. 1.

3. T. A. Hsia, *The Gate of Darkness,* p. 71. The Communist Youth League was, prior to 1925, known as the Chinese Socialist Youth League and founded by Ch'en Tu-hsiu and others.

4. Ibid., p. 72. Another version has it that upon his return to China

Chiang first served under Feng Yü-hsiang and was later transferred to Shanghai to teach because "his personality was unsuitable" for the job. Yang Ts'un-jen, "T'ai-yang she yü Chiang Kuang-tz'u," *Hsien-tai* 3.4:475 (August 1922).

5. T. A. Hsia, *The Gate of Darkness*, pp. 72—73.

6. C. T. Hsia, *A History of Modern Chinese Fiction* (New Haven, 1961), pp. 259—262.

7. T. A. Hsia, *The Gate of Darkness*, p. 100.

8. Chiang Kuang-tz'u, "Mo-ssu-k'e yin" (Hymn to Moscow), *Chiang Kuang-tz'u shih-wen hsüan-chi*, pp. 17—20.

9. Chiang Kuang-tz'u, "K'u Lieh-ning" (Bewailing Lenin), in ibid., 21—24.

10. See Chapter 9, note 80.

11. Chiang Kuang-tz'u, "Wo-shih i-ke wu-ch'an-che" (I am a member of the proletariat), *Chiang Kuang-tz'u shih-wen hsüan-chi*, p. 50.

12. Quoted and translated in Schultz, p. 68.

13. Chiang Kuang-tz'u, "T'ai-p'ing-yang chung ti o-hsiang" (Evil phantoms in the Pacific Ocean), *Chiang Kuang-tz'u shih wen hsüan-chi*, pp. 7—8.

14. Schultz, p. 68.

15. Chiang Kuang-tz'u, "Hung-hsiao" (Red smiles), *Chiang Kuang-tz'u shih-wen hsüan-chi*, p. 3.

16. Chiang Kuang-tz'u, "Shih-yüeh ke-ming ti ying-erh" (Children of the October Revolution), ibid., p. 28.

17. Chiang Kuang-tz'u, "Huai Pai-lun" (Recalling Byron), ibid., pp. 35—37.

18. See Chapter 4, note 30.

19. Huang Yao-mien, "Hsü" (Preface), *Chiang Kuang-tz'u hsüan-chi* (Peking, 1951), p. 18.

20. Chiang Kuang-ch'ih (tz'u), "Shih-yüeh ke-ming yü O-lo-ssu wen-hsüeh," *Ch'uang-tsao yüeh-k'an* 1.3:83 (September 1927).

21. Ibid., p. 85.

22. Ibid.

23. Ibid., p. 88.

24. Ibid., p. 83.

25. Ibid., p. 87.

26. T. A. Hsia, *The Gate of Darkness*, p. 81.

27. Ibid., p. 82.

28. Ibid., p. 80.

29. Chiang Kuang-tz'u, *Shao-nien p'iao-p'o che* (Shanghai, 1933), Sec. 11.

30. Chiang Kuang-tz'u, *Li-sha ti ai-yüan* (Shanghai, 1940).

31. Chiang Kuang-tz'u, *Ya-lu chiang-shang* (Shanghai, 1927), pp. 1—40.

32. Ibid., pp. 41—80.

33. Chiang Kuang-tz'u, "I-feng wei-chi ti hsin" (An unmailed letter), in ibid., p. 128.

34. Chiang Kuang-tz'u, "T'ien-yeh ti feng" (Wind across the fields), in *Chiang Kuang-tz'u hsüan-chi*, pp. 193–283.

35. Quoted in T. A. Hsia, *The Gate of Darkness*, p. 89.

36. Chiang Kuang-tz'u, "Tuan-k'u tang" (*Sansculottes*), in *Chiang Kuang-tz'u hsüan-chi*, pp. 85–192.

37. T. A. Hsia, *The Gate of Darkness*, p. 89.

38. Huang Yao-mien, Preface to *Chiang Kuang-tz'u hsüan-chi*, p. 18.

39. T. A. Hsia, *The Gate of Darkness*, pp. 90, 96–97.

40. Quoted in ibid., p. 80.

41. Yü Ta-fu, "Kuang-tz'u ti wan-nien," *Hsien-tai* 3.1:71 (May 1933).

42. Yang Ts'un-jen, p. 470.

43. Yü Ta-fu, "Kuang-tz'u ti wan-nien," p. 72.

44. Chiang Kuang-tz'u and Sung Jo-yü, *Chi-nien-pei* (Shanghai, 1931), p. 85. Selections from their love letters as well as those of other literary celebrities can be found in Yü Ta-fu, ed., *Hsien-tai ming-jen ch'ing-shu* (Shanghai, 1936).

45. Chiang Kuang-tz'u, "Yü An-na" (To Anna), in *Chiang Kuang-tz'u shih-wen hsüan-chi*, pp. 38–41.

46. *Chi-nien-pei*, pp. 18, 24, 127, 154–155, 158, 170.

47. Ibid., p. 126.

48. Ibid., p. 197.

49. Huang Yao-mien, "Chiang Kuang-tz'u hsiao-chuan," p. 2.

50. Lu Hsün, *Lu Hsün ch'üan-chi*, IV, 96.

51. Yang Ts'un-jen, p. 471.

52. Chiang Kuang-tz'u, "I-pang yü ku-kuo" (Foreign land and native country), in *Kuang-tz'u i-chi* (Shanghai, 1932), p. 49.

53. Ibid., pp. 58–59.

54. Ibid., p. 56.

55. Ibid., pp. 102–104.

56. Quoted in T. A. Hsia, *The Gate of Darkness*, pp. 55–56.

57. Wu Ssu-hung, "Kuang-tz'u hui-i lu," *Ta-feng* 74:2364 (Sept. 6, 1940).

58. Ibid., p. 2362.

59. Ibid., 75:2394 (Sept. 20, 1940).

60. Ibid., p. 2395.

61. Ibid., p. 2396.

62. Ibid., 76:2441 (Oct. 4, 1940).

63. Ibid., p. 2440.

64. Ibid., 77:2480 (Oct. 20, 1940).

65. Ibid., 78:2516 (Nov. 5, 1940).

66. Ibid., p. 2517.

67. Ibid., p. 2519.

68. Yang Ts'un-jen, p. 576.

69. T. A. Hsia, *The Gate of Darkness*, p. 65. A complete catalogue of Chiang Kuang-tz'u's works and translations has also been compiled and published. See *Chung-kuo hsien-tai wen-i tzu-liao ts'ung-k'an ti-i chi*, ed. Shanghai wen-i ch'u-pan she pien-chi pu (Shanghai, 1962).

70. Ting Yi, *A History of Modern Chinese Literature* (Peking, 1958), pp. 166–167. Quoted in T. A. Hsia, p. 66. For another sympathetic analysis, see Fan Po-ch'ün and Tseng Hua-p'eng, "Chiang Kuang-ch'ih lun," *Wen-hsüeh p'ing-lun* 5:42–58 (October, 1962).

11. Hsiao Chün

1. T'ien Chun, *Village in August*, trans. Evan King with an introduction by Edgar Snow (New York, 1942). The book has also been translated into Russian and German.

2. Edgar Snow, ed., *Living China* (New York, 1936), pp. 205–206.

3. Hsiao Chün, "Wo ti sheng-ya" (My life), quoted in Chou Li-po, "Hsiao Chün ssu-hsiang fen-hsi" (An analysis of Hsiao Chün's thought), *Chou Li-po hsüan-chi* (Peking, 1959), p. 262.

4. Hsiao Chün, "Wen-t'an shang ti 'Pu-erh-pa' ching-shen," *Chieh-fang jih-pao* (June 13, 1942), p. 4.

5. Quoted in Yuan Chia-hua and Robert Payne, eds., *Chinese Short Stories* (London, 1946), introduction, p. 12.

6. See, for instance, his *Ti-san-tai* (Shanghai, 1946), and the short stories included in *Chiang-shang* (Shanghai, 1936).

7. Hsiao Chün, Postscript to *Pa-yüeh ti hsiang-ts'un* (Peking, 1954).

8. Included in *Lu Hsün ch'üan-chi* (Shanghai, 1948), VI, 288.

9. C. T. Hsia, p. 273.

10. Hsiao Chün, *Pa-yüeh ti hsiang-ts'un*, p. 93.

11. Ibid., p. 36.

12. *Village in August*, pp. 125–127.

13. Hsiao Chün, "Lun t'ung-chih ti ai yü nai," *Chieh-fang jih-pao* (April 8, 1942), p. 4; reprinted in *Wen-i pao*, 2:19 (1958).

14. Ibid.

15. *Pa-yüeh ti hsiang-ts'un*, p. 137.

16. Translated by R. D. Charques as *The Nineteen* (New York, 1929). A comparison of these two works can also be found in Minoru Takeuchi, "Shō Gun to yu sakka ni tsuite," in *Tokyo Toritsu Daigaku soritsu jisshūnen kinen rombun shū—jimbunhen* (Tokyo, 1960), pp. 333–340.

17. Rufus W. Mathewson Jr., *The Positive Hero in Russian Literature* (New York, 1958), p. 243.

18. Ibid., p. 249.

19. Lo Pin-chi, *Hsiao Hung hsiao-chuan* (Shanghai, 1947), pp. 2–26.

20. Ibid., pp. 36–41.

21. Quoted in ibid., p. 41.

22. Ibid., pp. 44–64.

23. Hsü Kuang-p'ing, ed., *Lu Hsün shu-chien* (Peking, 1952), II, 773, 781.

24. There are altogether 53 letters to Hsiao Chün collected in the above volume. Only one other former protege, Hsü Mou-yung, has received from the master a comparable number of letters.

25. Hsiao Hung, *Hui-i Lu Hsün* (Peking, 1949).

26. See his stories included in the collection, *Yang* (Shanghai, 1935).

27. Reported by Nym Wales in Snow, *Living China*, p. 347. The other six best writers are Mao Tun, Ting Ling, Kuo Mo-jo, Chang T'ien-i, Yü Ta-fu, and Shen Ts'ung-wen.

28. Hsiao Chün, Preface to *Lu Hsün yen-chiu ts'ung-k'an ti-i-chi* (Yenan, 1941), pp. 2–3.

29. Ibid., p. 136.

30. Marx and Engels, *Literature and Art: Selections from Their Writings* (New York, 1947), appendix, p. 145.

31. Lo Pin-chi, pp. 90–100.

32. Ibid., p. 98.

33. Ibid., pp. 113–115.

34. Ibid., p. 159.

35. Chao Ch'ao-kou, *Yenan i-yüeh* (Nanking, 1946), p. 116; Chin Tung-p'ing, *Yenan chien-wen lu* (Chungking, 1945), p. 124.

36. Hsiao Chün's name is found in *Shan-Kan-Ning pien-ch'ü ts'an-i-hui wen-hsien hui-chi* (Collected documents of the Senate of the Border Regions of Shensi-Kansu-Ninghsia; Peking, 1958), p. 169.

37. *Chieh-fang jih-pao* (April 8, 1942); reprinted in *Wen-i pao*, pp. 19–20.

38. N. V. Gogol, *Taras Bulba*, trans. Isabel F. Hagood (New York, 1915). However, I have not found any mention of this incident. Hsiao Chün's memory might have been derived from a film version of this story.

39. *Chieh-fang jih-pao* (June 13, 1942).

40. *Chieh-fang jih-pao* (Jan. 1, 1942), p. 4.

41. Ibid.

42. Hsiao Chün, Preface to *Lu Hsün yen-chiu ts'ung-k'an ti i chi*, p. 1.

43. Mao Tse-tung, "Talks at the Yenan Forum on Literature and Art" included in *Mao Tse-tung on Art and Literature* (Peking, 1960), p. 77.

44. Hsiao Chün, "Tui-yü tang-ch'ien wen-i chu wen-t'i ti wo-chien," *Chieh-fang jih-pao* (May 14, 1942), p. 4.

45. Ibid.

46. Mao, "Talks at the Yenan Forum," pp. 111–112.

47. Yen Wen-ching, Kung Mu, "Hsiao Chün ssu-hsiang tsai pi-p'an," *Wen-i pao*, 7:36 (1958).

48. According to one source, the Communists turned over to Hsiao Chün printing equipment which they had confiscated. See Chao Chung, *The Communist program for Literature and Art* (Kowloon, 1955), pp. 56–57. He may also have held for a short period the position as dean of the Faculty of Liberal Arts of Northeastern University (Tung-pei ta-hsüeh). See Saburo Kukuchi, *Chūgoku gendai bungakū shi* (Tokyo, 1953), p. 567.

49. Hsiao Chün, "Wo ti sheng-ya" (My life) quoted in Liu Shou-sung, *Chung-kuo hsin wen-hsüeh shih ch'u-kao* (Peking, 1956), II, 222.

50. For a critical analysis of Hsiao Chün's humanistic attack against Russian imperialism, see T. A. Hsia, "Demons in Paradise: The Chinese Images of Russia," *Annals of the American Academy of Political and Social Sciences* (September, 1963), pp. 27–37.

51. Liu Chih-ming, *Ch'ing-suan Hsiao Chün ti fan-tung ssu-hsiang* (Hong Kong, 1949), p. 3.

52. Quoted and translated in Yang I-fan, *The Case of Hu Feng* (Kowloon, 1956), p. 8. The original article appeared in *Wen-hua pao* (Literary gazette), No. 8, under the title "Hsin-nien hsien-tz'u" (New Year greetings), under the pseudonym of Hsiu-ts'ai.

53. Quoted in Chou Li-po, p. 263.

54. Ibid., p. 268.

55. Liu Chih-ming, p. 62.

56. Goldman, p. 85.

57. Hsiao Chün, Epilogue to *Wu-Yüeh ti K'uang-shan* (Peking, 1954), p. 551.

58. Yen Hsüeh and Chou P'ai-t'ung, "Hsiao Chün ti 'Wu-yüeh ti k'uang-shan' wei shen-mo shih yu-tu ti," *Wen-i pao*, 24:43–47 (1955).

59. C. T. Hsia, p. 279.

60. Yen Hsüeh and Chou P'ei-t'ung, p. 43.

61. Li Hsi-fan, "Hsiao Chün ti 'Pu-erh-pa' ching-shen ti tsai-hsien" (The resurgence of Hsiao Chün's 'Bulba' spirit," in his *Kuan-chien chi* (Peking, 1959), p. 86.

12. The Modern Wen-jen and Chinese Society

1. Lu Hsün, "Na-han tzu-hsü," *Lu Hsün ch'üan-chi*, I, 5.

2. Yü Ta-fu, *Niao-lo chi*, pp. 192–193.

3. For an exposition and discussion of the alienation of the Russian intelligentsia, see Richard Pipes, ed., *The Russian Intelligentsia* (New York, 1961), which includes a comparative essay by Benjamin Schwartz, "The Intelligentsia in Communist China: A Tentative Comparison," pp. 164–181.

4. Shroder, p. 29.

5. Ch'eng Fang-wu, "Hsin wen-hsüeh chih shih-ming," *Ch'uang-tsao chou-pao*, 2:3 (May 20, 1923).

6. Yü Ta-fu, "Hsiao-shuo lun chi ch'i-t'a" (On fiction and other subjects), *Hung-shui* 2.1–7 (1926).

7. Han Shih-yen, "Ke-jen chu-i ti wen-hsüeh chi ch'i-t'a" (Individualistic literature and other subjects), *Yü-ssu* 4.21: 462 (May 28, 1928).

8. Ch'eng Fang-wu, "Chen ti i-shu-chia," *Ch'uang-tsao chou-pao* 27:3 (Nov. 11, 1923).

9. T. A. Hsia, *The Gate of Darkness*, p. 59.

10. Lu Hsün, "Wen-i yü ke-ming" (Literature and revolution), in *Chung-kuo hsien-tai wen-hsüeh shih ts'an-k'ao tzu-liao*, I, 240–242.

11. Ch'eng Fang-wu, "Hsin wen-hsüeh ti shih-ming," p. 3.

12. Kuo Mo-jo, "Wen-i chia ti chüeh-wu" (The awakening of the literary men), *Hung-shui* 2.4:135–136 (December 1926).

13. See T. A. Hsia, "Lu Hsün and the Dissolution of the League of Leftist Writers," in his *Gate of Darkness*, pp. 101–145.

14. Ibid., p. 71.

15. Kuo Mo-jo, *Ch'uang-tsao shih-nien hsü-pien*, p. 142.

16. See Yang Yin-fu, *Kuo Mo-jo chuan* (Canton, 1938), pp. 222–224.

13. The Journey of Sentiment

1. Chow Tse-tsung, *The May Fourth Movement*, p. 274.

2. Liang Shih-ch'iu, "Hsien-tai Chung-kuo wen-hsüeh chih lang-man ti ch'ü-shih," *Shih-ch'iu tzu-hsüan chi* (Taipei, 1954), p. 8.

3. Benjamin Schwartz, "Some Polarities in Confucian Thought," in David S. Nivison and Arthur F. Wright, eds., *Confucianism in Action* (Stanford, 1959), p. 54.

4. Wong Kai-chee (Huang Chi-ch'ih), "Li-hsüeh chia chih wen-i ssu-hsiang shih-lun" (Literary thought of the Neo-Confucianists: A preliminary survey), *The Chung Chi Journal* 7.2:187–195 (May, 1968).

5. Arthur Waley, *Yuan Mei: Eighteenth-Century Chinese Poet* (London, 1956), p. 168.

6. Chou Tso-jen, *Chung-kuo hsin wen-hsüeh ti yüan-liu* (3d edition, Peiping, 1934), p. 34.

7. Ibid., p. 44.

8. Hu Shih, "Chin wu-shih nien-lai Chung-kuo chih wen-hsüeh," in *Hu Shih wen-ts'un* (Taipei, 1953), II, 197–199.

9. Quoted in A Ying (Ch'ien Hsing-ts'un), *Wan-Ch'ing hsiao-shuo shih*, pp. 174–176.

10. Jaroslav Průšek, "Subjectivism and Individualism in Modern Chinese Literature," *Archiv Orientalni*, 25.2:266–270 (1957).

11. Yü Ta-fu, "Hsien-tai san-wen tao-lun" (Introduction to modern essays), in Cheng Chen-to, ed., *Chung-kuo hsin wen-hsüeh ta-hsi tao-lun*

hsüan-chi (Selected introductory essays from *A Comprehensive Compendium of Modern Chinese Literature,* Hong Kong, 1961), p. 150.

12. Chang I-p'ing, *Ku-miao chi* (Shanghai, 1929), pp. 103–104.

13. Yü Ta-fu, *Ch'en-lun,* p. 17.

14. See Chapter 8, note 9.

15. Liu Ta-chieh, "Ch'un-hen chih yü" (After "Scars of Spring"), *Ch'en-pao fu-k'an* 1422:15 (Jan. 11, 1926).

16. Hsia K'ang-nung, "Fang i Hsi-ha-no hsü" (Preface to Fang's translation of Cyrano), *Ch'un-ch'ao yüeh-k'an* (Spring tide monthly), 1.2:28 (Dec. 15, 1928).

17. Chang I-p'ing, *Ku-miao chi,* p. 78.

18. David E. Pollard, "Chou Tso-jen and Cultivating One's Garden," *Asia Major,* Vol. 11, Pt. 2 (1965), pp. 187–188.

19. Lang-hsün (Mao Tun), "P'ing ssu wu liu yüeh ti ch'uang-tso" (On creative writings produced in April, May, and June), *Hsiao-shuo yüeh-pao* 12.8:2 (Aug. 10, 1921).

20. Chu Hsi-chou, "Chu-shu chi," 3:13.

21. C. Vreni Merriam, "Love and Sex in Modern Chinese Literature" (unpublished seminar paper, Harvard University), pp. 3–4.

22. Shih Ping-hui, *Chang Tzu-p'ing p'ing-chuan* (Shanghai, 1932), p. 62.

23. Chang I-p'ing, "Ch'ing-shu i-shu san-pan tzu-hsü" (Preface to the 3d edition of A Batch of Love Letters), *Pei-hsin* 21:696 (Jan. 15, 1927).

24. Chang I-p'ing, *I-chen jih-chi* (Shanghai, 1931), p. 27.

25. Advertisement in *Hsin nü-hsing* 1.10:795 (October 1926).

26. Chao Ching-shen, "Chung-kuo hsin wen-i yü pien-t'ai hsing-yü," *I-pan* 4.1:204–208 (Jan. 5, 1928).

27. Chang Ching-sheng, "Hsing-mei," *Hsin wen-hua* 1.6:1–12 (June 1927).

28. Chang Ching-sheng, "Ch'ing-ai yü mei-ch'ü ti she-hui," *Ching-pao fu-k'an,* 263:60 (Sept. 8, 1925).

29. Chang Ching-sheng, "Mei chih cheng-ts'e," *Ching-pao fu-k'an* 283:218–219 (Sept. 28, 1925).

30. Hsü Chih-mo, *Ch'üan chi,* III, 54.

31. Ting Ling, "I-chiu-san-ling nien ch'un Shanghai," in *Ting Ling tuan-p'ien hsiao-shuo chi* (Peking, 1954), p. 154; English translation revised from T. A. Hsia, *The Gate of Darkness,* p. 188.

32. T. A. Hsia, *The Gate of Darkness,* pp. 186–187.

33. Mao Tun, *Shih* (Shanghai, 1930), Pt. 1, chap. 13.

34. Chu Tzu-ch'ing, "Na-li tsou," *I-pan* 4.3:372 (March 5, 1928).

35. Olga Lang, *Pa Chin and His Writings: Chinese Youth between Two Revolutions* (Cambridge, Mass., 1967), p. 242.

36. Quoted in T. A. Hsia, *The Gate of Darkness,* p. 60.

37. Ibid.

38. Ibid., p. 185.

14. The Romantic Heritage

1. *TH, X,* 355–379.

2. Bonnie S. McDougall, *The Introduction of Western Literary Theories into Modern China* (Tokyo, 1971), pp. 254–255.

3. See, for instance, Mao Tun, "Chin-tai Po-lan wen-hsüeh t'ai-tou Hsien-k'e-wei-chih" (The master of modern Polish literature, Sienkiewicz), *Hsiao-shuo yüeh-pao* 12.2:1–4 (Feb. 10, 1921).

4. McDougall, p. 82.

5. T'ien Han, "K'e-lien ti Lü-li-yen" ("Pauvre Lelian"), *Ch'uang-tsao chi-k'an* 1.2:1–2 (Winter 1922).

6. Kuo Mo-jo, T'ien Han, Tsung Pai-hua, *San-yeh chi* (Shanghai, 1925), p. 81.

7. Ou Meng-chüeh, *Wang Tu-ch'ing lun* (Shanghai, 1933), p. 73.

8. Průšek, "La Nouvelle Littérature chinoise," *Archiv Orientalni* 27:76–95 (1959), cited in McDougall, p. 213. But Průšek has over-extended his comparison between the lyricism and subjectivism of May Fourth literature, which is essentially romantic, and the avant-garde of Europe after the First World War. See Průšek, "A Confrontation of Traditional Oriental Literature with Modern European Literature in the Context of the Chinese Literary Revolution," *Archiv Orientalni* 32:365–375 (1964); also McDougall, p. 262.

9. Shroder, pp. 37–38.

10. Janko Lavrin, *Studies in European Literature* (New York, 1930), p. 20.

11. Shroder, pp. 39–40.

12. Lavrin, p. 21.

13. Quoted in ibid., p. 15.

14. Ibid.

15. Hsü Chih-mo in *Ch'üan-chi,* III, 138.

16. Ibid.

17. See Chapter 7, note 117.

18. Lavrin, p. 21.

19. Ibid., p. 22.

20. See Chapter 9, note 30.

21. Howard E. Hugo, "Components of Romanticism," in John B. Halsted, ed., *Romanticism: Definition, Explanation, and Evaluation* (Boston, 1968), p. 33.

22. Kuo Mo-jo, *Shao-nien Wei-t'e chih fan-nao* (Hong Kong, reprint, 1949), pp. 3–5.

23. Hsieh Ping-ying, *Autobiography of a Chinese Girl,* trans. Tsui Chi (London, 1943), p. 74.

24. Chang I-p'ing, *Ch'ing-shu i-shu* (Shanghai, 1937), p. 35.

25. Quoted in Průšek, "Subjectivism and Individualism," p. 263.

26. Peter L. Thorslev, Jr., *The Byronic Hero: Types and Prototypes* (Minneapolis, 1962), p. 88.

27. Johann Wolfgang von Goethe, *The Sorrows of Young Werther and Selected Writings,* trans. Catherine Hutter (New York, 1962), pp. 139–140.

28. Hermann J. Weigand, "Foreword" in ibid, p. *vii.*

29. Ibid., p. 131.

30. Liu Wu-chi, *Shao-nien Ko-te* (Shanghai, 1929), p. 132.

31. *Hsiao-shuo yüeh-pao,* 17.1 (Jan. 10, 1926), special page.

32. Harold March, *Romain Rolland* (New York, 1971), p. 57.

33. Ibid.

34. Ibid., p. 58.

35. Rolland's pacifist stance during the First World War nevertheless provoked an outburst of anger from his compatriots in France. See Maurice Nadeau, "Romain Rolland," *Journal of Contemporary History* 2.2:213 (1967).

36. Kuo Mo-jo, "Lo-man-lo-lan tao-tz'u" (Condolences for Romain Rolland), in his *Fei-keng chi* (Shanghai, 1951), pp. 273–274.

37. Ching Yin-yü, "Lo-man lo-lan" (Romain Rolland), *Ch'uang-tsao jih* collection (July 25, 1923), p. 118.

38. Stefan Zweig, *Romain Rolland: The Man and His Work,* trans. Eden and Ceder Paul (New York, 1921), pp. 189–190.

39. Ibid., p. 63.

40. Ibid.

41. Hsü Chih-mo, "Lo-man lo-lan" (Romain Rolland), in *Ch'üan-chi,* II, 286.

42. Kuo Mo-jo, "Ho-p'ing chih kuang" (The light of peace), in his *T'iao-t'ang chi* (Shanghai, 1948), p. 28.

43. Hsiao Chün, "Ta-yung-che ti ching-shen," p. 17.

44. Quoted in George Connes, *The Tragedy of Romain Rolland* (Buffalo, 1948), pp. 138–139.

45. Zweig, p. 190.

46. Weigand, "Foreword," *The Sorrows of Young Werther,* p. *ix.*

47. Zweig, p. 190.

48. A new translation by Fu Lei was published in 1937. Other works by Rolland which have been translated into Chinese include: *Beethoven, Goethe and Beethoven, Living Thoughts of Rousseau,* together with two biographies of Rolland by Zweig and Ronald Wilson.

49. *Hsiao-shuo yüeh-pao,* 15.4 (April 10, 1924), front page.

50. Ibid.

51. Ibid., p. 15.

52. Ibid., p. 2.

53. Liang Shih-ch'iu, "Pai-lun yü lang-man chu-i", *Ch'uang-tsao yüeh-k'an*, 1.4:98 (June 1926).

54. Ibid., 1.3:117 (May 1926).

55. Hsü Tsu-cheng, "Pai-lun ti ching-shen," *Ch'uang-tsao yüeh-k'an*, 1.4:75.

56. See Thorslev, Pts. 1, 2.

57. Mario Praz, *The Romantic Agony*, trans. Angus Davidson, 2d ed. (New York, 1951). For a collection of critical essays on Byron by recent Western scholars, see Paul West, ed., *Byron: A Collection of Critical Essays* (Englewood Cliffs, N.J., 1963).

58. *Lu Hsün ch'üan-chi*, IV, 170.

59. Hu Shih, *The Chinese Renaissance* (Chicago, 1934).

60. For the severest critique of the usefulness of romanticism as a historical and literary concept, see Arthur O. Lovejoy, "On the Discrimination of Romanticisms," in his *Essays in the History of Ideas* (Baltimore, 1948), pp. 228–253. For a rebuttal of Lovejoy's thesis by an eminent literary historian, see René Wellek, "The Concept of Romanticism in Literary History," and "Romanticism Reconsidered," in his *Concepts of Criticism* (New Haven, Conn., 1964), pp. 128–198, 199–221. See also Northrop Frye, ed., *Romanticism Reconsidered* (New York, 1963).

61. See Chapter 7, note 99.

62. Jacques Barzun, *Classic, Romantic, and Modern* (Garden City, N.Y., 1961), p. 7.

63. Ibid., p. 75.

64. Ibid., p. 83.

65. Chang Ching-sheng, "Chieh-shao lang-man-p'ai," *Hsin wen-hua*, 1.6:9 (June 1927).

66. Cheng Po-ch'i, "Tao-yen" (Introduction), *Hsiao-shuo san-chi* (Fiction, 3d series), *TH*, V, 3.

67. Liang Shih-ch'iu, "Hsien-tai Chung-kuo wen-hsüeh chih lang-man ti ch'ü-shih," p. 17.

68. Yang Chih-hua, *Wen-t'an shih-liao*, p. 311.

69. Ts'ao Chü-jen, *Wen-t'an wu-shih nien*, p. 143.

70. It would be most intriguing to compare the influences of European romanticism on China and Japan. If there was a romantic generation in modern Japanese literature, it had preceded the Chinese by at least one generation. A preliminary study by Yue Him Tam has established a romantic period in Meiji Japan from 1884 to 1908. The many similarities and differences between romantic writers in these two countries should constitute the subject of another monograph, yet to be written. For a concise introduction in English to Japanese romanticism, see Yue Him Tam, "A Study of Japanese Romanticism: Its Problems, Meanings, and Development" (unpublished M.A. thesis,

Department of East Asian Languages and Literatures, Indiana University, June, 1968).

71. Lavrin, p. 16.
72. See Merle Goldman, *Literary Dissent in Communist China.*
73. Ibid., pp. 246–247.

Bibliography

A Ying 阿英 (Ch'ien Hsing-ts'un). *Wan-Ch'ing wen-i pao-k'an shu-lüeh* 晚清文藝報刊述略(A short account of late Ch'ing literary journals and newspapers). Shanghai, 1958.

———— *Wan-Ch'ing hsiao-shuo shih* 晚清小說史 (A history of late Ch'ing fiction). Reprint. Hong Kong, 1966.

Akiyoshi Kukio 秋吉久紀夫. "Koku Matsu-yoku no romanchishizumu no seikaku" 郭沫若のロマンチシズムの性格 (Kuo Mo-jo's romantic personality), in *Kindai Chūgoku no shisō to bungaku*.

Ayers, William. "The Society for Literary Studies, 1921–1930," *Papers on China* 7:34–79 (February 1953).

Barzun, Jacques. *Classic, Romantic, and Modern*. Garden City, N.Y., Anchor paperback, 1961.

Birch, Cyril. "English and Chinese Meters in Hsü Chih-mo," *Asia Major*. New Series, Vol. 8, Pt. 2 (1961), pp. 258–293.

Bloch, Marc. *The Historian's Craft*. New York, Knopf, 1953.

Boorman, Howard. *Men and Politics in Republican China*. New York, Columbia University Press, 1960.

————, ed. *Biographical Dictionary of Republican China*. 4 vols. New York, Columbia University Press, 1967–1971.

Britton, Ruswell S. *The Chinese Periodical Press*. Shanghai, Kelley & Walsh, 1933.

Carr, E. H. *Romantic Exiles*. Boston, Beacon paperback, 1961.

Chang Ching-lu, ed., *Chung-kuo hsien-tai ch'u-pan shih-liao*, see *CPSL*.

Chang Ching-sheng 張競生. "Ch'ing-ai yü mei-ch'ü ti she-hui" 情愛與美趣的社會 (A society of love, beauty, and fun), *Ching-pao fu-k'an* 京報副刊 (Literary supplement of Ching-pao) 263:57–61 (Peking, Sept. 8, 1925).

——— "Mei-chih cheng-ts'e" 美治政策 (Rule by beauty policy), *Ching-pao fu-k'an* 281:201–203 (Sept. 26, 1925), 283:217–219 (Sept. 28, 1925).

——— "Hsing-mei" 性美 (Sexual beauty), *Hsin wen-hua* 1.6:1–12 (June 1927).

——— and Hua Lin 華林. "Chieh-shao lang-man-p'ai" 介紹浪漫派 (Introducing romanticism), *Hsin wen-hua* 1.6:9–11 (June 1927).

Chang Chün-ku 章君穀. *Hsü Chih-mo chuan* 徐志摩傳 (Biography of Hsü Chih-mo). Taipei, 1970.

Chang Hao. *Liang Chi-chao and Intellectual Transition in China 1890–1907*. Cambridge, Mass., Harvard University Press, 1971.

Chang I-p'ing 章衣萍. *Ku-miao chi* 古廟集 (Old temple). Shanghai, 1929.

——— *I-chen jih-chi* 倚枕日記 (Diary written while leaning on a pillow). Shanghai, 1931.

——— "Ch'ing-tai shih-jen Huang Chung-tse p'ing-chuan" 清代詩人黃仲則評傳 (A critical biography of the Ch'ing poet, Huang Chung-tse), *Hsüeh-lin tsa-chih* 學林雜誌 (Hsüeh-lin magazine) 1.12:1–16 (June 1935), 2.2:1–14 (August 1935).

——— *Ch'ing-shu i-shu* 情書一束 (A batch of love letters). Shanghai, 1931.

Chang Jo-yin 張若英. *Chung-kuo hsin wen-hsüeh yun-tung shih tzu-liao* 中國新文學運動史資料 (Source materials on the history of the new literature movement in China). Shanghai, 1934.

Chang K'e-piao 章克標. *Wen-t'an teng-lung-shu* 文壇登龍術 (The trick of succeeding on the literary scene). Hong Kong, reprint, 1966.

Chao Ch'ao-kou 趙超構. *Yenan i-yüeh* 延安一月 (One month in Yenan). Nanking, 1946.

Chao Chia-pi, ed., *Chung-kuo hsin wen-hsüeh ta-hsi*, see *TH*.

Chao Ching-shen 趙景深. "Chung-kuo hsin-wen-i yü pien-t'ai hsing-yü 中國新文藝與變態性慾 (Modern Chinese literature and perverted sex), *I-pan* 一般 (General) 4.1:204–208 (Jan. 5, 1928).

Chao Chung. *The Communist Program for Literature and Art*. Kowloon, Union Research Institute, 1955.

Chao Ts'ung 趙聰. *Wu-ssu wen-t'an tien-ti* 五四文壇點滴 (Vignettes of the May Fourth literary scene). Hong Kong, 1964.

Ch'en-pao fu-chüan 晨報副鐫 (Literary supplement to the morning news, Peking).

Ch'en Ts'ung-chou 陳從周. *Hsü Chih-mo nien-p'u* 徐志摩年譜 (Yearly record of Hsü Chih-mo). Shanghai, 1949.

Cheng Chen-to 鄭根鐸. "Lin Ch'in-nan hsien-sheng" 林琴南先生 (Mr. Lin Ch'in-nan), *Hsiao-shuo yüeh-pao* 15.11:1–12 (Nov. 10, 1924).

Ch'eng Fang-wu 成仿吾. "Shih chih fang-yü chan" 詩之防禦戰 (The defensive battle of poetry), *Ch'uang-tsao chou-pao* 1:2–12 (May 13, 1923).

——— "Hsin wen-hsüeh chih shih-ming" 新文學之使命 (The mission of new literature), *Ch'uang-tsao chou-pao* 2:1–7 (May 20, 1923).

——— "Chen ti i-shu chia" 眞的藝術家 (True artists), *Ch'uang-tsao chou-pao* 27:1–3 (Nov. 11, 1923).

——— "Ch'uang-tsao she yü Wen-hsüeh yen-chiu-hui" 創造社與文學研究會 (The Creation Society and the Association for Literary Studies), *Ch'uang-tsao chi-k'an* 1.4:12–20 (Feb. 28, 1924).

Chesneaux, Jean. *The Chinese Labor Movement, 1919–1927*, trans. H. M. Wright. Stanford, Stanford University Press, 1968.

Chiang Kuang-tz'u 蔣光慈. "Shih-yüeh ke-ming yü O-lo-ssu wen-hsüeh" 十月革命與俄羅斯文學 (The October revolution and Russian literature), *Ch'uang-tsao yüeh-k'an* 1.2–4, 7–8 (1926–1927).

——— *Ya-lu-chiang shang* 鴨綠江上 (On the Yalu). Shanghai, 1927.

———— *Kuang-tz'u i-chi* 光慈遺集 (Posthumous works of Chiang Kuang-tz'u). Shanghai, 1932.

———— *Shao-nien p'iao-po che* 少年漂泊者 (The youthful tramp). Shanghai, 1933.

———— *Ch'ung-ch'u yun-wei ti yüeh-liang* 衝出雲圍的月亮 (The moon forces its way through the clouds). Shanghai, 1939.

———— *Li-sha ti ai-yüan* 麗莎的哀怨 (The sorrows of Lisa). Shanghai, 1940.

———— *Chiang Kuang-tz'u hsüan-chi* 蔣光慈選集 (Selected works of Chiang Kuang-tz'u). Peking, 1951.

———— *Chiang Kuang-tz'u shih-wen hsüan-chi* 蔣光慈詩文選集 (Selected poetry and prose of Chiang Kuang-tz'u). Peking, 1955.

———— and Sung Jo-yü 宋若瑜. *Chi-nien pei* 紀念碑 (Monument). Shanghai, 1931.

Chiang Mon-lin. *Tides from the West: A Chinese Autobiography*. New Haven, Yale University Press, 1947.

Chiang Shu-ko 姜書閣. *T'ung-ch'eng wen-p'ai p'ing-shu* 桐城文派評述 (On the T'ung-ch'eng school of literature). Shanghai, 1930.

Ch'ien Hsing-ts'un 錢杏村. *Hsien-tai Chung-kuo wen-hsüeh tso-chia* 現代中國文學作家 (Contemporary Chinese writers). 2 vols. Shanghai, 1929.

Chin Tung-p'ing 金東平. *Yenan chien-wen lu* 延安見聞錄 (Yenan notebook). Chungking, 1945.

Ch'iu Chu-shih 邱竹師. "Huang Ching-jen chi ch'i lien-ai shih-ko" 黃景仁及其戀愛詩歌 (Huang Ching-jen and his love poetry), *Hsin-yüeh* 2.10:1–29 (Dec. 10, 1929).

Chou Li-po 周立波. *Chou Li-po hsüan-chi* 周立波選集 (Selected works of Chou Li-po). Peking, 1959.

Chow Tse-tsung. *The May Fourth Movement*. Cambridge, Mass., Harvard University Press, 1960.

———— *Research Guide to the May Fourth Movement*. Cambridge, Mass., Harvard University Press, 1963.

Chou Tso-jen 周作人. *Chung-kuo hsin wen-hsüeh ti yüan-liu* 中國新文學的源流 (The origins of modern Chinese literature). Peiping, 1934.

Chu Tzu-ch'ing 朱自清. "Na-li tso" 那裏走 (Where to go?), *I-pan* 4.3:368–384 (March 5, 1928).

Ch'uang-tsao chi-k'an 創造季刊 (Creation quarterly).

Ch'uang-tsao chou-pao 創造周報 (Creation weekly).

Ch'uang-tsao jih 創造日 (Creation day).

Ch'uang-tsao yüeh-k'an 創造月刊 (Creation monthly).

Ch'un-ying Hung-yü 春英紅雨. "Wen-kai chieh-chi lun" 文丐階級論 (On the class of literary beggars), *Wan-jen tsa-chih* 萬人雜誌 (Multitude magazine, Canton) 1.1:1–23 (April 1930).

Chung-kuo hsien-tai wen-hsüeh ch'i-k'an mu-lu 中国现代文学期刊目錄 (A catalogue of Chinese literary periodicals), ed. Hsien-tai wen-hsüeh ch'i-k'an lien-ho tiao-ch'a hsiao-tzu 現代文學期刊联合調查小組 (Joint Research Committee on Contemporary Literary Periodicals). 2 vols. Shanghai, 1961.

Chung-kuo hsien-tai wen-hsüeh shih ts'an-k'ao tzu-liao 中国现代文学史参考資料 (Research materials on the history of modern Chinese literature), ed. Peking Shih-fan ta-hsüeh Chung-wen hsi hsien-tai wen-hsüeh chiao-hsüeh kai-ke hsiao-tsu 北京师范大学中文系现代文学教学改革小組 (Committee on the Revision of Teaching of Modern Literature, Department of Chinese Literature, Peking Normal University). 2 vols. Peking, 1959.

Chung-kuo hsien-tai wen-i tzu-liao ts-ung-k'an ti i chi 中国现代文芸資料叢刊第一輯 (Anthology of modern Chinese literary materials, first collection), ed. Shanghai wen-i ch'u-pan she pien-chi pu 上海文芸出版社編輯部 (Editorial board of Shanghai Literature Publications). Shanghai, 1962.

Cohen, Morton. *Rider Haggard: His Life and Works.* London, Hutchison, 1960.

Connes, George. *The Tragedy of Romain Rolland.* University of Buffalo Studies. Buffalo, N.Y., University of Buffalo Press, 1948.

CPSL: Chung-kuo hsien-tai ch'u-pan shih-liao 中國現代出版史料 (Historical materials concerning contemporary Chinese publications), ed. Chang Ching-lu 張靜廬. 4 vols. (1, 2, 3 and Addenda). Peking, 1954–1957.

Dickens, Charles. *Dombey and Son.* New York, Dell paperback, 1963.

Doležalová, Anna. *Yü Ta-fu: Specific Traits of Literary Creation.* New York, Paragon, 1971.

——— Quelques Remarques sur la question de l'Auto-description chez Yü Ta-fu," *Asian and African Studies* 2: 56–61 (Bratislava, 1966).

Doležalová-Vlačková, Anna. "Remarks on the Life and Work of Yü Ta-fu up to 1930," *Asian and African Studies* 1: 53–80 (1965).

Dowson, Ernest. *Poems of Ernest Dowson.* London, John Lane, 1909.

Elmhirst, Leonard K. "Recollections of Tagore in China." Mimeographed transcript (taped on March 3, 1959).

———, ed. "Letters from Hsu Tsemou" (manuscript).

Erikson, Erik H. *Young Man Luther.* New York, Norton, 1958.

——— *Childhood and Society.* New York, Norton, 1963.

——— *Gandhi's Truth.* New York, Norton, 1969.

Fadeyev, A. *The Nineteen,* tr. R. D. Charques. New York, International Publishers, 1929.

Fairbank, John K., Edwin O. Reischauer, and Albert Craig. *East Asia: The Modern Transformation.* Boston, Houghton Mifflin, 1965.

Fang, Achilles. "From Imagism to Whitmanism in Recent Chinese Poetry: A Search for Poetics That Failed," in Horst Frenz and G. A. Anderson, eds., *Indiana University Conference on Oriental-Western Literary Relations.* Chapel Hill, N.C., University of North Carolina Press, 1955.

Fang Ch'ing 方青. *Hsien-tai wen-t'an pai-hsiang* 現代文壇百象 (Myriad phenomena on the contemporary literary scene). Hong Kong, 1953.

Ford, George, and L. Lance, Jr., eds. *The Dickens Critics.* Ithaca, Cornell University Press, 1961.

Forster, E. M. *Goldsworthy Lowes Dickinson.* New York, Harcourt, Brace, 1934.

Frye, Northrop, ed. *Romanticism Reconsidered.* New York, Columbia University Press, 1963.

Goethe, Johann Wolfgang von. *The Sorrows of Young Werther and Selected Writings,* trans. Catherine Hutter, New York, Signet paperback, 1962.

Gogol, N. V. *Taras Bulba,* trans. Isabel F. Haggood. New York, Knopf, 1915.

Goldman, Merle. *Literary Dissent in Communist China.* Cambridge, Mass., Harvard University Press, 1967.

Guerard, Albert. *Thomas Hardy.* New York, New Directions, 1964.

Halsted, John B., ed. *Romanticism: Definition, Explanation and Evaluation.* Boston, Heath paperback, 1968.

Hay, Stephen N. *Asian Ideas of East and West: Tagore and His Critics in Japan, China, and India.* Cambridge, Mass., Harvard University Press, 1970.

Ho Yü-po, ed. 賀玉波. *Chung-kuo hsien-tai nü tso-chia* 中國現代女作家 (Contemporary Chinese women writers). Shanghai, 1932.

——— *Hsien-tai Chung-kuo tso-chia lun* 現代中國作家論 (On contemporary Chinese writers). 2 vols. Shanghai, 1936.

——— *Yü Ta-fu lun* 郁達夫論 (On Yü Ta-fu). Shanghai, 1936.

House, Humphrey. *The Dickens World.* London, Oxford University Press, 1941.

Hsia, C. T. *A History of Modern Chinese Fiction, 1917–1957.* New Haven, Yale University Press, 1961.

———, ed. *Twentieth Century Chinese Stories.* New York, Columbia University Press, 1971. Translation of "Sinking," pp. 3–33.

Hsia, Tsi-an (T.A.) "Demons in Paradise: The Chinese Image of Russia," *Annals of the American Academy of Political and Social Sciences* (September 1963), pp. 27–37.

——— *The Gate of Darkness: Studies on the Leftist Literary Movement in China.* Seattle, University of Washington Press, 1968.

Hsiao Chün 蕭軍. *Yang* 羊 (Sheep). Shanghai, 1935.

——— *Chiang shang* 江上 (On the river). Shanghai, 1936.

———, ed. *Lu Hsün yen-chiu ts'ung-k'an ti i chi* 魯迅研究叢刊第一輯 (Series on the Study of Lu Hsün, first collection). Yenan, 1941.

——— "Lun t'ung-chih chih ai yü nai" 論同志之愛與耐 (On love and patience among comrades), *Chieh-fang jih-pao* 解放日報 (Liberation daily; April 8, 1942).

——— "Tui-yü tang-ch'ien wen-i chu wen-t'i ti wo-chien" 對於當前文藝諸問題的我見 (My views concerning current problems in literature and art), *Chieh-fang jih-pao* (May 14, 1942).

——— "Wen-t'an shang ti 'Pu-erh-pa' ching-shen" 文壇上的'布爾巴'精神 (The "Bulba" spirit on the literary scene), *Chieh-fang jih-pao* (June 13, 1942).

——— "Ta-yung-che ti ching-shen" 大勇者的精神 (The spirit of the great brave men), *Wen-ts'ui* 文萃 (Literary digest) 1.1:17–19 (Oct. 9, 1945).

——— *Ti san tai* 第三代 (The third generation). Shanghai, 1946.

——— *Pa-yüeh ti hsiang-ts'un* 八月的鄉村 (Village in August). Peking, 1954.

——— *Wu-yüeh ti k'uang-shan* 五月的礦山 (Coal mines in May). Peking, 1954.

Hsiao Hung 蕭紅. *Hui-i Lu Hsün* 回憶魯迅 (Reminiscences of Lu Hsün). Peking, 1949.

Hsiao-shuo yüeh-pao 小說月報 (Short story monthly).

Hsieh Ping-ying 謝冰瑩. *Autobiography of a Chinese Girl,* trans. Tsui Chi. London, Allen & Unwin, 1943.

Hsin nü-hsing 新女性 (New women).

Hsin wen-hua 新文化 (New culture).

Hsin yüeh 新月 (Crescent moon).

Hsü Chih-mo 徐志摩. *Hsü Chih-mo ch'üan-chi* 徐志摩全集 (The complete works of Hsü Chih-mo), ed. Chiang Fu-ts'ung 蔣復璁 and Liang Shih-ch'iu 梁實秋. 6 vols. Taipei, 1969.

Hsu Kai-yu, ed. and trans. *Twentieth Century Chinese Poetry: An Anthology.* Garden City, N.Y., Doubleday & Co., 1963.

Hsü Kuang-p'ing, ed. 許廣平. *Lu Hsün shu-chien* 魯迅書簡 (Letters of Lu Hsün). 2 vols. Peking, 1952.

Hsü Tsu-cheng 徐祖正. "Pai-lun ti ching-shen" 拜輪的精神 (The spirit of Byron), *Ch'uang-tsao yüeh-k'an* 1.4:73–94 (June 1926).

Hu Shih 胡適. *The Chinese Renaissance.* Chicago, University of Chicago Press, 1934.

——— "Chin wu-shih nien lai Chung-kuo chih wen-hsüeh" 近五十年來中國之文學

(Chinese literature in the past fifty years), in *Hu Shih wen-ts'un* 胡適文存 (Collected works of Hu Shih), Vol. 2. Shanghai, 1926.

Hu Tao-ching 胡道靜. *Shanghai ti ting-ch'i k'an-wu* 上海的定期刊物 (The periodicals of Shanghai). Shanghai, 1935.

Hu Yü-chih 胡愈之. *Yü Ta-fu ti liu-wang yü shih-tsung* 郁達夫的流亡與失踪 (The escape and disappearance of Yü Ta-fu). Hong Kong, 1946.

Huang Ching-jen 黃景仁 (Chung-tse 仲則). *Liang-tang hsüan shih-ch'ao* 兩當軒詩鈔 (Poetry collection of the Liang-tang balcony). 1833.

Huang Jen-ying, ed. 黃人影. *Ch'uang-tsao she lun* 創造社論 (Essays on the Creation Society). 2d ed. Shanghai, 1936.

Huang Ming-ch'i 黃鳴岐. *Su Man-shu p'ing-chuan* 蘇曼殊評傳 (A critical biography of Su Man-shu). Shanghai, 1949.

Huang, Philip. *Liang Ch'i-ch'ao and Modern Chinese Liberalism.* Seattle, University of Washington Press, 1972.

Huang Sung-k'ang. *Lu Hsün and the New Culture Movement of Modern China.* Amsterdam, Djambatan, 1957.

Hummel, Arthur, ed. *Eminent Chinese of the Ch'ing Period.* 2 vols. Washington, D.C., Library of Congress, 1943.

Hung-shui 洪水 (*Deluge*).

Itō Toramaru 伊藤虎丸. "Iku Tappu ni okeru josei" 郁達夫における女性 (The female characters of Yü Ta-fu) in *Kindai Chūgoku no shisō to bungaku.*

——— "Chinrin ron" 沈淪論 (On "Sinking"), *Chūgoku bungaku kenkyū* 中國文學研究 (Studies of Chinese literature), 1:51–92 (April 1961).

——— and Inaba Shōji 稲葉昭二. "Iku Tappu kenkyū shiryō shokō" 郁達夫研究資料初稿 (First draft of research materials concerning Yü Ta-fu), *Chūgoku bungaku kenkyū* 1:93–121 (April 1961).

——— Inaba Shōji, and Suzuki Masao 鈴木正夫. *Iku Tappu shiryō* 郁達夫資料 (Materials concerning Yü Ta-fu). Tokyo, 1969.

Johnson, Edgar. "The World of Dombeyism," in Austin Wright, ed., *Victorian Literature.* New York, Oxford University Press, 1961.

Juan Chi-ming 阮无名. *Chung-kuo hsin wen-t'an pi-lu* 中國新文壇秘錄 (Secret record of the new literary scene in China). Shanghai, 1933.

Kindai Chūgoku shisō to bungaku 近代中國思想と文學 (Modern Chinese thought and literature), ed. Tokyo Daigaku bungakupo Chūgoku bungaku kenkyū shitsu 東京大學文學部中國文學研究室 (Research Bureau on Chinese Literature, Division of Humanities, Tokyo University). Tokyo, 1961.

Kuo Mo-jo 郭沫若. "Ku hung" 孤鴻 (Solitary letter), *Ch'uang-tsao yüeh-k'an* 1.2: 127–139 (August 1927).

——— "Ke-ming yü wen-hsüeh" 革命與文學 (Revolution and literature), *Ch'uang-tsao yüeh-k'an* 1.3:1–10 (September 1927).

——— *Ch'uang-tsao shih-nien hsü-pien* 創造十年續編 (Sequel to *Ten Years of the Creation Society*), Shanghai, 1929.

——— *Nü-shen* 女神 (Goddesses). Shanghai, 1929.

——— *P'iao-liu san-pu ch'ü* 漂流三部曲 (Trilogy of wandering). Shanghai, 1931.

——— *Ku hung.* Shanghai, 1933.

——— *Kuo Mo-jo shu hsin chi* 郭沫若書信集 (Collected letters of Kuo Mo-jo). Shanghai, 1937.

———— *Ch'uang-tsao shih-nien* 創造十年 (Ten years of the Creation Society). Chungking, 1943.

———— "Lun Yü Ta-fu" 論郁達夫 (On Yü Ta-fu), in his *Li-shih jen-wu* 歷史人物 (Historical personalities). Shanghai, 1947.

———— *Pao-chien chi* 抱箭集 (Holding the arrow). Shanghai, 1948.

———— *Shao-nien shih-tai* 少年時代 (Age of youth). Shanghai, 1948.

———— *T'iao-t'ang chi* 蜩螗集 (Cicada). Shanghai, 1948.

————, trans. *Shao-nien wei-t'e chih fan-nao* 少年維持之煩惱 (The sorrows of Young Werther). Hong Kong, reprint, 1949.

———— "Tsai-lung Yü Ta-fu" 再論郁達夫 (More on Yü Ta-fu), in his *T'ien-ti hsüan-huang* 天地玄黃 (Primordial universe). Shanghai, 1951.

———— *Fei-keng chi* 沸羹集 (Boiling broth). Shanghai, 1951.

———— *Ke-ming ch'un-ch'iu* 革命春秋 (Chronicles of revolution), contains "Hsüeh-sheng shih-tai" 學生時代 (Student years), "Ch'uang-tsao shih-nien," "Ch'uang-tsao shih-nien hsü-pien," and "Pei-fa t'u-tz'u" 北伐途次 (On the journey of the Northern Expedition). Shanghai, 1951.

———— *Mo-jo wen-chi* 沫若文集 (Collected works of Kuo Mo-jo). 17 vols. Peking, 1958–1963.

———— T'ien Han 田漢, and Tsung Pai-hua 宗白華. *San-yeh chi* 三葉集 (Three leaves). Shanghai, 1925.

Kikuchi Saburō 菊池三郎. *Chūgoku gendai bungaku shi* 中國現代文學史 (History of contemporary Chinese literature). Tokyo, 1953.

Lai Kuang-lin 賴光臨. *Liang Ch'i-ch'ao yü chin-tai pao-yeh* 梁啟超與近代報業 (Liang Ch'i-ch'ao and modern journalism). Taipei, 1968.

Lang, Olga. *Pa Chin and His Writings: Chinese Youth between Two Revolutions.* Cambridge, Mass., Harvard University Press, 1967.

Lavrin, Janko. "Romantic Mentality," in his *Studies in European Literature.* New York, Richard R. Smith, 1930.

Lee, Leo Ou-fan 李歐梵. "Hsiao Chün: The Man and His Works." Seminar paper, Harvard University, 1964.

———— "Lin Shu and His Translations: Western Fiction in Chinese Perspective," *Papers on China* 19:159–193 (December 1965).

———— "Wu-ssu yün-tung yü lang-man chu-i" 五四運動與浪漫主義 (The May Fourth movement and romanticism), *Ming-pao yüeh-k'an* 明報月刊 (Ming-pao monthly, Hong Kong) 41:17–25 (May 1969).

———— "The Romantic Temper of May Fourth Writers," in *Reflections on the May Fourth Movement: A Symposium,* ed. Benjamin I. Schwartz. East Asian Research Center, Harvard University, 1972.

Li Ho-lin, ed. 李何林. *Chung-kuo wen-i lun-chan* 中國文藝論戰 (Literary polemics in China). Shanghai, 1929.

———— *Chin erh-shih nien Chung-kuo wen-i ssu-ch'ao lun* 近二十年中國文藝思潮論 (On intellectual trends in Chinese literature in the recent twenty years). Shanghai, 1945.

Li Hsi-fan 李希凡. *Kuan-chien chi* 管見集 (Personal views). Peking, 1959.

Li Lin, ed. 李霖. *Kuo Mo-jo p'ing-chuan* 郭沫若評傳 (Critical biographies of Kuo Mo-jo). Shanghai, 1932.

Li Ping-jen 李冰人 and Hsieh Yün-sheng 謝雲聲 eds. *Yü Ta-fu chi-nien chi* 郁達夫紀念集 (Memorial volume on Yü Ta-fu). Singapore, 1958.

Liang Shih-ch'iu 梁實秋. "Pai-lun yü lang-man chu-i" 拜倫與浪漫主義 (Byron and romanticism), *Ch'uang-tsao yüeh-k'an* 1.3:103–121 (May 1926); 1.4:94–101 (June 1926).

———— "Hsien-tai Chung-kuo wen-hsüeh chih lang-man ti ch'ü-shih" 現代中國文學之浪漫的趨勢 (The romantic tendencies in contemporary Chinese literature), in his *Shih-ch'iu tzu-hsüan chi* 實秋自選集 (Selected works of Liang Shih-ch'iu). Taipei, 1954.

———— *T'an Hsü Chih-mo* 談徐志摩 (Discourse on Hsü Chih-mo). Taipei, 1958.

———— *Wen-hsüeh yin-yüan* 文學因緣 (Associations with literature). Taipei, 1964.

Lin Shu 林紓, trans. *Ping-hsüeh yin-yüan* 冰雪因緣 (Dombey and Son), in *Shuo-pu ts'ung-shu* 說部叢書 (Compendium of fiction), 2d collection. Shanghai, 1915.

———— *Wei-lu wen-chi* 畏廬文集 (Collected essays of Lin Shu), Shanghai, 1910.

———— *Wei-lu hsü-chi* 畏廬續集 (Collected essays of Lin Shu, second series), Shanghai, 1916.

———— *Wei-lu man-lu* 畏廬漫錄 (Random notes of Lin Shu). Shanghai, 1922.

———— *Wei-lu shih-ts'un* 畏廬詩存 (Collected poems of Lin Shu). Shanghai, 1923.

———— *Wei-lu so-chi* 畏廬瑣記 (Fugitive notes of Lin Shu). Shanghai, 1922.

———— *Wei-lu san-chi* 畏廬三集 (Collected essays of Lin Shu, third series). Shanghai, 1924.

———— *Lin Ch'in-nan hsien-sheng hsüeh-hsin p'u-chi ssu-chung* 林琴南先生學行譜記四種 (The life and works of Mr. Lin Ch'in-nan, four records), ed. Chu Hsi-chou 朱羲冑; includes "Cheng-wen hsien-sheng nien-p'u" 貞文先生年譜 (Yearly record of Lin Shu), 2 chüan, and "Ch'un-chüeh chai chu-shu chi" 春覺齋著述記 (Works from the Ch'un-chüeh study), 3 chüan. Taipei, 1961.

Lin Yutang. *A History of the Press and Public Opinion in China*. Shanghai, Kelley & Walsh, 1936.

Liu Chih-ming 劉芝明. *Ch'ing-suan Hsiao Chün ti fan-tung ssu-hsiang* 清算蕭軍的反動思想 (Liquidation of Hsiao Chün's reactionary thought). Hong Kong, 1949.

Liu Chün-jo. *Controversies in Modern Chinese Intellectual History*. Cambridge, Mass., East Asian Research Center, Harvard University, 1964.

Liu Hsin-huang 劉心皇. *Yü Ta-fu yü Wang Ying-hsia* 郁達夫與王映霞 (Yü Ta-fu and Wang Ying-hsia). Taipei, 1962.

———— *Hsü Chih-mo yü Lu Hsiao-man* 徐志摩與陸小曼 (Hsü Chih-mo and Lu Hsiao-man). Taipei, 1965.

———— *Yü Ta-fu shih-tzu hui pien* 郁達夫詩詞彙編 (Collected poetry of Yü Ta-fu), Taipei, 1970.

Liu Shou-sung 劉綬松. *Chung-kuo hsin wen-hsüeh shih ch'u-kao* 中國新文學史初稿 (History of modern Chinese literature, preliminary draft). 2 vols. Peking, 1956.

Liu Wu-chi 柳無忌. *Shao-nien ko-te* 少年哥德 (Young Goethe). Shanghai, 1929.

———— *Su Man-shu*. New York, Twayne Publishers, 1972.

————, ed. *Su Man-shu nien-p'u chi ch'i-t'a* 蘇曼殊年譜及其他 (A yearly record of Su Man-shu and other items). Shanghai, 1927.

————, ed. *Man-shu ta-shih chi-nien chi* 曼殊大師紀念集 (Memorial collection of Reverend Man-shu). 2d ed. Shanghai, 1949.

Liu Ya-tzu 柳亞子, ed. *Man-shu ch'üan-chi* 曼殊全集 (The complete works of Su Man-shu). 5 vols. Shanghai, 1929.

Lo Pin-chi 駱賓基. *Hsiao Hung hsiao-chuan* 蕭紅小傳 (A short biography of Hsiao Hung). Shanghai, 1947.

Longaker, Mark. *Ernest Dowson*. Philadelphia, University of Pennsylvania Press, 1945.

Lovejoy, Arthur O. "On the Discrimination of Romanticisms," in his *Essays in the History of Ideas*. Baltimore, Johns Hopkins University Press, 1948.

Lu Hsün 魯迅. *Lu Hsün ch'üan-chi* 魯迅全集 (The complete works of Lu Hsün). 10 vols. Peking, 1957.

McAleavy, Henry. *Su Man-shu; A Sino-Japanese Genius.* London, China Society, 1960.

March, Harold. *Romain Rolland.* New York, Twayne Publishers, 1971.

McDougall, Bonnie S. *The Introduction of Western Literary Theories into Modern China, 1919–1925.* Tokyo, The Centre for East Asian Cultural Studies, 1971.

Mao Tse-tung. *Mao Tse-tung on Art and Literature.* Peking, Foreign Language Press, 1960.

Mao Tun 茅盾 (Shen Yen-ping 沈雁氷). *Shih* 蝕 (Eclipse). Shanghai, 1930.

Marx, Karl, and Friedrich Engels. *Literature and Art; Selections from Their Writings.* New York, International Publishers, 1947.

Mathewson, Rufus W. Jr. *The Positive Hero in Russian Literature.* New York, Columbia University Press, 1958.

Meisner, Maurice. *Li Ta-chao and the Origins of Chinese Marxism.* Cambridge, Mass., Harvard University Press, 1967.

Melyan Gary G. (Mei Ch'i-jui 梅其瑞). "Yü Ta-fu yü-hai chih mi" 郁達夫遇害之謎 (The riddle of Yü Ta-fu's death), *Ming-pao yüeh-k'an* 5.11:31–37 (November 1970) 5.12:53–61 (December 1970).

Merriam, C. Vreni. "Love and Sex in Modern Chinese Literature." Seminar paper, Harvard University, 1965.

Mizener, Arthur, ed. *F. Scott Fitzgerald: A Collection of Critical Essays.* Englewood Cliffs, N. J., Prentice-Hall paperback, 1963.

——— *The Far Side of Paradise: A Biography of F. Scott Fitzgerald.* 2d ed.; Boston, Houghton Mifflin, 1965.

Moy, Clarence. "Kuo Mo-jo and the Creation Society," *Papers on China* 4:131–159 (April 1950).

Murray, Henry A. "American Icarus," in Arthur Burton and Robert E. Harris, eds., *Clinical Studies of Personality.* New York, Harper, 1955.

Nadeau, Maurice. "Romain Rolland," *Journal of Contemporary History* 2.2:209–220 (1967).

Ostrovsky, Nikolai. *The Making of a Hero,* tr. Alec Brown. New York, Dutton, 1937.

Ou Meng-chüeh 區夢覺. *Wang Tu-ch'ing lun* 王獨清論 (On Wang Tu-ch'ing). Shanghai, 1933.

Pao T'ien-hsiao 包天笑. "Hsin-hai ke-ming ch'ien-ho ti Shanghai hsin-wen chieh" 辛亥革命前后的上海新聞界 (The journalistic scene in Shanghai at the 1911 Revolution), in *Hsin-hai ke-ming hui-i lu* 辛亥革命回憶錄 (Reminiscences of the 1911 Revolution), ed. Chung-kuo jen-min chen-chih hsieh-shang hui-i ch'üan-kuo wei-yüan hui wen-shih tzu-liao yen-chiu wei-yüan hui 中国人民政治協商會設全国委員會文史資料研究委員會 (Committee on the Study of Historical Materials, National Committee of the Chinese Peoples' Political Consultative Conference), Vol. IV. Shanghai, 1962.

Payne, Robert, ed. *Contemporary Chinese Poetry.* London, Routledge, 1947.

Pei-hsin 北新 (New north).

Pipes, Richard, ed. *The Russian Intelligentsia.* New York, Columbia University Press, 1961.

Pollard, David E. "Chou Tso-jen and Cultivating One's Garden," *Asia Major,* New Series, Vol. 11, Pt. 2 (1965), pp. 180–198.

Praz, Mario. *The Romantic Agony,* trans. Angus Davidson. 2d ed. New York, Oxford University Press, 1951.

Průšek, Jaroslav. "Subjectivism and Individualism in Modern Chinese Literature," *Archiv Orientalni* 25.2:261–283 (1957).

———— "La Nouvelle Littérature chinoise," *Archiv Orientalni* 27:76–95 (1959).

———— "A Confrontation of Traditional Oriental Literature with Modern European Literature in the Context of the Chinese Literary Revolution," *Archiv Orientalni* 32:365–375 (1964).

————, ed. *Studies in Modern Chinese Literature*. Berlin, Akademie-Verlag, 1964.

———— *Three Sketches of Chinese Literature*. Prague, Oriental Institute, 1969.

Roy, David T. *Kuo Mo-jo: The Early Years*. Cambridge, Mass.; Harvard University Press, 1971.

Schultz, William R. "Kuo Mo-jo and the Romantic Aesthetic: 1918–1925," *Journal of Oriental Literature* 6.2:49–81 (April 1955).

Schwartz, Benjamin. "Some Polarities in Confucian Thought," in David S. Nivison and Arthur F. Wright, eds., *Confucianism in Action*. Stanford, Stanford University Press, 1959.

———— "The Intelligentsia in Communist China: A Tentative Comparison," in Lichard Pipes, ed., *The Russian Intelligentsia*.

———— *In Search of Wealth and Power: Yen Fu and the West*. Cambridge, Mass., Harvard University Press, 1964.

Shih Chien 史劍. *Kuo Mo-jo p'i-p'an* 郭沫若批判 (A critique of Kuo Mo-jo). Hong Kong, 1954.

Shih Ping-hui 史秉慧. *Chang Tzu-p'ing p'ing-chuan* 張資平評傳 (A critical biography of Chang Tzu-p'ing). Shanghai, 1932.

Shinobu Ono 小野忍. *Gendai no Chūgoku bungaku* 現代の中國文學 (Contemporary Chinese literature). Tokyo, 1958.

Shroder, Maurice Z. *Icarus: The Image of the Artist in French Romanticism*. Cambridge, Mass., Harvard University Press, 1961.

Snow, Edgar, ed. *Living China*. New York, Reynal & Hitchcock, 1936.

Su Ya 素雅 ed. *Yü Ta-fu p'ing-chuan* 郁達夫評傳 (Critical biographies of Yu Ta-fu). Shanghai, 1931.

Sun Pai-kang 孫百剛. *Yü Ta-fu yü Wang Ying-hsia* 郁達夫與王映霞 (Yü Ta-fu and Wang Ying-hsia). Hong Kong, 1962.

Tagore, Amitendranath. *Literary Debates in Modern China, 1918–1937*. Tokyo, The Centre for East Asian Cultural Studies, 1967.

Takeuchi Minoru 竹內實. "Sho Gun to yū sakka ni tsuite" 蕭軍という作家について in *Tokyo Daigaku sōritsu jisshūnen kinen rombun shū—jimbun hen* 東京都立大學創立十周年紀念論文集—人文篇 (Collection of papers in celebration of the 10th anniversary of the founding of Tokyo Metropolitan University—volume on humanities). Tokyo, 1960.

Tam Yue Him (T'an Ju-ch'ien 譚汝謙). "A Study of Japanese Romanticism: Its Problems, Meanings, and Development," M.A. thesis, Department of East Asian Languages and Literatures, Indiana University, June 1968.

TH: Chung-kuo hsin wen-hsüeh ta-hsi 中國新文學大系 (A comprehensive compendium of modern Chinese literature), ed. Chao Chia-pi 趙家璧. 10 vols. Shanghai, 1935–1936.

Thorslev, Peter L. Jr. *The Byronic Hero: Types and Prototypes*. Minneapolis, University of Minnesota Press, 1962.

T'ien Chun (Hsiao Chün). *Village in August*, trans. Evan King with an introduction by Edgar Snow. New York, Smith & Durrell, 1942.

Ting Ling 丁玲 "I-chiu-san-ling nien ch'un Shanghai" 一九三〇年春上海 (Shanghai, spring 1930), in *Ting Ling tuan-p'ien hsiao-shuo chi* 丁玲短篇小說集 (The short stories of Ting Ling). Peking, 1954.

Ts'ao Chü-jen 曹聚仁. *Wen-t'an san i* 文壇三憶 (Three reminiscences of the literary scene). Hong Kong, 1954.

——— *Wen-t'an wu-shih nien* 文壇五十年 (Fifty years of the literary scene). Hong Kong, 1955.

——— *Shan-shui ssu-hsiang jen-wu* 山水思想人物 (Landscape, ideas, and personalities). Hong Kong, 1956.

Tseng Hua-p'eng 曾华鹏 and Fan Po-ch'un 范伯群. "Yü Ta-fu lun" 郁达夫論 (On Yü Ta-fu), *Jen-min wen-hsüeh* 人民文学 (People's literature) 91:184–204 (May/-June 1957).

——— "Chiang Kuang-ch'ih lun" 蔣光赤論 (On Chiang Kuang-ch'ih), *Wen-hsüeh p'ing-lun* 文学評論 (Literary commentary) 5:42–58 (October 1962).

Tso Shun-sheng 左舜生. *Chung-kuo hsien-tai ming-jen i-shih* 中國現代名人軼事 (Anecdotes of modern Chinese celebrities). Hong Kong, 1951.

Waley, Arthur. *Yuan Mei: Eighteenth-Century Chinese Poet*. London, Allen & Unwin, 1956.

——— "Notes on Translation," *Atlantic Monthly* 202.5:107–112 (November 1958).

Wang Che-fu 王哲甫. *Chung-kuo hsin wen-hsüeh yün-tung shih* 中國新文學運動史 (A history of the new literature movement in China). Hong Kong, 1965.

Wang P'ing-ling 王平陵. *San-shih nien wen-t'an ts'ang-sang lu* 三十年文壇滄桑錄 (Changes on the literary scene in thirty years). Taipei, 1965.

Wang Tu-ch'ing 王獨清. *Wo tsai Ou-chou ti sheng-huo* 我在歐洲的生活 (My life in Europe). Shanghai, 1932.

Wang Yao 王瑤. *Chung-kuo hsin wen-hsüeh shih-kao* 中國新文學史稿 (A draft history of modern Chinese literature). 2 vols. Shanghai, 1951.

Wellek, René. "The Concept of Romanticism in Literary History," and "Romanticism Reconsidered," in his *Concepts of Criticism*. New Haven, Yale University Press, 1964.

Wei Shao-ch'ang 韋紹昌. *Yüan-yang hu-tieh p'ai yen-chiu tzu-liao* 鴛鴦蝴蝶派研究資料 (Research material concerning the Butterfly School). Shanghai, 1962.

Wen Kung-chih 文公直 ed. *Man-shu ta-shih ch'üan-chi* 曼殊大師全集 (The complete works of Reverend Man-shu). Reprint. Hong Kong, n.d.

Wen Tzu-ch'uan 溫梓川. *Yü Ta-fu nan-yu chi* 郁達夫南遊記 (The southward journey of Yü Ta-fu). Hong Kong, 1956.

West, Paul, ed. *Byron: A Collection of Critical Essays*. Englewood Cliffs, N.J., Prentice-Hall, 1963.

Wong Kai-chee (Huang Chi-ch'ih 黃繼持). "Li Hsüeh chia chih wen-i ssu-hsiang shih-lun" 理學家之文藝思想試論 (Literary thought of the Neo-Confucianists: A preliminary survey), *The Chung Chi Journal* 7.2:187–195 (May 1968).

Wong Yoon-wah. "A Study of Yü Ta-fu's Life in Singapore, Malaya, and Sumatra, 1939–1945." Seminar paper, University of Wisconsin, 1969.

Wu Ssu-hung 吳似鴻. "Kuang-tz'u hui-i lu" 光慈回憶錄 (Reminiscences of Kuang-tz'u), *Ta-feng* 大風 (Great wind semi-monthly), Nos. 74–78 (Sept. 6–Nov. 5, 1940).

Yang Chih-hua 楊之華, ed. *Wen-t'an shih-liao* 文壇史料 (Historical materials on the literary scene). Shanghai, 1944.

Yang Shih-chi 楊世驥. *Wen-yüan t'an wang* 文苑談往 (Discourse on the past of the literary scene). Chungking, 1945.

Yang Ts'un-jen 楊邨人. "T'ai-yang she yü Chiang Kuang-tz'u" 太陽社與蔣光慈 (The Sun Society and Chiang Kuang-tz'u), *Hsien-tai* 現代 (Contemporary), 3.4:470–476 (August 1932).

Yao Nai-lin 姚乃麟 ed. *Chung-kuo wen-hsüeh-chia chuan-chi* 中国文學家傳記 (Biographies of Chinese literary men). Shanghai, 1937.

Yen Hsüeh 晏學 and Chou P'ei-t'ung 周培桐. "Hsiao Chün ti *Wu-yüeh ti k'uang-shan* wei-shen-mo shih yu-tu ti" 蕭軍的'五月的礦山' 爲什么是有毒的 (Why is Hsiao Chün's *Coal mines in May* poisonous?), *Wen-i pao* 文藝報 (Literary gazette) 24:43–47 (1955).

Yen Wen-ching 严文井 and Kung Mu 公木. "Hsiao Chün ssu-hsiang tsai p'i-p'an" 蕭軍思想再批判 (Re-criticism of Hsiao Chün's thought), *Wen-i pao* 7:36–41 (1958).

Yuan Chia-hua and Robert Payne. *Chinese Short Stories*. London, Routledge, 1946.

Yuan Yung-ch'ao 袁昶超. *Chung-kuo pao-yeh hsiao-shih* 中國報業小史 (A short history of Chinese journalism). Hong Kong, 1957.

Yü Mu-hsia 郁慕俠. *Shanghai lin-chao* 上海鱗爪 (Tidbits of Shanghai). 2 vols. Shanghai, 1935.

Yü-ssu 語絲 (Thread of talk).

Yü Ta-fu 郁達夫. *Niao-lo chi* 蔦蘿集 (Wisteria and dodder). Shanghai, 1923.

—— *Chi-chin chi* 鷄肋集 (Chicken ribs). Shanghai, 1928.

—— *Mi yang* 迷羊 (Stray sheep). Shanghai, 1928.

—— *Pi-chou chi* 敝帚集 (Battered brooms). Shanghai, 1928.

—— *Ch'i-ling chi* 奇零集 (Fugitive fragments). Shanghai, 1930.

—— *Han-hui chi* 寒灰集 (Cold ashes). Shanghai, 1931.

—— "Wu liu nien lai ch'uang-tso sheng-huo ti hui-ku" 五六年來創作生活的回顧 (Reminiscences of my writing career in the past five or six years), in his *Kuo-ch'ü chi* 過去集 (The past). Shanghai, 1931.

—— *Ch'an-yü chi* 懺餘集 (After the confession). Shanghai, 1933.

—— *Jao liao t'a* 饒了她 (Forgive her). Shanghai, 1933.

—— *Jih-chi chiu-chung* 日記九種 (Nine diaries). Shanghai, 1933.

—— "Kuang-tz'u ti wan-nien" 光慈的晚年 (The last years of Kuang-tz'u), *Hsien-tai* 3.1:71–75 (May 1933).

—— *Tuan ts'an chi* 斷殘集 (Broken fragments). Shanghai, 1933.

—— *Chi-hen ch'u-ch'u* 屐痕處處 (Footprints here and there). Shanghai, 1934.

—— "Tzu-chuan" 自傳 (Autobiography), serialized in *Jen-chien shih* 人間世 (Human world) 2.17–26 (Dec. 5, 1934–April 20, 1935). Contains the following fragments:
"Pei-chü ti ch'u-sheng" 悲劇的出生 (Birth of a tragedy) 2.17:11–14 (Dec. 5, 1934).
"Wo ti meng wo ti ch'ing-ch'un" 我的夢我的青春 (My dreams, my youth) 2.18:28 (Dec. 20, 1934).
"Ssu-shu yü hsüeh-t'ang" 私塾與學堂 (Private tutor and public school) 2.19:29–31 (Jan. 5, 1935).
"Shui-yang ti ch'un-ch'ou" 水樣的春愁 (Watery spring melancholy) 2.20:35–38 (Jan. 20, 1935).
"Yüan i-ch'eng tsai yüan i-ch'eng" 遠一程再遠一程 (Farther and farther away) 2.21:29–31 (Feb. 5, 1935).
"Ku-tu che" 孤獨者 (The loner) 2.23:33–35 (March 5, 1935).

"Ta-feng ch'üan-wai" 大風圈外 (Outside the great whirlwind) 2.26:25–28 (April 20, 1935).

"Hsüeh-yeh" 雪夜 (Snowy night), *Yü-chou feng* 宇宙風 (Universal wind), Vol. 1 collection, pp. 520–522 (May 1936).

———— *Hsien-shu* 閒書 (Idle notes). Shanghai, 1936.

———— "Huai ssu-shih sui ti Chih-mo" 懷四十歲的志摩 (Remembering Chih-mo at forty), *Yü-chou feng*, Vol. 1 collection, pp. 364–365 (May 1936).

———— *"Ch'en-lun" chi ch'i-t'a* 沈淪及其他 ("Sinking" and other stories). Shanghai, 1947.

———— *Chüeh-wei chi* 蕨薇集 (Ferns). Shanghai, 1947.

———— *Ch'un-feng ch'en-tsui ti wan-shang* 春風沈醉的晚上 (That intoxicating spring night). Reprint. Hong Kong, 1959.

———— *Yü Ta-fu jih-chi* 郁達夫日記 (The diaries of Yü Ta-fu). Reprint. Hong Kong, 1961.

———— *Yü Ta-fu shih-tz'u ch'ao* 郁達夫詩詞鈔 (Collected poetry of Yü Ta-fu), ed. Lu Tan-lin 陸丹林. Hong Kong, 1962.

———— *Ta-fu san-wen chi* 達夫散文集 (Collected essays of Yü Ta-fu). Taipei, 1965.

———— *Wen-hsüeh man-t'an* 文學漫談 (Random talk on literature). Hong Kong, n.d.

————, trans. *Ta-fu so i tuan-p'ien chi* 達夫所譯短篇集 (Collected short stories translated by Yü Ta-fu). Shanghai, 1935.

————, ed. *Hsien-tai ming-jen ch'ing-shu* 現代名人情書 (Love letters of contemporary celebrities). Shanghai, 1936.

Zweig, Stefan. *Romain Rolland: The Man and His Work*, trans. Eden and Cedar Paul. New York, Thomas Seltzer, 1921.

Glossary

A-li-ssu Chung-kuo yu chi 阿麗思中國遊記
Ai Ch'ing 艾青
Akuyama 岡山
An-ch'ing 安慶
Ao-fu-ho-pien 奧伏赫變
Arishima Takeo 有島武郎

Bungei sensen 文藝戰線

Chang Chi 張繼
Chang Chia-ao 張嘉璈
Chang Chia-chu 張嘉鑄
Chang Chien 張謇
Chang Chün-mai 張君勱
Chang Hen-shui 張恨水
Chang Nai-ying 張廼瑩
Chang Ping-lin (Tai-yen) 章炳麟(太炎)
Chang Shih-chao 章士釗
Chang Tung-sun 張東蓀
Chang Yu-i 張幼儀
Chao Lien 趙廉
Chao Yüan-jen (Yuenren) 趙元任
Ch'ao-yin chi 潮音集
Ch'en Ch'i-hsia 陳企霞
Ch'en Meng-chia 陳夢家
Ch'en Shao-pai 陳少白
Ch'en Tu-hsiu 陳獨秀

Ch'en Yi 陳毅
Ch'en Yi 陳儀
Ch'en Yüan (Hsi-ying) 陳源(西瀅)
cheng-fa 政法
Cheng Po-ch'i 鄭伯奇
Ch'eng-ch'eng (Seizo Gakko) 成誠
Ch'eng Shih-ch'un 程世淳
ch'i 氣
ch'i-p'ao 旗袍
Chia-hsing 嘉興
Chia Pao-yü 賈寶玉
Chia-ting 嘉定
Chia-yin 甲寅
Chiang-hsüeh she 講學社
Chiang Pai-li 蔣百里
"Chiang-sha chi" 絳紗記
Ch'iang-meng 強猛
chieh 刦
Ch'ien Hsüan-t'ung 錢玄同
Ch'ien-lung 乾隆
chin-shih 進士
ch'in-fang-nan 沁芳南
Ching-ling 竟陵
Ching-p'ai 京派
Ching-shih i-shu ch'ü 京師譯書局
Ching-tzu (Shizuko) 靜子
Ching Yin-yü 敬隱漁

ch'ing 情
Ch'ing-i pao 清議報
ch'ing-t'an 清談
Chou Ch'üan-p'ing 周全平
Chou Kuei-sheng 周桂笙
Chou Shou-chüan 周瘦鵑
Chou Yang 周揚
Chu Chen-tan 竺震旦
Chu Ching-wo 朱鏡我
Chu Hsi-tsu 朱希祖
Chu-ko Liang 諸葛亮
Chu Te 朱德
Chu Yün 朱筠
Chuang-tzu 莊子
Chung-hua jih-pao 中華日報
Chung-shan 中山
Chung-yung 中庸
chü-jen 舉人
chü-k'an 劇刊
Ch'ü Ch'iu-pai 瞿秋白
Ch'ü Shih-ying 瞿世英
Ch'ü Yüan 屈原
Ch'üan-chün 荃君
Chueh-wu 覺悟

Erh-shih nien mu-tu chih kuai hsien-chuang
　二十年目睹之怪現狀

Fan Chung-yen 范仲淹
Fang Wei-te 方瑋德
Feng Hsüeh-feng 馮雪峯
feng-liu 風流
Feng Nai-ch'ao 馮乃超
Feng Tzu-yu 馮自由
Feng Yü-hsiang 馮玉祥
feng-yü mao-lu 風雨茅廬
Fu-sheng liu-chi 浮生六記
Fu Ssu-nien 傅斯年
Fu-yang 富陽
Fujimori Seikichi 藤森成吉
Fukuoka 福岡

Hai-p'ai 海派
Han-shu 漢書
Han Yü 韓愈
Hangyakusha 叛逆者
hao-han 好漢
Hen-hai 恨海
Ho Li-yu 何麗有
Ho Wei 何畏

Hsi-hsiang chi 西廂記
Hsi-hu chi 西湖記
Hsi-hu chia-hua 西湖佳話
Hsi-yang lou 夕陽樓
Hsi-yu jih lu 西遊日錄
Hsia-sheng 俠生
Hsia-shih 硤石
Hsiang-shan 香山
Hsiang Yü 項羽
Hsiao Ming 蕭明
Hsiao-nü nai-erh chuan 孝女耐兒傳
Hsiao-shuo lin 小說林
Hsiao-shuo shih-chieh 小說世界
Hsiao-shuo shih-pao 小說時報
hsieh-ch'ing hsiao-shuo 寫情小說
Hsieh Ping-hsin (Wan-ying) 謝冰心
　（婉瑩）
Hsieh-shih chu-i 寫實主義
Hsien-Ch'in cheng-chih ssu-hsiang shih
　先秦政治思想史
Hsien-tai p'ing-lun 現代評論
Hsin-ch'ao 新潮
Hsin ch'ing-nien 新青年
Hsin hsiao-shuo 新小說
Hsin-liu 新流
Hsin-wen pao 新聞報
Hsing-chou jih-pao 星洲日報
Hsing shih 性史
Hsiu-hsiang hsiao-shuo 繡像小說
hsiu-ts'ai 秀才
Hsü Chen-ya 徐枕亞
Hsü Shen-ju 徐申如
Hsü Ti-shan 許地山
Hsü Yu-shen 徐栖森
Hsü Yü-no 徐玉諾
Hsüeh Ch'iu-yün 薛秋雲
Hsüeh-heng 學衡
Hsüeh-hung 雪鴻
Hsüeh-mei 雪梅
Hsüeh Meng-chu 薛夢珠
Hsüeh Pao-ch'ai 薛寶釵
Hsüeh-teng 學燈
Hsün-tzu 荀子
Hu Ch'iu-yüan 胡秋原
hu-tzu 胡子
Hu Yeh-p'in 胡也頻
Hua-chi wai-shih 滑稽外史
Hua yüeh hen 花月痕
huai-ts'ai pu-yü 懷才不遇
Huan-chou 幻洲

Huang Ch'ao 黃巢
Huang Lu-yin 黃廬隱
Huang-p'u 黃浦
Huang T'ing-chien 黃庭堅
Hui Shih 惠施
Hung-ch'i 紅旗
Hung-ch'i jih-pao 紅旗日報
Hung-ch'iao 虹橋
Hung Liang-chi 洪亮吉
Hung-lou meng 紅樓夢
Hung mei-kuei 紅玫瑰
Hung tsa-chih 紅雜誌
hung-yen po-ming 紅顏薄命
Huo ti-yü 活地獄

I-ke nü-ping ti tzu-chuan 一個女兵的自傳
I-ta-li san-chieh chuan 意大利三傑傳

Jao Meng-k'an 饒孟侃
Jih-ch'u 日出

K'ai-ming 開明
K'ang Pai-ch'ing 康白情
K'ang Yu-wei 康有爲
Kao Ch'ang-hung 高長虹
Kao-ch'un 高淳
kao-liang 高粱
Kawai-sen 河合仙
Kawakami Hajime 河上肇
Ke i so ch'ang, hsiang-ch'ing so tuan
　各以所長，相輕所短
Keng Chi-chih 耿濟之
Ku Chieh-kang 顧頡剛
Ku Hung-ming 辜鴻銘
Ku-kuei i-chin chi 古鬼遺金記
K'uai-jou yü-sheng lu 塊肉餘生錄
Kuan-ch'ang hsien-hsing chi 官塲現形記
Kuang-hsü 光緒
Kuang-hua 光華
K'uang-p'iao 狂飇
K'un-ch'ü 崑曲
Kung-an 公安
Kuo-chia chu-i p'ai 國家主義派
Kuo-min jih-jih-pao 國民日日報
Kuo Shao-yü 郭紹虞
Kurahara Korehito 藏原惟人

Lao She 老舍
Lao Ts'an yu-chi 老殘遊記
Leng-hung-sheng 冷紅生

li (rites) 禮
li (principle) 理
Li Chi 李濟
Li Chi-yeh 李霽野
Li Ch'i 澧溪
Li Chin-fa 李金髮
Li Ch'u-li 李初黎
Li Ho 李賀
Li Hsiao-feng 李小峯
Li Li-san 李立三
Li Lieh-wen 黎烈文
Li-pai liu 禮拜六
Li Pao-chia (Po-yüan) 李寶嘉(伯元)
Li Po (Tai-po) 李白(太白)
Li Shang-yin 李商隱
Li Shih-ch'en 李石岑
Li Ta-chao 李大釗
Li T'ieh-sheng 李鐵生
Liang Ch'i-ch'ao 梁啟超
liang-chih 良知
Liang Ssu-ch'eng 梁思成
Liang-tang hsüan ch'üan-chi 兩當軒全集
Lin Ch'ang-min 林長民
Lin Hui-yin 林徽音
Lin Tai-yü 林黛玉
Lin Yutang 林語堂
Ling Shu-hua 凌叔華
Liu E (T'ieh-yün) 劉顎(鐵雲)
Liu Fu (Pan-nung) 劉復(半農)
Liu ts'ai-tzu 六才子
Liu Tsung-yüan 柳宗元
Liu-an 六安
Lo Chia-lun 羅家倫
Lo Lung-chi 羅隆基
lo-sung 羅宋
Lun-yü 論語

Mang-yüan 莽原
Mei-chou p'ing-lun 每週評論
Mei Kuang-ti 梅光廸
Mei-ti shu-tien 美的書店
Meng Ch'ao 孟超
Meng Hao-jan 孟浩然
Mi-ssu 蜜絲
Mi-ssu-t'o 蜜斯脫
Min-kuo jih-pao 民國日報
ming-shih 名士
Miu-ssu 繆思
mo-erh-teng 摩爾登
Moji 門司

mo-teng 摩登
Mo-tzu 墨子
Mu Mu-t'ien 穆木天
mu-yu 幕友

Nagoya 名古屋
Nan-k'ai 南開
Nan-kuo 南國
Nan-t'ai 南臺
Ni I-te 倪貽德
Nu-li chou-pao 努力週報
Nü-ke-ming 女革命

Ou-yang Hsiu 歐陽修
Ou-yang Yü-ch'ien 歐陽于倩
Owaka 合子

Pa Chin 巴金
pai-hua 白話
Pan Chao 班昭
Pan Ku 班固
Pan-yüeh 半月
P'an Han-nien 潘漢年
P'an-ku 盤古
P'an Kuang-tan 潘光旦
Pei-hai 北海
Pen-liu 奔流
P'eng K'ang 彭康
Pi Yüan 畢沅
Pu-lun-k'e-ssu 布倫克斯
p'u-lo 普羅
P'u-t'ien chung-fen chi 普天忠憤集

Saburō 三郎
san-kang 三綱
Satō Haruo 佐藤春夫
Satō Tomiko 佐藤富子
Sha-wan 沙灣
Shang-shu 尚書
Shang-wu yin-shu kuan 商務印書館
Shen-chou jih-pao 神州日報
Shen Fu 沈復
Shen-pao 申報
Shen Ts'ung-wen 沈從文
Shen Yin-mo 沈尹默
Sheng-huo pao 生活報
Sheng-ssu ch'ang 生死場
Shih-chi 史記
Shih-ching 詩經
Shih-k'an 詩刊

Shih-li yang-ch'ang 十里洋場
Shih-pao 時報
Shih-shih hsin-pao 時事新報
Shih-tai wen-i 時代文藝
Shih-wu pao 時務報
Shina 支那
Shishōsetsu 私小說
Shui hu chuan 水滸傳
Ssu-ma Ch'ien 司馬遷
Ssu-ma Hsiang-ju 司馬相如
Ssu-ma Kuang 司馬光
Su Chieh-sheng 蘇傑生
Su-pao 蘇報
Su Tung-p'o 蘇東坡
Sui-tsan chi 碎簪記
Sun Ch'uan-fang 孫傳芳
Sun Fu-hsi 孫伏熙
Sun Fu-yüan 孫伏園
Sung Chih-ti 宋之的
Sung Ch'ing-ling 宋慶齡

Ta-chung wen-i 大衆文藝
Ta feng 大風
Ta-hsia 大夏
Ta-kung pao 大公報
ta-ling 大令
ta-t'ung 大同
Tai Chen 戴震
Tai Wang-shu 戴望舒
T'ai-hsi li-shih yen-i 泰西歷史演義
T'ai-p'ing-yang pao 太平洋報
T'ai-tung 泰東
T'ai-yang yüeh-k'an 太陽月刊
T'ai-yüan 太原
T'ao Ch'ien (Yüan-ming) 陶潛（淵明）
Ti Ch'u-ch'ing 狄楚青
T'i-yung 體用
Ting Hsi-lin 丁西林
Ting Wen-chiang 丁文江
T'o-huang-che 拓荒者
tsa-wen 雜文
tsai-tao 載道
"Ts'ai-shih chi" 采石磯
ts'ai-tzu chia-jen 才子佳人
Ts'ai Yüan-p'ei 蔡元培
Ts'ao P'i 曹丕
Ts'ao Ts'ao 曹操
Tsei-shih 賊史
Tseng Ch'i 曾琦
Tso-chuan 左傳

351

tsu 族
Ts'ui-hua 翠花
Tu Fu 杜甫
Tuan Ch'i-jui 殷祺瑞
Tuan-hung ling-yen chi 斷鴻零雁記
Tuan-mu Hung-liang 端木蕻良
Tung-pei 東北
Tung-pei jih-pao 東北日報
t'ung-jen 同人
Tzu-chih t'ung-chien 資治通鑑
tzu-jan 自然
Tzu-lo-lan 紫羅蘭
Tzu yu-t'an 自由談

Uchiyama 內山

Wan-lung 萬龍
Wang Ching-wei 汪精衛
Wang Erh-nan 王二南
Wang I-jen 王以仁
Wang Keng 王廣
Wang Shih-wei 王實味
Wang T'ung-chao 王統照
Wang Tzu-jen 王子仁
Wang Wei 王維
Wang Yang-ming 王陽明
wei ch'ing ch'iu-tao 爲情求道
Wei-li 唯力
Wei-ming 未名
Wei Su-yüan 韋素園
Wei-t'e 維特
Wen-hsüeh chou-pao 文學週報
Wen-hsüeh hsün-k'an 文學旬刊
Wen-hua pao 文化報
Wen-hua p'i-p'an 文化批判
Wen I-to 聞一多
wen i tsai-tao 文以載道
wen-kai 文丐

wen-jen 文人
wen-jen hsiang-ch'ing 文人相輕
Wen-ming hsiao-shih 文明小史
wen-t'an 文壇
wen-yen 文言
Wu-chin 武進
wu-jen 武人
Wu Ju-lun 吳汝論
Wu Shu-t'ien 吳曙天
Wu Wei-yeh (Mei-ts'un) 吳偉業 (梅村)
Wu Wo-yao (Yen-jen) 吳沃堯 (研人)
Wuchin 武進

Ya-tung 亞東
yang-wu 洋務
Yeh Ch'u-ts'ang 葉楚傖
Yeh Kung-ch'ao 葉公超
Yeh Ling-feng 葉靈鳳
Yeh Shao-chün 葉紹鈞
Yeh Ting-lo 葉鼎洛
yen-chih 言志
Yen-chiu hsi 研究系
Yen Fu 嚴復
yen-shih-p'i-li-ch'un 烟式披里純
Yen Tu-ho 嚴獨鶴
"Yin-hui-she ti ssu" 銀灰色的死
Yin-t'ieh-li-keng-chui-ya 印貼利更追亞
Ying hsiao-tzu huo-shan pao-ch'ou lu
    英孝子火山報仇錄
Yokohama 橫濱
Yu-hsi pao 遊戲報
Yung-lo 永樂
yü 慾
Yü P'ing-po 俞平伯
Yü Shang-yüan 余上沅
Yü Yu-jen 于右任
Yüan Mei 袁枚
Yüan Shih-k'ai 袁世凱
Yüeh-yüeh hsiao-shuo 月月小說

Index

HARVARD EAST ASIAN SERIES